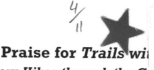

Praise for *Trails wi*
History Hikes through the Ca
Saratoga, Berkshires, Catskills &

D0827673

This is a refreshing twist on the traditional guidebook. —**Adirondac**

To me, this book is full of old friends, whether places, people or stories. It also includes several distant acquaintances, and (especially pleasing) even a few complete strangers. To find such a wide and eclectic variety between the covers of one book, and also within an easy drive of home, is a wonderful gift.

—**Karl Beard, New York Projects Director of the Rivers, Trails & Conservation Assistance Program of the National Park Service**

Even if you don't plan on taking the hikes, the book offers Dunn's always-entertaining descriptions of each destination's significance, making it a prime candidate for any history lover's bookshelf. —**Hudson Valley magazine**

Trails with Tales ... *invites you back in time, not just historically, but personally, to a time in your life when your imagination could people the landscape.*
—**Berkshire HomeStyle**

These twin passions—history and hiking—make for a perfect marriage.
Kaatskill Life magazine

Throughout, the book is enhanced with interesting current and old photos. ... Dunn and Delaney were extremely thorough in their research. —**The Saratogian**

Whether your interest is architecture or industry, waterfalls or caves, religion or vistas, Trails with Tales *has paths and walks that will lead the reader and the hiker, literally, through the physical remnants of years gone by. ... No matter if the only hike you take with this book is to the armchair, it will be an engaging and enjoyable walk, and a path you will return to stroll many times.*
—**Catskill Daily Mail**

Trails with Tales *not only gives you some of the best hikes in the Hudson Valley, it also adds value by giving you the history of each area within the hike. As a reference tool, it is excellent. ... the historical insight gives local hikers a broader understanding and appreciation of the land under their feet.*
—**Times Herald-Record**

Places with historically compelling pasts are brought to life; people with peculiar stories live again in this satisfying and enlightening book.
—**River Reporter, Literary Gazette**

Praise for Russell Dunn's *Adirondack Waterfall Guide*

Many of the falls are well known, but this is an especially good guide to cataracts that hikers might otherwise miss. —**Adirondack Life**

Also by Russell Dunn and Barbara Delaney:

Trails with Tales
*History Hikes through the Capital Region, Saratoga,
Berkshires, Catskills & Hudson Valley*

Also by Russell Dunn:

Catskill Region Waterfall Guide
Cool Cascades of the Catskills & Shawangunks

Hudson Valley Waterfall Guide
From Saratoga and the Capital Region to the Highlands and Palisades

Mohawk Region Waterfall Guide
From the Capital District to Cooperstown and Syracuse

Berkshire Region Waterfall Guide
Cool Cascades of the Berkshire & Taconic Mountains

ADIRONDACK

Trails
with
TALES

ADIRONDACK Trails with TALES

HISTORY HIKES

through the Adirondack Park and the Lake George,
Lake Champlain & Mohawk Valley Regions

Russell Dunn and Barbara Delaney

BLACK·DOME

Published by
Black Dome Press Corp.
1011 Route 296, Hensonville, New York 12439
www.blackdomepress.com
Tel: (518) 734–6357

First Edition Paperback 2009

Library of Congress Cataloging-in-Publication Data

Dunn, Russell.
  Adirondack trails with tales: history hikes through the Adirondack Park and the Lake George, Lake Champlain, and Mohawk valley regions / Russell Dunn and Barbara Delaney. — 1st ed. pbk.
       p. cm.
  Includes bibliographical references and index.
  ISBN-13: 978-1-883789-64-0 (trade paper)
  ISBN-10: 1-883789-64-8
  1. Hiking—New York (State)—Adirondack Mountains—Guidebooks. 2. Adirondack Mountains (N.Y.)—Guidebooks. 3. Historic sites—New York (State)—Adirondack Mountains—Guidebooks. 4. Adirondack Mountains (N.Y.)—History, Local. I. Delaney, Barbara. II. Title.

  GV199.42.N652A34265 2009

  917.47'5—dc22

                                        2009015976

Outdoor recreational activities are by their very nature potentially hazardous and contain risk. See "Caution: Safety Tips," page xvii.

Cover painting: Winslow Homer, *Two Guides,* 1877, oil on canvas, 1955.3. © Sterling and Francine Clark Art Institute, Williamstown, Massachusetts.

Maps created with DeLorme Topo USA® 7.0, copyright 2007 DeLorme (www.delorme.com)

Design: Ron Toelke Associates

Printed in the USA

10 9 8 7 6 5 4 3 2 1

To Dan, Matt, & Mike Canavan—
three wonderful sons who appreciate hiking,
paddling and bike riding in the Adirondacks

Map Key

1. Valcour Island (Lake Champlain)
2. Coon Mountain (Westport)
3. Crown Point: Fort St. Frederic & His Majesty's Fort of Crown Point (Crown Point)
4. Fort Ticonderoga (Ticonderoga)
5. Ironville & Penfield Homestead (Ironville)
6. Rock Pond (Chilson)
7. Rogers Rock (Hague)
8. Shelving Rock Mountain & Shelving Rock Falls (Shelving Rock)
9. Prospect Mountain (Lake George)
10. Fort George and Bloody Pond (Lake George)
11. Cooper's Cave & Betar Byway (South Glen Falls)
12. John Brown's Farm (North Elba)
13. Mt. Jo & Mt. Van Hoevenberg (Heart Lake)
14. Adirondac & Indian Pass (Adirondac)
15. East Branch of the Ausable River & Adirondack Mountain Reserve (St. Huberts)
16. Santanoni (Newcomb)
17. The Sagamore (Raquette Lake)
18. Paul Smiths (Paul Smiths)
19. Hooper Garnet Mine (Thirteenth Lake)
20. Chimney Mountain (Indian Lake)
21. Kunjamuk Cave (Speculator)
22. Griffin, Griffin Falls, & Auger Falls (Griffin)
23. Moss Island (Little Falls)
24. Tufa Caves & Waterfalls of Van Hornesville (Van Hornesville)
25. Canajoharie Gorge (Canajoharie)
26. Wolf Hollow (Hoffmans)

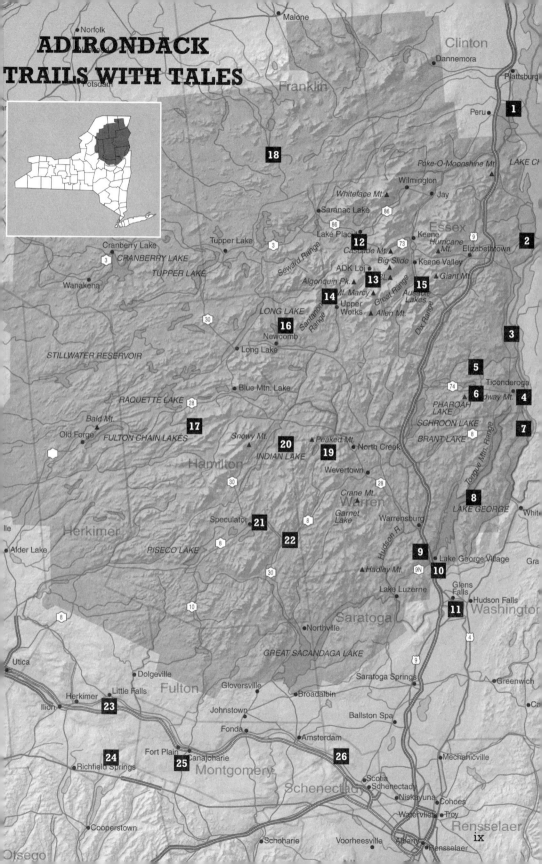

Contents

Map		ix
Foreword		xii
	by Joe Martens, President, Open Space Institute	
Preface: Evolution of a Hiking Guidebook		xiv
	Mileage	xvi
	Degree of Difficulty	xvi
Caution and Safety Tips		xvii
Acknowledgments		xx
List of Hikes by Theme		xxi
List of Hikes According to Level of Difficulty		xxiv

Part I: Champlain Valley Region — 1

1. Valcour Island (Lake Champlain) — 5
2. Coon Mountain (Westport) — 22
3. Crown Point: Fort St. Frederic & His Majesty's Fort of Crown Point (Crown Point) — 32
4. Fort Ticonderoga (Ticonderoga) — 42
5. Ironville & Penfield Homestead (Ironville) — 58
6. Rock Pond (Chilson) — 64

Part II: Lake George/Eastern Adirondacks Region — 71

7. Rogers Rock (Hague) — 73
8. Shelving Rock Mountain & Shelving Rock Falls (Shelving Rock) — 79
9. Prospect Mountain (Lake George) — 88
10. Fort George and Bloody Pond (Lake George) — 97
11. Cooper's Cave & Betar Byway (South Glen Falls) — 104

Part III: High Peaks Region — 119

12. John Brown's Farm (North Elba) — 121
13. Mt. Jo & Mt. Van Hoevenberg (Heart Lake) — 132
14. Adirondac & Indian Pass (Adirondac) — 141
15. East Branch of the Ausable River & Adirondack Mountain Reserve (St. Huberts) — 156

Contents

Part IV: Great Camps   **167**

16.   Santanoni (Newcomb)   168

17.   The Sagamore (Raquette Lake)   175

Part V: Route 30 Region   **185**

18.   Paul Smiths (Paul Smiths)   186

19.   Hooper Garnet Mine (Thirteenth Lake)   193

20.   Chimney Mountain (Indian Lake)   197

21.   Kunjamuk Cave (Speculator)   206

22.   Griffin, Griffin Falls, & Auger Falls (Griffin)   211

Part VI: Foothills of the Adirondacks:
     Mohawk Valley Region   **217**

23.   Moss Island (Little Falls)   219

24.   Tufa Caves & Waterfalls of Van Hornesville
     (Van Hornesville)   232

25.   Canajoharie Gorge (Canajoharie)   237

26.   Wolf Hollow (Hoffmans)   246

Postscript   **252**

Adirondack Museums, Historical Sites,
     Interpretive Centers, and Other Historical Resources   **253**

Endnotes   **257**

Bibliography   **280**

Index   **289**

About the Authors   **296**

Foreword

In the early 1980s I was invited on an adventure "north of 60" degrees parallel that retraced the route of French voyagers down the Natla, Keele and McKenzie rivers in the Northwest Territories. I'm not sure which excited me more—the raw wilderness of the trip or traveling in a landscape memorialized by the likes of the poet Robert Service who warned that "arctic trails have their secret tales that would make your blood run cold." Great landscapes are filled with great stories, some factual and some fictional. Our Adirondack landscape is a prime example, filled with natural and historic treasures and legendary personalities.

Adirondack Trails with Tales describes in detail that familiar landscape along with some familiar and not-so-familiar historical sites and persons, reminding me that although the Adirondack Park contains the largest wilderness area in the eastern United States, it was not always so wild. It once spawned mines and tanneries, sprouted communities that grew, prospered, and disappeared, leaving nary a trace, played a pivotal role in several wars, and attracted wealthy industrialists who built palatial retreats that blended in with the forested landscape. Now, thanks to Russell Dunn and Barbara Delaney, visitors to the Adirondacks, guidebooks in hand, will be able explore its rich past as well as its unequalled scenery ... and ponder its future.

An area like the Adirondacks that is so rich in natural resources should not suffer from high unemployment and limited economic opportunities, but it does. The Adirondacks are a challenging place to make a living. This is due in part to its geography, topography, and entomology (e.g., black flies and mosquitoes), but also to other, complex reasons that have been the subject of ongoing debate since the Adirondack Park was created in 1892. I've sensed a change in the debate in recent years, however, both in tone and in substance. Instead of fighting each other over whether or not excessive regulations are responsible for the economic malaise in the Park, the environmental community and Park residents have joined forces and found common ground rooted, in part, in protecting the Park's natural, cultural, and historic resources and promoting sustainable economic development that provides real opportunity for the Park's residents. *Adirondack Trails with Tales* will help do that, too. Its clear directions and vivid descriptions of important and beautiful places will bring more visitors to the Park and leave them with a deeper understanding of the relationship between man and nature.

That relationship is insightfully illustrated by the book's description of the Village of Adirondac. This abandoned mining town in the heart of the Park is being protected, restored, and interpreted by the Open Space Institute (OSI) working hand-in-hand with a variety of partners. The site is a national treasure. For years, however, its corporate owners kept it off-limits to local residents and Park visitors. Important historic resources on the site decayed slowly like autumn leaves. Now, thanks to OSI's acquisition of the property and help from staff at the New York State Department of Environmental Conservation, the New York State Office of Parks, Recreation and Historic Preservation, Town of Newcomb officials, local residents, and other nonprofit organizations, the site is open to the public. Its most important historic structures have been stabilized, but we have lots of work ahead of us. OSI is now partnering with the State University of New York College of Environmental Science and Forestry's Adirondack Ecological Program to use the natural and historic resources in and around Adirondac as an outdoor classroom.

Like the other sites described in *Adirondack Trails with Tales*, the Village of Adirondac teaches us more than interesting history. When Adirondac was in its heyday in the mid-1800s, the land around the village was largely cleared of trees for as far as the eye could see. Today, the forest has closed in around this former mining site and foundry, providing a lesson in natural succession and the restorative powers of nature.

In my fourteen years at OSI, I have purposefully sought out multidimensional land protection projects to not only protect beautiful landscapes, but to preserve important historic and cultural resources as well. Although invariably this makes for more challenging projects, it also makes the work more rewarding and beneficial to the local economy. OSI protects important presidential sites, Revolutionary War redoubts, historic fire towers and barns, and much more. The breadth and variety of our projects distinguish us from many other conservation organizations.

Similarly, the breadth and variety of the stories in this compilation distinguish *Adirondack Trails with Tales* from other trail guides. The authors provide the reader with much more than trail descriptions; they provide understanding and context. This wonderful book will better connect visitors and residents with very special places and help them learn from the land.

Joe Martens

President

Open Space Institute

April 2009

Preface

Evolution of a Hiking Guidebook

The end result of writing *Adirondack Trails with Tales* has been a deepening appreciation not only for the Adirondack wilderness, but for those early adventurers, writers, cartographers, photographers, illustrators, and stereographers who strove so diligently to make the wilderness accessible through words and pictures.

Our outdoor adventures as New York State-licensed hiking guides and our ongoing trips to libraries and museums prompted us to write a hiking guidebook like no other—a book designed to lure the reader from its pages into the Adirondack forest not merely to savor the sights and sounds along a trail in the gnarly woods, although the trails in this book were all chosen for their natural beauty and certainly provide adequate enticement to do just that, but also to describe twenty-six delightful walks, bike rides or paddles that reveal insights into fascinating past events that actually happened along the trails. *Adirondack Trails with Tales* is intended to guide your historical imagination as well as to provide you with clear directions and good maps to get your feet confidently to the desired trailhead. Within these pages we pay homage to all the woodsman guides and guidebook writers who have gone before us—and to all the heroes, patriots, and scoundrels who, wittingly or not, created a trail of history where they walked in the Adirondacks. For us, it is the natural evolution of a guidebook.

For the earliest explorers, there were no guides or guidebooks. Native Americans and early pioneers navigated a relatively wild and featureless wilderness by using its rivers and natural landmarks such as waterfalls, lakes, and giant boulders. This was particularly true in the Adirondacks, where the land was so untamed and so remote from early European settlements.

The first regional guides to emerge were Native American and colonial scouts for the French and British, and their importance increased through the military campaigns of the seventeenth and eighteenth centuries. These scouts were hardly the kind of guides with whom we are familiar today who take people into the wilderness for recreational purposes. This was a time for vigilance and stealth; one wrong encounter could mean the forfeiture of many lives.

By the early 1800s, however, after the American Revolution had been won and the Adirondack region had ceased to be a violent frontier, a number of colorful, eccentric, backwoods characters arose from the ranks of pioneers and trappers and began earning their livelihood by taking individuals and small parties into the wilderness for recreation. These included Oliver W. Whitman, John Cheney, Mitchell Sabattis, Orson Scofield Phelps, and Alvah Dunning, to name just a few. It would seem that the adventurous outdoor lifestyle enjoyed by these guides also offered health benefits, for most of them lived long lives—Cheney (1800–1887), Sabattis (1801–1906), Phelps (1817–1905), and Dunning (1816–1902).

For the most part, these early Adirondack guides led small groups or individuals on trips to hunt or fish where game was plentiful. But there were exceptions to this rule. One of the best-known examples was Adirondack guide Orson Scofield Phelps, or as he is better known, "Old Mountain Phelps." Phelps took his clients on "random scoots" to lakes or mountain summits simply for the sake of hiking and enjoying nature, rather than to provide the customer with a trophy buck or a kettle of fish.

The roots of this book can be traced back to guides like Old Mountain Phelps, for *Adirondack Trails with Tales* is most assuredly a *hiking* guidebook. Phelps, however, promoted guided hiking on a small scale, mostly through word of mouth. As an occasional hiking guide, he was limited in terms of the number of people he could introduce to the Adirondack wilds because he could only take out individuals or small groups at a time.

Then, in the 1870s, a number of authors and adventurers began to write books about the Adirondacks, exciting the public's imagination and urging readers to leave the cities and visit wondrous gorges, towering waterfalls, vast networks of lakes, and other natural wonders of the most magnificent kind. These books introduced many more people to the wilderness than any individual guide could ever hope to accomplish through guided treks alone.

A number of these authors are worth mentioning. William H. H. Murray wrote *Adventures in the Wilderness* in 1869, a small book credited with starting the influx of Adirondack tourists. Seneca Ray Stoddard, a premier photographer, stereographer, cartographer, illustrator, and author, wrote *The Adirondacks Illustrated* in 1874. Not wishing to be outdone by others, Old Mountain Phelps jumped onto the bandwagon and wrote *The Adirondack Mountains* from 1873 to 1874. In 1877 Nathaniel Bartlett Sylvester published *Historical Sketches of Northern New York and the Adirondack Wilderness*. And so it continued, right into the early 1900s when T. Morris Longstreth published *The Adirondacks* in 1917.

These books did much to popularize the natural beauty of the Adirondacks and encourage tourists to come to the region in increasing numbers, which they did. Still, these were not guidebooks. They described the Adirondack's natural wonders, but they didn't specifically tell the reader how to get to them.

The first really modern Adirondack guidebook appeared in 1934, published by the Adirondack Mountain Club (ADK) and edited by Dr. Orra Phelps. Although it may appear primitive by today's standards, the book included much relevant information about the hiking trails that were then in existence. As time went on, new editions of this guidebook were written and subsequently divided into a series of separate guidebooks, each exploring a different section of the Adirondacks as new areas became open to the public. Today, the ADK guidebooks provide extremely precise and detailed information on getting to the trailhead, trail mileages, and the key points of interest along the trail. Some history is also included to frame the areas being discussed.

It wasn't until the late 1970s and the appearance of Barbara McMartin's first hiking guidebook (later to evolve into the popular Discover the Adirondacks series) that history was interwoven into the text. McMartin's books also often provided leads to further historical research.

Taking this trend a bit further, *Adirondack Trails with Tales* combines history with hiking so that each is provided in a discrete, separate unit and yet the two are conjoined to create a marriage of physical outdoor adventure and historical appreciation. So, our concept of guiding has evolved. A hiker can enjoy this book strictly as a hiking guide. A lover of history can read it just for the historical content. And readers who enjoy both history and hiking are guided on hikes through history.

Mileage

The mileages given to the trailheads are accurate to within 0.1 mile; however, odometers will vary slightly from one car to the next.

Mileages given along hiking trails have been calculated using topographic software and thus are estimates; therefore, they may not be quite as precise as mileages determined by an odometer.

All distances are given in feet, yards, or miles. For visitors to the U.S.A, the following conversions may prove helpful: 1 foot = 0.3048 meter; 1 yard = 0.9144 meter; and 1 mile = 1609 meters (or 1.6 kilometers).

Degree of Difficulty

The degree of difficulty encountered on any given hike is inherently subjective, since individuals vary greatly in terms of age, ability, and conditioning. What is easy for one individual may prove difficult for another. Even so, general guidelines can be helpful when applied to the "average" hiker and are as follows:

Easy—A short distance, generally less than 1.0 mile, or where no significant effort is required to complete the hike.

Moderate—1.0–2.0 miles; trail crosses over mixed terrain; some effort required.

Difficult—Greater than 2.0 miles, or involving an appreciable ascent with increasing effort required.

There are gradients in between, such as "easy to moderate," "moderate to difficult," and so on. Most of the hikes in this book fall within the easy to moderate range, with the more difficult hikes being at Indian Pass, Roger's Rock, Valcour Island, Santanoni, and along the East Branch of the Ausable River.

Caution and Safety Tips

CAUTION: Recreational activities are by their very nature potentially hazardous and contain risk. All participants in such activities must assume responsibility for their own actions and safety. No book can be a substitute for good judgment. The outdoors is forever changing. The authors and the publisher cannot be held responsible for inaccuracies, errors, or omissions, or for any changes in the details of this publication, or for the consequences of any reliance on the information contained herein, or for the safety of people in the outdoors.

Safety Tips

1. Always hike with two or more companions. There is safety in numbers. Should an accident occur, one or more can stay with the victim while another goes for help.

2. Take a day pack loaded with survival items such as extra layers of clothes, matches, a compass, water, high-energy food (gorp or Power Bars), mosquito repellent, an emergency medical kit, moleskin, duct tape (for quick repairs), raingear, a whistle, and sunblock. Very few hikers are ever "over prepared."

3. When waterfalls are encountered, treat them with the respect they deserve. Don't get too close to the top, where an inadvertent slip can send you tumbling over the edge. Many waterfalls send up a spray, so keep an eye out for slippery rocks. Whenever possible, approach waterfalls from the base.

4. Apply ample portions of insect repellent to prevent mosquitoes and black flies from targeting you, and don't be stingy with sunscreen if you are going to be exposed to the sun for any length of time. Remember that you can get sunburned even on a cloudy day, if conditions are right. Wear a long-sleeved shirt and long pants.

5. Wear good hiking boots for proper traction and ankle support.

6. Be aware of the risks of hypothermia, and dress accordingly. Wear clothing that has the ability to wick away moisture (polypro, for instance), or dress in materials such as wool that will continue to insulate even when wet. Avoid wearing cotton (as the old-timers say, "cotton kills"). Keep in mind that the temperature doesn't have to be freezing to cause the onset of hypothermia. If you become accidentally wet or immersed while hiking

during the spring, fall, or winter, return to your car immediately unless the temperature is higher than seventy degrees. Also be cognizant of the dangers of hyperthermia (overheating) and always drink plenty of water when the weather is hot and muggy. Stay in the shade whenever possible and cool off in streams, ponds, and lakes if you begin to feel overheated. Be aware of the importance of staying hydrated even in the winter, particularly on long hikes.

7. Stay vigilant for others who may not be attentive to those around them. During hunting season wear bright colors and make frequent sounds so that you will not be mistaken for a wild animal (which you will be, if a hunter takes a shot at you!) If you are hiking to the base of a large waterfall, keep an eye out for people at the top, especially kids, who might impulsively toss a rock over the edge without first checking to see if there is anyone below.

8. Stay on trails whenever possible. When you head off-trail to explore old ruins and foundations, be sure to get your bearings first before you leave the trail.

9. Do not consider bushwhacking through the woods unless you are an experienced hiker, you have a compass with you and know how to use it, you are prepared to spend several days in the woods if necessary, you are with a group of similarly prepared hikers, and you have notified someone as to your destination and your estimated time of return from the hike.

10. Don't presume to be a master rock climber by trying to free-climb rock walls in any deep gorge. Many gorges have walls made of shale or slate—not particularly stable rocks to grab hold of if your life is depending on a firm support. Stay on the trails. When the going is steep, maintain three points of contact whenever possible.

11. Heed all signs and trail markers. Be on the lookout for possible changes in topography or trails following the date of this book's publications. Trails may be rerouted because of blowdown, heavy erosion, the sudden appearance of a lake or bog because of beaver activity, or any number of other unanticipated events. Trails or portions thereof occasionally become closed off. If you see a posted sign, go no farther.

12. Always let someone back home know where you are hiking and your expected time of return. Clearly discuss with this person what actions should be taken if you are not back at the appointed time.

13. Always know where you are. Guidebooks, topographic maps, and compasses are essential if you venture out into the wilderness. A GPS unit is also worth taking along. Nothing, however, is a substitute for good judgment and basic common sense.

14. When you visit waterfalls, never jump or dive off rocks or ledges into what may appear as an inviting pool of water. Too many people have slipped and tumbled onto the rocks below, or have collided with unseen and unknown hazards below the water's surface.

15. Stay away from overhanging ice. People have died when blocks of ice have suddenly broken off from the rock face and fallen upon them.

16. After the hike, check yourself thoroughly (and your partner, also!) for deer ticks, which can carry Lyme disease. Removing the tick within the first twenty-four hours after contact effectively minimizes your chances of contracting the disease.

17. Avoid cornering any wild animal. If the animal has nowhere to retreat and feels threatened, it may seek a way out that goes right over you.

18. Do not drink untreated water. Giardia is not a pleasant memento to bring back from your hike.

19. Be extra careful if you are making your way over terrain where freezing rain has fallen or melting snow has frozen into ice. This can be particularly dangerous along abandoned roads, which are more likely than are trails within the shelter of woods to be covered with ribbons of ice. In warmer weather always be on the lookout for slippery tree roots or loose gravel that can give way as you walk downhill.

20. Exercise caution around old ruins and foundations. Crumbling bricks, potholes, broken glass, and other debris can cause you to lose your footing and fall. Make sure that you are up-to-date with your tetanus shots.

Do not remove, disturb, or damage any structures, ruins, artifacts, or flora at historic sites. Leave the ground undisturbed.

And remember: If you carry it in, carry it out!

Acknowledgments

Many experts reviewed particular chapters related to their area of expertise. We are eternally indebted to: Beverly Bridger, Executive Director of Great Camp Sagamore, for reviewing the chapter on "The Sagamore"; Ken Helms Sr., operator of Circle 7, for reviewing the chapter on "Santanoni"; Teri Ulrich-Gay, Town Historian of Malta; Andy Flynn, Senior Public Information Specialist at New York State Adirondack Park Agency's Visitor Interpretive Center, for reviewing the chapter on "Paul Smiths"; Brendan Mills, Facility Manager at the John Brown Farm State Historic Site, for reviewing the chapter on "John Brown's Farm"; Joan Hunsdon, Crown Point Town Historian and President of the Penfield Homestead Museum Board, for reviewing the chapter on "Ironville & the Penfield Homestead"; Anita Abrams for reviewing the chapter on the "Hooper Garnet Mine"; Tony Tyrell, New York State Parks Ranger, for reviewing the chapter on "Valcour Island"; Connie Prickett, Director of Communications, The Nature Conservancy–Adirondack Chapter & Adirondack Land Trust, for reviewing the chapter on "Coon Mountain"; Chuck Porter, retired Hudson Valley Community College geology professor, for reviewing the chapter on "Chimney Mountain"; Joe Martens, President of the Open Space Institute, for reviewing the chapter on "Adirondac & Indian Pass"; Chris Moran, Champlain Valley Program Director, The Nature Conservancy–Adirondack Chapter and the Adirondack Land Trust, for reviewing the chapter on "Coon Mountain"; David C. Glenn, Gilliland Family Historian and genealogist, and author of the soon-to-be published *The Battle of Valcour—Myths, Mysteries and Misconceptions Explored,* for reviewing the chapters on "Coon Mountain" and "Valcour Island", and offering substantial textual changes; Edward J. LaFave, Trustee & Deputy Mayor, Village of South Glens Falls, for reviewing the chapter on "Cooper's Cave & the Betar Byway"; Susan R. Perkins, Administrative Director, Herkimer County Historical Society, for reviewing the chapter on "Moss Island"; Dudley Crauer for reviewing the chapter on "Wolf Hollow"; Kathleen Hanford, Canajoharie Town & Village Historian, for reviewing the chapter on "Canajoharie Gorge"; Nicholas Westbrook, Director, Ticonderoga, for his extensive review of the chapter on "Fort Ticonderoga" and suggestions of textual changes; Dr. Paul R. Huey, Scientist (Archaeology), Bureau of Historic Sites, New York State Office of Parks, Recreation, and Historic Preservation, for reviewing the chapter on "Crown Point: Fort St. Frederic & His Majesty's Fort of Crown Point" and for offering substantial textual changes; and author William Preston Gates for reviewing the chapter on "Prospect Mountain."

Further assistance was generously provided by: Raymond Banuls for sleuthing out some of the history regarding the old powerhouse at The Sagamore; Anne McCarty, Director of Membership and Special Initiatives,

Acknowledgments

Fort Ticonderoga; Matt Skinner, Director of Collections, Penfield Homestead Museum; and Faith Bouchard.

An earlier version of the chapter on Cooper's Cave appeared in the *Glens Falls Magazine* (Vol. 5, #5, spring 2004) and is reprinted with permission.

All photographs were taken by Barbara Delaney and Russell Dunn. The postcard illustrations are from the collection of Russell Dunn. The individual maps contained in each chapter were created by Barbara Delaney and Russell Dunn using Delorme 2007 software.

We are honored that Joe Martens, president of the Open Space Institute, has written the foreword to this book. His wonderful organization has been responsible for the preservation of many of the natural areas in New York State that we have come to appreciate and value over the years.

We are also deeply grateful to Fred LeBrun, Albany *Times Union* columnist, for his review of the book and insightful commentary.

We especially want to thank our editor, Steve Hoare, whose deft editorial touch is present throughout the book. Steve also makes sure that not only is the book clear and intelligible, but that all the minor details have been checked and double-checked with everything, suddenly and magically, falling into its proper place and order. Proofreaders Matina Billias, Richard Delaney, and Erin Mulligan were a great help in finding errors and improving the text.

As graphic designers, Ron Toelke's and Barbara Kempler-Toelke's contribution was essential. They gave the book its unique look and made the cover so appealing that it caught your eye in the bookstore and made you stop to take a closer look.

Last, but not least, we want to thank our publisher, Deborah Allen, who probably works too long and hard at what she does, but the outstanding quality of books produced by Black Dome Press is the end result—and who can argue with that?

Most early guides just took clients out hunting and fishing. Postcard ca. 1910.

Hikes by Theme

Battle Sites
1. Valcour Island
3. Crown Point: Fort St. Frederic & His Majesty's Fort of Crown Point
4. Fort Ticonderoga
7. Rogers Rock
10. Fort George & Bloody Pond
26. Wolf Hollow

Caves
1. Valcour Island
11. Cooper's Cave & Betar Byway
14. Adirondac & Indian Pass
20. Chimney Mountain
21. Kunjamuk Cave
24. Tufa Caves & Waterfalls of Van Hornesville
26. Wolf Hollow

Forts
3. Crown Point: Fort St. Frederic & His Majesty's Fort of Crown Point
4. Fort Ticonderoga
10. Fort George & Bloody Pond

Gorges
14. Adirondac & Indian Pass
20. Chimney Mountain
25. Canajoharie Gorge
26. Wolf Hollow

Great Camps
16. Santanoni
17. The Sagamore

Historical Eras
Colonial Settlement
2. Coon Mountain
French and Indian War
2. Coon Mountain
3. Crown Point: Fort St. Frederic & His Majesty's Fort of Crown Point
4. Fort Ticonderoga
7. Rogers Rock
10. Fort George and Bloody Pond
American Revolution
1. Valcour Island
2. Coon Mountain
3. Crown Point: Fort St. Frederic & His Majesty's Fort of Crown Point
4. Fort Ticonderoga
Civil War
12. John Brown's Farm
Nineteenth-Century Industry
5. Ironville & Penfield Homestead
6. Rock Pond
14. Adirondac and Indian Pass
19. Hooper Garnet Mine
22. Griffin
23. Moss Island
24. Tufa Caves & Waterfalls of Van Hornesville
Victorian Age
8. Shelving Rock Mountain & Shelving Rock Falls
9. Prospect Mountain
13. Mt. Jo & Mt. Van Hoevenberg
15. East Branch of the Ausable River & Adirondack Mountain Reserve
18. Paul Smiths
Gilded Age
15. East Branch of the Ausable River & Adirondack Mountain Reserve
16. Santanoni
17. The Sagamore
18. Paul Smiths

Islands
1. Valcour Island
23. Moss Island

Hikes by Theme

Lakes/ Ponds
5. Ironville & Penfield Homestead
6. Rock Pond
10. Fort George & Bloody Pond
13. Mt. Jo & Mt. Van Hoevenberg
14. Adirondac & Indian Pass
18. Paul Smiths
21. Kunjamuk Cave

Lake Views
Lake Champlain
  1. Valcour Island
  2. Coon Mountain
  3. Crown Point: Fort St. Frederic & His Majesty's Fort of Crown Point
  4. Fort Ticonderoga

Lake George
  8. Shelving Rock Mountain & Shelving Rock Falls
  9. Prospect Mountain
  10. Fort George & Bloody Pond

Heart Lake
  13. Mt. Jo & Mt. Van Hoevenberg

Lighthouses
1. Valcour Island
3. Crown Point: Fort St. Frederic & His Majesty's Fort of Crown Point

Mansions, Houses, & Estates
5. Ironville & Penfield Homestead
12. John Brown's Farm
14. Adirondac & Indian Pass
16. Santanoni
17. The Sagamore

Mines
6. Rock Pond
14. Adirondac & Indian Pass
19. Hooper Garnet Mine
21. Kunjamuk Cave
26. Wolf Hollow

Mountains/Hills
2. Coon Mountain
7. Rogers Rock
8. Shelving Rock Mountain & Shelving Rock Falls
9. Prospect Mountain
13. Mt. Jo & Mt. Van Hoevenberg
14. Adirondac & Indian Pass
15. East Branch of the Ausable River & Adirondack Mountain Reserve
19. Hooper Garnet Mine
20. Chimney Mountain

Potholes
8. Shelving Rock Mountain & Shelving Rock Falls
23. Moss Island
25. Canajoharie Gorge

Rivers/Creeks
5. Ironville & Penfield Homestead
8. Shelving Rock Mountain & Shelving Rock Falls
11. Cooper's Cave & Betar Byway
14. Adirondac & Indian Pass
15. East Branch of the Ausable River & Adirondack Mountain Reserve
17. The Sagamore
18. Paul Smiths
21. Kunjamuk Cave
22. Griffin, Griffin Falls, & Auger Falls
23. Moss Island
24. Tufa Caves & Waterfalls of Van Hornesville
25. Canajoharie Gorge

Rock Climbing
14. Adirondac & Indian Pass
23. Moss Island

Rock Formations
1. Valcour Island
7. Rogers Rock
15. East Branch of the Ausable River & Adirondack Mountain Reserve

23. Moss Island
24. Tufa Caves & Waterfalls of Van Hornesville
25. Canajoharie Gorge

Ruins

1. Valcour Island
3. Crown Point: Fort St. Frederic & His Majesty's Fort of Crown Point
4. Fort Ticonderoga
5. Ironville & Penfield Homestead
6. Rock Pond
8. Shelving Rock Mountain & Shelving Rock Falls
9. Prospect Mountain
10. Fort George & Bloody Pond
11. Cooper's Cave & Betar Byway
14. Adirondac & Indian Pass

18. Paul Smiths
22. Griffin
23. Moss Island

Waterfalls

5. Ironville & Penfield Homestead
8. Shelving Rock Mountain & Shelving Rock Falls
11. Coopers Cave & Betar Byway
14. Adirondac & Indian Pass
15. East Branch of the Ausable River & Adirondack Mountain Reserve
17. The Sagamore
18. Paul Smiths
22. Griffin, Griffin Falls, & Auger Falls
24. Tufa Caves & Waterfalls of Van Hornesville
25. Canajoharie Gorge

Hikes According to Level of Difficulty

Easy
3. Crown Point: Fort St. Frederic & His Majesty's Fort of Crown Point
4. Fort Ticonderoga
5. Ironville & Penfield Homestead
14. Adirondac (note that Indian Pass is difficult)
8. Shelving Rock Falls
11. Cooper's Cave & Betar Byway
12. John Brown's Farm
18. Paul Smiths
22. Griffin & Griffin Falls
24. Tufa Caves & Waterfalls of Van Hornesville
25. Canajoharie Gorge
26. Wolf Hollow

Easy to Moderate
19. Hooper Garnet Mine
23. Moss Island

Moderate
2. Coon Mountain
10. Fort George & Bloody Pond
17. The Sagamore
21. Kunjamuk Cave
22. Griffin Falls to Auger Falls

Moderate to Difficult
6. Rock Pond
8. Shelving Rock Mountain
9. Prospect Mountain
13. Mt. Jo
13. Mt. Van Hoevenberg
20. Chimney Mountain

Difficult
1. Valcour Island
7. Rogers Rock
14. Indian Pass
15. East Branch of the Ausable River & Adirondack Mountain Reserve
16. Santanoni

ADIRONDACK

Trails *with* Tales

Part I: Champlain Valley Region

The six hikes in the Champlain Valley region follow in the footsteps of the early Native Americans, European colonials, French and Indian War soldiers, Revolutionary War heroes and scoundrels, mining company entrepreneurs, and everyday industrious individuals who sought work and freedom on the scenic shores of Lake Champlain in the shadows of the Adirondacks.

Lake Champlain is the "Great Lake" of eastern New York/New England. In fact, except for the five Great Lakes, it is the largest body of water in the United States. It covers 440 square miles and is 128 miles long, with a maximum depth of nearly 400 feet. It contains 70 islands (of which Valcour Island holds the most significant naval history), and has 587 miles of shoreline.[1] It has also been called Corlear Lake, Lake Hiracois, and Lake Iroquois in days gone by.[2]

In 1609, when Samuel de Champlain—the first European to explore this magnificent body of water—sailed south on Lake Champlain, it was firmly controlled by two major tribes of Native Americans, the Mohawks and the Algonquins. With the arrogance typical of European explorers of that time, however, Champlain immediately claimed the lake for France. Soon thereafter the lake came to be known as Lake Champlain and provided the French with an excellent water route south from Canada and the St. Lawrence River to Lac du St. Sacrement (Lake George). Controlling the waterways was essential for transportation and trade, and was key to exploration and settlement. By the mid-1700s the French were using this route to invade the British colonies.

Unknown to Champlain at the time, that very year he "discovered" Lake Champlain, 1609, Henry Hudson, an Englishman in the employ of the Dutch, was sailing north up what would become known as the Hudson River. For the rest of the seventeenth century, the Dutch, British, and French flexed their muscles in the New World, intent on establishing trade routes and gaining territory.

By the early eighteenth century, boundaries were drawn. In 1730 the French had moved south on Lake Champlain to build a stone fort at Crown Point. The eastern coast of America was being settled by the British, whose

The Spirit of 1776. Long live Yankee Doodle! Postcard ca. 1930.

population south of the Canadian border had reached nearly one million people, not counting the Native Americans in their midst.[3] Regular stagecoach service had begun between Boston and Newport, Rhode Island.

Tensions had begun to simmer in the provinces by 1744, when King George's War extended to the British and French colonies. In 1754 the colonies erupted as the North American theater of what became known as the Seven Years War. In America this is often called the French and Indian War, referring to the royal French forces, the French Canadians, and the various Native American tribes who sided with the French and Canadians against the British, their American colonists, and the Native Americans who sided with the British. Although the official declaration of war between Britain and France came in 1756, and the war ended with the signing of the Treaty of Paris in 1763 (hence the name Seven Years War), it was a nine-year war in the colonies.

After the British claimed victory, there was a short time of peace in the Champlain Valley between the years 1764–1774 when settlers like William Gilliland, the subject of the Coon Mountain hike, sought to make their fortune as pioneers along the northern banks of Lake Champlain. A lively period of commerce commenced on the lake, but was soon cut short by the American Revolution. Lake Champlain once again became a military highway.

Some of the most fascinating history of the American Revolution occurred near the forts at Ticonderoga and Crown Point and is described in the chapters on hikes at those sites. In 1775–1776, Benedict Arnold and Ethan Allen became heroes of the Revolution while chasing the British up and down Lake Champlain. Valcour Island was an especially significant battleground.

Once the Revolution had been won, entrepreneurs in the nineteenth century remembered that there were veins of iron ore and other minerals that might be extracted from under the fertile soil of the Champlain Valley. The business of building America was now at hand. Its seemingly inexhaustible forests were being harvested, and iron ore was needed for implements and machinery. Railroads were built, and once again Lake Champlain became a commercial highway. Mines prospered at Hammondville and Ironville, as described in the chapters on walks to Rock Pond and the village of Ironville. Crown Point and Port Henry became significant ports for the nineteenth-century iron mines in the Champlain area. Gradually, however, the best veins of ore ran out and mining faded in the valley.

Today the mines are closed, and the mighty, renovated Fort Ticonderoga and the skeletal remains of the fort at Crown Point are preserved parks and visitor attractions. Valcour Island, silent witness to colonial America's first naval battle, sits peacefully a mile east from land once owned by William Gilliland, founder of Willsboro. Ironville is now an historic town, and the Penfield homestead is a museum dedicated to nineteenth-century mining in the Champlain Valley. Rock Pond, another mine site, is hidden in the forest, but luckily contained on state land accessible by a marked trail.

Lake Champlain and the surrounding shores and mountains remain beautiful, scenic areas for boating and hiking. The bridge at Crown Point and the ferries at Essex and Plattsburgh make it fairly easy to tack from the New York to the Vermont sides of the lake, enhancing recreational possibilities.

In this section, you will walk through at least 400 years of European history in the Champlain Valley.

Valcour Island: Visit a rugged island with naval history going back to the Revolutionary War. Although its many summer homes are gone, ruins remain, including a working nineteenth-century lighthouse that has been restored to full function.

Coon Mountain: When William Gilliland, founder of an eighteenth-century farming colony in the area, died from exposure on Coon Mountain, his name became forever linked with that mountain. Gilliland prospered following the French and Indian War, only to see his colony diminished after the Revolution. His saga as a colonial pioneer is a fascinating story of achievements and setbacks in the wild lands bordering Lake Champlain and extending into the heart of the Adirondacks.

Crown Point—Fort St. Frederic & His Majesty's Fort of Crown Point: This is an outstanding opportunity to see layers of history side by side—His Majesty's Fort of Crown Point (Fort Amherst), built in stages by the English between 1759 and 1763, and the earlier Fort St. Frederic, built by the French in the 1730s.

Fort Ticonderoga: Reconstructed in the twentieth century with painstaking attention to detail, Fort Ticonderoga provides the opportunity to experience what it must have been like living there during the 1700s when the fort was the site of major ongoing battles.

Ironville & Penfield Homestead: Walk through a preserved mining community that is considered to be the "birthplace of the electric age."

Rock Pond: Although now desolate and remote, at one time Rock Pond was a vibrant site of mining activity.

1 VALCOUR ISLAND

Location: Peru (Clinton County), Lake Champlain
DeLorme NYS Atlas & Gazetteer: p. 103, CD6

Fee: None

Hours: Daily, open continuously

Accessibility: The island can be reached by boat, canoe, or kayak during the spring, summer, and fall, or by foot, snowshoes, or cross-country skis during the winter when the lake has sufficiently frozen over with a covering of at least five inches of ice.

Degree of Difficulty: Difficult, because of the 1.0-mile traverse of water to reach island, followed by 7.5 miles of hiking around the perimeter of the island.

Restrictions: Camping is allowed by permit. Permits can be obtained from the caretaker at the Peru Dock or, if you have already selected a campsite, from the forest ranger that patrols the sites daily by boat.

Remarks: If you are crossing Lake Champlain in the winter, make sure that the ice is thick enough to support your weight. Ice-fishing season typically begins in mid-December at the northern end of Lake Champlain and advances south as winter progresses. Do not head out onto the lake unless the ice is five inches thick. Be aware of the possibility of open water near the mainland, the island, and where streams come into the lake, even when the rest of the lake is covered with ice.

Animals, especially deer, have been observed not only making their way to the island across the ice during the winter, but swimming between the island and the western shore during open water seasons (something humans should not attempt).

Highlights:
- Offshore site of 1776 naval battle led by General Benedict Arnold against British forces
- Several foundation ruins and stone artifacts
- Preserved stone exterior of the Seton Mansion

■ Bluff Point Lighthouse
■ Limestone caves

Description: This amazing paddle/hike combines natural beauty with the history of the American Revolution, Civil War and beyond.

Valcour Island, which lies within the boundaries of the Adirondack Park, sits less than a mile off the western shore of Lake Champlain and is about five miles south of Plattsburgh. It is two miles long and roughly one mile wide, containing 980 acres of New York State parkland with eleven miles of trails, a day-use picnic area, and twenty-six primitive campsites. The Perimeter Trail is 7.5 miles long.[1] The island, with its craggy cliffs that jut up high out of the water, was formed out of limestone bedrock that was deposited 450 million years ago.[2] The island is accessible only by boat or by crossing the ice in the winter. It serves as a permanent home for birds, especially great blue heron, and a variety of small animals, along with some deer that are tolerant of visiting humans.

Valcour Island's greatest historical claim to fame is the offshore naval battle that took place near the beginning of the Revolutionary War, when American Brigadier General Benedict Arnold squared off against British General Sir Guy Carleton and commander of the British fleet, Captain Thomas Pringle, during the Battle of Valcour Island. Although the Americans didn't exactly win the battle, they were effective in disrupting the progress of the British troops into the Hudson Valley, a result that many historians believe played a pivotal role in the eventual outcome of the war.

Directions: From the Adirondack Northway (I-87), take Exit 35 for Peru and Valcour, and drive east on Bear Swamp Road (Rt. 442) for 2.8 miles. Turn left onto Rt. 9 and drive north for 3.2 miles, then turn right at the sign for the Peru Dock Boat Launch.

For kayak or canoe rentals, continue north on Rt. 9 for another 0.3 mile from Peru Dock until you reach the Kayak Shack, which will be on your left.

To reach the island by boat, canoe, kayak, or x-country skies/snowshoes: Be sure to sign in at the DEC registry next to the launch site before setting out across the lake. From the Peru State Boat Launch, paddle southeast across the lake towards Valcour Island, using the lighthouse on Bluff Point as your reference. The high cliffs at Bluff Point prevent landing there, so keep the lighthouse to your left and follow the contour of the shoreline as it leads around the corner of Bluff Point into Bullhead Bay, south of the lighthouse. In Bullhead Bay, put in on the sandy beach roughly midway between the cove's two endpoints.

Valcour Island

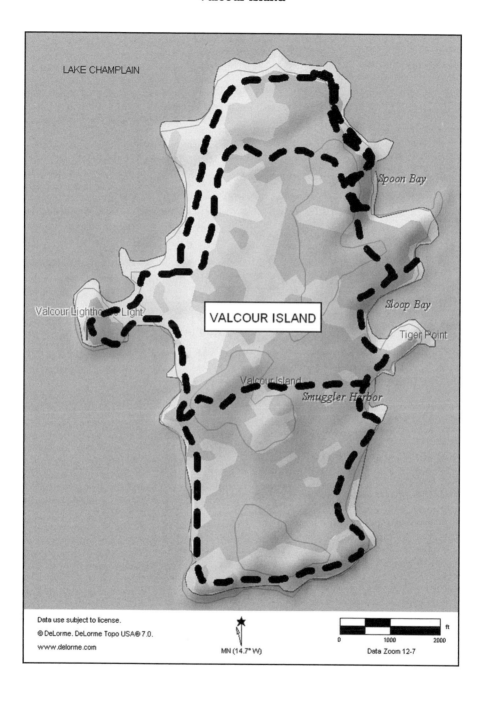

LAKE CHAMPLAIN

Spoon Bay

Sloop Bay

Tiger Point

VALCOUR ISLAND

Valcour Lighthouse Light

Valcour Island

Smuggler Harbor

MN (14.7° W)

0   1000   2000   ft

Data Zoom 12-7

The Hike

For this hike we will be following the perimeter trail as it winds around Valcour Island, bypassing the two connecting trails that span the island's width. The perimeter trail is far more interesting and enjoyable than the connecting trails as it provides ongoing views of the lake.

As you hike around the island, bear in mind that at one time several large farms operated along the western shore and numerous private cottages and camps could be found near many of the bays. Private landownership began to wane after 1963, however, as New York State started purchasing tracts of land. The state's grip on the island tightened further in 1972 when the boundaries of the Adirondack Park were extended to include Valcour Island. In the mid-1970s, work crews were sent to the island to demolish most of the private homes and other structures that had been purchased by the state and were not considered historically significant. This even included removing most of the foundations to allow the land to return to its original state.

As you get set to begin the hike, it's worth noting that the island's alpine-like flora is more characteristic of the Adirondack High Peaks region than of the Champlain Valley. The harsh winds that bear down on Valcour Island are undoubtedly responsible.

The trail that you will be following was completed by the Department of Environmental Conservation in 1976, the nation's bicentennial. The yellow decals marking the trail depict the *Royal Savage*, Benedict Arnold's flagship, which was sunk in shallow waters 150 feet from the island's southwest end during the Battle of Valcour Island. From the 1870s to the early 1930s, numerous artifacts, including cannonballs, bar-shot, and grapeshot material, were brought up from the ship. Finally, in 1934, Lorenzo Hagglund, a prominent East Coast salvage engineer, brought up what remained of the vessel, which further deteriorated upon drying out. Its surviving remnants were kept in storage in Pennsylvania for many years.[3]

Begin by walking south along the beach until you see a yellow-blazed path leading into the woods. This is the perimeter trail, which circles the entire island. Follow the trail south for 0.1 mile to the first junction. The path to the left leads in 0.4 mile to the Royal Savage Trail (one of two connecting paths that traverse the island's middle). Continue straight ahead on the perimeter trail. In another 0.1 mile you will come to a field on the left where an old foundation can be seen near the southwest corner.

At roughly 0.4 mile from the start, you will reach the first of two trails that cross the island from west-to-east. It is called the Nomad Trail and leads in 0.8 mile to the east side of the island and Smuggler Harbor. The path is named after the *Nomad*—a World War I vessel that was torpedoed in the North Atlantic and sank with its captain and crewmembers.

The Seton Mansion is one of only two surviving structures on the island. The others were razed years ago to conform to New York State's policy of "forever wild." Photograph 2008.

The trail to your right takes you in less than 0.1 mile to an open field with campsites next to Indian Point, which overlooks the waters where Benedict Arnold's fleet hid while waiting to do battle with the British navy. If you stand at Indian Point and look north, you will see that you are at the southwest end of Bullhead Bay.

Return to the perimeter trail. Continuing south, you will soon pass by a cistern, an old stone column, and faint ruins from a past boys' camp. In roughly 0.4 mile from the Nomad Trail junction, you will walk past a tiny sinkhole to your right, a reminder that you are walking on bedrock formed of limestone, a sedimentary rock that is readily eroded to produce caves and karst features.

In another 0.1 mile you will come to Seton Mansion—a two-story house constructed of limestone blocks, with a wooden awning overhanging the porch. This is one of the few structures on Valcour Island that was considered historically significant enough not to be demolished when the state came into possession of the land. All the windows and entrances have been boarded shut. Hikers should respect the "no trespassing" signs. Seton Mansion was built by Henry Seton in 1929 from stone quarried on the island. Seton's estate included 129 acres that he had purchased in 1919, part of which contained a 200-year-old blue heron rookery. In 1973 New York State acquired the property from Seton after finally agreeing to formulate a management plan for the island.

Walk down towards the lake and you will quickly reach a lower, 10-foot-square stone building that overlooks the lake. From this smaller structure a flight of stone stairs leads down to a concrete jetty.

Incoming boats can still put in at the jetty downhill from the Seton Mansion. Photograph 2008.

From the rear of the mansion, follow the perimeter path uphill through a cutout in the bedrock and then turn left as you begin to parallel the south end of Valcour Island. The island's southwesternmost extremity is called Cedar Point. Within 0.05 mile from Seton Mansion, you will come to a short side path on the right that leads to a high overlook of Lake Champlain. From the overlook, Garden Island looms large to the southeast of Valcour Island

Return to the main trail and proceed east, following the path as it takes you through a karst-like area where the bedrock is deeply fissured. (Watch your footing). In another 0.1 mile the trail leads steadily downhill and then levels off, taking you through a section of trail heavily covered with pine needles. While hiking along this portion of the trail, you can periodically bushwhack over to the cliff face if you wish to obtain slightly varying views from the top of the high bluffs. In many places enormous blocks of talus have splintered off from the cliff face and are visible in the shallows below. The bluffs at their highest point loom 191 feet above sea level (not to be confused with lake level). By comparison, the shoreline in general averages 96 feet above sea level.[4]

Approaching the southeast corner of the island, called Cystid Point by some (and by others Heron Point), you will pass by a considerable amount of blow-down. You will also see a sign that states "Islands End." Cystid Point is named after a type of fossil that abounds near the base of the cliffs at the southeast end.[5] Unfortunately, the trail never takes you to the very tip of the island; instead it rather sharply veers left and heads north, taking you deeper into the woods.

In 0.3 mile you will suddenly come out to a commanding view of the lake at a spot called The Garden Overlook, named for its perfect, southeast view of nearby Garden Island. Looking further east across the lake towards Vermont, you can see distant Providence Island, separated from South Hero (a very large island on the Vermont side) by a passageway called The Narrows. Garden Island has also been called Gunboat Island[6] because sailors have mistaken its shape in low light or in fog for a small battleship.

In another 0.1 mile the trail returns to being near the escarpment and then descends rapidly, bringing you closer to water level where you will see a rocky beach with huge rock slabs adorning the shoreline and tilting down into the water. After another 0.5 mile you will reach Smuggler Harbor, a well-protected bay shaped like the letter "C." On the beach near the southwest end of the harbor is a wrought-iron fence that encloses a memorial to Captain Gerald Walker Birks and the crew of the *Nomad*. According to the historic plaque set into the bedrock, the captain and crew "fell fighting with the Canadian and Imperial Forces in the Great War, 1914–1918." Captain Birks and his crew had often visited Valcour Island and enjoyed their time there.

From the memorial, continue north along the perimeter trail and you will immediately come to the junction with the Nomad Trail. The Nomad Trail leads west across the island, arriving at Indian Point, near where you initially started, in 0.8 mile. Behind you is Islands End, roughly 1.3 miles south; ahead are Sloop Cove & Paradise Bay, approximately 0.5 mile distant.

A view of Tiger Point from Smuggler Harbor. Photograph 2008.

11

Continue north on the perimeter trail. In 0.2 mile you will reach the northeast tip of Smuggler Harbor, where gorgeous views of the cove can be obtained from the rocky shoreline next to campsite #15. From the campsite, walk northeast for less than one hundred feet and you will see Tiger Point to the north, a tiny nub of rock that has nearly separated from the island proper. Directly east of Tiger Point, on the Vermont side of the lake, is Phelps Point on South Hero Island next to The Narrows.

Return to the perimeter trail and follow it as it takes you briefly through a wooded area between Smuggler Harbor and Sloop Cove, bypassing the huge mass of land that extends east out into the lake and culminates at Tiger Point. You will reach Sloop Cove in less than 0.2 mile.

Follow the trail as it leads around the bay about fifteen feet above the water. In 0.1 mile you will come to the Sloop Cove Overlook, where fairly unobstructed views of Lake Champlain and the distant islands of Vermont can be obtained.

In another 0.1 mile you will arrive at another junction, having gone 0.2 mile from Sloop Cove and 0.5 mile from Smuggler Harbor. From the junction, follow the trail to your right that leads in 0.1 mile to Paradise Bay. Along the way you will pass by a fifteen-foot-high chimney several hundred feet before reaching the lake. The chimney is all that has survived from a log cabin once owned by "Father Moore" (Monsignor Robert Edward Moore), a Catholic priest. Limbo Island, named by Father Moore, is close at hand, only 0.1 mile distant.[7]

From the chimney, walk north for several hundred feet and then descend to the stony beach of Paradise Bay, where massive cliff walls can be seen to the left.

Return to the perimeter trail and head northwest. The trail takes you through dense woods with no lake views, bypassing Paradise Bay and Cumberland Bluff. In 0.3 mile you will come to a junction where the Royal Savage Trail enters from the west. The Royal Savage Trail leads west across the island for 1.3 miles, emerging at Butterfly Bay (which is north of the Bluff Point Lighthouse). The trail to the right leads to Spoon Bay in 0.05 mile, where it dead-ends at the beach. There are good views of Spoon Island from the beach. The island is virtually connected to Cumberland Bluff. Approximately 3.0 miles off in the distance, east towards Vermont, is Jackson Point on South Hero Island.

In order to continue north on the perimeter trail, you will begin by following the Royal Savage Trail west for several hundred feet and then bearing right at a second junction, proceeding north. You are now roughly 0.8 mile from the north end of Valcour Island.

After walking through a long stretch of woods, you will emerge at Beauty Bay in 0.3 mile where a high, cliff overlook provides inspiring views of the bay and its surrounding landscape. From there, the perimeter trail heads back into the woods, descending in another 0.1 mile to a lower level via a switchback. More campsites are encountered here.

In another 0.3 mile you will reach the northeast end of Valcour Island, where 0.5-mile-long Crab Island can be seen to the northwest, 1.5 miles distant. It was between Crab Island and the western mainland in 1759 that the French scuttled three warships during the French and Indian War, throwing armaments and cannons overboard to be retrieved later. They never returned, however, and it wasn't until the 1960s that scuba divers discovered the lost wreckage.

A famous naval battle was fought near Crab Island during the War of 1812. The pivotal Battle of Plattsburgh was fought in Cumberland Bay on Lake Champlain on September 11, 1814, when American ships led by Commodore Thomas MacDonough decisively defeated the British, turning the tide of war. Prior to the naval engagement about 10,000 British troops had advanced out of Canada to the Plattsburgh area. The American army was heavily outnumbered, but fought bravely. Once the naval engagement was decided in favor of the Americans, however, the British army was left without naval support and hastily retreated back to Canada.[8]

Crab Island is the burial site for American and British seamen who perished in the War of 1812. Until recently, Crab Island was also part of the U.S. Air Force base located south of Plattsburgh. It has now become overgrown with poison ivy except for the monument area, which is kept perpetually mowed in recognition of its status as a National Veterans Cemetery. Be mindful of poison ivy if you venture off-trail to other parts of the island.

The largest of the red-roofed buildings discernible from Bluff Point looking northwest to the mainland was once the Delaware & Hudson Railroad Company's Hotel Champlain. The original hotel opened in 1890, serving as the summer White House for President William McKinley in 1897. It burned to the ground in 1910 and was rebuilt in 1911. This building, along with cottages from the original hotel and several newer structures, is now Clinton Community College.[9]

Follow the trail west as it parallels the shoreline. Gone are the rocky bluffs that have characterized much of the southern and eastern parts of the island. Valcour Island's north shoreline is essentially beach-like. As you continue, you will pass by a number of campsites.

The northwest tip of Valcour Island is reached in 0.4 mile. There, Mason's Reef extends about 200 feet out from shore. Its hidden boulders and ledge rocks have left many boats foundering after claiming their props.

Bear left, now heading south. The topography changes appreciably here, becoming essentially flat and covered with shrubs, bushes, and tall grass. In 0.2 mile you will find yourself following what was once an old road. At 0.4

The Bluff Point
Lighthouse
became fully
operational
again in 2004.
Photograph 2008.

mile you will emerge onto a grassy field where an old piece of farm machinery
can be seen to your left. When you come to the end of this field, you will see
to the right an unusual, tombstone-shaped rock that juts out vertically from
the water near the shoreline.

Soon you will reach a sign that tells you that you have gone 0.9 mile from
the northwest end of the island. From there, Butterfly Bay quickly comes into
view with its long beach and campsites. Many of the trees along the shoreline
look ready to topple because erosion has undermined their roots.

In another 0.2 mile you will reach North Bay, likely named because of its
location just north of the Bluff Point Lighthouse. Finally, 0.3 mile south of
Butterfly Bay, you will reach the lighthouse junction. Turn right and follow
the path as it wends its way up to the top of Bluff Point, where the Bluff Point
Lighthouse awaits, 0.2 mile distant.

The Bluff Point Lighthouse was completed in 1874. Fashioned out of dark blue limestone and crowned by a red-shingled roof, the structure is rectangular with an integrated octagonal tower approximately thirty-five feet in overall height rising out of the lakeside front. During the early years it used a 5th order Fresnel lens, which could be seen from a distance of eighteen miles.[10] Presently it uses a solar-charged, battery-powered light. [11]

In 1930 a steel tower was built to the south of the lighthouse, and the light was transferred to this new structure. The days of the lighthouse seemed to be over. In 1954, however, a Massachusetts dentist named Adolph Raboff purchased the lighthouse and thirteen acres of surrounding land for a summer residence. In the mid-1980s, Raboff agreed to sell the property to the Adirondack State Park, but only after the state agreed to maintain the structure. The state now owns the property, and Clinton County Historical Society maintains the lighthouse.[12] In the summer months the lighthouse is open to the public on Sundays. There is no entry fee, but donations are welcomed. A visit to the small museum in the lighthouse provides the opportunity to learn of the area's history from a Historical Society docent. In 2004 the light was transferred from the nearby skeletal tower back to the lantern room atop the lighthouse's octagonal tower.

From southwest of the lighthouse, pick up the trail again next to the steel tower. Follow it downhill for 0.1 mile to the base of Bluff Point and then head east. In 0.2 mile you will pass yet another junction and then reach Bullhead Bay at 0.3 mile (near the point where you started). You have circumnavigated the island in 7.5 miles, plus any additional miles logged by following side paths.

History: Valcour Island is the epitome of a history hike, combining natural beauty with a fascinating and historically important Revolutionary War saga. In addition, the island now serves as the station for a historic nineteenth-century lighthouse, which since 2004 has been restored as a functional beacon and also serves as a museum (another interesting chapter in the island's history). There are many fascinating ruins as well, some with known stories, and others remaining mysterious, mute remnants of the past.

As a geologic phenomenon, the island owes some of its natural beauty to the development of its limestone bedrock, which in combination with the constant action of wind and waves on Lake Champlain has created over the millennia a number of fascinating little caves along its rocky shore. The rugged landscape, home to birds and wildlife, also supports cedar, birch, and oak trees, as well as a variety of wildflowers.

The Native Americans were the first to explore and inhabit Valcour Island, whose present name was first noted by Samuel de Champlain in his journal.[13] Indian Point was named for a Native American summer campsite on the point.[14]

By 1609, when Samuel de Champlain made his foray south on the lake, Valcour Island was securely within the boundaries of the Algonquin tribes, with the Iroquois claiming the southern portion of the lake below Rock Dunder.[15]

During the French and Indian War, 1754–1763, the Algonquins aligned with the French, helping to secure Lake Champlain against the British. Ultimately, however, the French lost, and Lake Champlain and its surrounding territory became a British prize of war, as did the waterways of Lake George and the Hudson River. These vital water resources were not to remain uncontested spoils for long, as American patriots increasingly chafed under British rule and demonstrated their desire to become independent from Britain.

Lake Champlain and Valcour Island were hotspots in the American Revolution. There was no way to command the rich corridors of the Champlain and Hudson valleys without first controlling the fortifications and waterways along Lake Champlain. The American patriots fought in earnest to claim and maintain the forts on the lake. A young General Benedict Arnold was one of the first American military men to see the strategic importance of controlling Lake Champlain.

By 1776 the Americans had captured both Fort Ticonderoga and the fort at Crown Point. But the British were far from vanquished, in good part because of their strong navy, which they were readying to deploy south up the Richelieu River to the northern reaches of Lake Champlain. The odds of military success on the lake were strongly in their favor. They had more boats and seaworthy sailors; plus, they had centuries of experience in strategic naval warfare. They also had Montreal as an important British stronghold to supply them.[16]

In spite of their lack of experience in naval battles, Arnold and the other American generals knew they needed to block the invasion by the British fleet that was gathering to set sail from the northern end of the lake. Britain was preparing an offensive attack that, if successful, would gain them control of the Hudson Valley by way of Lake Champlain and the Hudson River. Their plan was to push British troops south and link up with other British-led troops advancing north from New York, with Albany being the point of convergence.

Benedict Arnold was in charge of adding to the existing American fleet, which consisted of the schooners *Royal Savage* and *Liberty*, and the sloop *Enterprise* that had been captured earlier from the British or their supporters. Arnold had to increase the fleet and then sail north on Lake Champlain to halt the British invasion. In Fort Ticonderoga the schooner *Revenge* was built. In Skenesborough (now Whitehall) Arnold hastily built a cutter, four galleys, and eight gondolas. All of the new vessels were rigged, outfitted, and equipped at Fort Ticonderoga.[17]

Meanwhile, General Horatio Gates—Arnold's superior at Fort Ticonderoga—was charged with sending Arnold's request for additional ship captains and supplies to the Continental Congress, which was not very forthcoming with money, men, equipment, or armaments, none of which were in abundance in the colonies. As late as ten days before the British attack, Arnold lacked anchors, anchor cables, nails, rope, cannon shot, and food rations and rum.[18] According to some accounts, Gates was not quick to respond to Arnold's requests for men and supplies and, in fact, often undercut Arnold with Congress.[19] In Gates's defense, part of his reluctance to muster supplies might have been his opinion that the British wouldn't attack that year. As late as August 5, Colonel James Wilkinson had written to Schuyler's aide Varick saying, "Our navy is in great forwardness but I seriously believe we shall have no other use for them as to transport our army to Canada".[20] Nevertheless, some capable men and stalwart craft did arrive—but not in the numbers that Arnold had requested.[21]

Perhaps the seeds of discontent were already being sown in Arnold's mind as he fought on with inadequate forces and perceived lack of support from his superiors. Arnold was never adroit at gauging the political climate or maneuvering in that arena.

On September 18, 1776, Arnold wrote to Gates that he would move the fleet to Valcour Island "where there is a good harbor and where we shall have the advantage ... and if there are too many for us we can retire."[22] Gates was ambivalent about giving the full go-ahead to Arnold, however, because his own style of warfare tended to be defensive. Nevertheless, in this case he acceded to Arnold.

Meanwhile, the British were assembling a fleet of thirty-three vessels at St. Johns in Quebec on the Richelieu River at the northern outlet of Lake Champlain. Some of the ships, like the nearly 100-foot-long *Inflexible*, were much larger than any American boat.[23] In addition to the *Inflexible*, the British commanded two schooners, a large floating gun platform (or *radeau*), a gondola, twenty-four gunboats, and four long boats.[24] The British had delayed their invasion in order to build more boats, because Arnold had cleverly "leaked" a report that the Americans were busily increasing their capacity for naval warfare.[25]

By late September Arnold sailed north on Lake Champlain to Valcour Island, awaiting the enemy as planned. All the ships were present except for the *Gates*, which was not yet ready, and the *Liberty*, which had gone south for provisions. Altogether, Arnold commanded fifteen vessels with a total of eighty-six cannons.[26]

On October 11, 1776, the battle of Valcour Island took place—the first naval engagement between an American and British fleet. The American vessels were manned by a little over 700 men, very few of whom had extensive knowledge of sailing or shipboard fighting. Previous to the forthcoming battle, there had been very little in the way of naval warfare in the colonies.

The British, under the command of General Sir Guy Carleton and Captain Thomas Pringle, had about 1,000 army men. Some were artillerists onboard the gunboats. Others were put ashore on the mainland and on Valcour Island to capture Americans should they try to escape on foot. Although the number of cannons between the two fleets seemed comparable at first glance, in actual fact the British cannons were twice as powerful and capable of inflicting much greater punishment. There were also an undetermined number of Indian war canoes at the disposal of the British; each was capable of holding up to thirty warriors. More Indians were concealed along the shorelines to harass and worry the American fleet.

As if that were not enough, the British had also deployed ground troops down the west bank of Lake Champlain. These were led by General John Burgoyne, the new commander sent from London. It was truly a fight of David against Goliath.[27]

The British found they faced greater difficulties than they'd anticipated, however. Arnold devised a clever strategy of surprising the British by positioning American boats in areas that were out of sight of the west side of the island. The British fleet had already sailed south past Arnold's hideout when Arnold sent out four vessels to entice them to turn around. Now sailing into the wind, the British vessels could only approach Arnold's line one at a time, thus evening out the odds a bit.[28]

Still, Arnold remained greatly outmatched in men and firepower, despite putting forth a valiant effort. The fact of the matter was that the British ship *Inflexible* alone was superior to the entire American fleet. At nightfall Arnold, in a daring move, pulled off a military stunt that has echoed down through history. His fleet was in shambles. One gondola had been sunk, and the *Royal Savage* had run aground early in the battle and was later burned by the British. Many other boats were badly damaged. Somehow, under the cover of fog and darkness, Arnold managed to sneak the remaining boats past the British line, rendezvousing eight miles south at Schuler Island. Two more gondolas were scuttled there.

Once the ruse was discovered the next morning, the British followed in hot pursuit. They chased Arnold's ten remaining craft for two days, with a subsequent battle erupting on the second day of running. More havoc was wreaked on the American fleet. Cornered and desperate, Arnold drove his galley *Congress* ashore in Ferris Bay (later renamed Arnold Bay in his honor), along with four gondolas, and set them on fire as he and his men took off on foot with British forces and Indians still in pursuit. Arnold and his men, including Bayze Wells (who kept a journal about the encounter), scrambled ten miles through the woods on the eastern shore of the lake. They camped overnight opposite Crown Point. After traveling further south to Putnam Point, they were ferried over to Fort Ticonderoga.[29]

The fort at Crown Point had never been rebuilt after being largely destroyed in the French and Indian War. It served as a small American outpost under the command of Lt. Thomas Hartley. Now that Lake Champlain was under the control of the British, Hartley and Arnold burned what was left of the fort and hastily retreated to the safety of Fort Ticonderoga.[30]

The British fleet anchored near Crown Point on October 13, 1776, and took possession of the now ruined fortress,[31] but General Carleton now had second thoughts about staying in the area with winter fast approaching. A siege of Fort Ticonderoga could be long and costly. The ruins of Crown Point offered little sanctuary for his forces during the winter and, once the lake froze over, communication and supply lines could be seriously hampered. For these reasons Carleton's forces sailed north on November 1, 1776, retreating back to winter quarters in Quebec.[32] That Arnold had successfully repelled the British was beyond dispute. That Carleton had made numerous errors, and then fudged his report to cover his own timidity, is beyond doubt. Many of Carleton's officers never forgave him.[33] But that's another story.

The Battle of Valcour Island had been a successful, strategic victory for the Americans. If not for the brave, calculated actions of General Arnold and his fleet, the British would surely have been unstoppable. At this point in his military career, Benedict Arnold was a patriot hero and admired by all.

The British now controlled Lake Champlain, but they had lost another year, and time was on the Americans' side. Carleton's withdrawal temporarily relieved enough pressure on Ticonderoga that General Gates was able to send troops south to fight under General Washington in his famous victory at Trenton, New Jersey, on the day after Christmas.[34]

The Americans gained strength in numbers by the spring of 1777 and had readied their forts and outposts along the Hudson River corridor for the next (and last) attempt by the British to gain control of these territories. On October 17, 1777, British General John Burgoyne surrendered (technically signing a treaty of convention) to General Gates after the American victory in the Battle of Saratoga, and the British attempt to cut the colonies in two had been thwarted.

Benedict Arnold was born into a seafaring family, but he was a pharmacist and bookseller before joining the military. British General John Burgoyne was formerly a playwright.[35]

Valcour Island stayed out of the limelight from 1777 to 1874, when Bluff Point Lighthouse was built and activated on the southwestern side of the island. The first lighthouse keeper was Major William Herwerth, a Civil War veteran who had been wounded in battle and remained sickly. Though his health continued to deteriorate, his wife Mary was up to the job and assumed most of the lighthouse responsibilities. In 1881, when William died, Mary was appointed keeper and kept the lighthouse until 1902. The lighthouse remained active until 1930, when a steel tower with an automatic light was established on the island.

In 1954, Dr. Adolph Raboff bought the lighthouse for use as a summer residence. He and his family decided to offer the historic building and property to the state of New York to be part of the Adirondack Park. The deal nearly fell through when they received word that the plan was to raze the structure. Fortunately, the Clinton County Historical Association offered to assist in the renovation and maintenance of the lighthouse. On June 11, 2005, a celebration was held to relight the light.

Valcour Island had a period of celebrity, or notoriety, in the 1870s when a controversial group known as the Dawn Valcour Agricultural and Historical Association settled in a commune on the island. The nineteenth century spawned a number of intentional communities,* including the Shakers and the Oneida communities. The Dawn Valcour community was similar to the Oneida group. They were primarily noted for espousing "free love" and being opposed to marriage.[36] The group, which never numbered more than twenty individuals at a time, only lasted about one year, failing for various reasons— the harsh winter climate, unfavorable regional public opinion, and landowner- ship issues.[37]

As a curious point of interest, a local Plattsburgh architect named William H. Prescott submitted a proposal to the Thousand Islands State Park Commission in 1968 to turn Valcour Island into a zoo, with giant movie screens set up on the northwest side of the island so that boaters could line up, as though at an outdoor movie theater, to watch educational films about activities in the western United States.[38] Fortunately, no action was ever taken on this proposal.

Caves: Valcour Island is home to a number of small joint caves, which have formed by weathering and freezing along vertical cracks in the rock. The island is essentially formed out of limestone (a very soluble rock) and, of course, surrounded by water (a weak acid that eventually wears down rock). The caves are located around the perimeter of the island at water level or

---

* Communities where people lived together to share a common lifestyle or belief system.

above, and were formed by the erosive action of waves against the rocky bluffs. The caves were first described by Dr. George H. Hudson in 1910 in a New York State Museum report entitled "Joint Caves of Valcour Island."[39] Dr. Hudson spent years studying and writing about the unique geology of Valcour Island. Since then, additional caves have been discovered through further exploration.

The largest cave is probably Tucker Cave, a maze with 430 feet of passageways. Several other notable caves are Bridge Cave, Darkroom Cave, and Spoon Pit Cave. For the most part, the caves are only visible from the water's edge, which means that they are best seen by canoe, boat, or sea kayak.

2 COON MOUNTAIN

Location: Westport (Essex County)
DeLorme NYS Atlas & Gazetteer: p. 97, BC6

Fee: None

Accessibility: There are two trails. The Summit Trail is 1.0 mile (one-way), with a 500-foot ascent. The Hidden Valley trail is about 0.5 (one-way) before it links with the Summit Trail.

Degree of Difficulty: Summit Trail—Moderate; Hidden Valley Trail— Easy

Restrictions: No camping or motorized vehicles. The trails are maintained for hiking only.

Additional information: contact Adirondack Land Trust, Box 65, Keene Valley, NY 12943. (518) 576-2082.

Highlights:
- 240-degree panorama of the Adirondack High Peaks, Lake Champlain, and Green Mountains of Vermont
- Site of William Gilliland's demise

Description: This scenic hike up a small mountain to a 1,030-foot-high summit (roughly 660 feet above Lake Champlain)[1] is on historic property that was owned by William Gilliland from the period following the French and Indian War until after the American Revolution. This land holds a story of brave immigrant settlers venturing into the Adirondack wilderness under the guidance of Gilliland, a natural leader who sought his fortune in founding the earliest colony on Lake Champlain, north of Crown Point. Coon Mountain, at one time the property of William Gilliland, later became the site of his demise. There was a plaque on Route 22 above Wadhams commemorating Gilliland's death. Unfortunately, the marker is no longer standing and is stored in the hamlet of Essex. The marker read: "Coon Mountain, near the northern base of this mountain, William Gilliland, early pioneer of Champlain Valley, met his tragic death in 1796".[2]

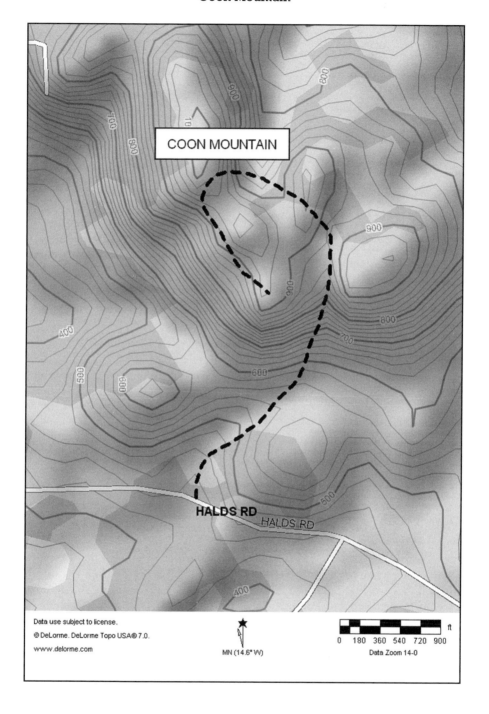

COON MOUNTAIN

HALDS RD
HALDS RD

Data use subject to license.
© DeLorme. DeLorme Topo USA® 7.0.
www.delorme.com

MN (14.6° W)

0   180   360   540   720   900   ft

Data Zoom 14-0

Coon Mountain today is a 246-acre preserve that is part of the Adirondack Land Trust's Champlain Valley Farm and Forest Project. In 2003 an additional 72 acres were acquired from the Ward Lumber Company.[3] You can readily hike to the top of the mountain to view the historic lands that were fought over in various times by Native Americans, Samuel de Champlain, French and British soldiers, and American patriots in order to control the important water route of Lake Champlain. The mountaintop consists of five rocky summits.

Directions: From the Adirondack Northway (I-87), take Exit 31 for Elizabethtown, Westport, and Rt. 9N. From the Northway overpass, drive east on Rt. 9N for 0.1 mile and turn left onto Youngs Road. Drive northeast for 2.6 miles. Turn right onto Elizabethtown-Wadhams Road (Rt. 8) and drive southeast for 0.1 mile. Turn left onto Rt. 22, cross over the Boquet River, and head northeast for 0.9 mile. At Morrison Road turn right and drive southeast. At 0.9 mile you will cross over a one-lane bridge spanning the Boquet River. Continue straight across River Road onto Halds Road and proceed east for 0.8 mile. The parking area will be on your left.

The Hike

The trail up Coon Mountain is indicated by green markers with white lettering and an arrow in the center to show direction.

As soon as you walk past the kiosk by the parking area, you will come to a junction where the Hidden Valley Trail goes left and the Summit Trail goes right. The Hidden Valley Trail provides a loop of roughly 0.5 mile and returns to the Summit Trail approximately 0.2 mile farther uphill.

For this hike, stay on the Summit Trail (the first part of which is an old road). After 0.1 mile the trail veers to the left and begins climbing steadily uphill as the old road (now blocked off) continues straight ahead. In 0.2 mile the upper section of the Hidden Valley Trail comes in on the left and provides an alternate route back to the parking area when you return from the top of the mountain.

Continue climbing uphill, now passing a forest directly on the right that is marked by posted signs. In 0.4 mile you will reach the beginning of a notch that breaks through the otherwise indomitable wall of the mountain. The trail continues up through this pass, gaining altitude steadily, with large stones placed strategically along the pathway to provide convenient steps for those who would otherwise find the going difficult. It is a very exciting climb, with vertical walls to the left towering over forty feet high. During the spring a small brook runs down through the notch, deriving its waters primarily from a tiny vernal pool that you will pass by near the summit.

In 0.6 mile you will reach the top of the pass, where the trail turns left and enters a small ravine. Although the ravine can be seasonally wet, stones have been thoughtfully placed to provide steps from one rock to the next.

In 0.7 mile, just after you pass by a vernal pool of water, the trail turns left and wends its way around a rocky mass, spiraling its way up to the summit and seemingly following the natural architecture of the mountain.

In another 0.1 mile you will come up to an area of flat rock near the top with great views of the surrounding lands. Continue on the path for several hundred feet more and you will reach the highest point on this section of the mountain, where an expansive area of exposed bedrock provides 240-degree views of the Green Mountains to the distant east, Lake Champlain (particularly Northwest Bay) and the Champlain Valley relatively close by, and the Adirondack High Peaks (Dix, Giant, and others) to the southwest.[4] A swamp is visible to the northeast, roughly 1.0 mile away.

Hidden Valley Trail—This trail provides an alternate route from the parking lot to the Summit Trail. It follows several seasonal brooks and passes through a biologically rich valley, a number of huge rock outcroppings, and then through a relatively young forest before intersecting with the Summit Trail. If you traverse either of these trails in the early spring, you may see a wide array of wildflowers including trillium, trout lily, Jack-in-the-pulpit, hobblebush, and foamflower.

Views from the summit of Coon Mountain looking southeast toward Lake Champlain. Photograph 2008.

History: The preserve was created through the generosity of Peter S. Paine Jr. and is owned by the Adirondack Land Trust. Today, the preserve is part of a small patchwork of protected lands. To the northeast a working farm is protected under a Land Trust easement, and a small woodland area is protected by a conservation easement held by the Northeast Wilderness Trust. New York State's Split Rock Mountain Wild Forest, which is the largest undeveloped property along Lake Champlain and includes Webb Royce Swamp, is a short distance to the northeast. It also has hiking trails.

Coon Mountain and the land bordering Lake Champlain near Westport are rich with stories about early settlers and mythical panthers that roamed the mountains. It is, in fact, an area bordering the Adirondacks that was on its way to prosperity before the Revolution and the birth of America. When the Treaty of 1763 was ratified, signaling the end of the Seven Years War and ceding Canada to Great Britain, Lake Champlain was no longer the portal between hostile nations, at least for the moment.[5]

It is hard today to imagine just how wild and inhospitable the shores and inland woods above Crown Point must have been around the time of the French and Indian War. Nevertheless, under the authority of colonial British offices, land grants along Lake Champlain were offered to officers and soldiers who had fought the wars against the French. It is no wonder that many grantees had second thoughts and decided to sell their land titles. Land speculation was rampant, with many landowners hoping to make a profit while retreating to the relative comforts of Albany, Boston, or New York. It would take a hardy man of vision to think in terms of buying vast acreage in the wilderness and then encouraging good numbers of other individuals to join him in settling this picturesque, but untamed, territory. And that is precisely what William Gilliland set out to do.

Gilliland's story is in some ways typical of immigrants of the time. He left Ireland under some duress to seek his good fortune in the colonies. He might have stayed happily in Ireland, however, if the wealthy father of his true love hadn't refused Gilliland his noble-born daughter's hand in marriage. Shortly thereafter, circa 1754, Gilliland set sail for New York. It was not an easy journey, nor one that guaranteed business success at the end of the line, but Gilliland seemed to be highly intelligent and willing to work hard. He was employed in the mercantile trade in New York City and established his own business there by 1759. That same year he married Elizabeth Phagan, an orphan with a considerable dowry, who had been under the guardianship of two respected gentlemen of the city.[6] Other sources state that Gilliland's first employ was with Mr. Phagan, an established merchant, and that he quickly achieved favorable notice and was promoted. These sources say that soon afterward he married Elizabeth, the boss's daughter, and received a large dowry.[7]

The story might have ended there. But William was not content to remain simply the successful prosperous New York merchant. He had greater dreams and ambitions and thought, why not become feudal lord of his own colony? He seized the opportunity at hand to acquire land in the uncharted wilderness on the upper reaches of Lake Champlain.

In 1765, William Gilliland bought twelve large land tracts on Lake Champlain above Crown Point to establish a farming colony.[8] The French and Indian (or Seven Years) War had concluded, and there were vast tracts of land in the northern regions open for speculation and purchase.[9] Up until that time Crown Point was the most northern community established on the lake, originally having been a French settlement surrounding Fort St. Frederic and built by Canadians under the French flag. The lands Gilliland proposed to settle were virgin territory.[10]

He was ambitious, and hoped to become wealthy while creating his empire. Luckily for future generations, he kept a meticulous journal titled the *Willsborough Day Book* over a two-year period. The journal describes his purchase, the journey north, the surveys of land, building the settlement of Willsborough (now Willsboro), named after him, and all his successes and tribulations. It is an amazing and fascinating document. In summing up the story of William Gilliland, Winslow Watson said in 1863, "His life was a romance—basking in brilliancy and hope—steeped in adversity—culminating in the highest prosperity, it closed its infinite vicissitudes in darkness and gloom and by a tragic end."[11]

According to Gilliland's journal, after buying up land from numerous officers and privates, he gave a talk before The Society for Promoting Arts and Agriculture and Economy in the Province of New York and proposed to establish a colony of sorts for farming and raising sheep. He no doubt made a favorable impression.

On May 10, 1765, he set out with thirteen men, three women, and assorted cattle. Traveling by river, lake, and land, they arrived at the mouth of the Boquet River on June 8. After resting and scouting, they prepared to build a settlement named Milltown, about 0.5 miles below the falls at Willsboro. By the end of June they had erected a house for Gilliland measuring forty-four feet by twenty-two feet. This was the first substantial colonial dwelling on the western side of the lake between Crown Point and the Canadian border. By mid-July of that year, a sawmill was established.[12]

Gilliland owned thousands of acres and roamed extensively, surveying the land from the Boquet River to Saranac River and from Westport, Essex, Elizabethtown and Willsboro (using their current names) north to the Canadian border. In his journal he described the abundance of fish and game in the region.[13] While engaged in exploring, Gilliland advanced up the Ausable River as far as its walled banks, now named Ausable Chasm. He provided a correct and highly graphic description of that amazing natural wonder, and his notations are the earliest descriptions that exist of that area.[14]

Gilliland and his small band of settlers managed to clear and plant the land around Willsboro Falls, as well as erect several mills for lumber and wheat. It was becoming a paradise in the wilderness. One author writes: "He had encompassed a stretch of land as far and fertile as any in the world, rolling from the lake shore to the foot of the mountains, well watered, richly wooded, close under the protection of the fort at Crown Point, and if ever a beautiful prospect had power to touch an Irish heart, how much his must have swelled with joy as he measured those acres for himself."[15]

In 1766, Gilliland returned to New York for his family and then, accompanied by his wife, sister, mother and brother, made the slow and arduous journey back to Willsboro.[16] He evidently suffered from a bout of illness, and his five-year-old daughter drowned when the bateaux in which she was riding capsized. It was a difficult trip.

When they finally arrived in Willsboro, they found there was some dissent among the tenants. After all, they were in the middle of the wilderness, and pioneer life wasn't easy. In the end Gilliland convinced most of them to stay. He saw the colony and the settlements from the perspective of a feudal "lord of the manor," which isn't surprising, considering that it was the most available community model for him to follow. According to one (disputed) account, Gilliland had even designed a coat of arms—a silver lion on a shield of blue emblazoned with the motto *"Dieu et mon pais"* (God and my peace).[17]

By April 1766 a house was built for Robert McAulay and was rapidly succeeded by others until the whole territory between the Boquet and Split Rock, including Gilliland's more northern settlement at the Salmon River, called Janesborough, was studded by neat pioneer cabins. By 1772 the settlement was thriving. There were homes, mills, a school—and no external disturbances to bother the colony. The result was that Gilliland became a wealthy landlord. Most of his tenants found him fair and just, but there were a few others that complained.

On March 17, 1775, an interesting incident occurred in the colony. All of the settlers convened by general consent and in effect constituted themselves into a pure democracy by which they instituted a local government and drafted social regulations ratified by individual signatures of the settlers. They sanctioned a free, self-imposed government. This was a remarkable occurrence for a humble little colony.

All might have continued well for the settlement had it not been for the outbreak of war between the British and the American colonists. Unfortunately for Gilliland, Willsboro was right in the pathway of battle, whether it was the Redcoats marching down the Champlain Valley from Canada or American patriots marching northward to defend Lake Champlain and the forts on its shores. Willsboro was caught in the middle.

The British put a price on Gilliland's head after he, Benedict Arnold, and others signed the Declaration of Principles, a precursor to the Declaration of Independence, on June 15, 1775, at Fort Ticonderoga. As signatories to the declaration, they were considered traitors by the British. As a result, an attempt was made to capture Gilliland at Willsboro that August by the Loyalist Sheriff of Tryon County, who sought to collect the bounty. His party was captured by Gilliland, some of his tenants, and a group of American soldiers who were visiting.[18] It was said that some of Gilliland's tenants also might have tried periodically to collect the bounty. Later, Benedict Arnold accused Gilliland of being a traitor. Gilliland was definitely between a rock and a hard place.

We do know that early in the war Gilliland was an active patriot who took 3,000–4,000 American soldiers into his settlement in order to nurse them or provide them with sustenance, a testament to his patriotism. During 1775, Gilliland's sawmills provided 5,000 board feet of lumber for Major General Philip Schuyler's emerging navy. Gilliland claimed to have personally escorted General Richard Montgomery to St. Jean, Quebec. He also established a band of Minute Men and penned a letter to the Continental Congress supporting Ethan Allen's request for the Green Mountain Boys to become a paid regiment in the northern theater.[19] Gilliland seemed authentically generous on most occasions. However, at one point he wrote a letter to General Gates complaining about the rapacious behavior of General Benedict Arnold's men. He was angry that they had damaged crops and property. This may be the cause of Arnold's later casting suspicion on Gilliland as being a traitor. As a result, Gilliland was arrested and brought as a prisoner to the fort at Crown Point.[20] While he was in prison, his daughter Elizabeth was sent to live with her grandmother in Albany.[21]

Gilliland was released by General Gates at Fort Ticonderoga and moved with the rest of his family to Albany in the fall of 1776. While there, Gilliland was again arrested, twice, by the Albany Committee of Correspondence, first in early December of 1777 for picking up battlefield remnants at Saratoga, and second on a charge brought by Gates concerning one of Gilliland's slaves. These charges were ultimately dropped, and he was released on February 5, 1778, after fifty-three days in jail.

The war devastated the Willsboro colony. For the previous eleven years Gilliland and his tenants had worked hard to tame the wilderness and create a successful community. There were farms teeming with flocks and herds, fields redolent with promising harvest. From Split Rock to the Boquet, including the more northern settlement of Janesborough, there were orchards, gardens, outbuildings, roads, bridges, twenty-eight dwellings, forty other buildings, two gristmills, two sawmills, and a school. Gilliland, as landlord, enjoyed a very handsome income of $1,000 a year.[22]

But by 1777 it was a dangerous place to live. Most settlers hastily abandoned their farms, leaving behind years of toil and expenditures, and fled with what little they could carry. The Gilliland family stuck it out the longest, finally sinking machinery and iron implements from the mills to the bottom of the lake for safekeeping, to be retrieved when they returned. Unfortunately, a recreant tenant revealed the hiding places to the enemy, who confiscated the cache.[23]

After the Revolution ended in 1783, Gilliland immediately returned from Albany to his estate in Willsborough. He found his farmhouse in ashes.[24] Nevertheless, Gilliland remained hopeful that he could reclaim his property and start afresh. That was not to be, however. Realizing that times had changed and that he could no longer remain a baronial landlord, he set about to sell most of his lands, which amounted to approximately 50,000 acres, and to deed some to his surviving children. He petitioned the new government for his lands. Several patents had clear title, having been approved by the New York colonial government before the Revolution. However, there were legal problems with his not yet approved patents. As a result, there were a number of legal suits against him, including legal tangles in 1786 over slave ownership, which was still legal at that time in New York State. Gilliland refused on principle to pay the fine levied against him in the slavery case and was confined to the New York City jail. During this time in prison, he had his portrait painted by the renowned artist Ralph Earl. During the latter part of his confinement, he became very ill, losing his ability to write and think clearly.

He had managed to maintain a confident optimism until his prison confinement and illness. When he was released in 1791, however, his spirit had been broken. He took up residence with his daughter and son-in-law, Daniel Ross, in nearby Essex on land he had given them. It was said that he was a bit deranged and thought he still owned townships. Nevertheless, he was an expert in surveying land and was frequently hired in that capacity.

As if his life hadn't been diminished enough, his final hours were terrible. On a cold day in February 1796, he left the house of a friend, Platt Roger, to walk home by way of Coon Mountain, as was his custom. When he did not arrive home as expected, a search party was sent out. Gilliland was found several days later, frozen on the mountain. He may have become disoriented, and he had apparently lost the ability to walk—his excoriated hands and knees were worn down to the nerves and muscles, attesting to his final struggle with hunger, cold, and exhaustion. Such was the final scene in an amazing frontier drama.[25] He is buried at Lakeview Cemetery in Willsboro in the Cuyler plot that overlooks land he once owned.[26]

But William Gilliland lives on, in a manner of speaking. The town of Willsboro is named after him, and Elizabethtown is named after his wife Elizabeth.

Coon Mountain carries the legend of the Coon Mountain panther. According to an oft-recounted folk tale, the Coon Mountain panther would lure men into the woods by its cry, which sounded like a damsel in distress. The men would then become easy prey for the beast.[27] Dogs were sent out to hunt the creature, but none ever returned. Finally, one hunter spied the creature and shot it in mid-leap. Falling, the beast tumbled over a cliff and sank into one of the tarns along the summit ridge. The panther's body was never recovered, which only adds to the myth.[28]

During the Civil War era, Coon Mountain was logged extensively for charcoal. Nearby Merriam's Forge used the charcoal to produce the intense heat needed in its forge, which was located on the Boquet River at Little Falls near the north town line of Westport.[29] The forge was part of a settlement that included a blacksmith shop, sawmill, a store, and over thirteen houses where the workers lived.[30] The forge was built in 1845 and consisted of "three fires, one hammer and two wheels. It consumed charcoal, burned in kilns on the Iron Ore tract owned by the company, and also in many a solitary kiln in the forest." It lasted until around 1870.[31]

3 CROWN POINT
Fort St. Frederic &
His Majesty's Fort of Crown Point

Location: North of Crown Point Village (Essex County)
Delorme NYS Atlas & Gazetteer: p. 97, D6

Fee: Modest admission fee on weekends

Hours: Open daily from 10 AM to 5 PM

Accessibility: 0.5–1.0-mile hike, depending on sections of grounds visited

Degree of Difficulty: Easy

Additional information: Crown Point State Historic Site Museum,
739 Bridge Road, Crown Point, New York 12928. (518) 597-4666 or
(518) 597-3666. www.nysparks.com/sites/info.asp?siteID = 8. Pick up a
"Walking Tour" brochure, available either at the tollbooth (when open)
or at the museum. The museum is open May to October, Wed.–Mon.,
9 AM–5 PM.

Highlights:
■ Ruins of Fort St. Frederic
■ Ruins of His Majesty's Fort of Crown Point
■ Old kiln
■ Windmill site (now occupied by a lighthouse)
■ Lighthouse

Description: The ruins of two eighteenth-century forts can be found at
the Crown Point State Historic Site. Each played a significant role in battles
fought between the French and British, and later between the British and the
American colonists. These forts were important to the historical development
of northeastern New York State.

Directions: *Adirondack Northway (I-87 from the south)*—Take Exit 28 for
Paradox/Crown Point. From the junction of Rtes. 9 & 74, proceed east on Rt.
74 for approximately 17.5 miles. At the junction of Rtes. 74 & 22 (north of
Ticonderoga), turn left onto Rt. 22 and drive north for approximately 11.5
miles (or roughly 3.5 miles north from the village of Crown Point). Turn right
onto Rt. 17 and proceed northeast for 3.6 miles. At the Crown Point State

The ruins of Fort St. Frederic are visible in the foreground, with the Crown Point Bridge in the near distance. Postcard ca. 1920.

Historic Site sign, turn left and follow a winding road for 0.6 mile to the parking lot on the right, just past the museum.

Adirondack Northway (I-87) from the north—Take Exit 31 for Elizabethtown and Westport. Turn onto Rt. 9N and head southeast. After 4.1 miles Rt. 9N is joined by Rt. 22. Continue south on Rtes. 9N/22 for a total of 18.5 miles from the Adirondack Northway (or 3.8 miles from the center of Port Henry at Broad & Main streets). Turn left onto Rt. 17 and proceed northeast for 3.6 miles to the Crown Point State Historic Site entrance, on your left.

The Hikes

Hike #1, Fort St. Frederic

The walk begins from the parking lot across from the museum. As you look east towards the Crown Point Bridge, you will see the ruins of Fort St. Frederic[1] several hundred feet away from where you are standing. Before starting the hike it is very helpful to pick up a "Walking Tour" brochure at the museum.

Proceed across an open field towards the fort ruins. You will pass by a plaque that provides historical information about the ruins, including a drawing of the fort as it once looked.

When you reach the edge of the ruins, walk to the middle of the northwest wall where the entrance is located. Keep in mind that the entry at one time was protected by a twelve-foot-deep, dry moat and that access into the fort was by drawbridge. The drawbridge vanished centuries ago, and during the 1900s the moat was filled in with earth to prevent the walls from collapsing. Stones on the ground surface now mark the outline of the filled-in moat.

Once inside the fort, there is much to see, including four beehive ovens where bread was baked. Just as intriguing is the main part of the fort, known as the Citadel, or Redoubt, which is at the north corner of the fort ruins.

The "Walking Tour" brochure and an informational plaque near the center of the ruins provide specific information about the various sites within the fort.

Looking east from the fort, past the south end of the Crown Point Bridge, also known as the Champlain Bridge, you can see the site of the historic windmill, now occupied by the Champlain Memorial Lighthouse.

According to legend, a French-occupied village surrounding Fort St. Frederic may have contained as many as 1,500 inhabitants living in a community of paved streets, crude dwellings, and gardens.[2] So far, however, this legend is not supported by archaeological evidence.

Upon exiting the fort (leaving where you entered), walk northwest for roughly a hundred feet, veering slightly towards the lake. You will come to a kiln (Exhibit #7), set into the side of a little hill, that the fort used to make mortar out of limestone. The base of the kiln is nearly at the edge of the lake.

The brick-lined ovens are still clearly identifiable at Fort St. Frederic. Photograph 2006.

Hike #2, His Majesty's Fort of Crown Point

The walk begins a couple of hundred feet southwest of the parking lot, at sign #8. At this marker you will see a map of the fort with information provided.

Continue walking west until you reach sign #9, located in front of the entrance to His Majesty's Fort of Crown Point.[3] A twelve-foot-deep moat has been filled in here (just as at Fort St. Frederic) to allow ready access to the fort. During the days when the fort was occupied, a wooden bridge spanned the moat.

As you enter you will be struck by the sheer enormity of the earthen mounds that encircle the fort and create a perimeter wall. Keep in mind that the walls were in actual fact much higher during the eighteenth century, when a twenty-seven-foot-high rampart of squared logs rose up from the earthen mounds. The walls enclose approximately six acres of land.

The best-preserved structures found at His Majesty's Fort of Crown Point are the two barracks, located in the east half of the fort. The one with the stone chimneys and fireplaces was the soldiers' barracks, and the one with no chimneys remaining served as the officers' barracks, which originally had fine brick fireplaces and chimneys.[4] A third barracks, along the west wall, was never completed and little of it remains aboveground today.

Near the southeast corner of the southeastern (soldiers') barracks, at a height of about six feet, can be seen an inscription chiseled into the stone— "G.R. 1759". The letters stand for *Georgius Rex* (King George) and marked the structure as English property. Additional figures are cut underneath this inscription.[5]

Be sure to climb up the wooden stairs to the top of the encircling mound. You will be rewarded with stupendous views of the surrounding countryside as well as a view of the moat directly below, which eighteenth-century soldiers blasted out of the bedrock around the fort's perimeter to increase the height of its walls.

The rocky floor in the open "parade" section of the fort is contoured and fissured, with tiny potholes eroded into its surface. This is visible evidence that the site was once under water.

Exit the fort at sign #13. The path takes you along the base of the southeast wall of the fort, straight through the moat. When you come to sign #14, follow a stone walkway that leads down past the museum to the parking area. A visit to the museum before returning to your car is highly recommended.

Hike #3, Site of the Fortified Windmill

From the ruins at Fort St. Frederic, walk carefully across Rt. 17 past the south end of the Crown Point Bridge and Visitors Center, and continue straight, paral-

The Crown Point
Lighthouse occupies
the site where a wind-
mill stood in the 1700s.
Photograph 2006.

leling Lake Champlain, until you reach the Crown Point Public Campgrounds, just southeast of the bridge. (Take note that Rt. 17 can be heavily trafficked, especially in summer.) If you have returned to your car, drive 0.2 mile east from the Crown Point State Historic Site entrance and turn right into the Crown Point Public Campgrounds. Roughly 0.2 mile past the entrance booth you will come to a parking area next to the lighthouse.

If you hope to find the actual windmill, or any ruins of the windmill that may have survived from the eighteenth century, your efforts will be in vain. All aboveground traces of the windmill vanished centuries ago. Only a lone sign mentions that a fortified windmill stood here in 1737. The windmill survived until 1759, when it was intentionally destroyed by the retreating French so that it would not fall into the hands of the English.

In 1759 the site of the destroyed windmill was turned into the Grenadiers' Redoubt (one of the smaller satellite forts of His Majesty's Fort of Crown Point). The ditch east of the lighthouse is all that remains visible of this earlier structure.

The main structure still evident today is a towering, fifty-five-foot-high lighthouse that was erected in 1858 and operated until 1926, after which the property was transferred to New York State. One tall vertical structure had been replaced by another one.

One more interesting piece of historical information is that the site may have been where the initial battle between the Algonquins (accompanied by the French with their arquebuses) and Mohawks took place, turning the Mohawks forever against the French from that point on.[6]

History: The Crown Point State Historic Site consists of the ruins of two stone forts separated by a distance of just several hundred yards. Unlike Fort Ticonderoga (farther south on Lake Champlain), which was recreated using historical information available in the nineteenth and twentieth centuries, the two forts at Crown Point remain as unreconstructed ruins and therefore more historically pure. To understand the role these forts played, it is necessary to have a general sense of the region's historical events in the seventeenth and eighteenth centuries.

Today, we give little thought to just how important waterways were before the construction of roads and the advent of automobiles. Waterways were ready-made corridors through the wilderness, enabling passengers and freight to be transported easily and efficiently over great distances. They who controlled the waterways controlled the region.

Crown Point was strategically located at a site on Lake Champlain where the lake narrows to a width of one-quarter mile. Military strategists refer to such narrowings as "choke points," because advancing ships are forced into the range of land-based cannon fire, restricting further advance.

Lake Champlain was part of a strategic north-to-south waterway starting in Canada, continuing up the Sorel River (Richelieu River) into Lake Champlain, and from there to Lake George via the LaChute River to the southwest and along Wood Creek (the southeast finger of Lake Champlain) and over to the Hudson River (eventually passing through Eastern New York State into the Atlantic Ocean). Except for portages at Chambly on the Sorel River, along the La Chute River between Lake Champlain and Lake George, and the "carrying place" between Wood Creek and Fort Edward, it was a fairly direct and relatively easy route of travel.

Lake Champlain had been coveted as a natural resource by the competing countries of France and Great Britain ever since Samuel de Champlain first explored the valley in 1609 just two months before Henry Hudson made his way up the Hudson River. Early Native Americans had occupied the Champlain Valley for thousands of years prior to Samuel de Champlain's arrival, but their lack of a written language and their hunting-gathering lifestyle have resulted in our knowing little of their history.

Crown Point proved to be militarily significant, occupying a "choke point" on the lake. Photograph 2006.

Champlain's goal was to attack the enemies of his Algonquin Indian allies in order to strengthen his alliance with them. When the French and Algonquins encountered a Mohawk war party during Champlain's foray into this new world, a battle erupted, possibly at Crown Point, in which the overpowering arquebus fire of the French effectively brought it to a quick end and carried the day for the Algonquins. The Mohawks would never forget this incident in the years to come and perpetually held it against the French.

Many years and battles later, in 1734, a stone fort, Fort St. Frederic, was built by the French on what is now called Crown Point.[7] It was named in honor of Frederic Maurepas, Secretary of the Department of the Marine. The fort served as a nucleus around which some settlement may have occurred, with farms established on both sides of the lake. The extent of this settlement, however, is in dispute. In 1737 a windmill for grinding grain into flour was erected outside the fort walls to the south.[8]

The fort usually maintained a garrison of 80 to 100 men and was used as a base for launching military excursions. Raids were conducted into surrounding New England and New York, making Fort St. Frederic such a thorn in the side of Great Britain and its colonists that the British finally resolved that something had to be done.

In 1755, William Johnson and an army comprised of Iroquois and provincials (troops raised in America) headed north to try to overrun the French and take Fort St. Frederic. They never made it. After defeating a small army led by Baron Dieskau that was sent out from Fort St. Frederic to stop the advancing troops, Johnson decided to halt his advance and build Fort William Henry instead, attempting thereby to ensure that the south end of Lake George was safe from conquest.

In the autumn of 1755, the French began construction of a fort at Ticonderoga, called Carillon [see "Fort Ticonderoga" chapter], which was to be Fort St. Frederic's first line of defense against British attempts to advance north. The period from 1754 to 1763, during which the French and English fought over control of the New World, became known in North America as the French and Indian War. It is also often referred to as the Seven Years War, as it was indeed linked to that conflict in Europe between the French and the British, which began in 1756 and ended in 1763 with the signing of the Treaty of Paris. But the battles between the French and British in North America erupted two years before the official declaration of war in Western Europe.

The French achieved a number of victories in the early years of the war in North America, principally through the brilliance of the Marquis de Montcalm. But they were greatly outnumbered by the British and knew that defeat was ultimately inevitable.

In January 1759 a British force of about 15,000 men, fielded by General Jeffrey Amherst, marched through the valley to drive the French north. The French, seeing the advancing army, wisely retreated from Fort Carillon, setting it on fire as they departed. Then, on July 31, they blew up the citadel and windmill at Fort St. Fredric as they retreated farther to Canada.[9] As a result, Amherst secured Britain's position at what remained of both Fort Ticonderoga and Fort St. Frederic with little loss of life on either side. Amherst had been well-prepared, perhaps even over-prepared; he did not want to repeat the embarrassing and bloody defeat incurred by British General James Abercromby and his army at Fort Carillon the previous year.

Amherst decided to build a new and bigger fort at Crown Point—"His Majesty's Fort of Crown Point," or simply "Crown Point" as it was more commonly called.

His Majesty's Fort of Crown Point—The new fort was elaborately conceived and consisted not only of the main, massive fortress, but three redoubts (smaller, satellite forts) and a line of blockhouses across the southern end of the peninsula (where Rt. 17 now passes close by). It would become the largest British fort in North America.

Work continued on the fort until 1763, which marked the end of the French & Indian War. During this time, it is speculated by some that an entire village grew up under the protection of the fort's walls, including houses, a tavern, an apothecary, and a variety of stores. Except for the third barracks (which was never finished), the fort had essentially reached a state of completion.

In 1773 a chimney fire started in the barracks and spread through the log walls into the powder magazine room, blowing up the bastion that contained the powder.

In 1775 the American Revolution broke out, bringing with it one of the strangest sagas in Crown Point's and Fort Ticonderoga's history. Joining forces with Benedict Arnold, Ethan Allen and his Green Mountain Boys captured not only Fort Ticonderoga, but the British fortification at Crown Point as well—possibly without a single life lost on either side. This was partly thanks to the element of surprise; just as important, however, was the fact that neither fort was sufficiently garrisoned to repel an attack—Ticonderoga had thirty-nine soldiers, Crown Point only nine. By taking Fort Ticonderoga and the fortification at Crown Point, the American forces had seized control over the Champlain Valley.

In September 1775, Crown Point became the launching base for a failed attack on Quebec by General Richard Montgomery, who died in the assault. Benedict Arnold, commanding another American force at Quebec, was severely wounded in the same battle. What remained of the American army after this attack retreated to Crown Point. From there, the sick and wounded were transported to Fort George (at the southern end of Lake George), where more medical services were available (see "Fort George & Bloody Pond" chapter).

After a major naval battle in 1776 near Valcour Island (see "Valcour Island" chapter)—which the Americans lost militarily, although they succeeded strategically in thwarting the further advance of the British—the British recaptured Crown Point. In 1777, General John Burgoyne, commanding an army of nearly 8,000 British, Hessian and Native American forces, drove southward from Canada to Crown Point. Burgoyne's plan was to attack the colonial army from the north, while Colonel Barry St. Leger invaded New York from the west, sweeping through the Mohawk Valley from Lake Ontario, and General William Howe moved his forces from the south, up the Hudson Valley from New York City to Albany.

It was a monumental plan, but one that ultimately failed. St. Leger was bloodied at the Battle of Oriskany and his siege of Fort Stanwix stalled. Howe was distracted from his course and ventured into Philadelphia in a vain attempt to capture members of the Continental Congress. And Burgoyne was defeated at the Battle of Saratoga, after capturing Fort Ticonderoga (again, with nary a shot fired!)

The British continued to occupy Crown Point until the end of the war, but the ruined fort was not much of a prize. Benedict Arnold and his crew had burned what remained of the old fort in his hasty retreat after the Battle at Valcour Island. In 1783, with the Treaty of Paris approved by Congress, the fort at Crown Point was relinquished once and for all to the Americans.[10]

At the end of the Revolutionary War, all military activities ceased at Crown Point. Much of the stone from the forts served as building materials for new structures in the local area. In 1801, New York State granted the land around Crown Point to Columbia College and Union College. Then, Sylvester Churchill purchased the property in 1828. When Churchill sold the property to Samuel Murdock in 1839, he stipulated in the deed that the ruins were to be protected.

In the late 1800s the following description of the fort was written: "Two of the barracks remain in partial preservation, one, one hundred and ninety-two feet and the other two hundred and sixteen feet in length. The ramparts were about twenty-five feet thick and nearly the same in height, of solid masonry. The curtains varied in length from fifty-two to one hundred yards, and the whole from circuit, measuring along the ramparts, and including the bastions, was eight hundred and fifty-three yards, a trifle less than half a mile. A broad ditch cut out of the solid limestone surrounded it."[11]

In 1910 the mining company of Witherbee, Sherman & Company from Port Henry gave the property to New York State for historical preservation. Since then, only basic preservation work such as stabilizing walls to prevent collapse has been undertaken. The ruins will continue to be stabilized, routinely repaired, and maintained as a ruin until the elemental forces of nature eventually reduce them to unrecognizable rubble. In 1966 the agency that has become the Bureau of Historic Sites of New York State Office of Parks, Recreation, and Historic Preservation took over responsibility for overseeing and interpreting the fort ruins.

During the nineteenth century, a ferry was established at Crown Point connecting New York with Vermont. The former ferry tollhouse is now the Lake Champlain Visitors Center.[12] By the 1920s increasing numbers of automobiles made the narrow point between the two states the ideal location for the first of two bridges to span the lake (the second bridge being farther north). The bridge at Crown Point, built in 1929, is high enough to allow tall ships to pass beneath it. It is virtually a stone's throw away from the two forts at Crown Point.

4   FORT TICONDEROGA

Location: East of Ticonderoga (Essex County)
DeLorme NYS Atlas & Gazetteer: p. 89, B6

Hours: Fort Ticonderoga—Open May 10 through October 20, from
9:00 AM to 5:00 PM
Mount Defiance—Open from May 10 to October 20, 9:00 AM to
5:00 PM

Fee: Admission is charged to enter Fort Ticonderoga; there is no fee to
walk around the grounds or to visit the gift shop. There is no fee to access
the summit of Mount Defiance.

Accessibility: Road leading to Fort Ticonderoga—1.0-mile walk, bike,
or car ride (one-way), with brief side trips extending from the side of the
road; King's Gardens—0.1-mile walk (one-way) to garden from lower
parking lot; Mount Defiance—Several-hundred-foot walk to summit from
parking lot

Degree of Difficulty: Easy

Restrictions: No metal detectors allowed; no artifact collecting permitted

Additional Information: Fort Ticonderoga, P.O. Box 390, Ticonderoga,
NY 12883, (518) 585-2821, www.fort-ticonderoga.org. The fort is open late
May to late October, daily from 9:30 AM to 5 PM.

Highlights:
- Reconstructed Fort Ticonderoga
- Breastworks
- King's Garden
- Views of Fort Ticonderoga & Lake Champlain from Mount Defiance

Description: Fort Ticonderoga (known as Fort Carillon when built by the
French in the 1755) was the site of epic struggles in the eighteenth century
between France and Great Britain as they competed for territory in the New
World, and shortly thereafter between Great Britain and American rebel forces who were striving for freedom. The forts on Lake Champlain served to

protect and control the vital waterways that were keys to travel and transport for early colonists.

Directions: *Fort Ticonderoga*—From the Adirondack Northway (I-87), take Exit 28 for Paradox & Crown Point and drive east on Rt. 74 for approximately 17.5 miles until you reach the traffic light at the junction of Rtes. 74 & 22/9N, north of Ticonderoga. Cross over Rt. 22/9N and continue east on Rt. 74 for another 1.7 miles. When you come to a second traffic light, turn left, following Rt. 74 as it heads east. After another 0.5 mile, turn right into the entrance to Fort Ticonderoga. From there, a 1.0-mile-long road leads to the parking lot next to the fort. Along the way are many stops where you can park and get out of your car (or off your bicycle) to look at historical markers and the 300-year-old earthen breastworks.

Mt. Defiance—From the Adirondack Northway (I-87), take Exit 28 for Paradox & Crown Point and drive east on Rt. 74 for approximately 17.5 miles. When you come to the traffic light at the junction of Rtes. 74 & 22/9N, turn right and follow Rt. 22/9N/74 south for 0.7 mile to Moses Circle. From the circle, proceed east on Montcalm Street for over 0.5 mile. When you come to a traffic light, turn right onto Champlain Avenue and drive south for 0.2 mile. At a fork in the road, bear left onto The Portage (this is the actual name of the street) and continue for 0.2 mile farther. Turn left onto Mount Defiance Street. After driving another 0.3 mile, you will come to the gate entrance to Mount Defiance on your right, open seasonally from 9:00 AM to 5:00 PM. Set your odometer to 0.0 and begin heading uphill. At 0.8 mile you will come to an overlook on your left, where there are superb views of Lake Champlain. At 1.0 mile, you will reach the parking area. From there, walk several hundred feet uphill to the top of the mountain, where you will have higher views of Lake Champlain as well as of Fort Ticonderoga. The elevation is 853 feet above sea level, or roughly 750 feet above the lake surface. Take a moment to imagine the Herculean effort required in early July 1777 for 400 British soldiers to cut a trail through dense woods and then drag massive cannons by backbreaking soldier power up to the top of the mountain so that heavy artillery could be trained on Fort Ticonderoga, below in the distance. No wonder that the American commander at the fort was taken by surprise.

Mount Defiance can also be reached directly from Fort Ticonderoga. Upon leaving the grounds of Fort Ticonderoga, drive west on Rt. 74 for 0.5 mile, cross over Rt. 22 at the traffic light and continue west on Montcalm Street for nearly 0.7 mile until you reach Champlain Avenue. Along the way, at 0.4 mile, you will have a great view of a robust waterfall on your right called LaChute Falls. This is one of five waterfalls on the river draining Lake George into Lake Champlain. The scenic LaChute River Walk Interpretive Trail starts in Bicentennial Park below the falls, and runs upstream for over two miles along the LaChute from the upper side of the falls. The River Walk includes twelve wayside exhibit signs. At Champlain Avenue turn left, go 0.2 mile, and then bear left onto The Portage (street) at a fork in the road. After another 0.2 mile, turn left onto Mt. Defiance Street. From there it is 1.3 miles to the top of the mountain.

Kings Garden & The Pavilion—From the northeast end of the parking lot at Fort Ticonderoga, follow directional signs down a gravel road downhill for 0.2 mile. When you come to the base of the hill, turn right and drive 0.2 mile to the parking area for the gardens, on your left.

Ticonderoga Heritage Museum—This museum is not part of Fort Ticonderoga, but is an interesting addition to your historical tour of the area around Ticonderoga. From the junction of Champlain Avenue and Montcalm Street (virtually at the center of town), drive east on Montcalm Street for 0.1 mile and turn in to the museum parking lot, which is on the left side of the road.

The Hike/Bike

This trek through colonial and Revolutionary War history begins at the entrance gate leading in to Fort Ticonderoga. The 1.0-mile-long road today is a quiet, tree-covered lane with monuments and markers that signify the many battles fought to gain control of Fort Ticonderoga. This peaceful byway belies the harried action of earlier centuries. Long gone are the days when Native Americans, French, British, and colonial troops skulked in the bushes and marched to breach the walls of the fort.

It is said that Fort Ticonderoga is the most faithfully restored French and Indian War or Revolutionary War fort in America, and that it contains the greatest collection of Revolutionary War artifacts.[1] It is worth keeping this in mind when you visit; allow sufficient time to take in all that the fort structure and its grounds have to offer.

On your walk you will come to a number of significant stopping points. (Note: if you are driving, set your odometer to 0.0 at the gatehouse, bearing in mind that the mileages indicated can vary slightly depending upon individual odometers.)

At 0.1 mile: You will see a large boulder to your right, flanked by cannons and with a historic plaque set into the rock face. The plaque, dedicated in 1900, commemorates Samuel de Champlain and the Huron's defeat of the Iroquois in 1609; it also commemorates Amherst's capture of Fort Carillon/Ticonderoga.

0.15 mile: The monument to the right, erected by New York State in 1925, calls attention to the beginning of Colonel Henry Knox's journey, which started here during the winter of 1775–76, to deliver artillery to

French line sign. Photograph 2005.

General George Washington outside of Boston. The cannons were used to force the British out of Boston, which the Redcoats had occupied since the end of the French and Indian War. Today, the route taken by Knox is known as the "noble train of artillery."

0.25 mile: The tablet to the right commemorates the gallantry of the Black Watch (the 42nd Regiment of Foot). On July 8, 1758, Major Duncan Campbell of Inverawe, Scotland, second-in-command of the Black Watch on the field, was mortally wounded here. Campbell became the hero of Robert Louis Stevenson's famous ghost story *Ticonderoga: A Legend of the Western Highlands.*

0.3 mile: You will come to a paved pull-off on your right where you can see the monument commemorating the death of George Augustus Viscount Howe, Brigadier General and inspired leader of the British forces. He was killed near Trout Brook two days before the battle at Ticonderoga, and his loss irreparably damaged the British offensive.

Right behind the monument are eighteenth-century breastworks from the French Lines. You can walk around the large mounds, but stay off of the historically significant earthworks. A historic marker gives information about the Carillon battlefield, with the opposing forces of Abercromby and Montcalm depicted in a map of the area. Mention is made of the Seven Years War between France and Great Britain for control of the Lake George/Lake Champlain region. The breastworks were constructed in less than forty-eight hours by 3,400 French regulars and a handful of Canadians commanded by Louis-Joseph de Gozon, the Marquis de Montcalm. When the battle erupted,

During the 18th century these breastworks provided cover for defending troops. Photograph 2007.

the French should have lost immediately, for Montcalm was outnumbered by the British five to one. For a number of reasons, including some possible ineptness on Abercromby's part, the tide turned against the British attackers. The breastworks were later used by the British in 1759 when they gained control of Carillon. It then became their defensive line when attacked by the French later that same year. During the Revolutionary War, the breastworks were rebuilt and further fortified by Americans troops in 1776, but abandoned in 1777 as British troops advanced.

Across the street, on the left side of the road, is a twelve-foot-high circular cairn with the inscription, "Sacred to the memory of the Gallant Highlanders of the 42nd Regiment of Foot 'the Black Watch'." Out of 1,000 soldiers of the Black Watch regiment, two-thirds became casualties. More breastworks can be seen on this side of the road, although they are not as prominent or as numerous.

0.35 mile: A stone monument to Louis-Joseph de Gozon, Marquis de Montcalm is on the right-hand side of the road. Behind it is an earlier monument to Montcalm, also made of stone, with a large wooden cross, a replica of the one erected by Montcalm in August 21, 1758, at the center of the French lines following his victory over British forces.

0.4 mile: A marker indicates that American troops occupied 150 log and canvas huts across a half-mile radius here from 1775–1777 during the Revolutionary War. The American forces were ultimately forced to abandon these defensive works as the British, led by General Burgoyne, advanced up Lake Champlain.

0.6 mile: You will see more breastworks near the left side of the road.

0.8 mile: A roadside monument to Major General James Abercromby and Lt. General Jeffrey Amherst is on the right, with an eagle adorning the top of the monument. It commemorates the British and American regiments' efforts to drive the French out of the Champlain Valley in the late 1750s.

Walk across the huge, grassy field behind the monument to a state historic marker next to the Garrison Cemetery. Buried here are several hundred officers and men of the colonial American Army—principally militiamen from New York, New Jersey and Pennsylvania—who served during 1775–1777. There are more breastworks in this area, most notably a large rectangular-shaped mound, or redoubt. Walk to the right of the redoubt until you come to a tablet inscribed, "R.I.P. Here are interred the bones of 18 colonial soldiers found near the Old Military Road in Ticonderoga Village on November 1st 1924." The remains were buried in May 1925. Nearby is a large limestone slab with the engraving, "Here lie the bones of a soldier of France found under the northwest bastion of the fort in December 1909. Rest in peace". The bones were uncovered during work on the fort. Next to the slab is a grave marker that reads, "Isaac Rice died 8/11/1852, Soldier of the Revolution." Rice was Fort Ticonderoga's first interpreter.

From the mound, walk south and downhill to a large field to your right that slopes towards the lake. From the lower section of the field, you can look up at the massive walls of Fort Ticonderoga. The huge fields are used by the fort for tactical demonstrations during battle reenactments.

Black Watch Monument. Postcard ca. 1940.

On the opposite side of the road (left) from the memorial to Abercromby & Amherst is a reconstruction of an eighteenth-century soldiers hut. Huts like this one were used here by up to six lucky soldiers through the winter of 1776–77; the unfortunate others tented here during that winter. Volunteers constructed this replica in 2004.

0.85 mile: You will come to another memorial on your right to Montcalm, this time written in French.

0.9 mile: You will see a clay bread oven on your right, which from roadside can easily be mistaken for a well. This is a terrific example of a French/Breton temporary army bread oven of the 1750s. Usually ovens like this were the first construction assignments for a newly arrived army. Armies built many similar ovens in the near vicinity during the twenty-year contest for Ticonderoga.[2]

1.0 mile: The main parking area for Fort Ticonderoga is reached.

History: Fort Ticonderoga, because of its strategic position at a narrowing on Lake Champlain, has been the site of many historic battles, starting in the French and Indian War (also called the Seven Years War) and then continuing during the American Revolution. Whichever force or country controlled the important Lake Champlain waterway was certain to rule the surrounding territory. Even before the European invasion of the region that began in 1609 with Samuel de Champlain and Henry Hudson (approaching from opposite directions and two months apart), northern tribes of Native Americans contested the waters of the great lake—the Hurons and Algonquins, advancing from the north, and the Mohawks, making their way up from the south. The territorial marking place in the lake at that time was a large, jagged, rocky outcropping, called Rock Dunder, off Shelburne Point. Split Rock, off the Plattsburgh shore, later set the European boundary according to the Treaty of Utrecht, ending Queen Anne's War in 1713.

This territory became hotly contested amongst the competing Dutch, French, and British commercial interests, although the northern lake territory remained relatively quiet for most of the seventeenth century with the exception of the martyring of Father Isaac Jogues at Auriesville. Father Jogues stirred up a hornet's nest and got stung in his zeal to convert the "heathen" Native Americans. The incident of the capture and torture of Father Jogues brought increased attention to the region from French, Dutch, and British colonists, as well as Native American tribes. The issue of territorial status for the various European interests in the Lake Champlain region marched to center stage.

The stage was set for conflict between the British and French as soon as claims were made by the British on the Mohawk and Hudson rivers, and by the French on Lake George and Lake Champlain. By 1689, New France and Britain were building armies and skirmishing on the borders of their claimed territories. Neither country wished to be in checkmate status in the game of New World conquest.

By 1754 the skirmishes had broken out into all-out warfare and the French and Indian War, or Seven Years War, had commenced. (In actuality, the war lasted nine years in North America. The official declaration of war between Britain and France didn't come until 1756. The war ended in 1763 with the signing of the Treaty of Paris.)[3] Ticonderoga, because of its strategic position at the headwaters of Lake Champlain, was a desirable military conquest for whichever nation meant to rule the northeastern territories. As a result, between 1755 and 1777, Fort Ticonderoga was attacked six times and changed from French to British hands, then to American, back to British, and finally back to American possession (though in ruins).[4]

The original fort at Ticonderoga was built beginning in 1755 by the French and was called Fort Carillon. It was made of earth and logs, and boasted thirty-six cannons. By 1757 it was in reasonable enough condition to withstand an enemy assault, should one occur.

General Montcalm and his aide de camp, Bougainville, however, found the fort far from complete when they returned from their victory over the British at Oswego. This caused much consternation for Montcalm, who seemed mystified as to the delays caused by the chief engineer, de Lotbinière. Thanks to Bougainville's detailed record of the life and times of early Fort Carillon, we have some insight regarding the construction problems. A soldier, sailor, mathematician and scholar by background, Bougainville kept his commander's

Fort Ticonderoga, N. Y. in 1777

The bastions and protective redans of Fort Ticonderoga are clearly evident in this ca. 1930 postcard.

daily journal, which contained astute observations about the goings-on at the fort. Evidently, many delays were caused by rampant corruption among the contractors. Bougainville records that "the soldier, corrupted by the money he receives and by the example set by the Indians and Canadians, breathes an air impregnated with independence, works with languor." Bougainville goes on to criticize chief engineer de Lotbinière for building with timber, when stone, limestone and sand were so abundant. He also states that the chief engineer was almost never on site supervising construction, but instead devoted energy to conducting a handy side-business selling wine at high prices to the soldiers. Worst of all, de Lotbinière was taking advantage of the soldiers. Bougainville writes: "Odd business! This engineer gives the workmen certificates which have the value of money without anyone assigned to control them, and all these certificates come back to him." Clearly, de Lotbinière was an opportunist.[5] It is thanks to journal writers like Bougainville that we have such insight into the daily life of the past. It would seem that in the era of exploration and conquest, the time was ripe for opportunists and profiteers, as well as for patriots and heroes.

Despite the obstacles, the fort became serviceable according to plan by the end of 1758. De Lotbinière had been ordered in 1755 to build a fort sufficient to house a garrison of 400. He did that. He also made plans to eventually defend the nearby high ground—the heights—but only when necessary. That moment came in early July 1758.

At that point Montcalm had about 3,500 men, but the fort could accommodate only 400 men within its walls, so he built a huge log wall at the heights of Carillon along a narrow ridge about 0.5 mile back from the fort to protect his troops. Officers and men hacked down virgin timber, some three feet or more in diameter. These were placed horizontally, two and three logs deep, and pierced with loopholes for musketry.[6]

The first major attempt by the British to capture Fort Carillon occurred in 1758. It is famously said of British General James Abercromby that he somehow managed to snatch defeat from the jaws of victory, given that he presided over a force of over 6,367 regular troops, 9,024 provincials and 400 Indians from Massachusetts, Connecticut, Rhode Island, New Hampshire, New York and New Jersey, led by senior British officers. Possibly the battle was lost at the very beginning, when Abercromby's second-in-command on the field and military strategist, Lord Howe, was killed by a bullet that struck him in the chest and tore out through his back.[7] At the moment of attack, Fort Carillon/ Ticonderoga was still under construction and low on rations. It was defended by General Montcalm, his officers, and 3,200 troops.

At the end of the day, thanks to a series of unwise decisions, Lord Abercromby and his British troops had sustained enormous loss of life and retreated, leaving Fort Carillon to remain in French hands. Military historians are still scratching their heads about this one. It remains one of the most famous and perplexing battles of this period.[8]

It must be added, however, that none of these hard-fought battles in the New World were easy for either party. The terrain was rugged and inhospitable. The waterways were easier to traverse than the land, but boats had to be built, supplies carried, and portages made. Couple that with the imprecision of navigation and the difficulties of communication, and it is easy to understand how things might become muddled.

Nevertheless, the next attack against Fort Carillon by the British, in 1759, used exactly the same attack plan and was successful. This time the British were led by General Jeffrey Amherst who, unlike Abercromby, was deliberate and cautious. The French fort was then under the command of Brigadier General Bourlamaque. In the end, the main reason for Amherst's success was thanks in good part to the French not sending the necessary troops and resources south from Canada to maintain the fort. The clear strategic objective of Canadian Governor-General Vaudreuil was to preserve the metropolitan centers of French Canada—Montreal, and Quebec—even if it meant that the outer defenses of New France needed to be sacrificed.[9]

Events in Europe had left the French king with little desire or capacity to divert manpower and supplies to hold the borders of New France. Governor-General Vaudreuil realized that the Ticonderoga frontier was not sustainable. As a result he ordered Bourlamaque to hold the fort as long as possible, and then to abandon the fort and blow it up as soon as the British were at its gates, leaving a force of only 400 French to stall the enemy. Amherst, perhaps unaware of the French strategy, stolidly and solidly continued on his robust course of action, determined not to repeat the failures of Abercromby. He may not have known it at the time, but Fort Carillon was ripe for the picking.

Amherst was ready on any account. In March 1759 he had Lieutenant Dietrich Brehm scout the fort in advance under the protection of Robert Rogers and 300 of his rangers. Amherst led an army of 11,000—half of them British regulars, and half provincials—slogging up the shores of the Hudson in June and July. This sizable army required huge supplies to maintain their advance—barrels of pork and beef, bread, rum, clothing, tents, heavy cannon and powder, shot and shell. Provisions accompanying the march included 13,000 barrels of meat and bread, 1,000 bateaux, 800 wagons, and 1,000 oxcarts. It was a slow, tedious march and bateaux ride on the way to Ticonderoga.[10]

Meanwhile, Brigadier Bourlamaque remained at the fort with a force of 2,300 men under orders to withdraw at the approach of the enemy. They had no intention of staying to fight a proper battle. As the British drew near, the bulk of Bourlamaque's command slipped away, leaving 400 French soldiers behind as a rearguard action. They blew up the powder magazine, destroying much of the

Although not apparent at first, Fort Ticonderoga has undergone massive reconstruction. The original fort was reduced to rubble in the 18th century. Postcard ca. 1920.

fort. On July 26, 1759, the fort (or what remained of it) fell into the hands of the British. It took the British soldiers nearly a week to put out the fires.

In spite of the victory, or perhaps because the French theater of war shifted away from the Champlain Valley, Fort Carillon, which was renamed Fort Ticonderoga by Amherst in 1759, lazily languished on the shores of the lake for seventeen years before it again took center stage.

In autumn 1759 Amherst decided to move his headquarters about twelve miles north to where Fort St. Frederic had formerly stood. The French in their retreat in 1759 had also blown up Fort St. Frederic. There, Amherst began to build a large, elaborate fortress that he would call His Majesty's Fort of Crown Point. Unfortunately, His Majesty's Fort of Crown Point suffered a major disaster in 1773, when a washerwoman's fire got out of control and ignited the tarred wooden outer walls. The blaze eventually reached the powder magazine and caused a huge explosion. The fort was unsalvageable after this final blast.[11] Once again, by necessity, British headquarters moved back to Fort Ticonderoga.

Amherst and his men had repaired the damage done by the French to Fort Ticonderoga in 1759, but years of lack of maintenance were evident. The fort had steadily declined to the point where walls had collapsed and the parapets that sheltered cannons on the ramparts were a mass of rotting wood and dirt.[12] The garrison was composed of a motley crew of forty-two men and a few dozen women and children.[13] But, no matter, all was peaceful on the shores of Lake Champlain.

By 1775 the political climate had changed. The grumbling of the Americans against British rule was turning into a roar. Increasing numbers of American patriots were speaking out against British taxes. Many felt it was time to throw off the yoke of crown rule. In April 1775 the battles of Lexington and Concord were fought—a successful defensive battle for the New England patriots. It was the dawn of the American Revolution. Enter center stage, once again, Fort Ticonderoga.

Fort Ticonderoga came to the attention of Ethan Allen and Benedict Arnold, who both realized that it would be an easy target. These two spirited and ambitious American patriots were not eager to do battle on the same team (that is a story in itself), but together they attacked the fort and took it from the British on May 10, 1775.[14] Many historians call this battle the first American victory of the Revolution. It was an important battle in that it captured British cannons and firearms to help sustain the Revolution. It also established an American military presence on the lake. Benedict Arnold made good use of his time on the lake and his experience as a seasoned sailor to build the first American navy during the following year. (See "Valcour Island" chapter.)

As the American Revolution grew more serious on the patriots' part, so did the resolve of the British. Britain definitely wanted to hold on to the American colonies. Even some of the colonists preferred to remain on the side of Britain, choosing to fight against their patriot neighbors. They were known as Loyalists, or Tories. Controlling the waterways of Lake Champlain by capturing Fort Ticonderoga once again became part of the British military strategy. They thought that by holding Lake Champlain they could separate New England from the rest of the American colonies, and thus more readily suppress the insurgency.

In 1777, British General John Burgoyne captured the fort to use as a base camp. The British plan for 1777 was for Burgoyne to advance south from Canada through the Champlain Valley to the Hudson River as far as Albany. Lieutenant Colonel Barry St. Leger was to march from the west to meet him, and General William Howe was to march north from New York City. The British had amassed considerable troops to complete their mission. Overpowering the defenses of the Americans at the narrows of Lake Champlain was the first objective, which Burgoyne successfully did in taking Fort Ticonderoga.

Given the success of the Americans under Benedict Arnold in impeding the British at Valcour Island in 1776, only a year earlier, it may seem surprising that Fort Ticonderoga fell so easily. The simple explanation would seem to be that Arnold's navy had been battered and sunk at Valcour, and there had been no time to rebuild the fleet. There were no attempts to bolster the scant troops on the lake; men and supplies were being deployed further downstate.[15]

There was also the fact that General George Washington initially didn't believe that the main thrust of the British would come from the north. He banked on British troops coming from the south, heading north up the Hudson River, and therefore put his resources into the forts on the lower Hudson. By mid-June, Washington had suspicions that the northern forts were in trouble, but there was no way to move men and supplies there fast enough. Military intelligence was slow and wanting in eighteenth-century America, and Washington simply did not have sufficient troops to maintain every line of defense.

The British were on a winning streak. They were once again in charge of Fort Ticonderoga and Mount Defiance as Burgoyne continued his push south to the Hudson Valley. There were problems ahead for the British, however. A skillful American defense slowed the forward progress of the British troops, creating a supply problem. The British had consumed three months of supplies, but had only advanced fifty miles. This, coupled with the lack of expected reinforcements from the west and south, was eroding their morale. Their grand strategy was failing.

On the American side there was renewed enthusiasm as volunteers and militias swelled the ranks of the American army at Saratoga. After a series of battlefield setbacks, Burgoyne was forced to surrender to General Horatio Gates on October 16, 1777.

While Burgoyne was trying to push south to Albany, British Brigadier General Powell had been left in charge of Fort Ticonderoga and of Mount Independence to the southeast across the narrows. In September 1777 there were some skirmishes against the British positions on the part of American troops led by Colonel John Brown, but the fort held. It wasn't until Burgoyne's surrender in October that General Powell burned and abandoned the fort. From that day forward, Fort Ticonderoga ceased to be maintained as a military garrison.[16]

After the conclusion of the Revolution, Americans migrated to the Champlain Valley to farm and later to work in the mines. It was common practice for these settlers to build their homes using the readily available stone blocks from the ruins of Fort Ticonderoga, rather than quarry new stone. The fort was gradually stripped of much of its stone as it languished under the sun and harsh winters. One can imagine it being an enticing playground for neighboring children—and that may have been what saved it.[17]

Two youngsters who loved to scale the ruins were the Pell cousins, Stephen and Howland. As the popular story goes, they were cavorting on ruined walls one day in 1888 when Stephen spied an object that turned out to be an old bronze tinderbox. This buried artifact kindled the boys' imaginations and that of their families. Fast-forward to 1908: Stephen and his wife decide to raise funds and reconstruct the fort, and they hire the English architect Alfred Bossom. Bossom had been working on his vision of restoring the fort since at least 1904. He presented his architectural drawings at a clambake sponsored by the Ticonderoga Historical Society held on the front lawn of The Pavilion on September 2, 1908. There were no actual historical drawings of the plans for the original fort, so Bossom had studied comparable forts in America and abroad. He corresponded with archivists in France and Great Britain. He had also drawn in detail and carefully mapped the surviving ruins of Fort Ticonderoga.[18]

After the west barracks were restored, the fort was opened to the public in July 1909 in conjunction with the 300th anniversary of Champlain's exploration of the lake. There was much fanfare. In attendance at the opening ceremonies were President Taft, the ambassadors of Great Britain and France, and the governors of New York and Vermont.

Today, the fort is preserved by the Fort Ticonderoga Association, a nonprofit educational organization established by the Pells in 1931. It remains a fascinating museum displaying relics of its many battles and relating the history of crucial chapters in the birth of our nation.[19]

Mount Defiance

Mount Defiance has been known by a number of other names—Sugar Hill (probably because its shape is similar to loaf sugar—a large, conical piece of concentrated, refined sugar—but it may also have harbored groves of sugar maple trees[20]), Rattlesnake Hill, and, by the French, Serpent-a-Sonette.[21] In 1777 it became one of the first mountains in the United States to have a road built to its summit. This was done out of military necessity. Under the direction of General Burgoyne, Lieutenant Twiss and 400 soldiers swinging axes and crowbars cut a road up to the top of the mountain in just thirty-six hours. Two heavy cannons were then dragged up this makeshift road and placed on top, creating a battery that overlooked Fort Ticonderoga. At the sight of these cannons gleaming in the sun, the officers at Fort Ticonderoga knew that they had been outmaneuvered and sensibly abandoned the fort without a fight.[22]

Interestingly, an officer at Fort Ticonderoga, Colonel John Trumbull, had repeatedly warned that Fort Ticonderoga might prove vulnerable if enemy cannons were established on top of Mount Defiance. He even proved his point by having a French gun at Mount Independence (across from Ticonderoga on the east side of Lake Champlain) double-shotted (loaded with two projectiles) and fired at Mount Defiance. The cannonballs hit the mountain midway up. To further make his point, he fired a six-pounder at the mountain from the ramparts at Fort Ticonderoga. It hit near the crest. Clearly, cannon fire from the top of Mount Defiance could reach Fort Ticonderoga. Trumbull recommended that a small, 500-garrison fort be built on top of Mount Defiance to defend the high ground and also to help guard the lake (this latter point, however, would have been a mistake; the mountaintop was too far away to train

A cannon on top of Mt. Defiance points threateningly at Fort Ticonderoga.
Photograph 2005.

accurate cannon fire at ships on the lake or to notice enemy ships sneaking
past under cover of darkness).[23] No one took Trumbull's concerns seriously
enough to take action.

As the years turned into decades and then centuries, the road to the top of
Mount Defiance became overgrown, but a path continued to the top and was
used by locals and others in the know. In the late 1800s the top one acre of the
mountain was owned by Reverend Joseph Cook. He called the spot Memorial
Acre, for it was always his intent to have a memorial tablet erected there, but
nothing came of his plans.[24] In 1950 a local businessman named James M.
Lonergan organized an area corporation to build a road up to the top of the
mountain, with a snack bar and souvenir stand at the summit. Lonergan also
constructed the parking area just west of the old battery where the cannons
had been placed.[25] The Fort Ticonderoga Association acquired the property in
1977 and maintains the site and road today.

The Gardens at Fort Ticonderoga

In 1755 the French established Fort Carillon and created a garden to help
feed the fort's garrison. They called the garden *le Jardin du Roi* (the King's
Garden). Crops were grown in this garden for the garrison throughout the
Seven Years War and the American Revolution.

In 1820, William Ferris Pell purchased the ruins of Fort Ticonderoga and
the adjacent lands. Pell built a summer home in 1826 called The Pavilion,

which later became a hotel that operated throughout much of the 1800s serving guests touring the ruins. Pell also established a garden and worked on landscaping the area. In 1909, after Fort Ticonderoga had been restored, a walled garden was established next to The Pavilion and called the King's Garden. In 1921, Marian Cruger Coffin, a landscape architect, redesigned the King's Garden in the form you see today.[26] Between 1997 and 2001 the King's Garden was reopened to the public.

The King's Garden provided produce for the soldiers garrisoned at Fort Ticonderoga during the 18th century. Today it has been turned into a beautiful garden walk. Photograph 2007.

5 IRONVILLE & PENFIELD HOMESTEAD

Location: Ironville (Essex County)
DeLorme NYS Atlas & Gazetteer: p. 89, A5

Fee: No fee to walk on the grounds; donations suggested for museum tour

Hours: The grounds are open daily from dawn to dusk. Tours of the Penfield Museum are conducted from 11:00 AM to 4:00 PM on Saturdays and Sundays from the first weekend in June to October 12; tours are also available by appointment. Gift shop on premises.

Accessibility: The village of Ironville and the grounds of the former forge and farm are fairly level, but not wheelchair-accessible.

Degree of Difficulty: Easy

Additional Information: Penfield Homestead, 703 Creek Rd., Historic Ironville, Crown Point, New York 12928, (518) 597-3804. Web site: www. penfieldmuseum.org.

Highlights:
- Marked sites of former forge and charcoal operation
- Millpond
- Penfield home and outbuildings dating from 1820s
- 1800s church (open when museum is open)
- Several buildings from the nineteenth-century mining days (some of which are private homes and not open to the public)
- Putts Creek Falls

Description: Ironville is a quaint little village consisting of a handful of white clapboard buildings that were originally part of a larger community centered around an early-nineteenth-century iron industry complex. The remaining cluster of buildings is near Penfield Pond at a height of land about seven miles on a quiet country road from the shores of Lake Champlain at Crown Point. Ironville has the look and feel of an old New England settlement.

Directions: From the Adirondack Northway (I-87), take Exit 28 for Paradox, Crown Point & Rt. 74, and drive east on Rt. 74 for 12.1 miles. Turn left onto

Rt. 2 and drive north for 3.5 miles to the tiny village of Ironville (which contains the Penfield Museum).

From north Ticonderoga (junction of Rtes. 22/9N & 74), drive west on Rt. 74 for 5.4 miles. Turn right onto Rt. 2 and drive north for 3.5 miles.

The Penfield Museum is located at 703 Creek Road (Rt. 2), to your left. Across the street are the millpond and walking sites.

The Hike

The walk begins at the old Penfield homestead in Ironville. By starting there when the homestead/museum is open, you can get a map of the marked sites and a tour of the Penfield home and outbuildings. You can also hear some of the history of the iron industry. There are six stations listed on the hamlet

The Penfield Homestead and Museum— "birthplace of the electric age."
Photograph 2007.

of Ironville walking tour map. The walk begins across the street from the Penfield homestead and to the right of the church.

Station #1. A sign states that the waterpower of Putnam (or Putts) Creek drove the iron industry on its shores for over sixty years. Although the structures disappeared nearly a century ago, many of the foundations remain visible today. Putnam (Putts) Creek is named after Major Israel Putnam, who was born in 1718 in Salem, Massachusetts. The major was known informally as "Put."[1]

Station #2. In 1876 the Crown Point Iron Company built a narrow-gauge railroad to carry ore from the mines to the foundry on Lake Champlain. Here, the path from town to the bridge crossed the rail line. You can still see the faint remains of the old narrow-gauge railroad bed. Over one hundred years ago you could have watched trainloads of iron ore coming from the Hammondville mines to Ironville to be crushed and forged into blooms of iron (raw iron). The processed iron would then be reloaded for transport to Lake Champlain, where it would be shipped by barge to Troy, New York, then on to other eastern markets.

Station #3. This is the site of the first dam, constructed by Timothy Taft in 1828 on Putnam Creek. The original dam held until 1862, when it was washed out by a flood that caused considerable damage to the mills along the creek for eight miles, all the way to Crown Point. In 1913 another flood caused a breach in the dam. As a result of major restoration in 1977, the stone facing and physical integrity of the dam is sound again. The dam pond covers over 100 acres, impounding water from an 18,500-acre watershed. In the days prior to electricity, setting up your business next to waterpower was absolutely necessary. Putnam Creek, which eventually empties into Lake Champlain, is said to have powered 101 waterwheels, driving sawmills, gristmills, woodworking factories and a woolen mill—all during the fifty-year period of the ironworks.

Station #4. This stone-lined pit marks the location of the scale used to weigh ore cars coming from the mines at Hammondville, three miles to the west.

Station #5. The water tower pictured at the site stored the water used to generate the steam for the train engines. The ore trains stopped in Ironville to process the iron ore. Passengers also rode the train from Hammondville to Hammond's Corners in Crown Point, with way stops in Ironville, Buck Hollow, and Bradford Corners.

Station #6. Sawmills and gristmills formed the nucleus of every nineteenth-century village. In 1809, Allen Penfield purchased waterpower rights along

Reflections of Ironville in the still waters of Penfield Pond. Photograph 2007.

Putts Creek and promptly built a sawmill and gristmill here. The timber that was cut up into lumber by the sawmill was used to construct all of the buildings in and around the forge.

If you walk downstream for about 0.2 mile, you will come to a pretty waterfall called Putts Creek Falls.[2] The waterfall, however, is most easily accessed by returning to the main road, walking east on Creek Road (Rt. 2) for less than 0.1 mile, and then bearing right onto Peasley Road. By proceeding downhill for 0.1 mile, you will reach a bridge spanning Putnam Creek from which the falls can be seen.

History: In the early nineteenth century the iron industry was important and prominent in the Champlain Valley. Today, one of the best-preserved examples of that early industry is the Penfield Museum in Ironville, near Crown Point. In 1974 the entire hamlet of Ironville was designated a Historic District on the National Register of Historic Places. The Penfield Foundation, established in 1962, now comprises 550 acres including the Penfield homestead, parsonage, church, Penfield farm barns, millpond, and the site of the Crown Point Iron Works along Putnam Creek. Membership in the foundation is open to all who share an interest in the history and heritage of the area.

Allen Penfield, one of the founders of the Crown Point Iron Company along with C. F. Hammond and Jonas Tower, moved from Pittsford, Vermont, to Crown Point in the 1820s to build the Penfield and Harwood Forge. By 1828, Allen Penfield and his wife Anna moved into their residence, which was originally an inn built in 1826. The Penfield inn served as the family home and business office, an unusual arrangement at the time.

By 1845 the iron industry had expanded significantly, and Penfield became one of the cofounders of the Crown Point Iron Works. The town of Ironville (at times called Irondale) was a booming company town. At its peak the iron works employed a large number of men. They, along with their families, lived in company-owned houses and bought their provisions at the company store.[3] The ore was mined in Hammondville, separated in Ironville, and then shipped by railroad to Crown Point.

A thirteen-mile narrow-gauge railway was built in the 1870s from Lake Champlain to the ironworks at Ironville and Hammondville. During this same period, forges were rebuilt at Ironville and two new blast furnaces were constructed near the docks on the lake. The remains of the forge and railway are still distinguishable.[4] Hammondville, a one-industry town whose sole focus was on the mining of iron, was the creation of John Hammond[5] and was located only a few miles west of Ironville.

Penfield is called "the Birthplace of the Electric Age," because it was the site of the first industrial application of electricity in the United States. It was also the site of the first attempt to use electromagnets to sort quality iron ore from chaff.

According to Dr. Eugene Barker:

> ... the iron ore, after being mined, was drawn to large open kilns, about 300 tons of it being piled upon twenty-five cords of wood. Heat caused the stone to lose its hold from the iron. The ore was then generally put through the water process of separation. It was placed in troughs with grate bottoms, in which it was stumped and screened, then passed through sieves through which water rose from the bottom. The iron being heavier sank through holes in the bottom of the sieve into a trough, while the pulverized rock was raised and carried off by the current of the water, often together with a considerable amount of the iron in fine particles.[6]

This was a wasteful process, so a separator came to be used at the Crown Point Iron Company. The separator was a cylinder about five feet in length and two and a half feet in diameter studded with magnetized bars on its surface. It revolved in a trough into which ore was shoveled. The iron particles were attracted to the magnetic charge of the bars and came out of the trough on the bars as the cylinder revolved. Stationary brushes then wiped the bars clean, and the iron fell into waiting receptacles. After a while the magnetic bars would lose strength and need to be recharged by the electromagnet.

Dr. Barker said that the electromagnet in use at Crown Point was secured in 1831 from Professor Joseph Henry of the Albany Academy at Albany, who later became director of the Smithsonian Museum. The electromagnet was worked by a galvanic cell (wet battery) for recharging the bar magnets of the separator and for detecting iron from the raw ore.[7]

Ironville and the Penfield Museum offer a fascinating glimpse into the nineteenth-century iron industry, and as an added bonus they are located in a very pretty area.

6 ROCK POND

Location: Ticonderoga (Essex County). Trailhead is in Putnam Pond Campground, New York State Park.
DeLorme NYS Atlas & Gazetteer: p. 89, AB5

Fee: There is a nominal seasonal entrance fee to state campground, or you can park outside the campground for free and walk an additional 0.3 mile to the trailhead.

Hours: Open continuously

Accessibility: 3.6-mile hike (round-trip); not wheelchair accessible

Degree of Difficulty: Moderate to difficult; well-marked trail over wooded terrain with no steep hills

Additional Information: Contact the Penfield Museum (see "Ironville & Penfield Homestead" chapter). Putnam Pond Campground, 763 Putts Pond Road, Ticonderoga, New York 12883, (518) 897-1309 (regional office), www.dec.ny.gov/outdoor/24492.html

Highlights:
- North Pond
- Rock Pond
- Remains of an old graphite/iron mine site, including a huge metal boiler, drainage tunnel, mine shaft, open pit mine, and stone foundations

Description: This is a delightful hike along a well-marked trail through pine forest and mixed hardwoods that skirts two picturesque Adirondack ponds—North Pond and Rock Pond. Each pond is a pleasant destination in itself. You can canoe to North Pond from the public beach located at the Putnam Pond Campground, a trip of roughly 1.3 miles. This is possible because the two ponds are connected by a short neck of water.

Although the location may seem remote, the remains of what at one time was a large mining operation tell a different story of teeming multitudes and endless hustle and bustle. Today you will see only faded traces of the graphite mine and of the roadways along which vast quantities of ore were hauled daily

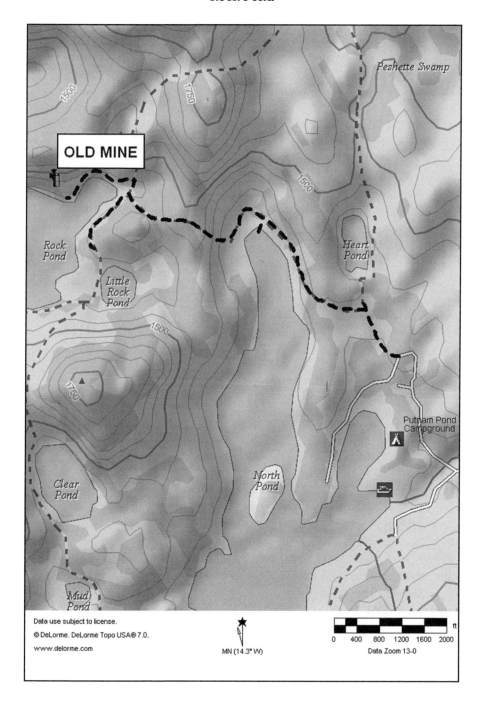

Data use subject to license.
© DeLorme. DeLorme Topo USA® 7.0.
www.delorme.com

MN (14.3° W)

0   400   800   1200   1600   2000   ft

Data Zoom 13-0

to Crown Point. Nevertheless, it is fascinating to see the rusted boiler and the crumbled stone walls in such a remote spot, so far from any enterprise today.

Directions: From the Adirondack Northway (I-87), take Exit 28 for Paradox, Rt. 74, & Crown Point. Proceed east on Rt. 74 for 12.6 miles and turn right onto Putnam Pond Road (Rt. 39) where a sign points the way to "Pharaoh Wilderness and Putnam Pond."

From northwest of Ticonderoga (junction of Rtes. 9N, 22, & 74), drive west on Rt. 74 for 4.9 miles. Turn left onto Putnam Pond Road.

Drive south on Putnam Pond Road (Rt. 39) for 3.7 miles until you reach the gatehouse entrance to the Putnam Pond Campground. During season, pay the entrance fee and drive in. As soon as you pass by the gatehouse, turn right to get to the campgrounds (should you proceed straight, you will end up at the boat launch). Drive or, during off-season, walk roughly 0.4 mile, always proceeding straight (north), avoiding side roads. Soon you will pass by a "Refuse Cycle" center on your left. Shortly after that, the road seemingly comes to an end (where another road goes off to the left). You have reached campsite #38. Park so that you don't block any of the campsites. Look for a red-blazed marker straight ahead at the end of the road where a path leads down a short embankment to the trailhead.

The Hike

Sign in at the trail register. The yellow-blazed trail to Rock Pond is 1.6 miles long; the hike to the old mine site is 1.8 miles.

The beginning of the hike takes you along the outlet stream from Heart Pond. As the hike continues you will begin to realize that part of the trail follows an old road. In fact, in several short sections the trail's inlaid stonework gives it the appearance of an old Roman road. At 0.3 mile you will come to a junction. Bear left, following the yellow-blazed trail and the sign that indicates "North Pond, Rock Pond, Clear Pond & Lily Pond." The other trail, heading right, leads to Bear Pond and, in a circular fashion, eventually to Rock Pond.

Following the yellow-blazed trail, proceed up a small hill, with Heart Pond in view to the right. The mixed forest has now changed to evergreens with a dense floor of pine needles. A view of Heart Pond continues for nearly 0.1 mile. Soon, after several ups and downs, you will descend to North Pond (which is actually a continuation of Putnam Pond). Your descent follows a road that was cut into the side of the hill.

When you reach the level of the lake, you will quickly come to a faint side path that takes you to the water's edge. Continue following the yellow-blazed trail, which takes you north and then south, back towards the northeast end of the lake. You will cross over a tiny footbridge in the process.

When you come to a trail junction, you will now be roughly 1.0 mile from the campground; Rock Pond is only 0.6 mile to the west. If you take the road to the left, inlaid with flat rocks, it will lead you immediately to North Pond and the site where canoeists from Putnam Pond generally disembark. Undoubtedly, this was a favored route in the past for moving ore to market via water instead of pulling it overland by ox or horse.

From the junction sign, continue southwest towards Rock Pond. Go uphill and then descend. You will come to a swampy area on your left with hundreds of dead trees. As you pull away from this desolate area, you will reach a junction where one of the signs indicates that you are now 1.4 miles from the campground. Another sign directs you to the left towards "Little Rock Pond & Lean-to." Don't take it! Instead, follow the sign that points straight ahead towards "Rock Pond & Lean-to" and "Bear Pond 1.9 miles."

Continue on the yellow-blazed trail. Within 0.05 mile you will come to yet another junction. One trail leads towards the "Rock Pond Lean-to"; the other takes you toward Bear Pond, where old mine ruins lie just ahead.

#1, Trail to Rock Pond Lean-to—Go left at the junction towards Rock Pond and the Rock Pond lean-to. Within 0.1 mile you will come to Rock Pond, which is stunning in its quiet beauty. Continue following the yellow-blazed trail, proceeding southwest along the east side of the pond. Within 0.2 mile you will see a faint side path to the left that leads within 25 feet to an interesting ruin. The small, intact basement and near-earth-level sidewalls suggest a once fairly imposing structure of brick and stone. The ruins are located in a flat area between the lake and the hillside, which rises steeply. The flat area is now filled in with tall, slender pines.

A view of Rock Pond with Peaked Hill in the background. Photograph 2006.

If you reach the lean-to at 0.3 mile without seeing the side trail, then you have gone too far.

#2, Trail to the Mine—From the junction, go slightly right, following the Bear Pond/Heart Pond trail, which is red-blazed. The trail leads downhill and then begins to arc around a swampy area towards the north end of Rock Pond.

In 0.2 mile you will come to another junction, where the Bear Pond/Heart Pond trail, now blue-blazed, goes right. Take the red-blazed "Trail Around Pond" path, and within 50 feet you will see a large, metallic cylinder (the boiler) to your right, resting on top of a stone foundation. Just west of the boiler are the foundation ruins of a large factory that once stood 50 feet high and 135 feet long. Thick cedar planks remain in evidence in places on the mortared rock walls.[1] Take time to walk through and around the ruins as you ascend the side of a hill. The larger and more intact walls are near the top.

There is still much more to see. Continue west along the red-blazed trail for another 100 feet and you will see a large mine shaft on your right that enters the side of the hill horizontally. The opening is six feet high and roughly six feet wide, almost square in shape. A small stream flows out from the mine. The bed of the creek is orange—rust-colored from the oxides, hydroxides and sulfates of the iron ore. It is best not to enter the mine, since its walls may be unstable.

If you scamper up the terrain above the mine opening and follow a tiny stream uphill, within several hundred feet you will come to the beginning of a large gorge that leads quickly to an enormous open pit mine where ore was quarried. The bottom of the pit is filled with water that the quarry siphoned off from the adjacent stream. The size of the quarry is impressive, rising up in the back to a height of at least fifty feet.

The quarry can also be reached from the old three-story foundation ruins near the boiler. From the uppermost level of the foundations, follow the outline of an old road northwest into the woods. You will immediately pass by a pile of rocks to your right, and then will see a (mostly) dry streambed to your left. Just a little farther up, cross over the streambed and you will come up to the east wall of the quarry, from where good views into its interior can be obtained.

History: The intriguing history at Rock Pond dates back to the early days of iron and graphite mining in the Adirondacks. There is a long history of iron mining in the Champlain Valley. As early as 1749, Peter Kalm, a Swedish naturalist, made reference to finding "iron sand" near Fort Frederic at Crown Point.[2] By 1775, when General Benedict Arnold was placed in command of the fort at Crown Point, he sent Philip Skene's slaves to dig iron ore on the fort property.[3] (Skene is reported to have freed his slaves after the war and settled them at Black Point in Ticonderoga.)

A quality vein of iron ore was discovered at Rock Pond in the 1870s. The Crown Point Iron Company began work at the Rock Pond site in 1878. They operated an open pit mine, and the big shaft (still visible today) was a drain from the pit. This was the primary mine operation established at Chilson Hill.

A road was built from Rock Pond across a marshy area near Bear Pond, eventually connecting to Ironville and Crown Point. In its heyday there was a boardinghouse and a hotel at Rock Pond in addition to the mine buildings. The successful mine provided jobs to the French settlement people as well as to builders and laborers from Crown Point and Ticonderoga.[4]

In the mid-to-late 1880s the huge boiler, which is still evident at Rock Pond, was hauled in over the Bear Pond Road. It is said that children were let out of school that day to watch the boiler being transported to the mine. It took twelve teams of horses to draw it to the pond, and it probably came by way of Ironville.

Reports state that 3,000 pounds of ore per day were hauled from the mine up an incline and down to a mill built above the shore of the pond. There, a ten-stamp mill crushed the ore, mixed it with water, fed it to "buddles" in which the ore was separated and shoveled out through the top. Tailings were shoveled from the bottom and dried.[5] The processed ore was then hauled, presumably to Crown Point, for further processing.

It is not clear exactly how long the mine prospered in extracting iron ore, but between 1900 and 1904 the operation converted to mining graphite, an

Russell Dunn perches for a moment before deciding on how he will get down from an abandoned piece of mining machinery. Photograph 2006.

important industrial product for lubricating gears, and for the "lead" in pencils. In January 1904 the mine was closed when a major piece of equipment, called a crusher, broke. The mine did not reopen. It had been a vital industry for nearly twenty-six years.[6]

There are pictures of the old mine buildings and boardinghouse.[7] If you visit the site today, however, you will have to use your imagination to reconstruct the buildings and the lively bustle of the nineteenth-century iron industry. What is visible is the abandoned pit mine, the drainage shaft, the tumbled furnace chimney, the magnificent but now rusted boiler machinery, and the impressive scope of the remaining old stone foundations. This somewhat obscured historic site makes for a wonderful hike; the ruins of the old mine are interesting, and the walk through the woods and along the ponds offers some of the most picturesque Adirondack scenery.

Iron Mining: Iron mined from north of Rock Pond, Ironville, and Moriah was used in the first American naval encounter, the Battle of Lake Champlain[8] near Valcour Island. The iron presumably was used for the ships' cannons and munitions as well as the nails and fittings of the ships themselves. By the nineteenth century the Champlain Valley had become a hub of iron mining activity. The population of the country had more than doubled following the Revolutionary War, expanding from an estimated 2,205,000 in the 1770s to 5,309,000 in 1800, according to the U.S. census data. There was a great demand for iron tools to clear the land, concomitant to the expansion westward into new territories. The British restrictions on the American manufacture of iron products had, of course, concluded with the end of the Revolutionary War. Since it had been established earlier that there were significant beds of high-grade iron ore in the Champlain Valley, the mining industry grew rapidly in that area.

Transportation advantages also contributed to the development of the industry in the Champlain Valley. Lake Champlain and its port communities of Port Henry and Crown Point were ideal for commercial shipping. When the Champlain Canal was completed in 1821, with its terminus at Westport, there was even smoother access to the Hudson River and, thereby, to the world trade in New York City. At nearly the same time railroads were developed, connecting the towns along the lake. Some of the immigrants who built the railroads stayed in the area and worked in the iron or phosphorous mines.

The mine at Rock Pond was but one of many iron mines that developed in the Champlain Valley. It was part of the subterranean strata of ore called the Penfield ore bed, named after Allen Penfield, co-owner of the Crown Point Iron Company (see "Ironville & Penfield Homestead" chapter).[9]

ADIRONDACK

Trails *with* Tales

Part II: Lake George/Eastern Adirondacks Region

L ake George is 32 miles long with 109 miles of shoreline, and contains over 170 islands of varying sizes. It is one the most beautiful bodies of water in the United States, if not the world. It has been called the "Queen of American Lakes." This magnificent lake played a strategic role in both the French & Indian War and the Revolutionary War.

The hikes selected in this region lead you to legendary sites of battle during the French and Indian War, to the famous cave featured in James Fenimore Cooper's *The Last of the Mohicans*, and to places where young America worked and played in Victorian times. Each trek provides a historical window through which you can glimpse how people from differing social strata lived in their time. The cultural dynamics of the post-Civil War era were particularly evident at splendid resorts and estates around Lake George.

You will walk in the very footsteps of early Native American dwellers and European colonial settlers, of soldiers, industrialists, and artists who came before you. The chapters on Fort George and Rogers Rock tell the stories of confusing but heroic battles of the eighteenth-century French and Indian War. In the mid-1800s, James Fenimore Cooper would write a number of tales, such as *The Last of the Mohicans*, romanticizing the men and women who struggled and forged early America. These stories were eagerly read by the habitués of the elegant Knapp estate at Shelving Rock or the travelers journeying to the magnificent resort on Prospect Mountain in the later part of the nineteenth century. Indeed, these stories, based on the history of our nation, endure today.

Rogers Rock: Climb to the top of Rogers Rock and decide for yourself: did Rogers actually slide down the incline of this cliff face in a fit of desperation?

Shelving Rock Mountain: Hike up to a fantastic vista overlooking Lake George and many of its islands. The mountain summit was once the exclusive domain and playground of George Knapp, a wealthy American businessman.

Shelving Rock Falls: Stroll to a lofty, tumbling waterfall that at one time powered the cable car and electric lights at the Knapp estate.

Prospect Mountain: Follow the bedding of an old cable car railroad to the summit of Prospect Mountain for panoramic views of Lake George.

Fort George & Bloody Pond: Bike or hike along a route that will take you past three separate battle sites that in the course of one frightful day became collectively known as the "Battle of Lake George."

Cooper's Cave & Betar Byway: Visit the legendary Cooper's Cave as described in James Fenimore Cooper's *The Last of the Mohicans* and walk upstream along a pathway that parallels the Hudson River, passing by beautiful scenery and industrial ruins.

7 ROGERS ROCK

Location: North of Hague (Warren County)
DeLorme NYS Atlas & Gazetteer: p. 89, B5–6

Fee: None for hike; day-use fee for camping at Rogers Rock Campground

Hours: Open year-round

Accessibility: 1.0-mile hike (one-way)

Degree of Difficulty: Difficult because of steep ascent, requiring some scrambling

Additional Information: Rogers Rock Campground, Route 9N, 9894 Lakeshore Drive, Hague, New York 12836, (518) 585-6746, www.dec. ny.gov/outdoor/24493.html

Caution: Timber rattlesnakes inhabit this region and like to sun themselves on exposed rocks. It is not likely that you will encounter a rattler—they avoid people, if possible—but you should be aware of their presence here and exercise extra caution.

Highlights:
■ Site of a (possibly apocryphal) feat of Captain Robert Rogers
■ Scenic views of Lake George from Rogers Rock

Description: Rogers Rock (roughly 1,075 feet in elevation) is an enormous shelf of rock dropping 750 feet to Lake George (elevation 318 feet). The Rogers Rock Campground derives its name from Robert Rogers, an English colonial fighter during the French and Indian War. Legend says that Major Rogers fled from his Indian and French pursuers to the top of what was then called Mt. Pelee (now Rogers Rock), above Trout Brook, where a cliff slopes abruptly into the waters of Lake George hundreds of feet below. One story is that he slid down the precipice to safety, a truly superhuman feat. Another is that he backtracked on reversed snowshoes so that his pursuers thought he made the fatal leap, descended a nearby path, picked up his pack and hightailed it out of there on a less precipitous route.

The land on which the campground is situated was purchased in 1936. The construction was started by the federal Civilian Conservation Corps and completed by New York State. The campground was opened in 1947.

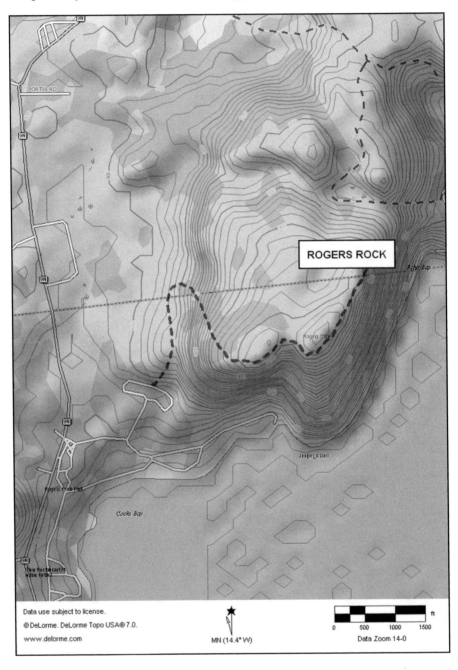

Directions: From the Adirondack Northway (I-87), take Exit 25 for Chestertown & Hague. Turn right onto Rt. 8 and drive northeast for 18.5 miles. When you reach Rt. 9N, turn left and proceed north, paralleling the shore of Lake George, for 3.9 miles.

Turn right into the Rogers Rock Campground. As soon as you pass by the gatehouse, turn left, following a small road that parallels Rt. 9N. In 0.2 mile you will pass by the Refuse Recycle Center. After you have gone less than 0.4 mile, turn left again, following signs pointing the way to campsites 178–244. At nearly 0.6 mile you will reach campsite #210, which is on your left. This is your starting point. If there is no place to park without obstructing other campsites, return to the bathhouse area near the recycling center and park there. It is a quick walk back to campsite #210.

From campsite #210, you will see a red-flagged trail leading into the woods. Keep in mind that the trail is not state-maintained. In fact, after roughly 0.05 mile, it crosses private property briefly, which the landowner fortunately has not posted and where travel limited to hiking is allowed.

The Hike

The trail, which begins as an old road, leaves Campsite #210 and gradually makes its way up to a large, rocky, dome-shaped hill in roughly 0.3 mile. As you begin to go around the base of the hill, look carefully and you will see that, although

Views of Rogers Rock and Rogers Slide from lakeside. Postcard ca. 1920.

the old road continues straight ahead, a red-flagged path goes off to the right, heading uphill. Follow the red-flagged path. The trail begins climbing steeply and does so relentlessly until you have climbed several hundred feet. Keep in mind that it is a scramble to the top section and not always clearly marked.

When you get near the upper part of the climb, you will see a cairn where one trail goes slightly to the left, the other to the right. Take the trail to the right, which is red-flagged (and occasionally marked by rectangular red bars painted on the rocks). It will quickly lead you around to the south side of the summit, where you are afforded one view after another of Lake George and the Rogers Rock Camping Area, looking south.

Stay on the trail as it guides you around the top to the east side of the summit and then northward. You will pass a number of large, glacial erratics along the way. After 0.2 mile the trail dips into a tiny valley momentarily, away from the views of the lake. Within several tenths of a mile, the trail climbs back up and reaches a junction. Bear right, following the red-flagged trail as it heads steadily downhill, dropping several hundred feet in over 0.2 mile. Eventually you will come to the end of the trail at the top of Rogers Slide, a fairly precipitous drop.

History: Rogers Rock, named for Major Robert Rogers, a hero of the French and Indian War, is a 1,075-foot-high mountain whose east side is a nearly vertical slab of rock called Rogers Slide, which drops into Echo Bay on Lake George. The rock slide is smooth and bare of vegetation, sloping down to the edge of the lake.[1] At one time the mountain was known as Mt. Pelee.[2] It was originally named Bald Mountain by Father Roubaud in the eighteenth century.[3]

Rogers Rock's main claim to fame is that it was at this site during the French and Indian War that Robert Rogers is said to have evaded capture at the "Battle on Snowshoes." The battle itself was a relatively minor skirmish; rather, it was the probably apocryphal story of Robert Rogers's daring slide down the rocky mountain on snowshoes to escape certain death at the hands of his pursuers that continues to capture the imagination of all who hear the tale.

Robert Rogers, originally from New Hampshire, was a flamboyant scout who organized and led a band of provincials, known as Rogers' Rangers, on scouting missions along the Lake George and Lake Champlain corridors on behalf of the British. What they lacked in military finesse, they made up for in aggressive derring-do. In the earlier years of battle, they succeeded in besting some of the French regiments. They were among the best at carrying out stealthy spying missions from the deep forest around the lakes. It was from these woodlands that they would watch for opportunities to gather information, hostages or supplies from the French forts.

One of their reputedly successful missions, in January 1756, was the surprise ambush at Five Mile Point of French sleighs headed for Fort St.

Robert Rogers was defeated at the Battle on Snowshoes, barely escaping with his life. He was luckier than most of his men. Postcard ca. 1930.

Frederic (later called Crown Point). Rogers and seventeen men captured a sleigh, took two prisoners, and sent the horse, sleigh, and provisions through a hole in the ice down to the bottom of the lake.[4] In June 1756, Rogers and his men managed to lug five whale boats (large canoe-like boats) overland from Lake George, near Hulett's Landing, to the shores of Lake Champlain. There, under cover of darkness, they captured and sank two provision-laden French bateau headed for Fort Carillon (later called Fort Ticonderoga). When the French later found the hidden whale boats, they assumed that the British must have discovered a secret passage from Lake George to Lake Champlain. They spent some time looking for the passage but, of course, never found it.[5]

In 1757 the rangers attacked Fort Carillon, but failed to gain access to the fort. Rogers and his rangers slaughtered many of the oxen quartered outside the walls and left behind a boastful note clipped to the horn of a steer. It was actions such as these that endeared Rogers to his fellow rangers, but also served to incense the French command.[6] Rogers's successful exploits gained him recognition and fame, at least for awhile. Newspapers of the day carried stories of his successes. It was inevitable, however, that he and his undisciplined crew of provincials would become something of an irritant to strait-laced British officers. The professional French military also became wiser to Rogers's tactics, making it more difficult for him to surprise them. Nevertheless, Rogers was a force to be reckoned with.

Views from the summit of Rogers Rock, looking south towards the campground. Photograph 2006.

The "Battle on Snowshoes" is Rogers's most famous military excursion, memorializing his escape near his namesake Rogers Rock on the northeastern shore of Lake George. In actuality, this was hardly a successful battle for the rangers. Their plan was to ambush a contingent of French Canadian provincials and Native Americans as they made their daily scouting rounds for Fort Carillon. Unfortunately for Rogers and his men, they were spied in the pass between what is now Cook Mountain and Rogers Rock. The rangers were vigilant and had a clear view of the trail passing the west side of Cook Mountain, where they expected to encounter the French, but the French at Fort Carillon, having been warned of the rangers' whereabouts, marched unseen along the lake from the eastern side of Cook Mountain. As a result, in the battle that ensued the rangers suffered considerable losses before hightailing it in retreat.[7]

It was Rogers's legendary retreat, supposedly off the cliff face of the mountain, that led to the naming of Rogers Slide. Did, or even, *could* Rogers have slid on snowshoes down the steep precipice? Most historians say, probably not.[8] Also, there is no record of Rogers ever stating that the incident had happened. Yet it can be imagined that, given conditions of very deep snow and by starting farther down from the top of the mountain, Rogers might have been able to manage the spectacular slide to make good his escape. He was, after all, a very tough man in prime condition. When you hike up to the famous rocky slide on the mountain, you can be the judge and form your own conclusions.

Robert Rogers died penniless in England in May 1795, his glory days behind him as though obliterated by the many blizzards that he and his men endured. Like many freedom fighters in America's early history, he was a complex, rough-and-ready leader of men. Rogers Island, which sits in the Hudson River near Fort Edward, was also named for Major Robert Rogers, another indicator of the admiration early colonists felt for this man.[9]

SHELVING ROCK MOUNTAIN & SHELVING ROCK FALLS

Location: Lake George (Washington County)
DeLorme NYS Atlas & Gazetteer: p. 89, D5

Fee: None

Hours: Open continuously

Accessibility: 1.7-mile hike to summit of Shelving Rock Mountain (one-way); 0.2-mile hike to Shelving Rock Falls (one-way)

Degree of Difficulty: Moderate to difficult to summit of Shelving Rock Mountain; Easy to Shelving Rock Falls

Highlights:
- Stunning views of Lake George
- A massive waterfall
- Carriage roads built in the nineteenth century

Description: *Shelving Rock Mountain* is one of several peaks along the southeast ridge of Lake George that serve to frame the lake's beautiful, deep waters.[1] Along this rocky spine is Buck Mountain to the south, Sleeping Beauty to the east, and Black Mountain to the northeast—each offering a notable summit hike.

The summit of Shelving Rock Mountain is 1,130 feet high and affords outstanding views of Lake George, the Narrows, and the Sagamore Hotel, which lies virtually straight across on the opposite side of the lake. The prettiest view, however, is actually found less than 0.4 mile below the summit, at a place where a side path leads out to a spectacular overlook of the Narrows and the Tongue Mountain range. The trail to the summit is a remnant of the carriage roads built on the property of the lavish nineteenth-century Knapp estate.

Shelving Rock Falls is a massive waterfall formed on a medium-sized stream that rises near Erebus and Buck mountains and flows into Lake George just downstream from the fall. The waterfall is seventy to eighty feet high, with a tiny dam running across its top.[2] "It is a very picturesque cascade, and is specially appreciated because there are few waterfalls in this immediate area. It is a beautiful spot, and much resorted to by picnic-parties."[3]

By descending along the west bank of the fall, you will come to a large pothole that is in the process of being further enlarged by the swirling waters.

Lake George

Lake George is thirty-two miles long and studded with over 170 wooded islands that congregate primarily in the shallow, central part of the lake called the Narrows. The lake was originally christened Lac du St. Sacrement in 1646 by Father Isaac Joques, a Jesuit priest who was subsequently martyred and later immortalized at the Auriesville Shrine in Auriesville, New York. A century later the lake was renamed Lake George in honor of King George II of England.

The waters of Lake George are unusually clear and pure because the lake's feeder streams drain over hard bedrock, where little sediment is picked up during the creeks' descent from the surrounding hills and mountains.

Lake George was the site of a number of epic battles because of its militarily significant position between the Hudson River and Lake Champlain. The lake provided good access to these bodies of water and became a vital link in the corridor extending from New Amsterdam (New York City) to Canada. The Hurons and Algonquins to the north, and the Mohawks to the south, were the first to fight over control of these lands and waterways. Soon after the arrival of Europeans, a series of minor wars ensued as the French and English battled each other for supremacy in the New World—King William's War, from 1689 to 1697; Queen Anne's War, from 1702 to 1713; and King George's War, from 1744 to 1748. These led up to the French and Indian War, which lasted in North America from 1754 to 1763, and then the Revolutionary War.[4]

Even one hundred years after the Revolutionary War, the shores around Lake George were virtually unchanged from the days when Father Joques first saw them in the seventeenth century. This was principally because the area's rugged terrain made farming unsuitable. The pristine nature of Lake George's lakefront changed forever in the nineteenth century, however, with the advent of the Delaware & Hudson Railroad and the construction of modern roads. These inroads made the lake accessible to hordes of tourists and big spenders, resulting in lavish camps and hotels quickly mushrooming up around the perimeter of the lake.

Directions: From the Adirondack Northway (I-87), take Exit 20 for Fort Ann and Whitehall, and proceed north on Rt. 9 for just over 0.5 mile. Turn right onto Rt. 149 and drive east for 6.0 miles. Turn left onto Buttermilk Falls Road, which soon merges with Sly Pond Road as you continue driving north. At 9.0 miles from Rt. 149, the road divides, with Hogs Town Road going off to the right. Go left (continuing straight) and proceed northwest for another 0.8 mile. At this point you will reach a parking area that lies directly ahead. Instead of proceeding straight into the parking lot, turn left and continue downhill for another 2.7 miles. You will come to a parking area on your right where a sign indicates "Shelving Rock Mt. 1.7; Black Mt. Pt. 4.8." Park there.

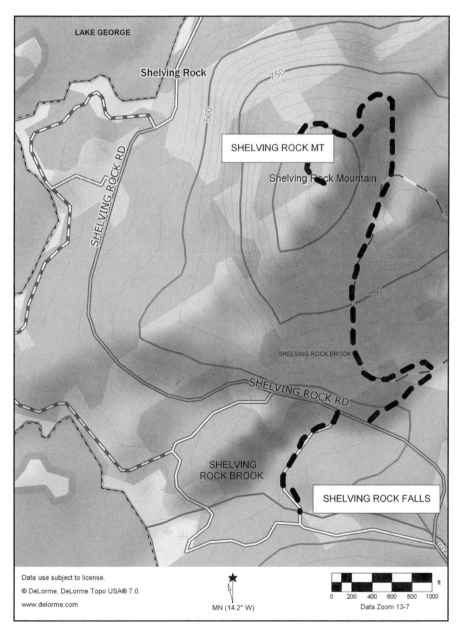

The Hikes

Both hikes begin from the lower parking area for Shelving Rock Mountain and Shelving Rock Falls, which is only a short distance uphill from the waters of Lake George.

Shelving Rock Mountain. The ascent to the summit of Shelving Rock Mountain involves a climb of 650 feet over a distance of 1.7 miles. The pathway follows an old carriage road with multiple switchbacks, thus ensuring a steady, but not overtaxing ascent.

Hike uphill on the carriage road. At 1.3 miles you will come to a secondary road on your right, which immediately leads to wonderful views of the lake. The lookout is created by a huge circular wall of stone that was built so that carriages could stop for a scenic view and rest before rounding the circle and continuing on the road to the top. The views from here include Lake George, the Narrows, and the Tongue Mountain range.

In less than 0.4 mile farther you will reach the summit of Shelving Rock Mountain, where there is a grassy clearing. Looking south, you can see Buck Mountain and Little Buck Mountain, as well as catch a glimpse of Pilot Knob Mountain. To the southeast and east you can see Sleeping Beauty (also known as Jack's Pinnacle, named after Jack Dacy)[5] and Erebus Mountain. To the

The views become more awesome the higher you go up Shelving Rock Mountain. Photograph 2002.

Shelving Rock Falls
was harnessed
by the Knapps for
hydroelectric power.
Photograph 2000.

northeast is Black Mountain. If you look directly across the lake to the opposite shore, you will see the Sagamore Resort on Green Island.

Imagine two of the central protagonists in James Fenimore Cooper's classic work of historical fiction, *The Last of the Mohicans*, locked in a struggle
to the death on this spot. The treacherous Magua is the winner, and Uncas's
lifeless body is thrown over the edge of the cliff. Some speculate that the summit of Shelving Rock Mountain is where this drama unfolded (fictitiously, of
course). You may have some difficulty visualizing this scenario as you stand on
top of Shelving Rock Mountain, however, because there is no significant cliff
face within sight that corresponds with the scene as described in the novel.

At one time a gazebo stood on top of the north-facing cliffs, containing a
beacon powered by acetylene gas. At night it could be seen from most sections
of the lake.[6]

It was once possible to visit the old foundations of the Knapp estate by following the Shelving Rock loop trail, which led down close to the lake and then
back up again. The land near the ruins is now posted, however, preventing
access, and part of the loop trail has been allowed to fall into obscurity.

Shelving Rock Falls. From the parking area, walk out to the main road and then downhill for several hundred feet. Take your first left onto an old carriage road and walk 0.2 mile to the fall. Along the way you will parallel a deep ravine to your right, where a tiny stream and dam can be seen far below.

The carriage road takes you directly to the top of Shelving Rock Falls, an especially pretty waterfall with several rocky granite outcrops and ledges. The proximity of conifers creates pleasant, pine needle-covered areas for picnicking. Do not attempt to cross over to the other side of the falls at the summit. If you wish to cross, do so downstream from the base of the falls.

Long ago a gazebo stood near the top of the waterfall, but it was later moved and placed on the shoreline opposite Fourteen Mile Island,[7] which is approximately fourteen miles from the ruins of Fort George, hence its name.

A rather steep path leads down along the west bank of the waterfall. Exercise caution in making your descent if you choose to take this path. Along the way you will see a huge pothole, which resembles a giant bathtub, carved into the west side of the fall.

At the bottom you will be rewarded with great views of Shelving Rock Falls as you crane your neck to look back up. You can also cross over the stream and follow a path along the east bank that leads in two directions—one

The Knapp estate ruins. Photograph 1990.

The Hundred Island House

The Hundred Island House (sometimes referred to as the Bradley House), located at the foot of Shelving Rock, was opened in 1875 and operated by Reuben Bradley.[12] The hotel could accommodate up to 100 guests and was notable for being the only hotel on Lake George with a water toboggan.

In 1894, George Knapp bought the hotel. By 1906, Knapp had the building destroyed in order to make room for other projects.[13] Henry E. Nichols, the former hotel manager, became the manager of Knapp's Shelving Rock estate.[14]

The Pearl Point House was built in 1876 and operated by Darwin W. Sherman, the son of a Glens Falls lumber tycoon. The hotel could accommodate up to 150 guests and had bedrooms furnished with East Lake style furniture.[15] It was torn down in the early 1920s. Now, only the old stone retaining wall exists at the edge of the lake.

takes you upstream to the top of the falls; the other takes you downstream to a carriage road that parallels the shore.

History: Shelving Rock Mountain's history is intimately associated with George Knapp, an industrialist and cofounder of Union Carbide Corporation.[8] Because of Knapp's enormous wealth and prestige, he was able to amass 7,600 acres of land along the east shore of Lake George. At one time he owned as much as ten miles of lake front.

Knapp used his personal steam yacht, the *Sayonara*, the largest privately owned steam-driven boat on the lake, to travel across Lake George to a boathouse near the base of Shelving Rock Mountain. From there, he and his guests would be hoisted up to a height of more than twenty stories by an electric cable car to reach his estate, Big Cottage, which overlooked the lake. The cable car actually went into the basement of Knapp's mansion, allowing guests to disembark without being exposed to the elements.[9] The mansion was built in 1901 and had a lovely Italian garden, called the Rose Garden, at the rear. At the very top of the mountain, a gazebo provided Knapp with unparalleled views of Lake George, particularly the Narrows. The mansion was destroyed by fire in 1918. Nothing remains of the estate now, except for old foundation ruins.[10] The stone arch facing the lake is where the cable car entered the basement.

After his death, Knapp's heirs sold over 7,400 acres of these lands to New York State in the 1940s to become part of the forest preserve. Many of the thirty to thirty-five miles of carriage and logging roads of yesteryear have become today's hiking trails, which currently form a vast interconnecting system of pathways. The building of some of these roads required a considerable amount of stonework, as can be seen on the hike to the summit of Shelving Rock. The job of constructing the roads had been given to Ed Benton, who lived nearby. Benton Pond, a small local body of water, carries his name.[11]

Before Knapp acquired the property, two hotels were built on the shore by Shelving Rock—the Hundred Island House, in 1875, followed by the Pearl Point House in 1876. Both of these establishments provided guests with a taste of the wilderness experience, but within a protective cocoon of elegance and comfort. Guests would arrive at the hotels either by steamers, or via the primitive roadway around the mountain that was first constructed and used by loggers and later by farmers.

Today, following the road to Shelving Rock from Rt. 149, you will notice a road sign for Hogstown when you come to a fork in the road at 9.0 miles. Hogstown was an old settlement that was inhabited by farmers and hog growers, many of whom would make the journey down the "Over the Mountain Road"—which descended nearly 1,000 feet to the hotels near the edge of Lake George—in order to sell their produce. Nothing remains of Hogstown today.

The Hundred Island House and Pearl Point House were once fashionable hotels along the lake shore. Virtually nothing remains of either today. Postcard ca. 1900.

The area was visited by Native Americans long before the old hotels and Knapp's acquisition of land. At Shelving Rock Bay, Indian artifacts have been uncovered that date back to 2500 BC.[16]

James Fenimore Cooper immortalized the area around Shelving Rock in his classic work of fiction, *The Last of the Mohicans*. In Cooper's story, Uncas, the son of Chingachgook—a noble Indian chief—is killed by Magua, an enemy warrior, and Uncas's lifeless body is hurled off the cliffs at Shelving Rock (leaving Chingachgook as the last of the Mohicans). In the Narrows several of the islands, such as Uncas Island and Mohican Island, have been named after characters and places in Cooper's book.

The Narrows

From Shelving Rock Mountain, the Narrows can be glimpsed in their entire splendor. The Narrows consist of a large number of small islands that rise above a shallow part of Lake George. The islands did not always exist as they appear today, however. During pre-glacial times, Lake George consisted of two separate lakes—north and south—divided by a narrow strip of land.

During the last glaciation this divide was both planed by glaciers and flooded when the south outlet, east of French Mountain, became blocked by moraines and drumlins (glacial fill left behind by retreating glaciers). This blockage caused the lake waters to rise significantly, leaving behind a series of small islands where a continuous segment of land had once been.

9 PROSPECT MOUNTAIN

Location: West of Lake George (Warren County)
DeLorme NYS Atlas & Gazetteer: p. 80, A4

Fee: None for the hiking trail; seasonal daily fee charged per vehicle for the toll road

Hours: Open continuously

Accessibility: 1.7-mile hike (one-way) with a 1,600-foot ascent

Degree of Difficulty: Difficult

Highlights:
- Remains of a railway cable car system
- Remnants of original bullwheel and housing
- Summit views of Lake George, distant mountains, and Lake George Village
- Site of the Prospect Mountain House

Description: The hike takes you uphill along the former bed of an old cable railway to the summit of Prospect Mountain for superlative views of Lake George and its surrounding mountains. Along the way you will see vestiges of the old cable railway. At the summit is the mighty bullwheel that pulled the two cable cars up and down the mountain. In addition, foundation ruins of Prospect Mountain House and other relics of the past can be seen while on the summit.

Directions: Exit the Adirondack Northway (I-87) at Exit 21 for Lake George Village and take Rt. 9N east for 0.1 mile to the junction of Rtes. 9N & 9. Turn left onto Rt. 9 and proceed north. At 0.5 mile you will pass by the entrance to the Prospect Mountain Memorial Highway on your left. This seasonal toll road can be taken if you wish to summit the mountain by automobile. The road is 5.5 miles long and follows a continuous uphill grade.

To access the hiking trail, continue north on Rt. 9. You will reach Beach Street at 1.3 miles from the junction of Rtes. 9 & 9N. Proceed straight on Rt. 9, continuing north, for another 0.1 mile until you reach a traffic light at the junction of Rt. 9 and Montcalm Street. Turn left onto Montcalm Street and drive west for 0.3 mile, traveling five blocks altogether. Take note that you will come to the first Prospect Mountain trailhead at the end of the street. This access is intended for hikers who are walking up from the village. Your destination is slightly higher. Turn right onto Cooper Street and drive north for less than 0.1 mile. When you come to West Street, turn left, drive west for less than 0.1 mile, and then turn left again, this time onto Smith Street. After proceeding south for

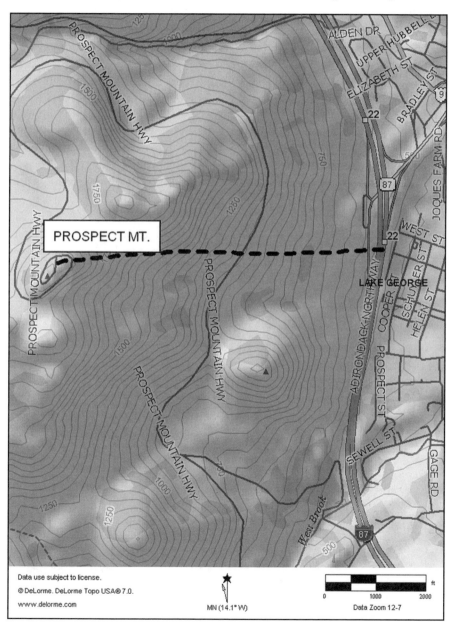

0.1 mile, you will come to a large flight of stairs to your right. Pull over to the side of the road as soon as you pass by the stairs. From the parking area, climb up the stairs and follow a footbridge that crosses over the Northway.

The Hike

For most of the hike up Prospect Mountain, you will be following the bed of an old cable car railway that led from the village of Lake George to a terminal at the summit of Prospect Mountain. At the top of Prospect Mountain, tourists would disembark from the cable car to enjoy stunning views of Lake George and its surrounding mountains. Some of them would continue over to the Prospect Mountain House for lodging and respite, while the rest would return to the base of the mountain after soaking in the views and basking in the balmy mountain air.

Although the cable car railway was a major improvement over the lengthy, winding carriage road that had previously taken passengers up to the Prospect Mountain Hotel and summit, it ultimately failed as a business venture and lasted only seven years.[1] It has been abandoned now for over a century.

The hike begins at the west end of the metal footbridge that spans the Northway. Take note that the cable car railway originally began from a terminal much closer to the lake than the starting point for this hike. The lower cable car bed, however, was eradicated when additional streets west of the village center were constructed, including, most prominently, the Adirondack Northway, which was built in 1967.

Prospect Mountain summit views of Lake George and the village.
Photograph 2006.

Vestiges of the old cable car railroad are visible along the hike. Photograph 2006.

As you begin your ascent you may be surprised at just how wide, rugged, and rocky the path is. The path's width is the result of the bedding having to be wide enough to accommodate a cable car's passage up and down the mountain. The rocky sections of the trail bed are the inevitable erosion that followed after a huge swath of land was cleared away, right down to the top-soil. It is also possible that many rocks never needed to be removed, since large sections of the track were elevated above the ground on wooden scaffolding.

The railway operated as a funicular, meaning that each end of the nearly mile-and-a-half-long cable had a passenger car attached to it; thus, when one car was ascending, the other one was descending, creating a counterbalance. You may be wondering, then, why the original rail bed wasn't twice its current width, since two cars were simultaneously going either up or down the mountain. The answer reveals the ingenious construction of the railway: Each car rode on the same track, except when the two reached the middle of the journey. There, the passing cars were momentarily diverted onto separate, parallel tracks, and then returned to a single track again as soon as they had passed each other.

Because each car was pulled up and down the mountain by a long cable under enormous tension, the railway had to run in a fairly straight line up the mountainside with a minimum of curves, and certainly no right-angle turns; otherwise, the torque would have been too great and the cable might have snapped or ripped out of its rigging. For this reason, even though the trail may seem to zig and zag abruptly on occasion, the cable car route itself remained fairly straight, without extreme turns in any direction. Whenever you depart from a relatively straight line as you hike the trail, you are bypassing the original rail bed in order to negotiate a more demanding section of terrain.

After 0.2 mile you will come to a four-foot-high stone wall to your right, with steps leading up and down at both ends. Look carefully and you will observe that these walls continue uphill in a parallel series, each separated from the other by a short distance. These stone walls once supported the tracks. Although the supports seem to lead away from the trail, in actuality it is the trail that temporarily pulls away from the railway bed.

Within a hundred feet you will notice that the red-blazed trail veers right and realigns itself with the original railway bed, while an unmarked path leads straight ahead, looking very much like a railway bed. Stay on the red-blazed trail.

As you continue your ascent pay close attention to your footing, for the bedding can be very rocky in places. Now and then you will see old wooden railway ties, wires, and even an occasional upthrusted beam along the railway bed. At each rock cut take a moment to imagine the dangers that workers were exposed to as they blasted through tons of solid bedrock to ensure that a relatively constant angle of ascent was maintained.

As you hike this lower section of the trail, you may only be subliminally aware of the constant background drone of cars wafting up from the Northway. During the tourist season the more distant sound of steamboat whistles in the village will occasionally punctuate the air. These sounds continue to recede as you make your ascent.

After 0.6 mile you will reach the Prospect Mountain Memorial Highway. Cross over the road, being mindful of oncoming traffic, and pick up the trail again on the other side. It quickly leads back to the old railway bed, but only for a moment. Be sure to look to your right at the stone supports, much like the ones you had seen earlier, partially concealed in the woods.

The trail quickly veers to the right and once again pulls away from the original rail bed to get around a rocky section ahead. You will cross over a tiny stream that is relatively dry in the summer and then follow the trail as it winds around a rocky bluff. Although you will pass by what looks like a shelter cave in the rock face to your left, approximately seventy-five feet from the trail, the cave is just an illusion created by shadows and lighting.

A minute or two later you should notice a large mound of white rocks off in the woods to your left. If you bushwhack over to this surface feature, you will find yourself at the edge of a deep ravine that was blasted out for the railway. It's a handy reminder that even when you're not following the actual rail bed, it is always close at hand. Return to the trail and continue ascending up the mountain.

Eventually the climb levels off momentarily, as if in preparation for the final assault. As you begin climbing again, look to your left at the point where the trail turns sharply right and you will see another large rock cut where bedrock was blasted out for the cable car railway.

Turning right and proceeding uphill, you will see more stone trestle supports, as well as old timbers with large rusted bolts extending from them.

Just above, the trail breaks out onto the Prospect Mountain Memorial Highway for the second time, at roughly 1.5 miles, directly uphill from the main parking area. Walk up the road for less than a hundred feet and then veer left, following a path up to the top of the hill where the bullwheel and housing ruins can be seen. Although rusted and derelict for many years, the bullwheel remains an impressive piece of machinery.

Several hundred feet farther uphill is a grassy knoll with picnic tables and grills, as well as a number of historic plaques recounting the history of Prospect Mountain and the cable car railway. At the summit, you will have gone roughly 1.7 miles with an ascent of 1,600 feet. When you are ready to depart, leave the way you came up, being careful of your footing as you proceed down.

History: Although the summit views alone are ample reward for the trek up the mountain, the experience is further enriched if you know a little about the mountain's history.

Prospect Mountain: According to early records the mountain was first called The Prospect.[2] In 1877, Dr. James Ferguson purchased the mountain and renamed it, somewhat immodestly, Mt. Ferguson, but the name didn't stick.[3] Today the mountain is known simply as Prospect Mountain.

Although Prospect Mountain, at 2,041 feet, is only half the height of an Adirondack High Peak, it looks much higher because of its steep ascent, dramatically rising up 1,950 feet from the shoreline of Lake George.[4] On a clear day from its summit, you can see as far away as Killington and Mt. Equinox by looking northeast into Vermont, Mount Marcy by gazing due north, and the northern Catskills by looking south.[5] Rattlesnake Cobble is visible in the distance below.[6] Thomas Jefferson once described Lake George as "the most beautiful water I ever saw."[7]

At one time a fire tower stood on top of the mountain. The tower was closed in 1970 and finally dismantled in 1984. You can still see where it was once mounted to the bedrock.

Prospect Mountain was also a downhill ski center for a short length of time. In 1938, Fred Pabst built a 2,400-foot-long, J-bar ski slope on the side of the mountain south of the old cable railway and just above the present-day Adirondack Northway. The ski center closed around the time of World War II.[8]

The Prospect Mountain House: In 1877 a retired Glens Falls physician named Dr. James Ferguson purchased the summit of Prospect Mountain, constructed a carriage road along a right-of-way to its top, and erected the Prospect Mountain House.[9] The hotel was a lavish, fifty-guest accommodation[10] and provided customers with great views of Lake George and the mountains surrounding it. The cost for staying at the hotel was $3.00 a day, which included meals. According to Seneca Ray Stoddard, a nineteenth-century writer, illustrator, and photographer, the hotel could be reached by a "road leading west, past the Indian encampment." There, "refreshments can be procured at the Mt. Ferguson House, on a point a little lower than the main mountain."[11]

Unfortunately, the hotel burned down three years later. Undeterred, Ferguson quickly rebuilt it,[12] this time electing to transform the building into a seasonal health resort where the invigorating benefits of balmy, pine-scented air and mountain solitude could be promoted. The resort only operated seasonally, however, because of winter's severity, and thus never made much of a profit.

In 1894, Ferguson sold the property to the Horicon Improvement Company, presided over by William Peck as president and A. B. Colvin as director.[13] Peck

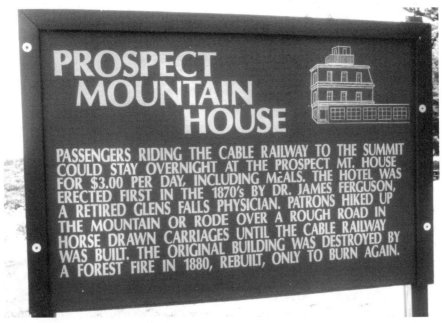

Prospect Mountain sign. Photograph 2006.

The powerful bullwheel single-handedly pulled the weight of the cable, cable cars, and passengers up and down the side of the mountain. Photograph 2006.

made improvements to the hotel and determined that a cable car system was needed to replace the much slower and more tedious trip up the mountainside by wagon or coach. To accomplish this end, he hired the Otis Engineering and Construction Company of New York City to build a cable railway to the top of Prospect Mountain.[14] This is the same company that constructed the world-famous funicular leading up to the Catskill Mountain House from Otis Junction near Palenville, New York, in 1892.

In 1904 the well-known philanthropist George Foster Peabody acquired the property and subsequently donated the hotel and 160 acres of land to the State of New York in 1925.[15] At the time, a rumor was circulating that the hotel might be turned into a gambling casino in the future, and Peabody wanted to ensure that this sad fate would never be the destiny of the Prospect Mountain House.[16]

In 1932 the hotel burned down a second time, and was never rebuilt. In its place was erected a steel fire tower (which was dismantled some years ago).

Cable Car Railway: It took only six months for the Prospect Mountain cable car railway to be constructed. Amazingly, much of the work was done during the harsh months of winter. As if to inaugurate the New Year, workers began their efforts on January 2, 1895, and continued right up until June 15, 1895, at which time the line was ready for business. The project cost a total of $120,000 from start to finish,[17] and during its first week of operation it carried over 5,000 people—a rather auspicious beginning.

The railway was 1.4 miles in length and went up at a steady incline of 40 vertical feet for every 100 horizontal feet of length.[18] Each cable car could seat 54 passengers and measured 32 feet long and 7.5 feet wide. Freight and baggage were carried outside on the conductor's platform at the front of the car.[19] The cars were pulled up the mountain by a bullwheel driven by two Otis compound engines. Two eight-foot drums that were attached to the bullwheel wound and unwound the cable, which was 7,150 feet long and weighed 5,438 pounds. The cars ran every half hour and cost passengers 50¢ for a round-trip (a substantial sum of money in those days, considering that the average worker earned $3.00 per week).[20]

The cars rode on a three-foot-gauge track that went fairly straight up the mountain except for some gradual curves. The running speed was 850 feet per minute (10 miles per hour), and the trip, each way, took eight minutes.[21]

The Otis Elevating Company took over the operation of the railway in 1902, but after a profitless year it was forced to shut down the line. The cable car railway never reopened. During World War I a shortage of steel and iron caused the rails to be sold as scrap metal.[22]

Memorial Highway: The Prospect Mountain Memorial Highway was created as a memorial to American war veterans. Opened in 1969, it follows the old carriage road[23] for 5.5 miles. Along the way there are three pull-offs for drivers to enjoy the views or to give their brakes a rest. The lowermost pull-off is near Rattlesnake Cobble, where a rocky outcrop 0.2 mile from the road provides great views to the northeast of Lake George and its village.

10 FORT GEORGE & BLOODY POND

Location: Lake George (Washington County)
Delorme NYS Atlas & Gazetteer: p. 80, A4

Fee: None

Hours: The Warren County Bikeway is open continuously.

Accessibility: 3.0-mile bike ride or walk (one-way) along black-topped bikeway between Fort George and the spur path to the Ephraim Williams Monument; 0.2-mile-long trail/old road between bike path and Ephraim Williams monument

Degree of Difficulty: Easy to moderate

Highlights:
- Ruins of Fort George dating from the French and Indian War
- View of Lake George from north end of bike path
- Bloody Pond, where a massacre occurred when a predominantly Canadian French and Native American force was ambushed by British troops, American colonists, and Native Americans sympathetic to the colonials
- Monument to Colonel Ephraim Williams, founder of Williams College, killed July 1755 in the battle of Bloody Pond

Description: This scenic 3.0-mile (one-way) or 6.0-mile (round-trip) hike or bike excursion takes you on an historic path near battle sites of the French and Indian War that were fought overlooking beautiful Lake George.

Directions: From the Adirondack Northway (I-87), take Exit 21 for Lake George Village and Lake Luzerne. The exit ramp will immediately take you down to Rt. 9N. Turn east and drive 0.1 mile. At the intersection of Rtes. 9N & 9, turn left onto Rt. 9 and drive north for 0.4 mile. Turn right onto Fort George Road and drive northeast for 0.5 mile. At 0.3 mile you will pass by the entrance to Fort George Park, which is open seasonally to cars. At 0.5 mile, just before the intersection of Fort George Road and Beach Road, you will cross over the Warren County Bikeway. No parking is available, so you must continue on. Turn left onto Beach Road and drive west for over 0.1 mile, then

The Battle of Lake George began on September 8, 1755. This statue memorializes two leaders who fought on the British side—King Hendrick and Gen. William Johnson. Postcard ca. 1930.

turn left onto West Brook Road (which is a continuous one-way loop). Park along the right-hand side of the road, either as you head southwest or, after you reach Rt. 9, by turning around and driving back in the opposite direction. The bike path begins from West Brook Road, near the intersection of West Brook Road and Beach Road.

The Bike/Hike

We will follow the Warren County Bikeway to Fort George, then on to Bloody Pond, and finally end at the point where Ephraim Williams was killed.

Starting at the northeast end of West Brook Road, proceed east on the bike path for 0.1 mile. As soon as you cross over Fort George Road, follow a paved walkway to your right that leads uphill in several hundred feet to a conspicuous memorial and statue of General Sir William Johnson and King Hendrick, a Native American who fought alongside the British in the French and Indian War. The statue commemorates the victory of the colonial forces, under the direction of Johnson, and their Mohawk allies, under King Hendrick, over the French regulars commanded by Baron Dieskau and their Canadian and Indian allies.

You are now in the northwest part of Fort George Park. Stay on the paved walkway until you reach the parking area. From there, follow the park road as it leads southwest towards the entrance, approximately 0.2 mile away. In 0.05 mile you will come to the ruins of Fort George, directly on your right.

Fort George was partially built in 1759 by British Colonel James Montresor under orders from General Jeffrey Amherst. The design was a traditional quadrangle used by European armies for eighteenth-century fortifications. The fort was intended to be garrisoned by 600 men, with bastions at each of its four corners. Each side was to be 100 feet long, with the entire structure built on a solid base of black limestone. It was positioned to command a view of the lake, looking north, to at least ten miles out.[1]

Retrace your steps, returning to the bike path at the junction of Fort George Road and Beach Road. From there, head south, proceeding steadily uphill. In 0.5 mile the bike path crosses over East Shore Road (Rt. 9L). In another 1.1 miles it comes out next to Rt. 9 and begins paralleling the highway, crossing over Bloody Pond Road in 0.1 mile. After another 0.1 mile the bike path veers left, leaving Rt. 9 behind and reentering the woods. If you wish to see Bloody Pond before entering the woods, continue straight ahead on Rt. 9 for 0.2 mile farther and you will come to a view of Bloody Pond next to a historical marker.

Years of sedimentation have virtually turned Bloody Pond into a bog, but during the spring the water level rises and it again becomes a little pond covered with lily pads and pond lilies.[2] According to an account by W. Max Reid, Bloody Pond "is nearly circular, about two hundred feet in diameter, with no apparent inlet or outlet. It is probably maintained by the drainage from hills to the south, or seepage from springs under the pond."[3] Seneca Ray Stoddard, the famous nineteenth-century Adirondack author, photographer, illustrator, cartographer, and stereographer, wrote before 1887 that Bloody Pond " is simply a stagnant pool that in the early part of the season is nearly covered with lily-pads and great white pond-lilies, and in the summer becomes almost dry."[4]

Return to the Warren County Bikeway and continue south. Within 0.2 mile after leaving Rt. 9, you will pass by a historic marker on your left that provides information on Bloody Pond, including photographs taken by Seneca Ray Stoddard. Just before the sign, you will pass by Bloody Pond off to the right in the woods, but virtually impossible to see from the bikeway except when there is no foliage.

From the historical marker, continue south on the bike path for 0.9 mile farther. You will come to a pull-off on your right where another historic marker gives a brief history of the Hudson Valley Railroad, whose railroad bed is now part of the bike path. There is also a bicycle rack located here. From the pull-off, follow a side path that leads steeply uphill in 100 feet to a power line corridor. Follow the path to the right, and then almost immediately to the left, as it pulls away from the power lines and begins heading uphill.

Within several hundred feet the path arrives at an abandoned road. Continue straight ahead, heading uphill on the road for another several hundred feet until you reach the Ephraim Williams Monument. This is as good a place as any to pause and meditate for a moment about the fortunes of war and the Battle of Lake George.

From the Williams Monument, continue following the road uphill for several hundred feet until you reach Rt. 9, 0.5 mile north of the intersection of Rtes. 9 & 149. Should you wish to visit Williams's gravesite memorial,[5] cross over Rt. 9 and proceed south for 100 feet. The memorial is at roadside to your right.

The Ephraim Williams monument.
Postcard ca. 1920.

History: A visitor to the Lake George Battlefield Park today will likely be entranced by the scenic views of Lake George and pay scant attention to the monuments and physical traces of the historical encampments. A careful exploration about, however, will reveal history dating from the French and Indian War and the American Revolution.

On September 8, 1755, the southern end of today's Lake George Village was the site of the Battle of Lake George, a fierce engagement during the French and Indian War. The battle actually consisted of three distinct encounters—the Battle of Bloody Morning Scout, the main battle fought at the British encampment on Lake George, and the infamous Battle of Bloody Pond three miles south of Lake George. This series of engagements pushed the French troops back to Lake Champlain, leaving the British and American colonists in control of the southern end of Lake George.

General Sir William Johnson, an influential colonist fighting for the British, arrived at the southern end of Lac du St. Sacrement in August 1755 and promptly renamed it Lake George in honor of King George II. Johnson's intention was to then proceed north along Lake George to capture Fort St. Frederic on the northwest shore of Lake Champlain, thereby stopping the advance of Baron Dieskau's French forces. The ultimate goal was to expel the French from North America.

On September 7, 1755, Baron Dieskau planned to curb Johnson's advance northward by marching south, circumventing Johnson at Fort George, and attacking the newly constructed Fort Edward south of Lake George. By raiding Fort Edward, a major supply depot for Johnson, Dieskau could seriously disrupt the British supply line. Dieskau's plans went awry, however.

Johnson was alerted by scouts to the presence of enemy forces marching towards Fort Edward. A messenger was quickly sent to warn the 500 men garrisoned at Fort Edward, but he was captured and prevented from sounding the alarm. Dieskau was then able to glean information from the captured messenger about the extent and placement of Johnson's troops, leading him to turn about from his march on Fort Edward and backtrack, marching his troops straight towards General Johnson's encampment at Lake George.[6]

On September 8, 1755, the fateful battles of Lake George took place. Johnson sent Colonel Ephraim Williams from Massachusetts with his 1,000-man regiment towards Fort Edward. They were ambushed in a ravine three miles south of Johnson's Fort George by French forces led by Baron Dieskau. A battle ensued between Williams's troops and the Canadian and Indian forces under French command. The battle came to be called "The Bloody Morning Scout," or "Early Morning Scout," so as not to be confused with the battle that took place later in the day called "Bloody Pond."

Although Colonel Williams and King Hendrick were killed, along with many of their men,[7] their regiment inflicted great damage to the Canadians and their Indian allies. It is thought that the battle of "The Bloody Morning Scout" also significantly delayed the French in reaching Fort George, giving Johnson more time to prepare its defense.

The remnants of Colonel Williams's regiment continued to fight bravely while retreating back to Fort George. By the time Dieskau's troops reached the fort, Johnson's force was prepared to join in battle. This main encounter is generally the one referred to as the "Battle of Lake George."

Unfortunately for the French, their Native American allies, who had helped ambush Williams's regiment and been pretty badly bloodied themselves, now balked at attacking Fort George, believing that they would encounter heavy artillery and suffer even greater casualties. They also may not have wanted to engage in fighting more of their fellow tribesmen, many of whom were sympathetic to Johnson. Many of the Native Americans in the French party refused to join in the ensuing battle.

The tide was now turning in favor of the British. The British were ready this time, and the French were defeated. The site of this second battle is now part of Fort George Park. Earth and stone embankments of the small fort can be easily distinguished today.

The third engagement of the battle is the one referred to as "Bloody Pond." The French and their Native American allies had retreated to a pond south of the lake, no doubt in need of rest and regrouping after the main battle, where they were surprised by colonial reinforcements coming up north along the military road from Fort Edward. The colonial forces opened fire and killed as many as 200 of the French and Indians. Afterwards, they dumped the bodies into what has been known ever since as Bloody Pond. It was said that the water turned blood-red from the carnage and remained so for many months.

Although there are discrepancies in the reports of the numbers of casualties inflicted on both sides, the Battle of Lake George was a major strategic victory for the British and their colonists. Johnson had not only weakened the French troops, but had halted the forward advance of Baron Dieskau.

More about Colonel Ephraim Williams: Colonel Williams's legacy did not end with his brave fight at the battle of the Bloody Morning Scout. He is remembered today as the founder and benefactor of Williams College. Before signing on as a colonel in General Johnson's regiment, Williams had the foresight to draft an elaborate will in which he left much of his estate to establish a college in western Massachusetts near his family homestead. Williams's brother faithfully carried out his wishes. Today, not only is the college named after Williams, but the village of Williamstown as well.

More about Fort George: With subsequent British military successes at Fort Carillon and Fort St. Frederic (renamed by the British as Fort Ticonderoga and His Majesty's Fort of Crown Point, respectively), the value of Fort George as a military base declined markedly and only the southwest bastion was ever completed. Nevertheless, a small British garrison remained there throughout the 1760s and into the next war, which pitted the American colonists against the British.

Seneca Ray Stoddard made this humorous comment about the defensibility of Fort George: "Although on an elevated piece of ground, it is commanded by others near by, and would not have been thought of at the present day, but in those times they had faith in the absent-mindedness of the enemy, who were expected to march regularly up to the places prepared for their reception."[8] Charles Posson commented in the same general period of time as Stoddard, "Years ago the lake could be distinctly seen from the fort, but the pines have since grown up and form a massive screen as if to shelter it from further damage from the elements and man."[9]

During the Revolutionary War, Fort George proved to be one of the easiest American victories. Only one British soldier, Captain John Nordberg, was manning the fort when it was captured. In July 1775, General Philip

The partial ruins of Fort George have survived into the present. Postcard ca. 1930.

Schuyler used Fort George as an outpost while building boats on Lake George. By 1776, Schuyler had established a large hospital at Fort George for smallpox victims, who were believed to have contracted the disease during the disastrous invasion of Canada by Generals Benedict Arnold and Richard Montgomery in 1775. The hospital was run by Dr. Jonathan Potts.[10] When British General John Burgoyne tried to attack Fort George in 1776, the fort was burned to the ground by patriots under Major Christopher Yates before they fled to Fort Edward.

In April 1776 an expedition of dignitaries visited the fort, including Benjamin Franklin and two commissioners appointed by Congress, named Chase and Carroll. Charles Carroll had this to say in his report to Congress: "Fort George is in as ruinous a condition as Fort Edward; it is a small bastion, faced with stone, and built on an eminence commanding the head of the lake.—There are some barracks in it. … About a quarter of a mile to the westward the small remains of Fort William Henry are to be seen across a little rivulet which forms a swamp."[11]

In 1780 a small band of patriots from Vermont held the diminished Fort George until it was attacked by a British raiding party. This ended once and for all the use of the fort as a military base.[12] During the late eighteenth century Fort George was visited by many dignitaries, including General George Washington in 1783, and James Madison and Thomas Jefferson in 1791.

Lake George Village has become a tourist attraction over the years, but Fort George has been mostly forgotten, overshadowed by historic Fort William Henry, which was reconstructed and returned to its original appearance. In the 1920s Fort George was partially reconstructed, but to no avail. All that now remains is part of the stone and earth ramparts, located within Lake George Battlefield Park and managed by The New York State Department of Environmental Conservation.

The Bike Path
This route follows along the abandoned bed of the Hudson Valley Railroad, which extended between Glens Falls and Warrensburg starting in 1902. The Hudson Valley Line (powered by electricity) made a round-trip between those two cities fourteen times a day! Line service ended by 1928.[13] A marker in Lake George Village refers to the bike path as the W. Keith Delarm Bikeway. Delarm was supervisor of the Town of Hague from 1958–1971 and 1973–1977.

COOPER'S CAVE & BETAR BYWAY

Location: South Glens Falls (Saratoga County)
Delorme NYS Atlas & Gazetteer: p. 81, B4–5

Fee: None

Hours: Cooper's Cave overlook is open seasonally from Memorial Day to October 31, 9:00 AM–8:00 PM.; Betar Byway, located at the South Glens Falls Historical Park, is open daily from 8:00 AM to dusk.

Accessibility: Cooper's Cave overlook—0.05-mile walk from River Road (one-way) along a paved road; there is limited parking at the bottom for people with disabilities. Betar Byway—0.7-mile walk (one-way) on a paved walkway eight feet wide, wheelchair accessible.

Degree of Difficulty: Easy walk or bike ride

Restrictions: Betar Byway—No motorized vehicles (except electric wheelchairs). No alcohol permitted. Dogs must be leashed. If you carry it in, you must carry it out.

Highlights:
- Cooper's Cave
- South Glens Falls Historical Park
- Betar Byway
- Historic ruins

Description: Cooper's Cave and the historic ruins along the Betar Byway are located along the Hudson River as it flows between Glens Falls and South Glens Falls. Cooper's Cave achieved fame and its name when it was written up in James Fenimore Cooper's thrilling novel, *The Last of the Mohicans*.

The Betar Byway, dedicated to the Betar family for their community services over the past seven decades, provides a very pretty walk along the bank of the Hudson River and is favored by many local residents who use it to jog, walk, bike, or to take the dog out for a leisurely stroll. It is an area also favored by birders. Along the river are forty-three different species of trees with much tangled undergrowth, providing an excellent habitat for ground- and low-elevation nesters. In the late nineteenth and early twentieth centuries this part of the Hudson River was a major corridor used by the logging industry.

Directions: From Glens Falls, drive south on Rt. 9, crossing over the Hudson River via the Cooper's Cave Bridge, which connects Glens Falls with South Glens Falls. As soon as you reach the south end of the bridge, turn right onto River Street. You will immediately see a sign for Cooper's Cave, and then a right-hand turn onto Cooper's Cave Drive leading down to the cave. Continue straight ahead on River Street for another 100 feet, however, to the large parking area to the left. River Road ends another 0.05 mile farther at a small boat launch. This parking site provides ready access to both Cooper's Cave and the Betar Byway, which are in opposite directions from one another.

To Cooper's Cave—Walk east, back down River Street, for over 50 feet and follow a secondary road to the left that leads downhill underneath Cooper's Cave Bridge to a platform overlooking Cooper's Cave at the base of the falls.

To the Betar Byway: North Entrance—From the parking lot, walk south, following a walkway past the Village Museum. The Betar Byway, a paved walkway, begins just south of First Street behind a large parking area.

To the Betar Byway: South Entrance—This requires driving to a different point of entry. From River Street, proceed south on Rt. 9 (Saratoga Avenue) for 1.1 miles. When you come to Beach Road, turn right and follow it downhill for 0.2 mile to the small parking area for the Byway. If you continue downhill for 0.2 mile farther, you will end up at the public beach on the Hudson River.

To Betar Byway Extension—In addition to the 0.7-mile-long section of the Betar Byway, there is another stretch that can be walked or biked. It is a dirt road that follows high above the Hudson River and provides limited views. When you turn onto Beach Road to reach the south entrance to the Betar Byway, drive less than 0.05 mile and, instead of bearing right and following Beach Road downhill, continue straight ahead into a small parking area next to the South Glens Falls Public Works. The path (actually an unpaved road) begins there.

Plans are underway to connect the Betar Byway to the Cooper's Cave Overlook area.

The Walk

Betar Byway—Beginning at the north end of the Betar Byway, proceed west past stone rollers where a plaque dedicating the byway to the Betar Family is mounted. Look to your right as you start down the walkway and you will observe an old foundation, 100 feet downhill from the Outdoor Entertainment Center (a large gazebo). Old deteriorated wooden steps lead to it. Farther downhill, by the river, is a huge pile of discarded stone rollers that were once used in the paper mills. You will see more of them along the side of the trail as you continue your walk. There are many benches along the walkway where you can stop to rest or contemplate the river.

You are in the general area where John Glenn established his sawmill(s) after receiving a patent in 1770 (and, unknowingly, giving his name to the

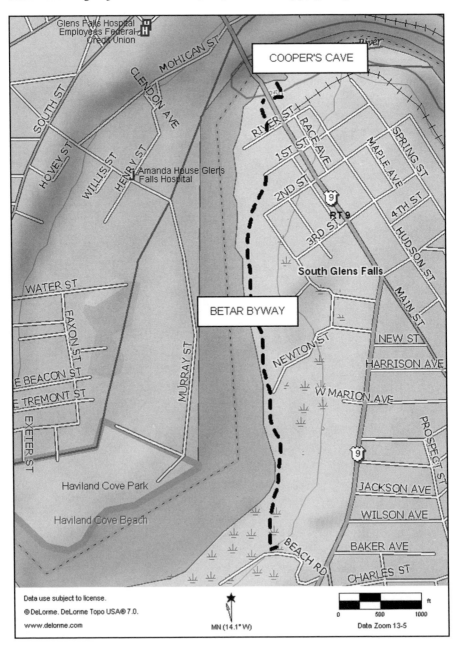

falls and to the city that would grow there). It was also in this general area that Daniel Parks built a gristmill in 1775, and Julius Rice, a village planner, erected his sawmill in 1839.

Follow the paved walkway as it veers to the left and begins paralleling the river. In 0.1 mile you will observe to your right an old dock-like area between two earthen mounds. Several stone pieces can be seen between it and the byway. In another couple of hundred feet, you will pass by a secondary paved path that veers off to your right, quickly leading to a deck overlooking the water. From there, excellent views of the river can be obtained both up and downstream.

As you continue along the main walkway, you will have periodic views of the East Cove public beach (identifiable by its sandy shoreline) over half a mile away. You will also see an occasional fire hydrant, relics from bygone days when there actually were buildings here to defend against conflagrations. Across the river, paralleling the Hudson River but out of sight, is the South Glens Falls Feeder Canal, which brought water down to the Champlain Canal, many miles distant east of Hudson Falls. The South Glens Falls Feeder Canal begins roughly 2.2 miles above the falls.

At over 0.3 mile you will pass by a sign on your right indicating "Hamilton's Boat Site. 1940." A road bearing off of Saratoga Avenue towards the river still bears the name Hamilton. Several hundred feet farther you will come to another sign on your right, this time indicating the 1940s "Old Beach Site." Whatever attraction this section of the river held for bathers is gone now, for the shoreline is indistinguishable from the rest of the river.

At 0.4 mile you will come to old foundations on your right, the site of the South Glens Falls Water Plant, which operated from 1895 to 1920. The foundation is what remains of a reservoir that once stood on this site. Water running downhill from several springs was dammed up at a point farther south along the byway (you will come to it in another 0.2 mile). From there, water was sent down to a filter house and then into the stone-walled reservoir where the present ruins stand. From the reservoir, the water was pumped up to a 120-foot stand pipe and, finally, transported to two distant water troughs for consumption by village residents.[1] The present waterworks system was built in 1973. Part of the new system is visible to the east as you walk along the trail—the huge South Glens Falls Water Tower, which holds up to one million gallons of water.

A second paved walkway goes off to the right next to the ruins and leads quickly to an observation deck overlooking the river.

After another 0.1 mile you will come to a third side path, this time unpaved, going off to the left. It leads east into the woods, circles around, and then takes you back out to where you started in 0.05 mile.

At roughly 0.6 mile you will come to the south end of the Betar Byway and the location of the old South Glens Falls Water Plant, which operated from 1920–1974, and parts of which are still used in the present water system. The well-preserved stone reservoir is visible behind a fenced-in area. It now serves as part of the watershed. Just south of the old reservoir is the modern South Glens Falls Water Works, located on Beach Road.

A small stream passes under the byway here and tumbles into the river after another hundred feet. Look towards the river and you will notice a sizeable island that parallels the east bank.

Historical Note: In the late nineteenth century this part of the Hudson River was pivotal to the logging industry. About 1.0 mile south of the remains of the foundation of the old reservoir was a section of the river called "the Big Boom," where logs that had been floated down from the upper Hudson were stored and sorted by various lumbering companies. According to *The New York Times* archives of March 12, 1893, the log drives down the Hudson began in earnest about April 1, when freshets set streams roaring. Logs were initially made into rafts of sorts at Schroon Lake and floated downstream.

Beginning in 1851, the "Big Boom" at Glens Falls was made by chaining large logs together across the river. This created an impassable barrier for the logs floating downstream from lumber camps. When danger of flooding was past, the "Big Boom" was opened and thousands of logs were floated down to the feeder dam, another general sorting place. Since each lumber company marked its logs, they were readily identified and claimed. By 1872 about one million logs per season were sorted there. Another "Big Boom" was located downriver at Fort Edward. Even then (1893), it was predicted that lumbering would deplete the forests near the rivers in the Adirondacks and become a thing of the past, which, of course, soon came to pass. As you walk Betar

Large millstones lie scattered about the Betar Byway. Photograph 2007.

The ruins of the old water cistern. Photograph 2007.

Byway today you might, with a little imagination, conjure up the image of the river at an earlier time when it teemed with thousands of logs awaiting their destiny to be metamorphosed as houses and furniture downstate.

Cooper's Cave—The walk to Cooper's Cave may be very short, but it is fascinating because it reveals the site of a memorable chapter in historical fiction that, after two hundred years, has become virtually accepted as fact.

Follow the signs from River Street leading down a side road to the base of the falls and to a viewing platform overlooking Cooper's Cave. Along the way you will pass by the Boralex South Glens Falls Hydroelectric Project, on your left.

You will find abundant historical plaques leading up to and around the viewing platform that tell the history of Cooper's Cave, the numerous bridges that have spanned the river by the falls, the Native Americans who occupied the area, and a brief biography of James Fenimore Cooper, who wrote so passionately about the falls and the cave.

From the platform, you will have an excellent view looking down and across at the opening of Cooper's Cave (this may prove disappointing if you are expecting something more spectacular) and of the falls (which generally are fairly insubstantial, because much of the river's water is diverted for power generation or to run the numerous factories along the north bank). If you look downstream for roughly 0.2 mile, you will see rapids that make advancement upriver to the falls extremely difficult.

The Boralex South Glens Falls Hydroelectric Project looms large along the south bank nearly under the south end of the bridge. Look for two massive black pipes, sixteen feet in diameter (called penstocks), which conduct water downhill for power generation.

The height of the falls at Glens Falls has been variously estimated by numerous visitors over the last three centuries. According to the historic plaque near the entrance to the Cooper's Cave overlook, the falls are thirty-six feet in height and formed out of Glens Falls limestone—a relatively hard black rock.

History: Cooper's Cave is located between Glens Falls and South Glens Falls at the base of the falls at Glens Falls, where the Hudson River tumbles over sixty feet in total before leveling off and continuing downstream.[2] Some speculate that Father Isaac Joques may have been the first white man to see the falls at Glens Falls and Cooper's Cave. This is assuming that his river crossing was made near the falls.[3]

Seneca Ray Stoddard, the famous nineteenth-century Adirondack author and photographer, gives this account of his visit to Cooper's Cave:[4]

> *At the south end of the long bridge, steps lead down to the flat rock, and, near the lower end where it is notched and broken out, we climb down to the level of the water, and enter the cave made memorable by Cooper in one of his wild Indian stories. We can pass entirely through this and a smaller one also, by crouching low at the entrance, and rising gradually as we advance to the south end, which opens over the gulf, where the face of the savage so startled Cora, and revealed the hiding place to their enemies.*

The city of Glens Falls has gone by other names as well—The Corners, Glenville, and Pearl Village.[5] It is a city whose growth was stimulated by its proximity to the waterfall and the many industries that were established along its banks. Bridges were erected across the Hudson River at Glens Falls to link the city to such other major centers as Albany and Schenectady. The first bridge, called the Old Toll Bridge, was constructed in 1803. It was replaced by a newer bridge, which was the one that Cooper and four English traveling companions saw in 1824. Then there was the wooden "Free" Bridge, of 1833, followed by a wooden covered bridge in 1842. Bridges didn't last long at Glens Falls, however, because raging annual floodwaters periodically destroyed them.

In 1890 an iron truss bridge was built, followed in 1913 by the Viaduct. Up until then, wooden stairs, and then iron steps, led down to the upper part of Pruyn's Island, from where Cooper's Cave could be accessed. With the completion of the Viaduct, this all changed. A circular stairway was built leading down from the bridge to the bedrock near Cooper's Cave. This endured until 1961, when the stairway was removed.

Cooper's Cave Fact & Fiction: When James Fenimore Cooper penned his series of five novels set within the mid-1700s and known as the *Leatherstocking Tales*, he made frequent use of local natural areas to flesh out his stories, giving his tales a character and believability that would otherwise have been lacking. In *The Pioneers*, for instance, Cooper set the action against the background of Kaaterskill Falls near Haines Falls, and in another section of the novel he set the scene at Natty Bumppo's Cave on the eastern hills above Otsego Lake in Cooperstown.

It is in *The Last of the Mohicans* (1826), Cooper's most famous novel, however, that he made use of a natural wonder that has become forever after identified with his name—Cooper's Cave. The existence of a cave at Glens Falls had been known for many centuries, probably as far back as when the earliest Native Americans began using the Hudson River as a waterway. Cooper visited the cave in 1824 (a year before the opening of the Erie Canal) and was clearly impressed by its natural beauty and the ruggedness of the surrounding gorge and falls, for he wrote his classic novel *The Last of the Mohicans* less than a year later, immortalizing the falls and the cave.

Because Cooper's Cave was in close proximity to the growing city of Glens Falls and, therefore, easily accessible to visitors, it rapidly became a tourist phenomenon attracting people whose imaginations were fired by Cooper's novel. To accommodate growing public demand for ready access to the cave, a spiral staircase was constructed from the top of the Glens Falls Bridge (called the Queensbury-Moreau Viaduct) in 1915 leading down to the falls and over to Cooper's Cave.[6] In 1961 the old bridge was replaced by a newer one, and the spiral staircase was eliminated. The State of New York had decided that continued erosion of the bedrock had made the cave unsafe and took the opportunity to permanently close off bridge access to it. In 2003 a new bridge was constructed, called Cooper's Cave Bridge, and an observation platform overlooking the cave was established in May of 2006 near the base of the falls at South Glens Falls. Unfortunately, direct access to the cave is still not possible, and one must remain content to look across at it from a short distance away.

Even so, it makes for a fascinating intellectual game to compare the Cooper's Cave of the nearly 200-year-old novel with the Cooper's Cave of today. Were Cooper's descriptions factual, or did he create a fictional cave and gorge that bears little resemblance to the one at South Glens Falls? And in regard to geology, how accurate was Cooper's description of the cave, the

In *The Last of the Mohicans* James Fenimore Cooper modeled his cave after the one at Glens Falls, now known as Cooper's Cave. Postcard ca. 1930.

falls, and the gorge? Finally, did Cooper use this particular cave and gorge to create a believable background for his characters?

For the answers to these questions, we turn to Cooper's novel, *The Last of the Mohicans*. The year is 1757, the third year of the French & Indian War. The story begins with the main protagonists—Cora and Alice Munro, Major Duncan Heyward (their escort), an itinerant named Gamut, and a Huron of dubious character named Magua—making their way through the woods towards Fort William Henry on Lake George, where Cora's and Alice's Scottish father, Colonel Munro, is the fort's commander. Heyward's mission is to make sure that the two young women arrive safely. On the way, the party is saved from a deadly ambush—and Magua's treachery—by Hawkeye, Chingachgook (a Mohican Sachem), and Chingachgook's son, Uncas. Their salvation is only temporary, however. In order to escape from a party of Huron warriors in close pursuit, Hawkeye leads the small party to a secret refuge, Cooper's Cave. They still have a long way to go to their final destination at Fort William Henry.

To get to the cave, Hawkeye and the others set off in a canoe paddling upstream on the Hudson River to the falls that are conveniently only a short distance away. Cooper's first description of the Glens Falls gorge is as follows:

> *the river was confined between high and cragged rocks ... As these, again, were surmounted by tall trees, which appeared to totter on the brows of the precipice, it gave the stream the appearance of running through a deep and narrow dell.*

Today there are no tall trees lining the top of the escarpment, but this is not to fault Cooper's description. He generally had a pretty good eye for detail. Where trees once flourished, an endless number of industries took root over the last several centuries and changed the topography.

The word "dell" is rather quaint today. The passage of time can change the meaning of a word, just as the actions of wind, rain, snow, moving water, and vegetation can alter geological features. Two hundred years ago the word commonly denoted a small, shady valley. The gorge, however, has never been small, although when lined with trees, it would have been cast into shadow. The glen, then and now, contains high walls with a fast-moving river and powerful cascades. Turbulent rapids exist just downstream from the falls, and it would have been extremely difficult to make headway against them. It was known to Native Americans at the time as *Chepontuo*, meaning the "difficult place to get around."

Cooper then describes the falls:

> *in front, and apparently at no great distance, the water seemed piled against the heavens, whence it tumbled into caverns, out of which issued those sullen sounds that had loaded the evening atmosphere.*

"Piled against the heavens" poetically describes how large waterfalls look when seen from below, as would be the case when Hawkeye's party advanced towards the base of Glens Falls. Since the falls at Glens Falls are nearly forty feet high and several hundred feet wide, they loom large when seen head-on from the level of the river below.[7] The falls are so large and powerful, in fact, that "the roar of the cataract sounded like the rumbling of distant thunder" and Hawkeye is able to speak "aloud, without fear of consequences with the roar of the cataract."

Paddling steadily up the river, Hawkeye unerringly guides his party through and around perilous rapids and eddies until they reach the base of the falls. Their fate has now become even more precarious, for they are in imminent danger of being capsized by the huge waves generated by the falls. Understandably concerned, Major Heyward demands to know, "Where are we? And what is next to be done?" This is the moment when the identity and location of the falls is finally revealed to the group by Hawkeye, who says, "You are at the foot of Glenn's."

Here, Cooper is playing fast and loose with the facts. John Glenn, for whom Glens Falls is named, hadn't yet acquired the land near the falls during Hawkeye's time, but Cooper's audience, of course, would not have known the falls by any other name. With the location of the falls now firmly established as Glenn's Falls, Hawkeye quickly outlines what their next course of action must be: "And the next thing is to make a steady landing, lest the canoe upset, and you should go down again the hard road we have traveled faster than you came up."

Cooper here accurately assessed the force of the river at Glens Falls. The Hudson is an immensely powerful river, especially after spring's melting of snow pack or following a major cloudburst. If the canoe were to capsize, the river would sweep the whole party downstream like pieces of bark at a velocity many times greater than they had traveled coming upstream.

After making a "steady landing" on the rocks by the falls, Hawkeye drops off his charges and then repeats the perilous journey, bringing back vital supplies and provisions so that they will be ready to face whatever comes next. At this point, Hawkeye and his two Mohican companions disembark from the canoe and with nary a word between them suddenly vanish into the rocks at the base of the falls while the rest of the party look on in helpless astonishment: "the whole three disappeared in succession, seemingly to vanish against the dark face of a perpendicular rock, that rose to the height of a few yards, within as many feet of the water's edge." Immediately, disembodied voices begin issuing from the rocks: "Smothered voices were next heard, as though men called to each other in the bowels of the earth."

Voices coming from inside the cave would sound muffled because of the placement of the rocks and the roar of the falling water, but why would Hawkeye's charges be unable to plainly discern the entrance to Cooper's Cave and instead just stand there mystified? Cooper's woodsmen on a previous visit had concealed the entrance to the cave by draping a blanket over it—a blanket which, by the way, would have needed to have been the size of a garage door, for the opening at Cooper's Cave is wider by far than several men standing side by side. A little poetic license, perhaps?

The blanket is removed momentarily, revealing the interior of the cave: "At the further extremity of a narrow, deep cavern in the rock, whose length appeared much extended by the perspective and the nature of the light by which it was seen, was seated the scout, holding a blazing knot of pine." Cooper's Cave, as we shall soon see, is not a cave with underground passages. It is strictly a surface phenomenon formed in the middle of a river bed.[8] Hence the interior of Cooper's Cave is dark and foreboding in the story only because the entrance has been covered by a blanket. This point is underscored when Hawkeye states, "Uncas, drop the blanket, and show the knaves [Hurons] its dark side."

The story continues with Major Heyward raising legitimate concerns over the indefensibility of their position. After all, haven't they merely succeeded in trapping themselves inside a tomb of rock, where they can neither see what is happening around them nor hear the sound of approaching warriors in the overpowering roar of the falls?

"'Are we quite safe in this cave?' demanded Heyward. 'Is there no danger of surprise? A single armed man, at its entrance, would hold us at his mercy.'"

If Cooper's Cave were a solutional cave (formed by running water), Heyward's statement would be unassailable, for there would be but one entrance. Most caves come to a dead end, either by their passageways pinching off (meaning that the crawlway becomes too tight for a caver to continue any further), sumping out when the water level rises to the height of the cave ceiling, or becoming obstructed by breakdown (jumbles of boulders). Most caves must be exited in the same manner as they are entered. But Cooper's Cave, both the real one and the fictional one, is an exception.

The secret to Cooper's Cave is now revealed. Chingachgook lifts up another blanket to reveal a second opening. "Then, holding the brand, he [Hawkeye] crossed a deep, narrow chasm in the rocks, which ran at right angles with the passage they were in but which, unlike that, was open to the heavens, and entered another cave, answering to the description of the first, in every essential particular." Cooper's Cave is a cave with two entrances!

The next paragraph is important if you're interested in geology, for in it Cooper describes how the falls came to acquire its irregular shape and offers some provocative views on the texture and composition of cave rock:

> *You can easily see the cunning of the place—the rock is black limestone, which everybody knows is soft; it makes no uncomfortable pillow, where brush and pine wood is scarce; well, the fall was once a few yards below us, and I dare to say was, in its time, as regular and as handsome a sheet of water as any along the Hudson. But old age is a great injury to good looks, as these sweet young ladies have yet to l'arn! The place is sadly changed! These rocks are full of cracks, and in some places they are softer than at othersome, and the water has worked out deep hollows for itself, until it has fallen back, ay, some hundred feet, breaking here and wearing there, until the falls have neither shape nor consistency.*

One can't help but wonder if Hawkeye is speaking tongue-in-cheek when he asserts that black limestone (a sedimentary rock) can be used as a substitute for a pillow of branches and brush. Even in its crushed form, for which the northern walls of Glens Falls gorge at one time were mined to fashion cement and lime, it would hardly make a comfortable headrest.

The remainder of Hawkeye's soliloquy describes how the falls were once "some hundred feet" downstream from its present location, with the further claim that the contours of Glens Falls have markedly been altered over time. We know for a fact that all waterfalls are gradually destroying themselves by wearing down the bedrock beneath them, thereby receding backwards over time. Cohoes Falls in Cohoes, New York, for example, originated about 2,000 feet downstream from its present location, nearly at the confluence of the Hudson and Mohawk Rivers. Glens Falls, likewise, started off significantly downstream from its current position and over the eons has worked its way upriver. Cooper states that the falls have receded some one hundred feet, but the length of the Glens Falls gorge speaks of a considerably greater recession.

Hawkeye's statement that Glens Falls was "once as regular and handsome a sheet of water as any along the Hudson" is intended to mean that the falls once possessed a continuous lip, much like the straight edge of a ruler. There is no question that the falls, as seen now, are jagged and discontinuous. Some sections have eroded more quickly than others. Some parts have developed huge cracks, forming miniature ravines. Still others have resisted the river's erosive action, leaving behind rocky abutments, virtual islands in the bedrock. Hawkeye's statement about the fall's past appearance, however, is mere speculation and nothing more. All traces of the waterfall's original appearance have long eroded away. Unless Hawkeye (or Cooper) could have seen the falls 10,000 years ago, there would be no way to be privy to this knowledge.

As the novel continues we now find Hawkeye and his companions making their final stand against the Hurons, who have caught up with them and are keen on extracting their pound of flesh. More information is now imparted about Cooper's Cave:

> "In what part of them are we?" asked Heyward.
>
> "Why, we are nigh the spot that Providence first placed them at, but where, it seems, they were too rebellious to stay. The rock proved softer on each side of us, and so they left the centre of the river bare and dry, first working out these two little holes for us to hide in."
>
> "We are on an island!"
>
> "Ay! There are the falls on two sides of us, and the river above and below."

Cooper's Cave, according to the novel, is located in a section of bedrock that has survived the erosive power of the Hudson River. Hawkeye and his companions are on an island, with the river rushing by on both sides. The real Cooper's Cave is also on an island of bedrock, one that is subject to seasonal flooding. In the early spring, when the Hudson River begins to swell after the release of snowmelt, Cooper's Cave can completely disappear under the high water. Cooper's Cave is still periodically inundated, but less frequently and less severely since the Great Sacandaga Lake (a man-made reservoir) was created in 1930 to control the waters of the Hudson River's main upper tributary, the Sacandaga River.

Hawkeye, seemingly untroubled that the Hurons may be ready to strike at any moment, describes the falls in greater detail now:

> *It falls by no rule at all; sometimes it leaps, sometimes it tumbles; there it skips; here it shoots; in one place 'tis white as snow, and in another 'tis green as grass; hereabouts, it pitches into deep hollows that rumble and quake the arth; and thereaway, it ripples and sings like a brook, fashioning whirlpools and gullies in the old stone, as if 'twas no harder than trodden clay. The whole design of the river seems disconcerted. First it runs smoothly, as if meaning to go down the descent as things were ordered; then it angles about and faces the shores; nor are there any places wanting where it looks backwards, as if unwilling to leave the wilderness, to mingle with the salt.*

Since the Hudson River at Glens Falls is broken up into a kaleidoscope of cataracts, with water tumbling every which way, it is easy for onlookers to feel that the river has become momentarily "disconcerted." What's more, the waters actually seem to pause and slow down for a fleeting moment at the base of the falls, as if "unwilling to leave the wilderness, to mingle with the salt." It is not until a short distance downstream from the falls that the waters reassemble and become ribbon-like again.

Cooper goes on to describe how the falls have fashioned "whirlpools and gullies" in a riverbed seemingly "no harder than trodden clay." In doing so, Cooper quite accurately captures how the force of falling water over centuries has scoured out potholes in the bedrock.

The real Cooper's Cave is markedly smaller than the fictional one. At best, judging from antique postcards and studying the cave from the present viewing platform, the cave is twenty to thirty feet in length. If you were to put seven people into the cave and then cover both entrances with large blankets (as Cooper does), you would quickly end up with seven claustrophobic people.

Perhaps the main problem with the fictionalized Cooper's Cave is that no experienced woodsmen would ever use it as a hide-out. The cave, as Major Heyward rightfully contended, is completely indefensible. Although Cooper's Cave possesses two openings, they are only about thirty feet apart, and neither one leads off the island. What is worse, the entrances directly face the sides of the gorge. If Hawkeye or any of his party were to emerge from either opening, they would be sitting ducks for arrows and gunfire from opposite sides of the river. But Cooper's Hurons are not simply content to outlast Hawkeye's party by camping out on the cliffs and pinning them down. They rush right in for the quick kill, attempting to swoop down on the cave from above the falls. The following description of the falls is now presented by Major Heyward:

> *The river had worn away the edge of the soft rock in such a manner as to render its first pitch less abrupt and perpendicular than is usual at waterfalls. With no other guide than the ripple of the stream where it met the head of the island, a party of their insatiable foes had ventured into the current, and swam down upon this point, knowing the ready access it would give, if successful, to their intended victims.*

This sounds more like an act of impatient foolishness or desperation on the Hurons' part, rather than a rational plan of attack. Here, Cooper has forsaken realism in favor of drama.

The story continues on, with some of the party escaping and the rest being captured, but the action quickly moves away from Glens Falls and no further information is provided on Cooper's Cave or the falls and gorge. We are left, then, with two Cooper's Caves to consider—one fictional and one based in fact—both located at the base of the waterfalls at Glens Falls.

Clay Perry, a well-known popularizer of caving in New York and New England, described Cooper's Cave as, "A shallow alcove which has resulted from stream erosion of the bedrock."[9] Louis Fiske Hyde writes that Cooper's Cave is "simply a cave excavated in the rock at the foot of the falls by the unending rush of water through soft limestone."[10] These descriptions apply equally well to the Cooper's Cave in *The Last of the Mohicans*. Cooper's notion of putting blankets over the entrances to hide the cave is pure hokum, since the ruse would be easily detectable in the daylight and would only serve to trap smoke from a fire inside the cave, making habitation unbearable.

Still, Cooper never took the liberties with the facts that many movie producers have when bringing *The Last of the Mohicans* to the big screen. Most film productions portray Cooper's Cave as a spacious cavern hidden behind a curtain of overhanging water. This is fiction—but not Cooper's fiction. Except for minor details and a little dramatic license here and there, Cooper's fictional cave and the real Cooper's Cave are one and the same.

Thousands of people every day drive across the bridge spanning Glens Falls and South Glens Falls without realizing that below them is one of the most famous caves in all of American literature, and one that just happens to really exist.

ADIRONDACK
Trails *with* Tales

Part III: High Peaks Region

Some of the most fascinating history of the High Peaks Region harkens back to its exploration and development in the nineteenth century, a time when the public first discovered the awesome beauty contained in this wilderness, as well as a time when the exploitation of its natural resources began. Oddly enough, a symbiotic relationship was maintained between those who came to plunder the land and the writers and artists who attempted to capture its picturesque appeal. At the root of it all was the tremendous zeal and excitement for determining the destiny of America, a new country with seemingly endless boundaries and a boundless future.

Quick on the heels of the earliest Adirondack settlers came the entrepreneurs. Although the rocky land racked by harsh climate might be unsuitable for farming, those with an eye for profit saw trees that could be harvested and buried iron that could be mined. Adirondac, a once hardscrabble, now nearly obliterated, small community in the high peaks was forged by the late-nineteenth-century iron mining industry. Although always a modest enterprise, it was nevertheless a lively, thriving town when the mines were booming. The rapidly disappearing remnants of what once was a village are located south of the terminus of Indian Pass, an amazing high-walled natural wonder.

Along with the developing mining and logging industries were the Adirondack hotels and resorts catering to an emerging clientele who sought the beauty and healthy air of the mountains. There were also the inquisitive, hardy painters who wished to capture the wild scenery on canvas, following in the manner of Thomas Cole, a nineteenth-century painter who in 1825 found a ready market for scenes of the Hudson Valley. Along with the painters came writers like James Fenimore Cooper, William H. H. Murray and Alfred Billings Street, who were only too eager to record droll tales of the early Adirondacks.

As a result, painters and writers were extolling the picturesque scenery at the same time that successful entrepreneurs were digging, chopping, and exploiting that very same scenery. After the industrialists had plundered the land and reaped their wealth, they sat back and wanted to live cultured lifestyles, buying paintings and reading the literature of the day. By all reports, many genuinely loved the Adirondacks. They had come to value the aesthetics of the wilderness and wanted to preserve and protect the beautiful land around them. Yet, a complex dichotomy continued between the practical use of the land and its aesthetic appreciation.

Some entrepreneurs like Paul Smith (see "Paul Smiths" chapter), a hunting guide turned grand hotelier, appreciated the pristine wilderness for its beauty and bountiful game. Smith built an empire while sharing the backwoods with city folk at his hotel. Henry Van Hoevenberg, a talented inventor but less astute businessman, built a rustic lodge in the High Peaks and established an intricate system of trails for his and his guests' hiking enjoyment. Others, like William Neilson and Robert DeForest, wealthy Adirondack industrialists and founders of the Adirondack Mountain Reserve and Ausable Club, were interested in buying land to create a permanent nature preserve while also establishing an exclusive club for rich families.

By the 1850s, the Adirondacks became a center of the Abolitionist Movement. John Brown, the most famous abolitionist, lived in North Elba near Lake Placid and used it as his base of operations. He was well-acquainted with Inez Mulholland and Garrit Smith, two other famous abolitionists who plied the Underground Railroad in the North Country.

The Adirondacks, though remote, have always managed to reflect the important trends of the day. This section includes:

John Brown's Farm: Walk on trails over lands farmed by John Brown, famous nineteenth-century martyr to the abolitionist cause, who was part of an experimental farming community of freedmen and former slaves on this site in North Elba.

Mt. Jo & Mt. Von Hoevenberg: Two mountains within view of each other were named for star-crossed lovers who met while hiking in the Adirondacks. Theirs is a mysterious, tragic story. Now their names are united throughout history, leaving you to reflect on the nature and meaning of their relationship as you hike up to the respective mountain summits.

Adirondac & Indian Pass: Walk through the abandoned village of Adirondac and then hike up through Indian Pass to Summit Rock, where you will find yourself immersed in the natural beauty and mining history of this area while traversing the most famous of the hikes written about in the early nineteenth century.

East Branch of the Ausable & Adirondack Mountain Reserve: This awesome hike along the East Branch of the Ausable takes you past a number of spectacular waterfalls and a towering cliff face—all located in the Adirondack Mountain Reserve (AMR), a wonderland of natural beauty managed by the Ausable Club, a story in itself.

12   JOHN BROWN'S FARM

Location: North Elba (Essex County), John Brown Farm State Historic Site
Delorme NYS Atlas & Gazetteer: p. 96, BC2

Fee: None for using grounds; modest admission fee to enter historic home

Hours: Grounds—open year-round; historic house & gravesite—open from May 1 to October 31, 10 AM–5 PM, closed Tuesdays

Accessibility: Immediate grounds around homestead—less than 0.3 mile walk; trails leading away from the homestead—variable; minimum of 0.4 mile walk

Degree of Difficulty: Easy

Additional information: John Brown Farm State Historic Site, 115 John Brown Road, Lake Placid, NY 12946. (518)-523-3900. www.nysparks.com/sites/info.asp?siteID = 14.

Highlights:
- Historic homestead of famous abolitionist John Brown and his family during the mid-1850s
- 244 acres of former farmland tilled by the Brown family, and site of a utopian community established by Gerrit Smith for freedmen and former slaves
- John Brown's grave and the graves of his sons Oliver and Watson, who were killed in Brown's raid at Harpers Ferry (Brown was hanged for leading the raid)

Description: John Brown, the famous abolitionist and antislavery martyr, was a catalyst for the American Civil War and the consequent freeing of slaves. These old farm roads in North Elba give hikers an opportunity to walk through woods that once were farmlands tilled by John Brown and by former slaves and freedmen who were part of a utopian community established by Gerrit Smith. It was here that Brown made plans for the raid on Harpers Ferry.

Unlike many other sites in New York State, Brown's farm was almost immediately recognized for its value to posterity and became a private historic site in 1870—only seven years after Mary Brown and her children had moved out.

John Brown, abolitionist, led the raid on Harper's Ferry, a flashpoint for the Civil War. Postcard ca. 1940.

Directions: From Lake Placid Village (junction of Rtes. 86 & 73), drive southeast on Rt. 73 for over 1.5 miles. Turn right onto John Brown Road, cross over Old Military Road (Rt. 35), and continue southwest for less than 0.7 mile until you reach the end of the road at a large cul-de-sac. Park off to the side of the road.

From the Adirondack Northway (I-87), take Exit 30 for Lake Placid. Drive northwest on Rt. 9 for 2.2 miles. At a junction of Rtes. 9 & 73, continue straight onto Rt. 73 and head northwest for over 26 miles. As soon as you pass by the Winter Olympic Ski Jumping Complex (on your left), veer left onto Old Military Road. Within several hundred feet turn left onto John Brown Road and head southwest for less than 0.7 miles to the historic farm.

The Hike

Standing at the cul-de-sac, take a moment to get oriented before starting off. Scanning left (south) to right (west) you will see: the graveyard where John Brown is buried along with two of his sons, Watson and Oliver, in addition to a number of the other Harpers Ferry raiders; the caretaker's cottage, built in the early 1920s a short distance behind the graveyard; the farmhouse where John Brown and his family lived; the wood shed; and, finally, the barn (behind the house and the shed), which was relocated to its present position in the 1920s/1930s. Far off in the distance, Mt. Marcy, New York State's highest peak, can be seen on a clear day.

In the middle of the cul-de-sac is a memorial to John Brown, erected in 1935 and sculpted by Joseph P. Pollia, depicting Brown with his arm around

Harpers Ferry

In October 1859, John Brown acted upon his long-held plan to raid the federal arsenal at Harpers Ferry, Virginia, and began freeing slaves in the surrounding area. He hoped to frighten Virginia slaveholders by inciting slaves to rebel and flee.

His plan in raiding the arsenal was to capture rifles and other weapons to arm the slaves, and to destroy whatever weapons he could not confiscate, along with arsenal machinery so that more weapons could not be manufactured there.

His small band of twenty-one men, consisting of five blacks and sixteen whites, did manage to capture the arsenal and to free some slaves from nearby plantations, but after thirty-six hours of battle with federal troops, Brown was captured and his sons Watson and Oliver were killed, along with others. Brown's plan had failed, but the raid on Harpers Ferry did succeed in ending slavery in the United States—but not in the way that Brown had anticipated.

Brown's behavior before, during, and after the raid focused the attention of both the North and the South on the issue of slavery with an intensity it had never before seen. Brown's well-articulated responses to his interrogators during his confinement and trial were covered by the press and inflamed opinion on both sides. Although he was convicted and hanged, he became a martyr to the antislavery cause and was a prime catalyst for the Civil War. He had lost the battle at Harpers Ferry, but he had won the war of words.

John Brown's gravesite as it looked ca. 1930s. Postcard.

a young black boy. To the east, towering above the tree line, are the 90-meter and 120-meter-high Olympic Ski Jumps.

To reach the trailhead, follow the path leading past the gravesite to the historic farmhouse, and then head down a slight grade through a wooden gate to the trail registry, a total distance of not more than a couple of hundred feet. The registry is located next to a small pond that was dammed up and made larger in the 1950s for use in the event of fire.

After signing in at the registry, follow the dirt road southeast for a couple of hundred feet. The basement of the old barn to your right has been modernized and can be visited in conjunction with touring the historic farmhouse. It contains additional information on John Brown and slavery in the 1800s.

As soon as you pass by the barn, you will come to an enormous boulder partially buried in the ground. From there you have three choices. The first is a walk around the perimeter of the cleared property, returning to the historic house, a trek of no more than 0.3 mile. As you circumnavigate the cleared property around the Brown farm, you will be struck by how the homestead seems to be situated on top of a dome, with the land going sharply downhill to the south, west, and (partially) to the north. Picnic tables are scattered. The zigzag wooden fences on the property may appear odd and quaint, but are perfectly in keeping with the harsh realities that the Brown farm had to face. The ground was simply too rocky to drive in fence posts.

The second choice is to continue straight ahead on the dirt road, initially heading west, and then north, as the road veers to the right and heads downhill. You will quickly cross over a small stream and then head steadily uphill for 0.1 mile. When you come to a fork in the road, bear right and continue uphill for another 0.2–0.3 mile. You will come to a metal barricade that makes for a good turnaround point. Trails on the property do continue beyond this point, but by now you probably have gotten a feel for what it must have been like to walk along the property many years ago when it was an active farm. It should be noted that this section of the property was primarily logged and used for maple sugaring, but was too rugged to be farmed. What you see today is a second-generation forest of birch and pine. Unfortunately, although you have gained a bit of altitude by the time you reach the metal barricade, there are no views that overlook the farm. Retrace your steps back to the homestead.

The third choice, starting again at the giant boulder, is to turn right and follow a dirt road that leads north across the clearing into the woods within a couple of hundred feet. In less than 0.1 mile, the road forks. Going right will return you immediately to the Brown Farm. Continue straight ahead, following the main road. In another 0.05 mile you will notice off in the woods to your right what at first appears to be a lean-to, but which upon closer examination turns out to be a springhouse. It is the current source of water for the caretaker's house. Continue north for another 0.1 mile and then bear right, following the trail. You are now on a section of land that was undoubtedly farmed, but would have yielded few crops, mostly potatoes. In 0.2 mile you will emerge from the woods at John Brown Road, a scant 0.05 mile from the cul-de-sac. From there you can either walk back on the main road or follow a grassy lane paralleling the main road to the right.

During the winter these wooded trails provide a marvelous opportunity for cross-country skiing or snowshoeing.

The pond was created in the 1950s for fire protection. The trail begins from here. Photograph 2008.

History: In 1849, John Brown,[1] the famous abolitionist and catalyst for the Civil War, chose North Elba for his family home. He may have initially sought to live in the north woods utopian community for ideological reasons, in hopes of assisting black settlers in honing their farming skills, but he also loved the Adirondacks for their beauty and splendor. He once said of the mountains, "Everything you see reminds one of omnipotence."[2]

By vocation Brown had been a farmer, tanner and maker of processed wool for yarn. But from an early age he despaired over the slavery of blacks and the unfair treatment freed slaves received at the hands of whites. These human rights sentiments led him to work zealously in the antislavery movement. Moving to North Elba (earlier called The Plains of Abraham)[3] presented Brown with the opportunity to eke out a living for his family while also fulfilling his dream of advancing the cause of freedom and equality for blacks.

In 1849 Brown traveled to Petersboro, New York, to meet with Gerrit Smith, a wealthy philanthropist and reformer who had established a farming settlement for free blacks and fugitive slaves in upstate New York. Brown proposed to Smith that he would survey the properties held by blacks in North Elba and instruct them in farming skills. It was the beginning of a lifelong friendship with Smith, a fellow abolitionist.

Smith granted Brown 244 acres at a dollar an acre in the remote Adirondack village of North Elba, and Brown promptly sent his family to live there in the rented Flanders house until he could join them to build a home of their own. Meanwhile, Brown needed to close down his wool business in Springfield, Ohio, an increasingly unprofitable venture for him.[4] It took him over a year of travels in England, Pennsylvania, Virginia, and Ohio to finally extricate himself from the wool trade. At last, in 1850, he returned to North Elba to attend his daughter's wedding to Henry Thompson, a North Elba neighbor and solid abolitionist. While there, Brown exhibited some of his prize Devonshire cattle at a country fair, demonstrating his pride in being part of the farming community.[5] But it was not until 1854 that Brown was finally able to resolve enough of his business problems to spend extended periods with his family in North Elba.

He had been an abolitionist activist for many years, but it was during this period of time that Brown became more convinced and resolute about the need for strong antislavery action. His destiny as a catalyst for the freedom of American blacks was formed when he began planning a raid on Harpers Ferry, a United States arsenal in Virginia. Many of the discussions and the development of fighting strategies for the raid on Harpers Ferry took place at his humble farmhouse in North Elba. It was here that he met with the famous black freedman and orator Frederick Douglass and others to initiate a plan of action.

It is said that in his role as mentor and farmer, Brown was kind and generous in his willingness to assist others. Many noted that he was truly egali-

John Brown's homestead as it looked ca. 1900. Postcard.

tarian and showed no racial preference in his relationships. He and his large family were welcoming to all. He had close friendships with many of his black neighbors and confided to them his Harpers Ferry plans.

Even in an era when large families were common, the Brown brood was unusual. Altogether he fathered twenty children by two wives. Only eight of the children would outlive him. Some died in accidents or succumbed to illness. Three of his sons—Frederick, Oliver and Watson—died fighting battles alongside him against slavery. Frederick was shot while walking on a road near Osawatomie.[6] Oliver and Watson died in the raid at Harpers Ferry.[7] Three of Brown's other sons—John Jr., Jason, and Owen—risked their lives fighting slavery, but survived the conflict. It is extraordinary how John Brown mounted antislavery battles in Kansas and Virginia with such strong family backing. Evidently, the same mix of Calvinist religion, racial tolerance, and antislavery passion was imbued in his offspring. The clan raised by John Brown in pre-Civil War America was willing not just to live with black people, but to die for them.[8]

The Brown homestead in North Elba was agreeably remote, set on land surrounded by the high peaks of the Adirondacks. Many of the most popular trails into the high peaks wilderness area started near Brown's farm and the Gerrit Smith-inspired settlement for freed men and fugitive slaves. By the mid-nineteenth century the Adirondacks were starting to become a popular area for adventurers and artists to explore. Farmers like Brown were often called upon to provide respite for hungry and weary travelers.

Henry Dana, author of *Two Years before the Mast,* recorded his visit in 1849 with his friend Theodore Metcalf to the Brown homestead in an article titled "How We Met John Brown," written for the *Atlantic Monthly* in 1871. After a lengthy trip to Burlington, Vermont, across Lake Champlain to Westport, and then by carriage to North Elba via Keene, Dana and Metcalf stopped at a cabin for breakfast. As luck would have it, they had arrived at the home of John Brown. Since Brown had arrived only a month before, this would have been the rented Flanders house on Cascade Road. In Dana's words:

> *In this remote region, almost every man who has a decent place takes strangers to lodge and eat, receiving compensation, rather in the way of a present than of regular pay. The place belonged to a man named Brown, originally from Berkshire, Massachusetts—a thin, sinewy, hard-favored, clear-headed, honest-minded man who had spent all his days as a pioneer farmer—He seemed to have an unlimited family of children, from a nice cheerful healthy young woman of 20 or so named Ruth, whom we all liked very much, and a full-sized red-head-ed son, Owen, who seemed to be foreman of the farm, down to every grade of boy and girl. He also had two Negro men, one called Mr. Jefferson, and a Negro woman. How on earth all these lived in that cabin was beyond our apprehension and almost beyond belief, and yet Aikens [Dana's guide] said he had often lodged here—in the garret to be sure—where were three beds beside his own.*[9]

Dana had come to the Adirondacks to hike some of the trails. Unfortunately for Dana and his party, they became disoriented on their hike back from Indian Pass. After some bushwhacking and backtracking, they spotted a cabin in the woods. Much to their relief it was the Brown domicile, where days earlier they had lodged for the night. Dana wrote:

> *We found them at breakfast in the patriarchal mode, Mr. and Mrs. Brown & their large family of children, with hired men and women, including three Negros, all at table together. Their meal was meat, substantial and wholesome, large quantities of the best of milk, good bread and butter, Indian meal and molasses.*[10]

These snippets of information recorded by Dana provide us with glimpses into the daily life of the Browns, which was probably comparable in most respects to the lives of other settlers in the area. The Brown family no doubt lived frugally, but had an abundance of food on the table.[11] It was years afterward that Dana realized he had visited with Brown the famous abolitionist.

Black settlers came to North Elba to take advantage of the land offered by Gerrit Smith, but not in the large numbers that Smith had envisioned. The North Elba census between 1850 and 1870 lists thirteen families. There may well have been additional families who did not stay long enough to show on the census. Most of the black settlers had not previously farmed. They had worked in cities as cooks, barbers, coachmen and the like. Some found the land, the climate, and the vocation of farming not to their liking.

Brown befriended his black neighbors and assisted them by teaching them farming techniques. One notable family was that of Lyman Epps. They were the only black family from this period of time to remain and become permanent residents in the Lake Placid area. Lyman Jr. stated that his father arrived in Westport at the same time as John Brown, and that they traveled together to North Elba.[12] The senior Epps and Brown became lifelong friends.

Lyman Epps Sr. had been born into freedom in Colchester, Connecticut, in 1815. No members of the Epps family were ever slaves. In North Elba they lived in a log cabin on lot #84 on Bear Cub Road until 1863. There is no plaque showing the exact location of the Epps home or of the homes of any of the other nineteenth-century black settlers on the Gerrit Smith lots. Brown's farm, however, would have been contiguous to those parcels of land. Bear Cub Road is off Old Military Road, west of the Brown property.

Later, the Epps family moved to Lake Placid. Lyman and his family ran a successful farm, and he further distinguished himself as an Adirondack guide in his early years, cutting the Epps trail through Indian Pass.[13] They were a prominent family in the community life of both North Elba and Lake Placid.

It is often stated that the Gerrit Smith settlement was not a success. It did not attract vast numbers of settlers or last very long. On the other hand, the fact that it came into being at all in the turbulent pre-Civil War era and offered a model of an integrated community is certainly an achievement. From that standpoint, it was one of the more successful nineteenth-century utopian communities. Plus, the black families of North Elba affected the course of American history by helping John Brown decide the direction in which his antislavery activities would take him—in particular the plan to raid Harpers Ferry.

The middle years of the nineteenth century were filled with strife and violence. Above all, John Brown was a product and a prophet of his time. While he loved the peaceful beauty of the Adirondacks and the bucolic farmlands, he was also drawn into the gathering fray surrounding the slavery issue, particularly as it raged in Kansas and Virginia. Brown had always been

It was at Deer's Head Inn in Elizabethtown that Mary Brown stayed while on her journey back to North Elba with her husband's body. Postcard ca.1930.

a staunch abolitionist. Now, living hand-in-hand with his black neighbors in North Elba, his thoughts and feelings crystallized. By 1850 he had formulated strategies for ending slavery. He concluded that violence was necessary to change the pro-slavery South and end slavery, and he acted on that conviction at Pottawatomie and Harpers Ferry.

Between 1850 and 1859, John Brown's speeches in the North and his skirmishes in the South captured the imagination of antislavery proponents. During that period he won the hearts of some of the most influential people in America.[14] He had the ear and support of Frederick Douglass, Henry David Thoreau, Ralph Waldo Emerson, Bronson Alcott, Thomas Higginson and countless others. Herman Melville called Brown "the meteor of the Civil War."[15] The east coast Transcendentalists supported Brown's message and antislavery actions. He also had financial backing from Gerrit Smith and the "secret six." By the time of his raid at Harpers Ferry on October 16, 1859, and his hanging for the deed on December 2, 1859, Brown had become a symbol and a martyr for the antislavery cause.

As a portent of things to come, Colonel Robert E. Lee was present at Brown's capture,[16] and Lee, Stonewall Jackson, and John Wilkes Booth were all present at Brown's execution. For the North, Brown's martyrdom tipped the balance of the scales in favor of civil war.

Brown's body was returned to North Elba where he had requested that he be buried. His wife Mary and abolitionist sympathizers, including Wendell

Philips, a famous antislavery orator, made the sad, dignified journey home from Harpers Ferry. Brown was applauded and eulogized along the way at stops in Philadelphia, New York City, Troy, Rutland, and Elizabethtown. In Albany, officials fired a 100-gun salute.[17]

In Elizabethtown, about fifteen miles northeast of North Elba, Brown lay in state at the Essex County Courthouse while Mary and company stayed across the street at the Deer's Head Inn. The inn still exists, although it has been renovated several times since the 1860s. A large portrait of John Brown painted by David C. Lithgow still hangs inside the Essex County Courthouse. The nearby Elizabethtown Town Hall, north of the courthouse, was formerly the Baptist Church where John Brown attended services.

There was a final funeral service at the Brown homestead in North Elba. Lyman Epps and his sons, noted local singers, sang hymns, including Brown's favorite, "Blow Ye Trumpets Blow."[18] Henry David Thoreau wrote the elegy, "The Last Days of John Brown," that was delivered by George Hinton at graveside.[19] Brown is buried alongside his sons Oliver and Watson, as well as others killed at Harpers Ferry and later surreptitiously transported to North Elba for burial.[20] The small cemetery also holds a memorial to his son Frederick, killed near Osawatomie.

The country was shocked and then galvanized by the death of John Brown and his cohorts. Shortly thereafter, troops from the North marched to do battle against the pro-slavery South in the Civil War, spurred on by singing the many verses of the song "John Brown's Body Lies A-moldering in the Grave."

The John Brown Farm State Historic Site consists of 244 acres of land, including the actual farm that John Brown and his family lived in and toiled over. The farm became a private historic site in 1870, fifteen years after it was built and a mere seven years after Mary Brown and her surviving children had left for more hospitable surroundings. It remained a private historic site for the next twenty-five years. In 1895 the site was acquired by the State of New York and has been a National Historic Site ever since. The bronze sculpture of John Brown created by Joseph P. Pollia was a gift from the John Brown Memorial Association, a group that had been making annual pilgrimages to the farm since 1922. The farm was restored to its present condition in the 1950s.

While visiting the grounds, be sure to take a guided tour of John Brown's homestead. You will walk away with a much deeper understanding of Brown's central role in ending slavery in this country, and how Harpers Ferry was one of the powder kegs whose explosion led to the Civil War.

13 MT. JO & MT. VAN HOEVENBERG

Location: North Elba, Heart Lake Wilderness (Essex County)
Delorme NYS Atlas & Gazetteer: p. 96, C2

Fee: Modest fee for parking by the High Peaks Information Center

Hours: Daily, open continuously

Accessibility: Mt. Jo—1.3 miles to summit via Long Trail; 1.1 miles return trip via Short Trail; (2.4 miles round-trip if following loop); 700 feet of ascent. Mt. Van Hoevenberg—2.2 miles (one-way); 740 feet of ascent.

Degree of Difficulty: Mt. Jo—Moderate to difficult; Mt. Van Hoevenberg—Difficult, because of length of hike

Restrictions: Observe posted rules & regulations

Highlights:
- Views of Adirondack High Peaks from summits of Mt. Jo and Mt. Van Hoevenberg
- Adirondak Loj
- Views of Heart Lake

Description: These two related hikes take you through some of the most beautiful scenery as well as some of the most fascinating history of the Adirondacks. The trails wind through the sites of many nineteenth-century stories of exploration, industrialization, and romance—in particular the poignant love story surrounding Mt. Jo and its companion peak, Mt. Van Hoevenberg, named for Josephine Schofield and Henry Van Hoevenberg, two people who were destined to become legends. The two peaks are perfect hiking destinations, following gnarly old trails to see picturesque views that entertained our forbears and continue to delight us today.

Directions: *To Mt. Van Hoevenberg*—From Lake Placid (junction of Rtes. 86 & 73), drive south on Rt. 73 for 3.3 miles. When you come to an open field where a sign points the way to the High Peaks Wilderness Area, turn right onto Adirondak Loj Road and drive south for 3.8 miles. Turn left onto a gravel road (which ultimately leads to South Meadows in over 1.0 mile) and drive east for less than 0.3 mile. You will see a sign on your left for the Mt. Van Hoevenberg Trail. Park in a pull-off if there is room; otherwise, park off to the side of the road.

From the Adirondack Northway (I-87), take Exit 30 for Lake Placid, drive northwest on Rt. 9 for 2.2 miles, and then follow Rt. 73 northwest for approximately 25 miles. Turn left onto Adirondak Loj Road and proceed south for 3.8 miles. Turn left onto South Meadows Road and drive east for less than 0.3 miles to park by the trailhead.

The road to South Meadows is seasonal; it is not maintained from November 1 to April 1. If you are taking this hike in the winter, be prepared to park along Adirondack Loj Road and add an extra 0.5 mile (round-trip) to the hike. Also bear in mind that, under the newly created High Peaks Wilderness Complex Unit Management Plan, the Town of North Elba-owned South Meadows Road may eventually be permanently closed and turned into a hiking trail.[1]

To Mt. Jo—Turn onto Adirondak Loj Road from Rt. 73 and drive south for 4.8 miles. Proceed past the entrance booth and park near the High Peaks Information Center (HPIC), where there is sufficient parking for up to 200 cars. Walk back up the road to the entrance booth. To your left is a turn-around. The red-blazed trail to Mt. Jo (and Indian Pass) begins there.

The Hikes

Mt. Van Hoevenberg

Follow the blue-blazed Mt. Van Hoevenberg Trail northeast along an old logging road that threads its way through a narrow corridor of tightly packed pines. This pine forest is so dense that it would be hard for even the most inattentive hiker to wander off from the trail.

After 0.7 mile you will emerge all at once from the pine forest into an open hardwood forest. At 0.9 mile you will reach a large swamp where beavers have been busy at work. Because of the deadfall and a huge swath of skeletal trees, Mt. Van Hoevenberg can easily be seen off in the distance. This first mile has little change in elevation and makes for a wonderful snowshoe or cross-country ski trek during the winter.

Depending upon prevailing conditions, the trail may become momentarily obscure at the edge of the swamp. If such is the case, bear left and circle around the swamp until you pick up the trail again on the opposite side. This will involve a bushwhack of less than 0.2 mile.

At approximately 1.0 mile, the path begins to ascend slowly at first and then more steeply, gaining altitude steadily. Soon, the way ahead, which up until now has been consistently oriented in a northeast direction, turns right and proceeds east, continuing in that direction from this point on.

At 2.1 miles you will come out to an open ledge where excellent views of Mt. Marcy (New York State's highest peak) and Algonquin Peak (New York State's second-highest peak) await you. What's more, the view also encompasses a veritable "Who's Who" of the Adirondack High Peaks. Pack a topographic map to facilitate identification. From left to right, you will see Saddleback,

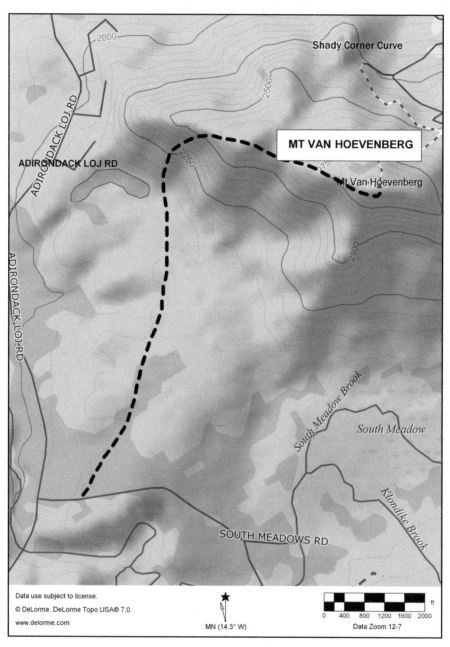

Basin, Phelps, Gray, Colden, Avalanche Pass (the huge notch between Wallface Mountain and Mount Marshall), Street, Nye, and Ampersand.[2] And, of course, there is Mt. Jo, just slightly to the right of Indian Pass, only 2.5 miles distant as you look southwest.

From the first ledge overlook, scurry up past two higher lookouts until you finally reach the summit, at 2.2 miles. From there, additional views of the High Peaks can be obtained, including sightings to as far southeast as Giant Mountain.

Mt. Jo

Start off from the trailhead following the red-blazed trail that ultimately leads to Indian Pass. In a moment or two the trail merges with a wide trail coming in on the left from the Adirondack Loj. Continue west, following along the perimeter of Heart Lake. In 0.4 mile you will come to a junction where the Short Trail (to your right) goes steeply up to the summit of Mt. Jo in 0.7 mile. The Long Trail goes straight ahead, taking you to the summit in 0.9 mile in a more leisurely fashion along a slightly more gradual route.

For this hike we will take the Long Trail. Initially, the path seems to go up and down, but without gaining much altitude. This is only temporary, however, for soon the trail begins to climb steadily. In 0.9 mile you will come to a junction at the base of a cliff where the Rock Garden Trail enters from your left. Continue climbing uphill steadily, heading north.

At 1.2 miles you will reach the upper junction with the Short Trail. Here, both trails become one again. Bear left and continue on to the summit, which is only 0.1 mile farther, heading east.

The view from the summit of Mt. Jo is truly inspiring. Looking into the immediate valley you will see Heart Lake. Off in the distance looms the High Peaks Range, circling around the lake like the cone of a massive volcano. Mt. Van Hoevenberg is visible to the northeast, dwarfed in size by the enormity of the peaks behind it. It has the appearance more of a ridge than a peak. Mt. Jo, when seen from Mt. Van Hoevenberg, is a more distinctive peak than is Mt. Van Hoevenberg when viewed from Mt. Jo.

To descend, follow the trail back for 0.1 mile to the junction. This time go straight, following the Short Trail as it takes you steeply down to the lower junction of the two trails in 0.7 mile. When you reach the lower junction, turn left and follow the path for 0.4 mile back to the trailhead.

The Long and Short trails, joining below and above, are a poetically apt symbol in this setting of the love story of Josephine Schofield and Henry Van Hoevenberg. The two trails circle in such a way as to form a ring, the universal symbol of unity and love.

The two summits are exactly 2.5 miles away from one another.

History: The stories surrounding the naming of Mt. Jo and Mt. Van Hoevenberg are poignant tales of love lost and dreams realized in nineteenth-century America.

Henry Van Hoevenberg was a resourceful inventor and entrepreneur. In 1876 he came to the Adirondacks primarily to relieve his vexing hay fever.

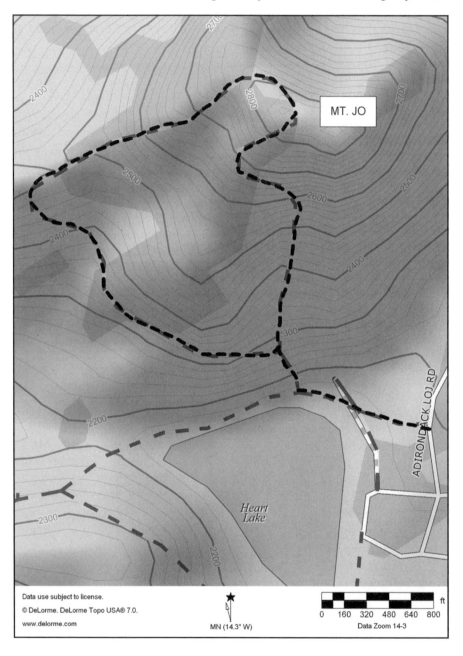

The venture proved to be a success, for his health seemed vastly improved. Perhaps it was the delectable combination of hiking endorphins and raging pheromones that affected the cure. Van Hoevenberg was later to become a prominent figure in promoting the Adirondacks, especially its trails in the High Peaks area. It is said that it was on this trip that he fell in love with Josephine Schofield.

What is known about Josephine is less well defined. The facts are as hazy as the views from Mt. Jo in the early morning mist. But then, maybe it is the very sketchiness of the facts and the mysteries surrounding the relationship that draw us into the ill-fated love story of Josephine and Henry.

Henry's trip to the Adirondacks began in Troy. Josephine's point of origin is uncertain. In some accounts, she traveled north from her home in Brooklyn. Other accounts say she was Canadian. What all the accounts do agree upon, however, is that Henry and Josephine were immediately smitten with each other. They spent two weeks trekking the mountains and enjoying the balmy, high-altitude air, which in the nineteenth century was highly recommended for its curative powers. One hike brought them to the top of Mt. Marcy. There they sat and scanned the terrain below, fantasizing about the place they would select to build their future home. Of the many choices, they spied a small heart-shaped lake nestled in the forest and surrounded by imposing lofty peaks. They decided that it would be on the shores of that lake that they would build their home. So far, so good for the romantic adventure.[3]

Winter views of Heart Lake and the High Peaks from the summit of Mt. Jo. Photograph 1998.

Mt. Jo as seen from Heart Lake. Photograph 2000.

After their romantic two-week sojourn, Henry left the Adirondacks to conduct business in New York City. Meanwhile, Josephine presumably returned to her day-to-day life. Some say that she, too, went to New York to continue in her employment as a telegrapher. The facts are hard to come by from this point on. What is known is that Josephine did not return to the Adirondacks to build and live in the lovers' dream home on the lake, but Henry did. He built a log lodge on Clear Pond—renamed Heart Lake—the lake he and Josephine had admired afar from Mount Marcy. Henry became rooted in the Adirondacks, first as the proprietor of the lodge on Heart Lake; then as the manager of the lodge and other properties that had been bought by the Lake Placid Club. All the while he continued designing inventions.

Henry's keen interest in the woods and mountains led him to blaze over fifty miles of trails emanating from his lodge. He named the small mountain with the wonderful view of Heart Lake and the high peaks Mt. Jo, in honor of Josephine Schofield. He evidently never forgot their sweet encounter. It is a gem of a peak. The famous nineteenth-century photographer and writer Seneca Ray Stoddard said of Mt. Jo, "The view from Lookout [Mt. Jo] toward the south is the finest mountain view in the Adirondacks."[4]

What happened to Van Hoevenberg's lost love? It would appear that she died mysteriously within a year after meeting Henry. The favored story is that she committed suicide by leaping from Niagara Falls, although her body was never found. Credence is given to this story because Seneca Ray Stoddard and Godfrey Dewey, both close friends of Van Hoevenberg, alluded to it as a possibility. Henry never made a public statement on the subject himself, but it was reported in the newspapers of the day that a Canadian woman named

J. J. Schofield was presumed to have jumped from the falls. Several items belonging to her were found on a rock near the top of Horseshoe Falls—a railway ticket, her bombazine purse, and a pair of black kid gloves.

But why would Josephine throw herself over the falls? Could it have been a dread of illness? Others in her family had succumbed to consumption, which she may also have contracted. She was engaged to a distinguished businessman whom her father wished her to marry. Had she met and fallen in love with Henry—an eccentric inventor—and feared her family would reject her for choosing a new sweetheart? It may have been a combination of circumstances that led her to despair. We'll never know for sure. Her family in Woodstock, Ontario, Canada never marked her grave, and only the solid presence of 700-foot-high Mt. Jo gives her ghost-like memory any substance at all. After the futile search for her body, no more was ever said of Josephine. Although Henry was a renowned storyteller, he never fully revealed the story of Josephine.

Van Hoevenberg was an ambitious, creative young man intrigued by apparatus and machinery. He was an inventor with many patents already to his credit when he made his first sojourn into the Adirondacks, and he had even gained some fame for inventing improvements to the telegraph. He continued to tinker with inventions throughout his life.

When he returned to the Adirondacks, however, he threw his energies into building a magnificent rustic lodge bordering Heart Lake. The lodge was built out of native spruce and was eighty-five feet long, thirty-six feet wide and three stories high.[5] At first the lodge was Henry's personal retreat; later

The current Adirondack Loj as viewed from Heart Lake. Photograph 1998.

he took in paying guests. His love of the forest was genuine, and he wanted his guests to enjoy hiking as much as he did. He built and improved the hiking trails on his property, creating broad, well-marked paths.

Van Hoevenberg's solid, comfortable lodge was popular with nature lovers, but Henry was more of a creator than a manager. Eventually, the lodge ended up sinking into debt. After some fumbled attempts to gain financial support, he sold the property to Melvil Dewey, the proprietor of the Lake Placid Club and a famous proponent of simplified spelling (hence Adirondack *Loj*—rather than *lodge*). Henry and Melvil became lifelong friends, and Henry stayed on as manager of the newly renamed Loj.

The Loj continued as an outpost of the Lake Placid Club until 1903, when it was razed by a ferocious fire that burned sixteen buildings and acres of property. The fire, ironically enough, started on Mt. Jo and then spread downward. As the lodge was becoming engulfed by fire, Van Hoevenberg threw the table silverware into the lake, set his telegraph invention on top of a rock, and escaped with his horses through Indian Pass.[6] It wouldn't be until 1927 that a new lodge was built on the original site of Henry's lodge.

Meanwhile, Henry moved to Lake Placid, where he continued to work for Melvil and resumed working on his inventions. Eventually, he severed his business relationship with Melvil and founded the Adirondack Electric Company, across Mirror Lake.

Henry was a primary mover in creating the Adirondack Camp and Trail Club, the forerunner of the Adirondack Mountain Club. He continued to hike and clear trails throughout the remainder of his life. He died on Sunday, February 17, 1918, after a day of hiking, and is buried in Oakwood Cemetery in Troy, New York. A Lake Placid newspaper account of the times described him as "machinist, electrician, boatman, guide, author, president of the Adirondack Camp and Trail Club, and all round genial gentleman."[7]

Van Hoevenberg's close friend Godfrey Dewey, Melvil's son, was on the committee for establishing the 1930 Olympics in Lake Placid. It was Godfrey who proposed renaming South Mountain as Mount Van Hoevenberg in recognition of Henry's efforts in establishing the Adirondack Camp and Trail Club and for being such a good steward of the Adirondacks. Today, the north side of Mount Van Hoevenberg is the slope that houses the Lake Placid bobsled run.

And so, although their own time together was short-lived, Henry and Josephine's mountain namesakes look silently at each other across the Adirondack meadows until the end of time.

14 ADIRONDAC & INDIAN PASS

Location: Tahawus (Essex County)
DeLorme NYS Atlas & Gazetteer: p. 96, CD1–2

Fee: None

Hours: Open year-round

Accessibility: Village of Adirondac—0.4-mile walk (round-trip);
Indian Pass—9.0 miles (round-trip)

Degree of Difficulty: The walk through Adirondac—Easy; the hike
through Indian Pass—Difficult

Highlights:
- Abandoned, historic, nineteenth-century mining hamlet, managed
  by Open Space Institute (OSI)
- Stabilized MacNaughton cottage, built in 1834, where Vice President
  Theodore Roosevelt stayed and hastily left upon hearing of the deteri-
  oration of President McKinley's condition following his assassination
- Largely intact remains of 1854 hot air blast furnace used in iron
  production
- Henderson Lake and upper origins of the Hudson River
- Indian Pass, famous geologic wonder

Description: This is a two-part adventure. The walk through the abandoned village of Adirondac takes you through the remains of a historic nineteenth-century mining hamlet, and the trek up through Indian Pass (also called
Adirondack Pass in past centuries) to Summit Rock leads you through what
is often touted as one of the most splendid geologic wonders in the eastern
United States.

The 4.5-mile-long trail from Adirondac to Summit Rock in the High Peaks
encompasses much of the natural, cultural, and art history of the Adirondacks.
Indian Pass, first walked by Native Americans, is a rough-cut thoroughfare
that leads from the heart of the highest peaks in the Adirondacks up to the
headwaters of the Hudson River. As such, it was inexorably linked to the early
mining village of Adirondac. This scenic pass first became famous when curious nineteenth-century explorers, artists, writers, loggers, and mining entrepre-

Take a walk down the main street of Adirondac—a true Adirondack ghost town. Photograph 2007.

neurs sought its picturesque beauty or hoped to plunder its potential resources. You may choose to hike it in one piece, or you may visit the lost village of Adirondac and Henderson Lake on one trip, and then hike into Indian Pass on a separate venture.

The historic site of Adirondac is being preserved by the Open Space Institute (OSI), in collaboration with other local, regional and state partners. In 2003, after negotiations spanning nearly ten years, OSI acquired the 10,000-acre Tahawus property from NL Industries, a Houston-based mining company. OSI, with support from a variety of partners, immediately took steps to prevent the continuing deterioration of the most historically significant structures. To this end, they secured funding to stabilize the MacNaughton Cottage, built in 1834; to reconstruct portions of a forty-five-foot-tall iron foundry blast furnace, originally completed in 1854; and to stabilize the abandoned fire tower atop Mt. Adams (the hike to the fire tower is not covered in this chapter).

Directions: From the Adirondack Northway (I-87), take Exit 29 and proceed west on Rt. 2 for 17.7 miles. When you come to Tahawus Road (Rt. 25), turn right and begin heading north. At 0.4 mile bear left at a fork in the road. When you come to a second fork, at 6.4 miles, bear left again, continuing on Rt. 25.

At 9.2 miles you will pass by a historic blast furnace on your right. There is a parking area just beyond the blast furnace, on the right, where you can pull over and walk back to the furnace. You can walk around the furnace, but don't get too close, because the structure is still being stabilized and there remains the possibility of falling brick and stone. If you walk over to the Hudson River, which is only several hundred feet behind the blast furnace, you can see the remains of a dam, a sluiceway, and various mechanical artifacts.

At 9.7 miles you will reach the south edge of the abandoned village of Adirondac. At 9.8 miles you will pass by the stabilized MacNaughton Cottage on your right, where Theodore Roosevelt stayed before being rushed by horse and carriage to North Creek and then by train to Buffalo to be sworn in as the new president of the United States. At 10.0 miles you will arrive at the Upper Works trailhead parking area.

The Hikes

Exploring the Deserted Village of Adirondac

Begin walking south from the parking lot, heading back the way you just came. On both sides of the road are abandoned buildings and homes in various stages of collapse. Some are next to the road, and some are farther into the woods (but still visible from roadside). After you pass by the first partially collapsed structure to your left, turn sharply left and follow a secondary road north between the collapsed building and the Hudson River. In a couple of hundred feet, you will reach a fairly intact cement structure next to the river that was used as a pump house. Close by, between the edge of the parking lot and the pump house, is a stone foundation, and next to it is an enormous mound of rocks that are the remains of the first iron furnace built on the site in the 1830s.

Return to the main road and continue walking south, passing between more old homes and buildings that once constituted Adirondac. Keep in mind that none of the buildings are safe to enter because of collapsing roofs and walls and deteriorating floorboards. Observe the buildings either from roadside or from the grounds around the buildings.

The house that Theodore Roosevelt stayed in, known as the MacNaughton Cottage, is located on the east side of the road approximately 0.2 mile from

The Open Space Institute is to be congratulated for preserving the historic MacNaughton Cottage. Theodore Roosevelt stayed here before his late-night flight to assume the presidency following William McKinley's assassination. Photograph 2008.

the parking lot. Like the rest of the houses in Adirondac, the structure was destined to collapse into rubble under relentless weathering. Fortunately, the Open Space Institute recognized the home's unique historical connection with Roosevelt's dramatic rise to the presidency and intervened to save the structure. In addition to being a residence, the building at other times also served

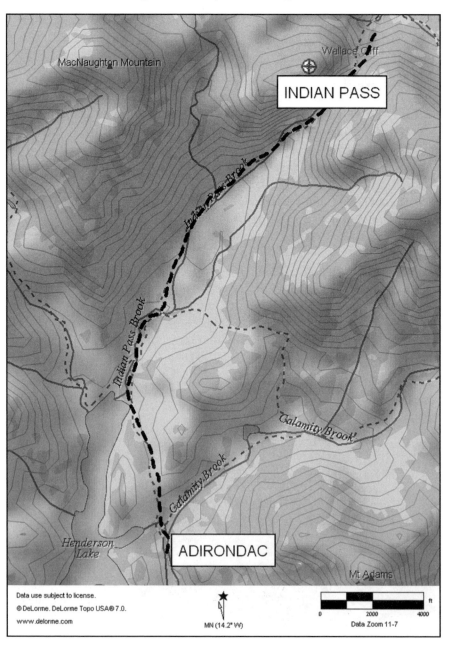

as a bank and post office. It is the oldest structure in the village (circa 1834) and the only residential building that dates back to the iron mine.

One hundred feet east of the MacNaughton Cottage is a pretty, two-tiered cascade on the Hudson River that was undoubtedly favored by anglers in the past—perhaps even by Theodore Roosevelt.

Exploring Indian Pass

From the parking lot, follow the barricaded gravel road (now a hiking path) north for 0.2 mile. As soon as you cross over the outlet stream from Henderson Lake, bear right and head northeast for 0.2 mile, following red- and yellow-blazed markers. When you come to the trail junction where the red-blazed Calamity Brook trail goes right, continue straight ahead on the yellow-blazed trail towards Indian Pass and Duck Hole.

At 1.5 miles you will come to your next junction. The trail to the left leads to Duck Hole. Continue straight ahead, following the red-blazed Indian Pass trail. In another 0.2 mile you will pass by the Henderson lean-to. Then, at 2.1 miles, you will come to another junction, where the Calamity Brook Crossover trail goes straight ahead. Turn left and cross over Indian Pass Brook, reaching the Wallface lean-to in 2.7 miles.

At approximately 3.0 miles you will get your first glimpse of Indian Pass with its west wall of rock—Wallface Mountain—rising imposingly into the sky from the floor of the valley. At around 4.0 miles the climb all at once grows steeper, and jumbles of rock begin to crop up around you, some the size of automobiles or larger. Ladders have been strategically placed in two places to help hikers over particularly tough climbs.

View of Indian Pass from Henderson Lake. Postcard ca. 1910.

At 4.4 miles you will come to a sign directing you left on a short side path to Summit Rock, from where you can obtain breathtaking views into the gorge and of Wallface Mountain, which forms the west wall of the gorge. Bear in mind, however, that Summit Rock is somewhat of a misnomer. The actual summit still lies another 0.5 mile farther up the trail. Views from Summit Rock were first painted by Charles C. Ingham (founder of the New York National Academy of Design) following a trip through the pass with geologist Ebenezer Emmons in 1837.

Directly in front of Summit Rock, at some distance below and towards the west wall of Wallface Mountain, is a gargantuan boulder with a flat top surface. Although there are no trails leading to this immense mass of rock, it is possible to get over to it by climbing down into the gorge, scrambling over other huge boulders and across yawning crevices, and then ascending at the base of the rock. The views from this boulder are even more awesome than those from Summit Rock, for you are now positioned inside the gorge instead of outside looking in. Extending in all directions, like a sea of icebergs, are the enormous boulders contained in this rock-strewn pass. This part of the hike, however, should be left to those who are very fit, nimble, and comfortable scrambling over and around huge rock formations.

If you wish to access Indian Pass from its north entrance, follow the directions given to Adirondack Loj at Heart Lake (see "Mt. Jo & Mt. Van Hoevenberg" chapter). From Heart Lake, follow the red-blazed trail south for over 5.0 miles. After a 400-foot rock scramble, you will be at the entrance to the notch. At 6.0 miles you will reach Summit Rock (the desired destination for most trekkers).

If you wish to make this a one-way hike north through Indian Pass to Heart Lake, you will need to position two cars, one at Adirondac and one at Heart Lake. Doing so will make it a 10.5-mile, one-way trek, but will involve a considerable amount of driving in order to place the two cars at opposite ends of the hike.

Canoe/kayak access to Henderson Lake—While visiting Adirondac you may wish to paddle on nearby Henderson Lake, named after David Henderson, who died tragically along Calamity Brook when his gun accidentally discharged. Although it is not a long carry to the lake, a canoe carrier would make the trek much more pleasant.

From the parking lot, head north along the barricaded road for 0.2 mile. After crossing the outlet stream from Henderson Lake and coming to a junction, turn left, proceeding west for less than 0.1 mile to the lake. Put in at an easy beach launch, roughly 150 feet north of the dam and spillway.

History: ***Abandoned Village of Adirondac***—The story of the hamlet of Adirondac is a tale of exploration and challenge. The former hardscrabble and

The remaining structures at Adirondac are slowly falling victim to the ravages of time. Photograph 2008.

now slowly vanishing little community was forged by the late-nineteenth-century iron mining industry. Although it was always a modest enterprise, nevertheless it was a lively, thriving hamlet when the mines were booming. The community consisted of sixteen dwellings and a multifunctional building with a cupola. The hamlet was surrounded by two farms, a blast furnace and forge, a puddling furnace, charcoal and brick kilns, and sawmills and gristmills. The rapidly disappearing remnants of this little hamlet are located at the southern terminus of Indian Pass, an amazing high-walled natural wonder.

In the early nineteenth century, David Henderson and Archibald McIntyre were scouting the Adirondacks for sources of ore to mine in order to develop lucrative iron industries. McIntyre had already established a mine in the town of North Elba, near Lake Placid and north of Indian Pass, but the output of high-quality ore had been disappointing. That mine only remained in operation from 1809–1813.[1]

According to an often-told story, in 1826 a Native American guide named Lewis Elijah Benedict approached Henderson with a shining rock of what appeared to be pure iron ore. Benedict offered to guide a party to the place where he had found the nugget. He boasted that there were large quantities of the shiny stuff lying about near a stream at the southern end of the great pass. (Incidentally, it was this same Native American guide who, in 1840, led geologist Ebenezer Emmons on the New York Natural History Survey of the central Adirondacks, part of a nationwide effort to identify and exploit natural resources.[2])

Starting from North Elba, near the northern terminus of Indian Pass, Henderson, Benedict, and a party of men including John McIntyre, Duncan and Malcolm McMartin, Dyer Thompson, and a black servant named Enoch, proceeded on their journey south through Indian Pass. It was an adventurous trip through the rocky gorge, but they were rewarded beyond their expectations when they finally reached the amazing cache of iron ore partially revealed in the bed of the outlet stream from what is now Henderson Lake. After some initial testing it was ascertained that it was indeed high-quality ore.[3]

Finding excellent iron ore south of Indian Pass during this period of America's early industrial expansion held great promise for these enterprising entrepreneurs. Once they had established the ore's unusually high quality, all they had to do was build the mines and tote the processed pig iron to Lake Champlain, where it could be shipped, mostly via waterways, to manufacturers of iron and steel implements. Unfortunately, transporting the processed ore to Lake Champlain turned out to be a continuing problem, but for the moment they were focused on the production of good iron.

They set about establishing McIntyre's Adirondack Iron and Steel Company, which remained in operation from about 1828 to 1858. The small hamlet of Adirondac, sometimes referred to as the Upper Works, quickly grew to surround the blast furnace and other machinery for processing the ore. There was also an iron operation about ten miles downstream, referred to as the Lower Works or Tahawus. Both the Upper and the Lower Works produced good processed ore.

The hamlet gradually grew to include a number of dwellings, a boarding-house, sawmills, gristmills, a school, churches, two substantial farms, and a bank and general store.[4] In 1849 the ever-hopeful McIntyre and Company built a new blast furnace. There were approximately 100 residents in Adirondac at that time, but it was indeed a rough backwater of a location.

Henry Dana, who visited the hamlet of Adirondac in 1849 after an arduous trip from North Elba through Indian Pass, described the community as having few comforts:

> *Mr. Portens, the agent, lives in half a house with one room serving as kitchen, parlor and nursery, which in Cambridge* [Massachusetts] *could only be let to the lowest class of Irish laborers. The only house at which strangers could be received was a boarding house for the hands, owned by the company. In this house were boarded and lodged 96 laborers.*

Dana went on to say that he and his four companions were accommodated in one room and slept on the floor after partaking of a meager dinner of pork and potatoes.[5]

Although Dana drew a grim picture of the town, it was visited and lauded by other visitors who at least credited it for its founders' ingenuity. One certainly could not fault the setting, as the surrounding waters reflected the glory of the High Peaks, including Mount Marcy.

One noted inhabitant was the famous Adirondack guide, John Cheney. For him this must have been an ideal location from which to lead fishing and hunting expeditions. No doubt his saddest trek, however, must have been in 1845 when David Henderson, son-in-law and partner of Archibald McIntyre, accidentally shot and killed himself at Calamity Brook. Henderson's young son was with the party at the time. Cheney recounted how he held the little boy through the night until a party of bearers could reach their camp and carry David's body on a bier back to Adirondac. Henderson Lake, near the now-abandoned hamlet, was named for David Henderson.

The mining community struggled on until 1858, when McIntyre decided that transporting the processed ore on roadways to Lake Champlain was a losing battle. There continued to be too few roads, and the ones that existed were in poor condition. That, coupled with floods on the upper Hudson River that washed out the dams, and the financial panic of 1857, finished off the iron industry at Adirondac.[6]

Although the closing of the Upper Works mine concluded an important chapter in the history of the hamlet of Adirondac and Indian Pass, the story continues. McIntyre might have retained some hope for the hamlet when Robert Hunter, a master bricklayer who worked on the construction of the blast furnaces, and his family stayed on in Adirondac as caretakers. The Hunters watched over the now-vacant buildings of the mining operation and hamlet until 1872, when Sarah Hunter died.

The lands bordering Indian Pass, Henderson Lake, the Hudson River, and the abandoned town of Adirondac were still owned by descendants of McIntyre and his partners in 1877 when they established a private sportsmen's colony, initially called the Preston Pond Club (later the Tahawus Club). The club used some of the vacant buildings in Adirondac, but also built some new and fancier cedar-shingled structures. It proved an ideal location for sportsmen seeking fish and game, as well as offering hiking trails to Mt. Marcy and the High Peaks.

Probably the most famous day in the annals of the Tahawus Club was September 13, 1901, when President McKinley, who had been recovering from a wound inflicted by an assassin's bullet, took a turn for the worse. Vice President Teddy Roosevelt was staying as a guest at Tahawus Club at the time, rooming at the MacNaughton Cottage. Reputably, they had to fetch Roosevelt from the trails of Mt. Marcy to alert him of McKinley's impending death. Sarah Hunter's son David, chief caretaker at Tahawus Club, drove Roosevelt on the first pell-mell leg of his horse and carriage journey from the club to North Creek, where a train was waiting to take him to Buffalo and the dying president. It was during the train ride that word came of McKinley's death, and Roosevelt was officially sworn in as president of the United States.

There are now markers along Route 28N (the Theodore Roosevelt Memorial Highway) indicating the names of the relay drivers who transported Roosevelt to the train station in North Creek. There is also a marker indicating where Roosevelt stopped to change horses.

Tahawus Club remained in Adirondac until World War II, when the National Lead Company (NLC) mined the area for titanium, a product used in whitewall tires and in paint used for battleships.[7] NLC built the railroad that finally made mining in Adirondac more feasible from a transportation standpoint. A company town called Tahawus was built near the former Adirondac community site, and the Tahawus Club was displaced in 1947 from that property (the club moved ten miles downstream to the Lower Works area, where it remains today).[8]

In 1963, NLC decided to end its landlord relationship with the workers, moving their homes on flatbed trucks fifteen miles to an area outside of Newcomb named the Winebrook Development. NLC ceased mining operations in 1989.

Forward-thinking individuals from the Open Space Institute (OSI) realized that the old nineteenth-century mining site was of great historical interest and negotiated with NLC to purchase the property. In 2003, the Open Space Conservancy, OSI's land acquisition arm, concluded its negotiations with NL Industries, Inc. (National Lead's successor) and acquired the 10,000-acre property for $8.5 million. OSI initiated an ambitious disposition plan for the property that included conveying nearly 7,000 acres to New York State as an addition to the Forest Preserve, nearly 3,000 acres to Finch Pruyn Paper Company for sustainable forestry, and retaining approximately 250 acres that contain all of the site's historic iron mining resources for OSI's own management and interpretation.[9] Part of the site was set aside as a historical district dedicated to preserving and interpreting the story of the nineteenth-century McIntyre mining enterprise.[10]

One of the historic buildings in today's Adirondac ghost town, the MacNaughton Cottage is the only extant building from the early mining days and has been stabilized by the Open Space Institute in collaboration with New York State. OSI has also been instrumental in securing funds for a major renovation project to stabilize the "new" blast furnace that was put into use in 1854. OSI also retained an old hunting cabin on Upper Preston Pond and an abandoned fire tower on Mount Adams, as well as the observer's cabin at the base of the mountain. It is an exciting prospect to think that within a few years visitors may be able to tour some of the hamlet sites with the benefit of descriptive signage or may even be able to enter the MacNaughton Cottage.

Blast Furnace—Roughly 0.5 mile south of the deserted village of Adirondac and virtually at roadside is the imposing blast furnace, built in 1849. A pull-off on the east side of the road provides ready access. Feel free to

The towering blast furnace, currently being stabilized by OSI, is passed just before reaching the village of Adirondac. Photograph 2008.

explore the grounds, but stay a safe distance away from the furnace itself since work is still being done to stabilize it. Portions of the Hudson River dam and spillway and huge pieces of old mining machinery as well as smaller pieces of artifacts may be seen behind the blast furnace. Directly in front of the blast furnace on the opposite side of the road is a hill lined with rows of large, terraced blocks, which were part of the charging bridge to the blast furnace.

History: *Indian Pass*—If one were to nominate contenders for the eight natural wonders of the Eastern United States, Indian Pass would surely be at the top of the list, right next to Niagara Falls. Indian Pass is a stupendous gorge formed between Wallface Mountain and Mount Marshall in the High Peaks Region. The pass possesses the highest vertical rock face east of the Rockies and quite possibly the largest mapped talus cave system in the world. Its tiny creek, Indian Pass Brook, is one of two headwaters for the Hudson River, New York State's largest river. Strewn with gigantic boulders, Indian Pass is larger than life in almost every respect.

In spite of its seemingly insurmountable, rocky obstacles, Indian Pass became a significant route for nineteenth-century iron industrialists as well as hardy travelers drawn by its rugged beauty. Alfred L. Donaldson, in *A History of the Adirondacks*, described Indian Pass as "a mighty chasm torn apart by the convulsions of nature," possessing a "large number of huge boulders, often

151

plumed with trees, that seem balanced in precarious poises, yet are found to be securely rooted against the powerful dislodging agents that attack them."[11]

Although originally known as Adirondack Pass, the name was later changed to Indian Pass in recognition of the fact that it was early Native Americans who established the notch's first trail, which provided them with a natural passageway through an otherwise impassable barrier of peaks. Native Americans had their own names for Indian Pass long before Europeans entered the scene. The passageway was variously called *He-no-do-as-da* or "path of thunder," *Os-ten-wanne,* meaning "Great Rock," or *Otne-yar-heh* for "Stonish Giants."[12] These are all apt descriptions of this enormous abyss where humans are dwarfed by huge boulders, where voices echo weirdly, with echoes seemingly coming out of nowhere, and where thunder rolls through like cannon fire.

The first white men to travel through Indian Pass were a party of mining entrepreneurs, including David Henderson, who followed an Indian guide from North Elba to present-day Tahawus in search of iron ore in 1826. Henderson and his party were successful in finding a bed of ore and, within a short span of time, iron mines began to be established several miles south of Indian Pass. Thus was born Adirondac and Tahawus (a mining town ten miles south of Adirondac).

Around the same time, the logging industry started advancing towards Indian Pass from the opposite direction, establishing outposts beyond Scott's Clearing near the northern end of Indian Pass. In the 1830s, Professor Ebenezer Emmons completed his survey of the Adirondacks, which included Indian

Pass. The notch was now officially on the map. Fortunately, despite these encroachments of civilization, the interior of Indian Pass was never mined or logged, in all likelihood because of a scarcity of harvestable resources within the gorge itself and the severity of the terrain.

For hikers climbing through the notch, one of the questions asked most often is, "How did such a huge pass come to exist?" Clay Perry, one of the earliest writers on caving in New York State and New England,

A strategically placed ladder helps a hiker negotiate a particularly difficult section of the climb. Photograph 1989.

stated in his 1948 classic, *Underground Empire*, that geologists believed that the pass had been "caused by an earthquake or earth tremor which split rock mountains open, then clashed them together and smashed the rocks into thousands of pieces, some of them huge."[13] Modern-day sources tell a slightly different story. Bradford B. Van Diver, geology professor and author, describes Indian Pass as a "deeply eroded northeast-trending fault zone" that developed during the Ordovician period when the Taconic Mountains to the east were being uplifted.[14] The fault zone was then widened and deepened by the grinding action of glaciers and the erosive power of streams that once raced through it at tremendous velocity.

Indian Pass, as it turns out, is but one of many northeast-trending faults that formed in the Adirondacks. These faults include Long Lake, Indian Lake, Avalanche Pass, the Ausable Lakes, and Cascade Lake. In all of these other faults, however, boulders and debris were swept away by energetic streams and the advance of glaciers, leaving behind scoured bedrock and glacial lakes. What's unique about Indian Pass is that its boulders were not carried away by natural forces, nor were any lakes or ponds left behind. All that remains today of the mighty waters that once rushed through the pass is a tiny creek called Indian Pass Brook and a huge number of massive boulders whose angular shape indicates that they have not been transported to their present location by glaciers.

It is speculated that, during the last glaciation, thousands of enormous boulders were calved off from the side of Wallface Mountain and lay suspended in the mass of glacial ice that had accumulated between Wallface Mountain and Mount Marshall. As time went on, the region warmed up and the last remaining glaciers retreated, exposing the Adirondack valleys and mountains again; still, one tongue of ice stubbornly remained in Indian Pass. When this last bastion of ice finally melted away, the suspended boulders dropped into the gorge. Since the glaciers had retreated long before, gone were the energetic, glacial-fed rivers that might have had the power to wash out the mass of rock debris giving Indian Pass a U-shaped glacial trough just like the fjords of Norway. Instead, the huge accumulation of boulders has deepened the notch by hundreds of feet.[15]

Perhaps Indian Pass's uniqueness also has to do with its height. At an elevation of 2,834 feet, the pass is over 655 feet higher than Heart Lake (a frequent starting point for hikers approaching from the north), making it a good deal higher, in fact, than the summit of many mountains in New York State.

People hike to Indian Pass today for a variety of reasons: hikers to marvel at what has been described[16] as an array of boulders "the size of tall city dwelling houses, hurled down from a mountain summit into a chasm a thousand feet in depth"; cavers to explore TSOD (Touchy Sword of Damocles) and the W. H. Lyman Talus Cave system, with 13,000 feet and 2,500 feet of passageway, respectively; and rock climbers to assail the vertical wall of anorthosite rock that is the eastern face of Wallface Mountain. Indian Pass has it all.

According to legend, the cliff face of Wallface Mountain was first climbed by a guide who was seeking treasure rumored to be located in a cave near the top. After much arduous climbing, the guide finally reached the cave only to be thrown off from the precipice by the demonic spirit of an Indian warrior guarding the treasure. Despite tumbling almost a thousand feet, his fall was broken by a hemlock tree and the guide lived to tell about his adventure (but, wisely, never to return). Today, rock climbers routinely ascend Wallface's sheer face—a rock buttress 2,500 feet wide and 800 feet high. For them, the real treasure is not to be found in a mythical cave, but in the accomplishment of scaling such legendary routes as Mental Break and reaching the top of the cliff.

The talus caves of Indian Pass are not solutional caves (formed by running water), but tectonic caves, formed by fallen jumbles of rocks. The caves offer an unusual opportunity for fun in the summer sun; as late as August, you can have snowball fights by scampering down into some of the deeper crevices and grabbing a handful of snow or ice. A. T. Shorey observed over half a century ago, "there are many grottoes and large holes and rock shelters, all filled with hard blue ice that never melts."[17] This phenomenon is the result of the sun's heat being unable to readily penetrate into the cave's deeper recesses. Some explorers have even speculated—rather fancifully—that the lower ice beds may date back to the last glaciation. Be that as it may, Indian Pass is a natural refrigerator and a good place to hike to on a hot summer's day.

Determined cavers seek out Indian Pass to explore the innumerable passageways that zigzag through the billions of tons of large boulders. Some of the passageways go down as far as 170 feet. In TSOD alone there are 355 entrances and over 455 intersections. Both TSOD and the W. H. Lyman Talus

The formidable cliffs of Wallface Mountain loom high above Indian Pass. Photograph 1998.

A solitary hiker contemplates the vast, rock-strewn abyss of Indian Pass. Photograph 2001.

Cave system contain huge chambers, pseudo-karst features, waterfalls, stalagmites and stalactites of ice, and other interesting speleo-features. Only experienced cavers should venture into either of these two massive cave systems, however. There are places where vertical lines must be rigged in order to exit, and other sections where boulders are so moss-covered and slippery that you may be unable to get an adequate handhold to pull yourself back out.

For most hikers, just hopping about on the boulders is the main attraction. And there are many massive boulders, indeed. One boulder alone, named Megaboulder, is estimated to weigh over 40,000 tons and to be 150 feet across. The most famous boulder of them all, and a must-see for hikers, is Sunset Rock, which is located near the south end of the pass. A side path heading west from the main trail leads directly to the top of this immense boulder, which is approximately thirty feet long and fifteen feet wide. From the top of Sunset Rock, there are fabulous views looking northward into the pass or southward down towards Henderson Lake.

It is very difficult to capture Indian Pass on film, for the area is so big that only small sections of it can be photographed at a time. In 1873, Seneca Ray Stoddard, the famous Adirondack landscape photographer, artist, writer, and lecturer, visited the pass and was able to capture some striking images of Indian Pass—pictures as fine in quality as any photographs taken today. An account of Stoddard's trek through Indian Pass, including several illustrations, can be found in his book *The Adirondacks Illustrated.*

In 1924 the Essex County Board of Supervisors proposed constructing a seven-mile-long road through Indian Pass. Fortunately, this proposal was never acted upon, and Indian Pass remains forever wild.

15   EAST BRANCH OF THE AUSABLE RIVER & ADIRONDACK MOUNTAIN RESERVE

Location: St. Huberts (Essex County)
Delorme NYS Atlas & Gazetteer: p. 96, CD3

Fee: None

Hours: Open continuously

Accessibility: 10 miles (round-trip). These are well-marked but rugged trails, and are not wheelchair-accessible.

Degree of Difficulty: Difficult, because of length of hike

Restrictions: The Ausable Club is privately owned, but public access to the trails via the Lake Road is allowed. Dogs, motorized vehicles, biking, and off-trail hiking are prohibited. Be sure to read the rules and regulations posted at the watchman's hut.

Highlights:
- A series of beautiful and renowned waterfalls on tributaries to the East Branch of the Ausable River, including:
  Pyramid Falls
  Wedge Brook Falls (lower, middle, and upper)
  Beaver Meadow Falls
  Rainbow Falls
- Scenic views of the East Branch of the Ausable River, including its own cascades
- Cathedral Rocks
- Bear Run
- The Ausable Club, a private club built in the nineteenth century
- Lower Ausable Lake

Description: This ten-mile round-trip hike along the East Branch of the Ausable River takes you through scenic forest past some of the Adirondacks' most famous and beautiful waterfalls. The trails found on this hike are on the property of the Adirondack Mountain Reserve (AMR), which is privately owned land with public access. The 0.7-mile-long road up to the AMR trail-head takes you past the Ausable Club, built in 1903 on the site of the Beede

House (a nineteenth-century hotel) and by numerous private homes that are also part of the club. You cannot linger at or enter any of these buildings; nevertheless, you can get a glimpse into days gone by.

Past the gatehouse (the watchman's hut) and trailhead registry is a dirt road, which is now closed to car and bike traffic. It may be used as a foot trail to Lower Ausable Lake. This is a long and uneventful walk, however, so it is not included in the hike description. The road is notable in that it was used by nineteenth-century guides and loggers to access the region around the Lower and Upper Ausable Lakes. It was originally a corduroy road, comprised of rough logs laid parallel, making for an exceedingly bumpy ride.[1]

The hike along the East Branch of the Ausable River described below is one of the most picturesque hikes found in the northeastern United States. It is, quite literally, a waterfall trail. Two of the falls, Beaver Meadow Falls and Rainbow Falls, have been the subjects of painters and photographers since Asher Durand and Seneca Ray Stoddard. You will definitely want to pack your camera for this hike.

Directions: From the Adirondack Northway (I-87), take Exit 30 for Lake Placid and drive northwest on Rt. 9 for 2.2 miles. At the junction of Rtes. 9 & 73, continue straight ahead on Rt. 73 and drive northwest for another 5.4 miles. At the bottom of a long winding hill, directly opposite the trailhead parking on Rt. 73 for Giant Mountain and Roaring Brook Falls, turn left onto a dirt road that leads to the Ausable Club. Park immediately to your left in an area designated for hikers.

If you are approaching from the junction of Rtes. 73 & 9N East (between Keene and Keene Valley), drive south on Rt. 73 for 6.1 miles and turn right onto a dirt road that leads to the Ausable Club. Turn immediately left into a large parking area.

Do not continue driving on the road leading up to the Ausable Club, because only members of the club are allowed to park on the grounds. For this reason you must proceed on foot from the parking area to reach the trailhead. It is a walk of 0.7 mile. When you reach the tennis courts, at 0.6 mile, turn left onto Lake Road Way and walk southwest for 0.1 mile, passing between private camps on both sides of the road. The hike begins from the watchman's hut. Before starting, be sure to familiarize yourself with the rules and regulations posted, and sign in on the trail registry.

The Hike

From the watchman's hut, follow a trail that leads northwest to the East Branch of the Ausable River in 0.1 mile. Cross the river via a footbridge to reach the junction of the West River Trail and the W. A. White Trail. (The

West River Trail follows the East Branch of the Ausable River up to Lower Ausable Lake. The W. A. White Trail leads northwest up to Lower Wolf Jaw, Snow, and Rooster Comb.) Turn left onto the red-blazed West River Trail and proceed upstream, heading southwest as you parallel the East Branch of the Ausable River.

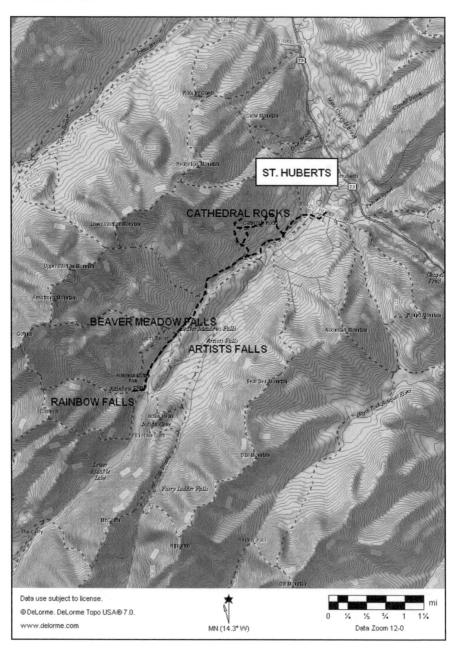

In 0.1 mile you will reach a point where the river is temporarily divided by an island. In 0.4 mile you will come to the first of two side trails leading up to Cathedral Rocks. The trail is opposite a footbridge crossing over the East Branch of the Ausable River. Hikers should take note that this footbridge can be used as a backup for accessing the West River Trail in the event that the first footbridge has been washed out.

Turn right onto the red-blazed Cathedral Rocks Trail. (For those who may choose to continue on the West River Trail, the second trail to Cathedral Rocks—and Pyramid Brook—is reached in another 0.7 mile.) Following the Cathedral Rocks Trail, you will immediately pass a grouping of large boulders. The trail then begins following a small stream as it climbs uphill. In 0.4 mile you will cross over one of the branches to this stream. At 0.5 mile a huge, fifty-foot-high rock face is reached. Near the end of this rock buttress, you will notice that a tiny, seasonal cascade comes down over the cliff face, producing the brook that you have been following. In another moment the huge rock face returns as you follow along its base. The wall of rock looms dramatically above you, again often attaining fifty feet or more in height. For decades this fortress-like wall has been known to hikers as Cathedral Rocks, but decades of guidebooks have seemingly had it wrong. According to an official-looking sign posted on a nearby tree, the real Cathedral Rocks is still farther ahead.

Continuing along the base of this rock face, you will soon pass by a more substantial seasonal cascade. It produces a twenty-five-foot-high cascade on your right, and then goes over a forty-foot-high drop on your left. After 0.8 mile you will come to a junction. Here the blue-blazed trail (the Bear Run Bypass) goes left and slightly downhill to Cathedral Rocks, while the red-blazed trail leads uphill to Bear Run. If you take the red-blazed Bear Run Trail, you will

The Ausable Club conjures up images of bygone years. Photograph 2003.

reach a second junction at the base of a large escarpment in 0.2 mile. Going left there will take you to the higher reaches of Pyramid Brook; turning right quickly leads up to Bear Run—an impressive valley overlook with views of the High Peaks that extend from Giant Mountain to Sawteeth.

Return to the junction of the blue-blazed and red-blazed trails. Following the blue-blazed trail downhill now, you will come to the base of Cathedral Rocks in 0.2 mile. This huge buttress of rock does not extend horizontally as far as the upper rock wall does (which, as mentioned above, was formerly thought to be Cathedral Rocks), but its massive bulk, reaching a height of over eighty feet, is sure to impress. Listen closely in the early spring and you will hear Pyramid Brook off in the distance, over the next notch.

From Cathedral Rocks, follow the trail as it starts uphill again. Although the path at first seems to lead towards the top of Cathedral Rocks, it soon pulls away from the mammoth rock face and heads directly over to Pyramid Brook, where it meets the red-blazed trail paralleling Pyramid Brook in 0.1 mile. At the red-blazed trail, turn left and start to descend. You will immediately pass by several small cascades, including a five-foot slide and a five-foot fall where the gorge narrows.

In less than 0.1 mile you will come to Pyramid Falls. The stream, having momentarily narrowed as it passes through a short ravine, emerges here into an open space and drops twenty feet down a nearly vertical rock face. Pyramid Falls starts off slender and then widens as it descends, forming a triangular (or pyramidal) shape. Just downstream from Pyramid Falls, the stream races through a descending flume and drops another ten feet.

From the bottom of the falls, follow the trail south for over 0.2 mile to return to the West River Trail, roughly 0.7 mile upstream from where you initially left it. From there, turn right onto the West River Trail and walk southwest for several hundred feet. You will reach a junction where a side trail, if taken, leads immediately to The Canyon—a third footbridge crossing of the East Branch of the Ausable River. Stay on the West River Trail, following it southwest as it climbs steadily above the East Branch of the Ausable River. In another 0.6 mile you will come to an overlook of the river where, far below, a pretty cascade on the East Branch of the Ausable River can be seen off in the distance.

In less than another 0.2 mile you will come to Wedge Brook, a small tributary of the East Branch that has produced three distinctive waterfalls. The middle fall is directly in front of a log footbridge crossing the stream. This ten-foot-high waterfall is broken into two rivulets by a large boulder, seemingly wedged at the top of the fall. It is this waterfall, split by a rock, which gives the stream its name. Immediately downstream is the lower fall—a graceful fifteen-foot-high cascade. There is much exposed bedrock between the two falls. The upper fall is quickly reached by following the Lower Wolf Jaw Trail uphill to your right as soon as you cross over Wedge Brook. Within two hundred feet

Twenty-foot-high Pyramid Falls is the largest of several cascades formed on Pyramid Brook. Photograph 1998.

you will come to views of the eighty-foot-high upper falls, where a faint path to your right leads down to the base of the cascade.

From Wedge Brook, continue southwest on the West River Trail for 0.7 mile farther until you reach Beaver Meadow Falls, a sixty-foot-high cascade that is one of the most widely photographed waterfalls in the Adirondacks. The trail passes directly in front of the cascade, affording wonderful close-up views of the waterfall. A fourth footbridge crossing of the East Branch of the Ausable River can be seen near this point.

From Beaver Meadow Falls, follow the West River Trail southwest for another 1.1 miles to reach Lower Ausable Lake, which is about 1.5 miles long and 0.5 miles wide. The north end of the lake is impounded by a large dam built in 2003–2004. There were earlier incarnations, however, and some had tragic histories. In 1856 torrential rains, possibly combined with a mudslide, caused the Wells Dam at the lake to rupture and send a tidal wave of water down the Ausable valley, killing eleven people and inflicting terrible damage to property. The Ausable River today usually appears peaceful and serene, making it hard to imagine just how ferocious and temperamental the river can become, particularly in early spring.

To get to Rainbow Falls, follow the Pyramid Peak/Sawteeth Trail west from the dam. In 0.1 mile you will reach a side trail for Rainbow Falls. Turn right and head northwest into a deep and foreboding box canyon littered with huge boulders. It is a place where snow and ice often remain until the warm days of summer. After 0.05 mile you will come to Rainbow Falls, produced

Lower Wedge Brook Falls is frequently overlooked by hikers in a rush to reach the bigger waterfalls waiting farther ahead. Photograph 2008.

by a 150-foot drop down a side wall near the end of the canyon.

Return to Lower Ausable Lake after you have enjoyed this magnificent waterfall. From there, you have three options for returning to the Ausable Club. The first is simply to retrace your steps, following the West River Trail back northeast, seeing everything in reverse order and from a new perspective. The second option is to cross over the East Branch of the Ausable River by the dam and follow the East River Trail as it heads downstream, paralleling the river (and the West River Trail on the opposite side of the river). This will provide new and exciting views of the East Branch. The third option is to cross over the East Branch and then follow the Lake Road back to the watchman's hut, a trek of 3.5 miles. Of the alternatives presented, this is the least attractive, for there is little to see. On the other hand, if you are weary or pressed for time, the Lake Road can provide an expeditious retreat back to civilization.

History: The story of the Adirondack Mountain Reserve and the Ausable Club in St. Huberts is a fascinating episode in nineteenth-century Adirondack history.

Keene Valley was where some of the earliest Adirondack settlers came in hopes of farming. It was also a region of unusual beauty and grandeur, which caught the attention of wealthy nineteenth-century businessmen who wanted to save the land from further encroachment by loggers and create a nature preserve for their own use and development. The preserve exists today as private land with public hiking access and a club with private membership. The story of how the Adirondack Mountain Reserve came to be mirrors the evolution of the Adirondack Park.

In 1797 settlers began to arrive in the valley to farm the land. By 1873 Keene Valley, then called Keene Flats, was a tiny farming community nes-

Beaver Meadow Falls is one of the Adirondacks' most photogenic cascades. Photograph 2001.

tled at the foot of the High Peaks.[2] The major roadways at the time, such as they were, bypassed this town altogether. The main route from downstate or from Vermont to Lake Placid and beyond was by way of boat on Lake Champlain to Westport and then by carriage to Elizabethtown. The mountainous route from Elizabethtown to the High Peaks paralleled what is now route 9N, bypassing Keene Valley and St. Huberts.

Farming in Keene Valley was not always profitable because of the harsh climate and short growing season. Hunting, trapping, and fishing helped supplement the farmers' incomes and their own tables. As the mountains became a destination for tourists in the second half of the nineteenth century, many Keene Valley farmers found that they could put their sporting skills to good use and make a profit by guiding tourists to prime hunting areas and fishing holes. Some guides, like Orson Phelps (Old Mountain Phelps), specialized in leading hikers up trails he cut to the peaks. Guiding became a way of life and a valued profession as the influx of tourists grew after the Civil War.

By the 1870s Keene Valley had become a favored destination of artists of the day. Following on the heels of the popular landscape painters dubbed the Hudson River School, aspiring artists sought fame and fortune farther up the Hudson River in the Adirondacks, which had recently been found to be at higher elevations than the formerly favored Catskills—a factor adding to their appeal. There suddenly was something akin to a mania for Keene Valley. The artist Roswell M. Shurtleff described one day in 1874 when he counted about forty artists in the hills overlooking Keene Valley, all diligently bent to their easels.[3] When these wonderful landscape paintings were displayed back in the cities, they no doubt served as further advertisement for the Adirondacks. Among the most renowned artists of this era to visit Keene Valley were Asher Durand, John Kensett, and John Casilear. Durand and his family enjoyed camping at Upper Ausable Lake, now part of the Adirondack Mountain Reserve (AMR).[4]

One-hundred-and-fifty-foot-high Rainbow Falls is magnificent in the early spring as it cascades into a snow- and ice-encased gorge. Photograph 1999.

Journalists and guidebook writers helped increase tourism, too. Seneca Ray Stoddard published his first guidebook to the Adirondacks in 1874, updating it annually until 1914.[5] Others, including William H. H. Murray, author of *Adventures in the Wilderness*, and Charles Fenno Hoffman, editor of the weekly *New York Mirror*, also extolled the majesty of the mountains and the town of Keene Valley in particular. With the influx of tourists, hotels were built and farms became boardinghouses.

By 1887, when the Adirondack Mountain Reserve (AMR) was founded, Keene Valley and the Adirondack Mountains had become an established destination for a discriminating and well-to-do clientele. Previously they had lived as summer residents in harmony with their guides and the general year-round population of the village. The venerable guides had come to rely on taking adventurous tourists to their quaint cabins in the wilderness for sport and recreation. But change would come when the founders of AMR and the Ausable Club ended up owning the land where the guides had established their rustic camps.

The twenty-nine primary founders of AMR were wealthy businessmen from New York City and Philadelphia. From the start, they saw the purchase of the land around Keene Valley in terms of potential land development, although they also wished to preserve the region around the Ausable Lakes and St. Huberts from being despoiled by logging operations. Their plan was to build a private club and construct their own summer residences on this property. That would give them control over who could buy land or become a member of the Ausable Club.

Initially they bought 28,625 acres, including property around the Ausable lakes that had been scheduled for clear-cutting by the Thompson & Armstrong lumber company.[6] The founders were spurred on to buy the land after William G. Neilson realized that Thompson & Armstrong Co. was prepared to put in a bid to buy the land for logging. Neilson responded by asking a few wealthy colleagues to contribute money towards a private preserve and land development company to thwart the logging company's plan. He met with great success, and the consortium acquired the desired property and more from the Beede family. In 1890 they bought the site of the venerable Smith Beede House, which had burned. The hotel was rebuilt and reopened in 1903 as the St. Huberts Inn. Although the Beedes had sold the land, they were among the stockholders of the hotel company and managed the hotel. In 1906, AMR purchased the inn and opened it as the Ausable Club, with Robert DeForest as president.[7]

Although the Adirondack Mountain Reserve and the Ausable Club were dedicated to protecting the forest and wildlife, within a short period of time it became clear that the towns of St. Huberts and Keene Valley were to face unforeseen problems resulting from the AMR's land purchase. The AMR and the Ausable Club signaled the end of an era. The reserve would protect the forest from the encroachment of the logging and mining industries and, from today's perspective, protecting the land would appear to have been a good thing, but in 1887 the local town inhabitants were often unhappily displaced. The farms and shanties that were thought quaint by visiting artists were an eyesore to wealthy Ausable Club members, the elite of Manhattan and Philadelphia. They set about buying and razing houses they found not to their liking. Probably the hardest pill to swallow for old-time residents, however, was the prohibition of hunting and fishing on the now-private reserve property—land they had roamed freely for generations. The town folk, particularly the guides, were not happy with this arrangement. The AMR also decided that the guides should demolish their long-established shanties around the Ausable lakes where up until then they had entertained their hunting and fishing clientele. To make amends, the reserve paid a sum of $50.00 per cabin They also employed most of the local guides, and hired one per year as overseer and gamekeeper.[8] There was also some genuine interest in improving education for the children of the town, and to that end a library (still in operation) was built in the village of Keene Valley.

During World War II, Secretary of War Henry Stimson and Assistant Secretary of War John McCloy, both club members, stayed at the Ausable Club for brief respite (apparently they didn't have to adhere to gas ration-

Views of the Great Range from Beaver Meadow. Photograph 2001.

ing policies), and they were there when the atomic bomb was dropped on Hiroshima. Stimson rushed back to D.C. when he realized that Truman planned to drop a second bomb on Kyoto, the cultural capital of Japan. Stimson intervened, and Truman changed the second target from Kyoto to Nagasaki. The death toll was just as horrific, but a significant portion of Japanese culture was spared. After the long war had ended on VJ Day, Stimson and McCloy returned to the Ausable Club, where Stimson was given a standing ovation as he entered the dining room. In response he said nonchalantly, "Let's have dinner," and sat down.[9]

The AMR and the Ausable Club were just one of a number of private organizations that owned land in the Adirondacks. According to William Chapman White, by 1892 one-quarter of the Great Forest was held in private reserve by clubs, associations, or individuals.[10] The most intense period of reserve development occurred between 1895 and 1910. The "blue line" was drawn in 1892, the Adirondack State Park was created in 1895, and the "forever wild" clause was added to the state constitution in 1896.

By 1910 the AMR had acquired 40,000 acres of land. These holdings included the upper watershed of the East Branch of the Ausable, the Ausable lakes, and a number of the highest peaks including Mount Marcy, the state's highest.[11] Since selling their high peaks holdings to the state in 1978, the AMR retains only a thin strip of land leading to and surrounding the Ausable Lakes.[12]

ADIRONDACK

Part IV: Great Camps

Whether through heritage or happenstance, the central Adirondacks were destined to become a mecca for extravagantly wealthy nineteenth-century families. They built large showy vacation compounds in the wilderness, and in so doing developed permanent year-round communities of workers who maintained and kept ready their "Great Camps." There were carpenters, cooks, blacksmiths, boat builders, livery drivers, gardeners, and housekeepers on hand should the masters decide to visit. Within a short time there followed stores, services, and schools to support the workers' communities built for the camps' upkeep. Although it would be an exaggeration to say that the relationship between the wealthy owners and their extensive staffs was a feudal model, it was certainly symbiotic.

Two interesting questions arise: why the Adirondacks, and why the distinctive Great Camp style of architecture? In a word, the answer is "Durant." But the full answer would be, "Durant, railroads, European heritage, roots in the northeastern states, and personal wealth." At least, all of these factors were primary to the origins of Sagamore, Santanoni, and most of the other Adirondack Great Camps. The following chapters visit two of these camps that are illustrative of the Great Camp phenomenon.

Santanoni: Walk a five-mile-long carriage road to one of the Adirondacks' most magnificent Great Camps, passing by the Santanoni farm and its buildings along the way.

The Sagamore: Visit one of the Adirondacks' surviving Great Camps whose interior is open to the public, hike along the Powerhouse Trail past ruins to a cascade by South Bay, and walk around Sagamore Lake for views of the lake and The Sagamore.

16 SANTANONI

Location: North of Newcomb (Essex County)
DeLorme NYS Atlas & Gazetteer: p. 95, D7

Fee: None

Hours: Open year-round

Accessibility: 5.0 miles (one-way). Trail is the former carriage road leading to the Santanoni estate on Newcomb Lake. The round-trip of 10.0 miles is not wheelchair-accessible. Arrangements can be made for horse-drawn wagons during summer months, however, by contacting Ken Helms at (518) 582-4191.

Degree of Difficulty: Moderate to difficult, because of length of hike and gradual, 200-foot change in elevation. The roadway, which is closed to motorized vehicles, can be walked, biked, skied, or snowshoed.

Description: This scenic five-mile-long trail on an old carriage road wends its way past former farm buildings and staff quarters, over quaint stone bridges, eventually leading to the remaining structures of what was once the Great Camp Santanoni on the shores of Newcomb Lake. It is a tantalizing destination, although the interiors of the beautiful rustic buildings are not open to the public for touring or shelter.

Highlights:
- Great Camp Santanoni
- Historic buildings (closed to the public) that were part of the Great Camp Santanoni, including the main camp complex, lakeside studio, boathouse, farm buildings, and stone creamery and shed
- Newcomb Lake

Directions: From Long Lake (junction of Rtes. 28N & 30), go east on Rt. 28N for 14 miles to Newcomb. When you see a sign for the Santanoni Preserve, turn left and then immediately left again, this time onto Newcomb Lake Road, and drive north for 0.3 mile until you reach the parking area for the preserve, which is on your right. (Note: the turnoff from Rt. 28N is approximately 1.0 mile east of the Visitor Interpretive Center in Newcomb). In the process of

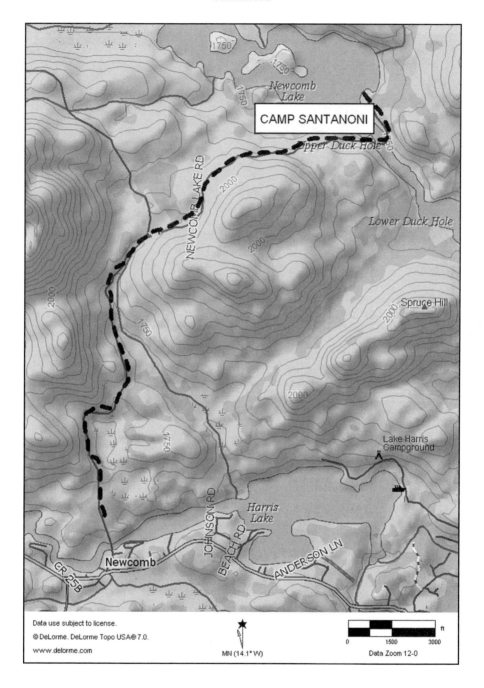

reaching the parking area, you will cross over a connecting stream between Rich Lake and Harris Lake

If approaching from the Adirondack Northway (I-87), take Exit 23. Drive through Warrensburg on Rt. 9, then take a left onto Rt. 28 north-

The farm at Santanoni is reached after a trek of 1.0 mile. Five buildings have survived from earlier days. Photograph 2006.

west of Warrensburg and follow Rt. 28 northwest for roughly 16.5 miles to North Creek. From North Creek, continue north on Rt. 28N for 27 miles. In Newcomb turn right at the sign for the Santanoni Preserve.

The Hike

Although the 5.0-mile-long trail (an unimproved dirt road) can be easily hiked, snowshoed, or cross-country skied, it is a passable road, so you may prefer to bike it or take the horse-drawn wagon. The hike is 10.0 miles round-trip.

Sign in at the trail registry. The road to Santanoni goes gradually uphill for the first three miles and then steadily downhill for the last two. At the beginning of the hike, you will pass by a sign that reads: "Farm, 1.0 mile; Newcomb Lake 5.0; and Moose Pond 7.0." The first two destinations are the focus of this trek.

At 1.0 mile into the hike, you will emerge from the woods into an open area, where the working farm for Santanoni once flourished. The area to the left is occupied by four main buildings—the red-colored home that housed the hired help, the stone creamery that stood across the road from the dairy barn, the gardener's cottage, and the herdsman's cottage (which is recessed from the road). The fifth, and northernmost stone structure—considerably smaller than the others—is the smokehouse.

To the right are the ruins of a large barn that burned down in 2003, victimized, it is believed, by an arsonist or a careless smoker. A historic marker states that the "farm once comprised more than a dozen buildings, about 200 acres of cleared land and provided dairy products, meats, vegetables, and fruits for the Pruyn Family and their guests." You can still see the stalls and stanchions where the cattle were kept.

At 2.0 miles you will come to Honeymoon Bridge, a distinctive stone bridge that crosses over a tributary to Harris Lake. Several hundred feet northeast of the bridge and off in the woods is the site where a sugar house, used for the making of maple syrup, stood many years ago. Up until fairly recent times, hunters could still readily locate the shack by its small foundation and scattering of old decaying buckets. It is no longer easy to find, however.

At 2.4 miles is a junction where a road to the left leads to Moose Pond in over 4.5 miles. A boathouse once stood on the lake.[1] Newcomb Lake and the great camp Santanoni are still 2.7 miles away. After gradually climbing uphill a short distance farther, you will see a giant boulder next to the road on your left, providing a handy landmark. Shortly after this rock, the road begins to descend for most of the rest of the journey until you reach the lake. Along the way you will pass by a red-blazed trail to your left. That trail leads to Moose Pond and a Loop Trail around Newcomb Lake.

At the bottom of the long hill, you will reach Newcomb Lake and will pass by a grassy picnic area to your left. Cross over a bridge that spans the outlet stream from Upper Duck Hole (a section of Newcomb Lake). Although it looks like you have reached the end of your trip, there is still another 0.3 mile to travel as you go around the southeast end of Newcomb Lake before reaching Santanoni.

The first thing you will notice when you arrive at Santanoni is that preservationists have done a remarkable job in restoring the buildings, which have lain dormant for many years. The structure to your left by the water's edge is

The stone creamery. Photograph 2006.

newly constructed and replicates the boathouse that once stood there. Straight ahead are the principal buildings of Santanoni—two sleeping quarters, a main meeting center, and the kitchen—all connected by roofed walkways. Farther to the right, initially out of sight (as intended), are the quarters of the hired help.

Of particular interest is the pump house, down near the edge of the lake behind the kitchen area. You can peer inside the pump house and see the old machinery. The Pruyns chose not to extract their drinking water from Newcomb Lake. Rather, a cistern on the opposite side of the lake collected water from Delia Spring,[2] and the spring water was then piped across the bottom of the lake to the pump house. Why the Pruyns avoided drinking from the lake has been the cause of some speculation. Ken Helms, who has been guiding tourists to Santanoni on a horse-drawn wagon for over twenty years, states that his horses refuse to drink water from a bucket when drawn from the lake. Perhaps the horses and the Pruyns know something we don't. There are minor structures off in the woods, fairly close to the main, interconnected buildings. There is truly much to see and many areas to explore.

The interiors of the main buildings are empty and devoid of furnishings. Still, take a look in through the windows and enjoy the craftsmanship that is plainly evident everywhere in the rooms' interiors.

History: The Adirondack Great Camps were a phenomenon of the latter part of the nineteenth century and crested with the "Gilded Age"—so-termed because of the immense wealth accumulated in the post-Civil War period and the conspicuous consumption that wealth generated. Industrialists and entrepreneurial tycoons were drawn to the beauty of the Adirondacks and established grand estates of rustic buildings. These "camps" were rustic in design, yet lavish and went way beyond the concept of a family compound. Often they were like small, self-sufficient villages with residences, cabins, dining buildings, blacksmith shops, carpentry sheds, stables, barns, boathouses, greenhouses, schools, and staff quarters. They represented a unique way of life, motivated by the challenge of relating man to the wilderness while maintaining a comfortable self-sufficiency in the face of a sometimes hostile environment.[3]

Santanoni is often considered to be the most magnificent of the remaining nineteenth-century Adirondack Great Camps, but unlike Camp Sagamore and White Pine, there is no public access to the interiors of its buildings. The camp lies due south of the Santanoni Mountain Range, a series of peaks that includes Little Santanoni, Panther, Couchsachraga, and Santanoni. Of these, Santanoni is by far the highest, at an elevation of 4,607 feet. It is the thirteenth-highest summit in the High Peaks Region. The name Santanoni is said to derive from the Native American pronunciation of the French "Saint Anthony."[4] The main inlets to Newcomb Lake are the Santanoni River and Sucker Brook. The lake drains into the Newcomb River.

The Santanoni camp complex was designed by the architect Robert Robertson for the Robert C. Pruyn family. The complex incorporated some elements of Japanese style, no doubt influenced by the Pruyn family's experiences in Japan when Robert's father, Robert H. Pruyn, served as ambassador to Japan in 1861 under the Lincoln administration. It was built on 12,500 acres (including Lake Newcomb) in 1892–1893 and constructed from native logs. It is said that over 1,500 trees were used in the log construction.[5] At the camp's completion it contained forty-five or more buildings.

Santanoni was heralded for its fine rustic workmanship, Japanese design features, and its large farm operation. In fact, the farm on the property was the largest family estate farm in the Adirondacks before or since. It served not only the camp compound, but the adjacent community of Newcomb as well. The farm complex included a massive set of barns, four farmhouses and workers' cottages, a stone creamery, workshop, chicken house, kennels, smoke house, root cellar, and other service buildings. There were imported and domestic breeds of cattle, sheep, goats, pigs, and poultry. The farm supplied the camp with its meat and produce, while surplus dairy products were sold in Newcomb or sent to Albany for the Pruyns and their friends. Many Newcomb residents today still own milk bottles with "Santanoni" embossed on them in raised letters.[6]

Robert C. Pruyn was an aide to Governor Dix, President of National Commercial Bank (now Key Bank) and Regent of the University of the State of New York.[7] Pruyn was one of the wealthy industrialists who made at least some of his fortune in the logging and paper industries. Though his business

A ride to Santanoni in a horse-drawn wagon takes you back to the old days and old ways. Photograph 2006.

interests no doubt despoiled some of the virgin forests of the Adirondacks, Santanoni was built with a keen eye for preserving the beauty of the land upon which it was built.

The Pruyn family occupied Santanoni for sixty years, from 1893–1953. They enjoyed the camp and invited many of the rich and famous of the day to stay there, including President Theodore Roosevelt and novelist James Fenimore Cooper. These luminaries would have stayed at the main lodge, which was the showpiece of the camp. The main lodge was actually a connected grouping of six separate buildings, in concept reminiscent of Japanese tea house design. You will be greeted by the sight of these structures on the lake at the end of your 5.0-mile bike ride or walk along the carriage road. When you peer through the dusty windows to the cobwebbed interior of the main building, you will wish you could explore inside. You will see an enormous fireplace, rustic railings, and birch-bark wallpaper.[8] Perhaps some day, if preservationists succeed in lobbying New York State, admission to the interiors will be possible. Still, even the dusty glimpses available today through the windows are a real treat, a genuine window to the past.

In 1953 the Pruyn heirs sold Santanoni estate to the Melvin family, wealthy entrepreneurs from Syracuse, New York.[9] The Melvins enjoyed the camp for over eighteen years, until 1971—when tragedy struck. Their eight-year-old grandchild, Douglas Legg, was lost in the forest and, in spite of a massive search, was never seen again. The family was devastated and could no longer bear to stay at the camp. They hastily sold it to the Adirondack Conservancy Committee of the Nature Conservancy. The Nature Conservancy, in turn, resold the property to New York State for incorporation into the Forest Preserve.

As a part of the "forever wild" State Forest Preserve, Santanoni languished and deteriorated for many years. Meanwhile, historic preservationists continued to make the case for saving the remaining structures of the former Great Camp. Since 1993, the New York State Department of Environmental Conservation, Adirondack Architectural Heritage, and the Town of Newcomb have partnered and begun to preserve some of the major buildings at Camp Santanoni. In 1998 this partnership launched Friends of Santanoni to provide long-term financial aid and volunteer support for the camp.[10]

17 THE SAGAMORE

Location: Sagamore Lake (Hamilton County)
Delorme NYS Atlas & Gazetteer: p. 86, BC3–4

Fee: None for hiking the Powerhouse Trail along the outlet stream from Sagamore Lake to a pretty cascade, or for hiking the perimeter trail around Sagamore Lake; there is a modest fee for touring the grounds and buildings of Great Camp Sagamore.

Hours: Powerhouse Trail—open continuously; Sagamore Lake perimeter trail—open continuously; Great Camp Sagamore—tours are provided daily from Memorial Day through Labor Day at 10:00 AM or 1:30 PM and during the fall at 1:30 PM only. Residential programs, including Grandparents'/Grandchildren's Camp, are conducted May through mid-October.

Accessibility: Powerhouse Trail—1.5 miles (one-way); Sagamore Lake Trail—3.5 miles (round-trip); the grounds of Great Camp Sagamore are generally wheelchair-accessible, with assistance, but the main buildings are not.

Degree of Difficulty: Powerhouse Trail to cascade—moderate; Sagamore Lake Trail—moderate; Great Camp Sagamore tour—easy

Additional Information: Great Camp Sagamore, Sagamore Road, Raquette Lake, New York 13436, (315) 354-5311, www.greatcampsagamore.org

Highlights:
- Remains of gatehouse, millrace, and powerhouse sluiceways along the outlet stream from Sagamore Lake
- Sagamore Lake
- Great Camp Sagamore
- Historic waterfall on outlet creek from Sagamore Lake

Description: These historic hikes explore land bordering the grounds of Great Camp Sagamore, which has been lovingly restored as an educational/recreational facility. By definition an Adirondack Great Camp is a self-sufficient complex (literally, a self-contained village), which Camp Sagamore was during its prime. In the late nineteenth century Camp Sagamore, built by William West Durant and later sold to Alfred Gwynne Vanderbilt, was a magnificent configuration of unique Adirondack structures that epitomized the lifestyle of wealthy individuals during the Gilded Age. It also reflected the humbler background of ordinary individuals who worked to build and maintain these lavish structures. It was, after all, the carpenters, blacksmiths, cooks, gardeners, liverymen, and other house staff that helped actualize the vision of the primary architect, Durant. Today, thanks to the preservation efforts of the Sagamore Institute of the Adirondacks, you can see and even visit the grand structures where Durant and Vanderbilt lived, as well as the outbuildings where craftsmen plied their trades.

Directions: From Blue Mountain Lake (junction of Rtes. 30 South & 28), drive southwest on Rt. 28 for 13.3 miles. Turn left onto Sagamore Road (opposite the right-hand turn to Raquette Lake).

If you are approaching from the center of Inlet, drive northeast on Rt. 28 for about 11 miles and turn right onto Sagamore Road (opposite the road to Raquette Lake).

To Powerhouse Trail: Follow Sagamore Road southeast for 3.0 miles. As soon as you cross over the outlet stream from Sagamore Lake, park in a small area to your left, just past the bridge. The blue-blazed Powerhouse Trail begins there.

There is also a drier, but less interesting, trail leading to the cascades at the terminus of the outlet stream. This trail begins just before the bridge is crossed and generally parallels the Powerhouse Trail, running nearby along the opposite side of the stream. Look for the trailhead next to large boulders on your left.

To Lake Trail around Sagamore Lake: From Rt. 28, proceed southeast on Sagamore Road and bear left when you come to a junction at 3.5 miles, following the way taken by registered guests of Great Camp Sagamore. After another 0.2 mile, stop before crossing a gated bridge spanning the outlet stream from Sagamore Lake and park off to the side of the road. Unless you are a registered guest of Great Camp Sagamore, you are not allowed to proceed any farther. The red-blazed Lake Trail begins from where you parked, at the north end of the bridge.

To Visitor's Center: From Rt. 28, follow Sagamore Road southeast for 3.5 miles. Stay to the right where the road divides, and you will reach the parking area opposite the Visitor's Center at 3.7 miles. This is the entry point for touring the grounds and buildings of Great Camp Sagamore.

The Hikes

There are two hikes: the Powerhouse Trail, following the outlet stream to South Bay on Raquette Lake, and the Lake Trail, which follows nearly around the perimeter of Sagamore Lake.

Hike #1, The Powerhouse Trail

The blue-blazed Powerhouse Trail parallels the outlet stream from Sagamore Road to South Bay. This is definitely a trek requiring hiking boots, preferably waterproof ones, for there are numerous wet areas year-round that must be negotiated. None are impassable, however.

Within several hundred feet after starting the hike, you will walk through an open field. Look toward the far right corner and you will see a makeshift cross that marks one of the spots where authorities dug up the earth in an attempt to locate the body of Sarah Anne Wood.[1] Sarah Anne Wood was twelve years old when she was abducted in 1993 while riding her bicycle home from a summer Bible school in Litchfield, New York. In 1996, Lewis S. Lent Jr. was charged with her abduction and murder. Although he told authorities that he had buried her body in the general area by the trail, he later recanted his story. Sarah Anne's body was never recovered.

From there, the trail continues straight ahead, paralleling the stream that is frequently visible. As you near 0.5 mile, the sound of rapids announces that you are approaching either a cascade or a dam. As it happens, in this case it's both. A little side path to your left leads you to a breached, cement dam. The part of the dam extending from the east bank is still fairly intact, although undermined by the stream; the section extending from the west bank is essentially gone, with parts of it having been washed into the stream. Here, the creek tumbles through a pretty, natural flume whose side walls almost look artificial at first glance. A sluiceway coming down from what was once an impoundment of water above the dam blocks you from crossing over to the dam.

Return to the trail. In twenty-five feet you will come to a red brick building on your left that stands next to the trail. The sluiceway runs directly beneath this building and then emerges on the other side of the structure to continue downhill, paralleling the stream for another 0.3 mile. The red brick building is roughly eight feet square and served as a gatehouse, where machinery would raise or lower a metal gate to allow water to either pass through or remain dammed at the pond. The front door to the building is gone, allowing you to peer into the interior. Don't step in for a closer look, however, for there are no floorboards and it is a drop of five or six feet to the bed of the channel below. Walk around to the left of the building and you can then proceed upstream between the sluiceway and stream for thirty feet to the east side of the breached dam.

The sluiceway (which technically becomes a millrace once it leaves the gatehouse) is lined with blocks. Parts of the sluiceway are filled in with debris—fallen tree limbs, bushes, and other materials; in some sections, the side walls themselves have caved in. At the underground entrance to the gatehouse, take note of the metal strainer that served to prevent debris from clogging up the millrace or doing damage farther downstream at the powerhouse, which is still another 0.3 mile downstream and set lower in elevation than the gatehouse so that water would rush down the millrace at increasing velocity to power the turbines.

Return to the main path. As you continue hiking north you will notice that you are paralleling not only the stream, but the millrace as well, for it continues

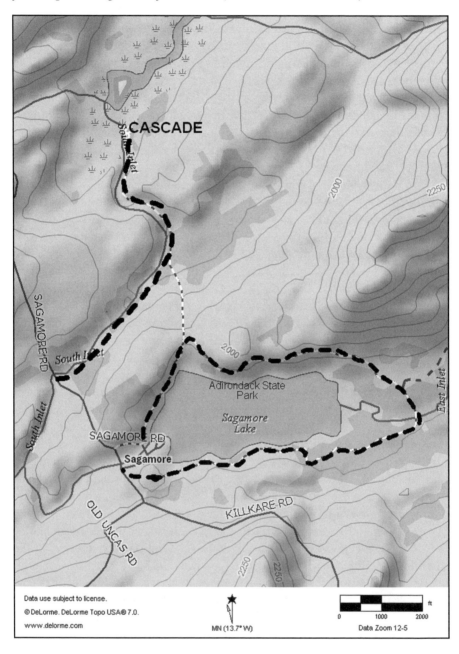

downstream for the entire distance to the powerhouse. After you have been walking for a few moments, the path momentarily veers left from the main trail to bypass a particularly boggy section. This slight detour leads you right next to the millrace, where you can observe barrel-like staves in the sluiceway that at one time encased a wooden penstock (pipe). The staves are prominent along the full length of the millrace, but most noticeable at this point.

About 0.3 mile from the gatehouse, you will come to a large, red-brick building down a steep embankment on your left. Look closely and follow a path to your left that leads down to the building. This second building, the powerhouse, is a much larger structure than the first one. It is roughly twelve feet high, thirty feet wide, and thirty feet long. It is a very imposing ruin and, most impressively, the exterior is still intact, despite the fact that slender, fifteen-foot trees are growing out of the roof! A side door and front windows allow you to peer into the interior, which houses large machinery including two old turbines that were state-of-the-art at their time. Do not attempt to go inside. The floor of the building consists of a metal plate. Its structural integrity is unknown, but has probably weakened significantly over the years through corrosion on its underside. Looking in, you will see walls of yellow brick and a ceiling fashioned out of cement. You can readily discern where the water from the millrace entered the building and where it exited via a sluiceway from the west side, ultimately entering the outlet stream a short distance downstream.

Return to the main trail. In a couple of hundred feet you will come to a fork. The right-hand trail leads toward Great Camp Sagamore (but is infrequently used). Stay on the main trail, continuing straight. After another half mile or so, you will notice a retaining rock wall to your right. You are now roughly 0.4 mile from the cascades. Continue following the trail as it parallels the stream. You will reach a small set of cascades, which block further passage up the outlet stream for paddlers and boaters coming in from Raquette Lake. It was here that the Vanderbilts would debark from their boat after leaving Raquette Lake and then make their way by carriage up to Great Camp Sagamore.

Look across the stream at the top of the cascade and you will see a stone abutment on the opposite bank where a bridge once spanned the fall. It is possible to cross the stream here, but only when the water levels are very low. Even then there is some risk of slipping.

You may also choose to approach these falls by water from Raquette Lake, following in the wake of the Vanderbilts. From the junction of Sagamore Road and Rt. 28, drive west on Rt. 28 for 2.5 miles. At the west end of the bridge, turn into a parking area, from where you can launch your canoe or kayak. Head south into South Bay and proceed southwest for 2.0 miles until you come to the end of navigable waters by the cascades. There are many places to pull over at the waterway's terminus if you wish to get out and hike along the trails.

Hike #2, Sagamore Lake Trail

This is a pleasant, 3.5-mile, loop walk on an old carriage road that circles the lake. Although there are not a great deal of tangible historical ruins to see as you follow the trail around Sagamore Lake, you do get occasional views of the lake through the trees. Periodically along the way you will see "borrow pits," where earth was removed during the construction of the carriage roads to smooth out the road surfaces. The trail is very much like a road at times, and at other times it is a mere path.

Excellent views looking across the outlet stream emanating from Sagamore Lake are available at the very beginning of the hike, and a great view of the lake from a rocky bluff that looms twenty feet above the water on the right, next to the trail, can be had about 0.3 mile farther.

In less than 1.0 mile into the hike, you will see through woods on your left a large open area in the distance. This open area was once a farmed meadow, part of the farm that supplied hay for the horses and some basic cold-weather crops for the workers at Great Camp Sagamore. This can be a fun area to explore if you have the time.

Shortly beyond this area you will come to a small iron cross on your left, commemorating the spot where a coach driver named Johnny Hoy was killed when a tree fell across the road and crushed him. The memorial is easy to miss, so don't be surprised if you hike right by it without taking notice.

At roughly 2.0 miles you will come to the inlet stream to Sagamore Lake and the footbridge crossing. This is a good place to turn around and start the return trip to your car. Otherwise, you can continue around the lake on the Lake Trail, exiting onto the road just above the Sagamore Shop and tour parking area. Remember: you are not allowed to cross the grounds of the Sagamore complex unless you are a guest.

These old generators once powered The Sagamore. Photograph 2008.

Sagamore's most recognizable structure. Photograph 2006.

History: The public hiking trails that abut the private property of the historic Great Camp Sagamore were once part of the Sagamore lands walked by the Durants, Vanderbilts, and their rich and famous guests. The Lake Trail was their carriage road.

Great Camp Sagamore is the epitome of the ornate and lavish nineteenth-century camps established in the wilds of the Adirondacks. It was the largest of the Great Camps and was built by William West Durant.[2] Its conception and construction represent a peculiarly American venture into the wilderness that perhaps could only have come to fruition during the "Gilded Age," a time when there was plenty of new money and vast reaches of virgin forests to buy in the North Country. Couple that with most of the wealth coming directly from transportation industries concentrated in the Northeast, and there you have it—have money, will travel. And so, what in the earlier nineteenth century had been literally "in the middle of nowhere" was by 1897 a fashionable Adirondack address.

It may have been the freshness and remoteness of the territory that led these entrepreneurial pioneers to explore, challenge, and domesticate the craggy Adirondack landscape. They were determined to expand roads, waterways, and railroads into the interior of the valleys and up the sides of the mountains, initially to facilitate mining and logging operations, and later to provide access to hotels and opulent residential hideaways.

The history of Great Camp Sagamore is a particularly American saga in which fortunes were gained and lost, and a vast swath of American wilderness was tamed. The pivotal characters—Thomas Clark Durant, his son William West Durant, and Alfred Gwynne Vanderbilt—were railroad men of intelligence and vision. Their stories are tales of powerful nineteenth-century entrepreneurs who lived off of fortunes made in the industrial cities, but sought to vacation in rustic luxury in the wild Adirondacks.

William Durant first went to the Adirondacks to look after the entrepreneurial interests of his wealthy father, Thomas Durant, who was general manager of the Union Pacific Railroad and who later cut a deal to build a railroad into the Adirondacks from Saratoga Springs to Ogdensburg. Thomas Durant had only gone as far as North Creek, however. Up to that point, he led the family business interests while William lived in Europe pursuing the cultured life of a wealthy gentleman.

William had been born in Brooklyn, New York, in 1850. His mother, Heloise Hannah Timbrel, was from England and was instrumental in moving with him to England at the outbreak of the Civil War. William received his education in England and Germany, traveled extensively in Europe and Africa, and was friendly with European aristocracy.[3]

Fast-forward to the year 1873. The economy was shaky. Thomas Durant's holdings were beginning to crumble. His health was also failing, and he found himself needing assistance. He owned miles of real estate in the Adirondacks, which he had planned to develop. Though William had known little but the life of a European bon vivant, he crossed the Atlantic and joined his father's enterprises. He was twenty-three years old.

One of the largest assets of the Durant family was their immense land holdings in the Adirondacks—700,000 acres of tax-exempt land. In 1876, William made the arduous journey to Raquette Lake by boat, railroad, and coach and took charge of the Durant empire. William's scheme was to interest the extremely wealthy in buying lavish rustic compounds to be built on extensive acreage in the Adirondack forest owned by the Durants. It was a promising idea. The Durants were well-connected to other wealthy families. There were seemingly endless tracts of woods and an abundance of wealthy families. The natural beauty of the Adirondacks was already drawing the emerging middle class as well as the very wealthy, all seeking clean mountain air and grand green scenery, a welcome respite from the crowded, unsanitary cities of the industrial age.

William quickly made his mark. He used native materials such as cedar, birch, and stone to build very elegant homes with a rustic flavor. It is thought that he may have been influenced by the Swiss chalets and lavish hunting lodges he undoubtedly visited during his early years in Europe. He built several noteworthy complexes between 1879 and 1890, including camps Pine Knot and Uncas.

Between 1897 and 1899, William embarked on building Sagamore. It was not his first venture in building a great camp in the wilderness, but it proved not to be a prudent move on his part. He had started his building career as an extremely wealthy man, and he established a fine reputation for himself as the designer of a unique Adirondack style of architecture, but the unstable economy of the time and his overextension of personal finances ultimately toppled his building empire in the Adirondacks.

Powerhouse Ruins

In 1915 the Vanderbilts constructed an elaborate system to divert some of the water from the outlet stream for hydroelectric power generation. They built a dam to impound the stream, thus ensuring the availability of water on a continuous basis. Water from the impoundment was next channeled down to the gatehouse, which controlled releases of the water, and from there the water was then carried 0.3 mile downriver via a millrace to the powerhouse, accelerating and gathering power in the process. Finally, the energized water would race into the powerhouse and drive two turbines, each of which powered a generator. The electricity subsequently produced was then channeled through a control panel and exited the building through a single-pole line up to Great Camp Sagamore.[5] The power plant was overseen by W. C. M. Ryan, an employee of the Vanderbilts, and continued operating until about 1930. The uniqueness of the Sagamore hydroelectric plant is put into perspective when you realize that it wasn't until sixteen years later that electricity was available in the village of Raquette Lake, a mere five miles away.

In 1900, Durant was forced to sell Sagamore to his friend and colleague Alfred Gwynne Vanderbilt for $162,500. And a steal it was—1,526 acres of land, the entire lake, and all of the buildings. Although it was already an extravagant camp, Vanderbilt continued to expand and embellish the Sagamore complex.

The personal stories of the two men, legendary entrepreneurs even in their own time, are fraught with heady successes and the cold touch of an often cruel and whimsical fate. After losing first his fortune, and then his wife to divorce, Durant ultimately ended up managing a hotel in the Adirondacks, serving people who had once worked for him. He also had tried his hand earlier at unsuccessful ventures in the optical business and mushroom farming. By all accounts, however, he was neither bitter nor unhappy with this life. Observers said that he was cordial and seemed content. He once said, "I was handicapped by having been brought up in wealth without being taught the value of money."[4]

Vanderbilt continued to prosper after a scandalous divorce and a happier second marriage, but met a tragic and untimely death in 1915 aboard the luxury ocean liner *Lusitania*, sunk by a German U-boat during World War I.

Margaret Emerson, Vanderbilt's widow, enjoyed and maintained Sagamore for many years, entertaining movie stars, politicos and, of course, her wealthy contemporaries. Songwriter Hoagy Carmichael said that he wrote the song "Stardust" while on the way to Sagamore.

In 1953–1955, Emerson gave the land and property to Syracuse University for use as an educational and recreational facility. The university kept the property until the 1970s, when the upkeep and repairs became too costly and daunting. They then transferred the property to New York State. For a time it seemed that the Sagamore buildings would be demolished by the state under its "forever wild" provisions. Fortunately, however, the fate of the Sagamore buildings came to the attention of a group of savvy individuals who had an interest in Adirondack architecture and historic preservation. Following swift and complex negotiations, the Preservation League of New York State and the National Humanistic Education Center took title to the Sagamore property under the restrictions placed on it by the state. The Education Center was renamed Sagamore Institute.

The new owners managed to save many of the grand structures from the Gilded Age, along with some of the simple outbuildings where the craftsmen and daily staff labored. Thanks to the preservationists' efforts, twenty-seven of the original sixty buildings of the combined Durant/Vanderbilt eras now remain, including the centerpiece main lodge, designed and built by William West Durant.

Today, Sagamore Institute of the Adirondacks, a not-for-profit educational organization, cares for and maintains the remaining buildings and grounds through sponsoring educational and recreational programs, as well as through paid house tours and fundraising activities. It is well worth the time to take a tour of the Great Camp Sagamore at the nominal fee charged. There is also a gift shop, the proceeds of which further benefit Camp Sagamore. Information about events, activities and programs can be found on the Great Camp Sagamore Web site: www.sagamore.org.

Gilded Age
A period of American history from 1878–1889 defined by extravagant displays of wealth by the super-rich. The term "Gilded Age" was coined by Mark Twain and Charles Dudley Warner in their book, The Gilded Age: A Tale of Today *(1873).*

A D I R O N D A C K

Trails *with* Tales

Part V: Route 30 Region

R oute 30 runs through the central Adirondacks, skirting lakes and cloud-splitting mountains, and winding through valleys of incomparable beauty. It is an area that has been home to tanneries, mines, and lumber operations whose stories are told in the following five chapters.

Paul Smiths: Paul Smith was many things to many people—Adirondack guide, land developer, hotel proprietor, raconteur, and hydroelectric entrepreneur. Underlying it all was an abiding love of the Adirondacks and a desire to share it with others.

Hooper Garnet Mine: The Adirondacks were not only harvested for timber, but mined for ore as well. The Hooper Garnet Mine near Garnet Hill Lodge is a perfect example of how open pit mining took place in the Adirondacks. (For more on mining operations in the Adirondacks, see chapters "Adirondac & Indian Pass" and "Ironville & Penfield Homestead.")

Chimney Mountain: Hike to the summit of Chimney Mountain, where powerful geological forces have split the top in half as though by a giant cleaver. There are talus and tectonic caves to explore, enormous boulders to scramble around, a deep chasm to peer into or walk through and, most of all, the chimney rock formation that gave the mountain its name.

Kunjamuk Cave: Is this a natural cave or was it made by man? You be the judge. Kunjamuk Cave provides a marvelous destination for hikers, bikers, cross-country skiers, and paddlers, and is located near Speculator, a small, historic town in the Adirondacks.

Griffin, Griffin Falls, & Auger Falls: Explore quiet, beautiful woods that were once the scene of a bustling nineteenth-century town of 300 residents and visit two waterfalls, one at each end of a mile-long hike.

18 PAUL SMITHS

Location: Paul Smiths (Franklin County)
Delorme NYS Atlas & Gazetteer: p. 95, A6–7

Fee: None; but donations can be made at the Adirondack Park Agency Visitor Interpretive Center to benefit the Adirondack Park Institute, Our Friends Group, and are used to help support programming.

Hours: Trails—open daily from dawn to dusk; Adirondack Park Agency Visitor Interpretive Center—open daily from 9 AM to 5 AM, except on Thanksgiving & Christmas.

Accessibility: 1.5-mile hike (round-trip)

Degree of Difficulty: Easy

Restrictions: During spring, summer, and fall, dogs must be leashed; during winter, dogs are not allowed on the property. No natural objects can be removed. Wildlife must be left undisturbed.

Additional information: Paul Smiths, PO Box 3000, 8023 State Route 30, Paul Smiths, NY 12970. (518) 327-3000. www.adkvic.org.

Highlights:
- Shingle Mill Falls
- Site of the Lester Homestead
- Heron Marsh, an artificially created pond
- Visitor Interpretive Center

Description: The walk beginning at Adirondack Park Agency Visitor Interpretive Center takes you by some interesting sites dating back to the heydays of the famous Paul Smith's Hotel, established in the mid-nineteenth century.

Directions: From Saranac Lake (junction of Rtes. 86 West & 3 East), go northwest on Rt. 86 for 12 miles. At the junction with Rt. 30, turn right onto Rt. 30 and drive north for 0.9 mile. Turn left at the sign for the Adirondack Park Agency Visitor Interpretive Center at Paul Smiths and drive west for less than 0.3 mile to the parking area for the center.

The Hike

The walk begins from the rear of the Adirondack Park Agency Visitor Interpretive Center, overlooking Heron Marsh approximately fifty feet below (on your right). The walk follows the green-blazed Heron Marsh Trail as it

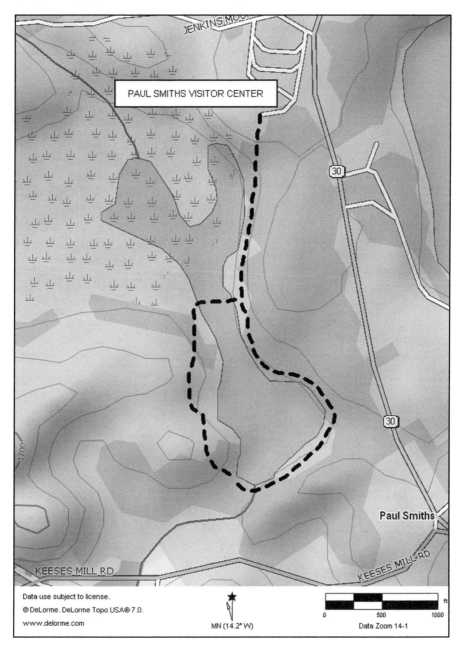

From a fifteen-foot-high observation platform, Barbara Delaney scans the quiet waters of Heron Marsh. Photograph 2007.

leads steadily downhill. In 0.1 mile you will reach the level of the marsh. As you continue you will pass by two side trails on your right, consisting of boardwalks that lead to views of the marsh and then back to the main trail again. You will also pass by an elevated platform at the edge of the marsh, from where higher views of the pond, aided by a telescope, can be obtained. In addition you will pass by two Adirondack lean-tos on your left.

In less than 0.4 mile the trail comes to the junction with the blue-blazed Shingle Mill Falls Trail, where a trailside plaque displays a picture of how the mill next to Shingle Mill Falls once looked. Continue straight ahead (going south), with the pond to your right. You will now be following a 0.7-mile-long loop trail clockwise that circumnavigates this portion of the pond, returning you to the junction with the Heron Marsh trail via a 300-foot-long pontoon bridge.

In less than 0.4 mile you will come to the dammed outlet to Heron Marsh, where a pretty, natural waterfall can be observed. Just before you cross over the bridge, look to your left and you will see a small pit where part of the hill was excavated. Standing on the bridge, you can obtain great views of the pond as well as the ten-foot-high cascade just below the bridge. The shingle mill that once operated on the west bank next to the cascade is long gone, literally vanishing without a trace. Try though you may, you will be hard-pressed to find any evidence that a fairly sizable building once stood there. In the summer of 1988, the present bridge was constructed and the dam rebuilt in anticipation of the May 24, 1989, opening of the Adirondack Park Agency Visitor Interpretive Center.

Continue along the Shingle Mill Falls Trail, now heading northwest. In less than 0.1 mile you will come to an historic plaque on your left that tells you about the Lester Homestead (consisting of two adjacent houses) that was located in the woods directly in front of you until the twentieth century. A fading picture on the plaque shows how the homestead once looked. The scene is convincing proof of just how fast the creations of humans can vanish under steady weathering and the relentless advancement of forest growth. By walking into the woods for less than fifty feet, you will see a 10-by-20-foot rectangular pit, which presumably served as an earthen basement. No stone or cement retaining walls are visible.

Continue north along the trail and you will pass by two huge boulders to your left. Then, in less than 0.2 mile, you will reach the 300-foot-long pontoon bridge that takes you back to the Heron Marsh Trail and then back up to the Adirondack Park Agency Visitor Interpretive Center.

Take note that, in addition to the Heron Marsh and Shingle Mill Falls trails, there are a total of 14 miles of hiking trails offered during the summer and 9.5 miles of snowshoe/ski trails available in the winter.

History: The most interesting historical feature of this hike is that it is on land once owned by Paul Smith, a fascinating nineteenth-century woodsman and hotelier who developed much of the area that today is called Paul Smiths.

Paul Smith, born Apollos Smith in 1825, was destined to become a legend in his own time. Originally a Vermonter, Smith as a young man began his career as an Erie Canal boatman. Later, Smith was drawn across Lake Champlain from Vermont to its western shores and the bountiful hunting in the Adirondacks. He soon developed such prowess as a hunter that he was a much-sought-after hunting guide. By all accounts he was also an accomplished raconteur and storyteller as well. Soon he had a loyal following that was happy to stay in the wilderness with him at Hunter's Home, the rustic camp he first

The waterfall at the outlet to Heron Marsh. Photograph 2007.

built in 1852 on Loon Lake. It was said that this men's-only place consisted of a first floor with a kitchen and a living room and a second-floor bunk room. For 4¢ a drink the men could help themselves to whiskey in a barrel, using a dipper that hung on the side. It was a wildly successful venture.[1]

In fact, it was so successful that his all-male clientele asked that Smith consider building another place to which they might bring along their womenfolk. So, in 1858, with some financing from his patrons, Smith bought the property, and erected a hotel in 1859 on Lower Saint Regis Lake. It was initially called the St. Regis Lake House, but everyone called it Paul Smith's. Smith started with a modest building of seventeen rooms. Over the next three decades the hotel grew to 500 rooms that sprawled along the lakeshore. It became the most renowned hotel in the Adirondacks. It is said that Mrs. Smith's cooking was famous, Paul Smith's stories were famous, and many of the regular patrons were famous.[2]

Apparently Smith never ran out of good stories, some of which have been passed down through the years. One that he loved to recount was about two Englishmen who arrived at the hotel wearing spats and sporting monocles. Naturally, in the rough and rustic Adirondacks they were irresistible targets for fun. So Paul and some guides told them that the best way to catch trout was to go out in the late evening and sprinkle snuff on the water. When the snuff sank down to the fish and got in their nostrils, they would give a big *ker-choo!* and you could note where they were by all the bubbles coming to the

The college at Paul Smith's now occupies the site where the hotel, shown above, once stood. Postcard ca. 1900.

surface. Supposedly, the Englishmen went to the general store and bought a large quantity of snuff to give it a try. This, of course, created no end of amusement for the guides and the savvier hotel guests. In telling these stories Smith would spin them out to become quite long yarns.[3]

Along with Smith's dynamic personality and skills as a storyteller, guests were treated to excellent cuisine prepared first by, and then under the tutelage of, Lydia Smith, Paul's wife. During the heyday of Paul Smith's resort, the meals were elegant and sumptuous. One hotel menu of the period lists the following: raw oysters, clear consommé, boiled salmon with hollandaise, roast turkey with cranberry jelly, potatoes prepared in various ways, spiced plums, Charlotte Rousse, assorted cakes and pies, fruits, nuts and so on.[4] The famed meals were said to be comparable to those offered in the finest New York City restaurants. Long gone were the days when a simple stew and a keg of spirits would do.

The famous clientele that flocked to the hotel included P. T. Barnum, Theodore Roosevelt, and Grover Cleveland. Roosevelt stayed at the hotel as a teenager in 1874, 1875, and 1877, and made numerous birding observations. Later, those observations were incorporated into a book that he cowrote with H. D. Minot entitled *Birds of the Adirondacks in Franklin County, N.Y.*[7]

Stoddard, in his book *Adirondacks: Illustrated*, wrote: "Paul Smith's is a surprise to everybody; an astonishing mixture of fish, fashion, pianos, and puppies; Brussels carpeting and cowhide boots; out of the way of all travel save that which is its own ... and a table that is seldom equaled in the best of city hotels, set right down in the midst of a howling wilderness."[5] Truly, those were the days.

Smith had a strong hand in developing the North Country. He was always ready to take advantage of the newest technology. In 1874 a telegraph line was brought to Paul Smith's. That same year Dr. Edward Livingston Trudeau spent the winter with the Smith family for health reasons and told of learning Morse code so that he could carry on conversations and get news from operators in Plattsburgh.[6]

In 1878, Smith brought electric power to the hotel and the surrounding communities by harnessing the power of Franklin Falls into a 150-kilowatt hydroelectric plant. By 1906, in recognition of the need for better transportation for his New York City guests, he built a seven-mile railroad extension that connected Paul Smith's to the Lake Clear station. Initially the train used steam power, but in 1908 it converted to electric power. General Electric Company even designed a special train that was one of a kind in the entire history of railroading. Guests could leave New York in the morning and have dinner at Paul Smith's in the evening, a timetable that can barely be matched today. Many wealthy guests even came to the hotel in their own railway cars. The railroad was eventually abandoned in 1932 when the tide of fortune had turned against the luxury resort business in the Adirondacks.[8]

Paul Smith's operated from 1859–1930, a good long run for a hotel by any standards. After Paul's death in 1912, his son, Phelps Smith, continued the business. During its later years, however, the hotel operated on a more modest scale because of a dwindling clientele and a fire in 1930 that destroyed the main building. The cottages continued to be rented through 1937, until Phelps's death.

Paul Smith and his family left a strong legacy and lasting impression on the North Country. Many of the families who now reside in the area descended from families who at one time had links to Paul Smith's hotel. Some were guides or members of the hotel staff, others worked in building and maintaining the electric company, the railroads, mills or supply services. Today the name Paul Smiths lives on, not as a swanky resort, but as a well-respected community college established according to Phelps Smith's will, which stipulated that a college in his father's name be built on the grounds where the hotel had once stood. The college opened in 1946 and operated the original Smith family cottage as a small hotel until 1962, when that structure also burned to the ground.[9]

Most of the historical ruins have long since been obliterated. If you keep a sharp eye, however, you can still discern some physical evidence of days gone by. The hike around the pond at the Adirondack Park Agency Visitor Center leads past a waterfall that was dammed to create the water supply system for the hotel. You can also still see cellar holes that were part of a family farm supplying produce to the hotel. And, although it is not on the hike described in this chapter, you can visit Franklin Falls where the power was once harnessed for Paul Smith's Power and Electric.

If you should visit Paul Smith's College today, turn your back to the buildings and face the Lower St. Regis Lake and you will see much the same view as P.T. Barnum and Teddy Roosevelt did more than a century ago.

19 HOOPER GARNET MINE

Location: North River (Warren County)
Delorme NYS Atlas & Gazetteer: p. 88, C1

Fee: None

Hours: Open daily

Accessibility: 0.3-mile ascent to Hooper Mine + 0.1 mile to upper views

Degree of Difficulty: Easy to moderate

Restrictions: As a matter of courtesy, notify the lodge or ski center of your intention to hike up to the Hooper Mine.

Additional information: Garnet Hill Lodge, Cross-Country Ski Center, and Gift Shop, Thirteenth Lake Road, North River, NY 12856. (518) 251-2444. www.garnet-hill.com.

Highlights:
- Open pit mine at Hooper Mine site
- Garnet Hill Lodge

Description: This walk takes you to an abandoned garnet mine now on property that is part of the Siamese Ponds Wilderness Area. The nearby Garnet Hill Lodge caters to hikers, mountain bikers and cross-country skiers, as well as other recreationists. The lodge, as well as some outbuildings, was formerly part of the nineteenth–twentieth-century Hooper Garnet Mine complex. Today you may visit the abandoned pit mine and imagine life and work in an earlier time.

Directions: From the Adirondack Northway (I-87), take Exit 23 for Warrensburg. From near the center of Warrensburg (junction of Rtes. 9 & 418), drive northwest on Rt. 9 for 3.4 miles. Turn left onto Rt. 28 and proceed northwest. When you eventually come to North Creek (junction of Rtes. 28 & 28N), continue northwest on Rt. 9 for 5.2 miles farther. As soon as you cross over Thirteenth Lake Brook, turn left onto 13th Lake Road, where a sign indicates that you are entering the Siamese Pond Wilderness Area. Drive southwest for 4.5 miles, staying on the main road, until you reach a fork in the road. If you go left, it will take you up to the Garnet Hill Lodge in 0.2 mile. Unless you are staying at the lodge, turn right and proceed downhill for 0.2 mile to the Garnet Hill Cross-Country Ski Center. Park next to the ski center.

The Hike

Begin by walking uphill on the road directly across from the front of the ski center. While this at first appears to be a private driveway, you will soon see signs pointing the way to the Hooper Mine. As you start your journey up the road, there is an old cement foundation to your right.

Within 200 feet, veer right from the road and begin following a hiking trail (formerly a dirt road) that leads uphill to the Hooper Mine. The trail initially parallels the road. In 0.1 mile the path veers sharply right, however, and then begins ascending steeply.

In 0.2 mile you will see a small path going off to your right. Make a mental note of it, but for the time being stay on the main trail, which immediately takes you out onto the floor of the open pit mine—a huge, 600-foot-diameter expanse of flat bedrock with piles of rock rubble randomly scattered about. An informal path leads around the perimeter, where you can scurry between or over rock rubble. All around, the walls of the pit rise up nearly vertically to as high as 80–100 feet. You may see a couple of pipes, but little else remains from the days when the pit was mined.

Exit from the floor of the mine where you entered it and begin to descend back down the trail. Immediately take the secondary path that you previously noted to your left. This path leads up to the top of the open pit mine within 0.1 mile. There are several spur paths to the left from this trail that lead to the rim of the pit, from where you can look directly down into its gaping interior and beyond. Off in the distance, slightly southeast, can be seen the grayish-colored walls of the Barton Garnet Mine and, most notably, Gore Mountain, which is dominated by its downhill ski center. Some of these spur trails are hard to see because of blowdown and overgrowth.

You will also note along the trail three metal shacks in various stages of deterioration. One of the structures contains the legend, "Magazines—Explosives." It was in these small shacks that the miners stored materials for blasting.

History: Hooper Garnet Mine on Ruby Mountain was established by Frank Hooper in 1894. By 1908 he had transferred his base of operation to 13th Lake, the site of the abandoned mine near Garnet Hill Lodge.

Garnets are ruby-colored crystals that are popular jewelry stones, but the prime purpose of the garnets mined in the southern Adirondacks was, and still is, for industrial use, primarily in the making of sandpaper. The twelve-sided crystal is commonly found in the Adirondacks and is especially prevalent in the hills near North Creek.

Frank Hooper was a mining engineer, and an innovative one at that. He had devised a way for improving the process of separating the garnet from the ore by taking advantage of the specific gravity of garnet in a special water-

The Hooper Mine is an open pit dug into the side of a hill. Photograph 2008.

swirling device. By today's standards the process might seem crude, but it enabled Hooper to harvest most of the high-quality garnet from the mine.

Before Hooper developed his new garnet-mining process, it was a time-consuming chore to extract garnet from ore. In the 1880s, when garnet production in the Adirondacks began, the only known method was to break out garnets using a small hand pick. At the Barton mines established on Gore Mountain by Henry Barton in 1878, huge rocks containing garnet first had to be split by inserting explosives. Then, workers used their small picks on the smaller rocks created by the blast. You may still visit the site of the former Barton Mine on Gore Mountain. The mine is commercially maintained as a tourist attraction from June until September. Currently there is also an operational Barton Mine located on Ruby Mountain, but it is closed to the public. Today, Barton Mines is the world's largest supplier of industrial garnet.

In 1908, Frank Hooper's North River Garnet Company was a vital new industry and employed over one hundred men. Hooper built roadways into the interior of the Thirteenth Lake/Garnet Hill area and established a town for the mine workers. The town grew to forty-five buildings, including a school, blacksmith shop, and boardinghouse. It is said that Zora Brown, the mine's cook, prepared on a daily basis, six days a week, forty loaves of bread, thirty-five pies, and a washtub of beef for the five meals a day consumed by two shifts of millworkers.

Hooper's and Barton's mines were the primary commercial enterprises in the Johnsburg area well into the twentieth century, but by 1928 the supply of good ore on Garnet Hill had diminished and Hooper's mine closed. He owned promising garnet rights on nearby Ruby Mountain, but decided to leave the mining business and sold the Ruby Mountain property to the Barton Mine Corporation.[1] Hooper later served as a New York State assemblyman.[2]

Hooper built the Garnet Hill Lodge in 1936 soon after his mine closed. He named it Log House. Today, the lodge offers sixteen guestrooms, dining and recreational facilities, and is run by Joe and Mary Fahy.

20 CHIMNEY MOUNTAIN

Location: Southeast of Indian Lake (Hamilton County)
Delorme NYS Atlas & Gazetteer: p. 87, C7

Fee: Modest day fee per car

Hours: Daily

Accessibility: 1.0-mile climb to Chimney Formation (one-way) + additional mileage for exploration; 760-foot ascent

Degree of Difficulty: Difficult

Restrictions: The caves are off-limit from mid-September to mid-May because of bat hibernation. Hikers are advised not to enter these caves at any time unless with a caving group.

Highlights:
- Huge rift near top of mountain
- Unusual chimney formation
- Tectonic caves
- Shelter caves
- Enormous boulders

Description: Near the top of Chimney Mountain (2,721 feet), the peak has been split apart as though cleaved by an enormous hatchet wielded by a giant.[1] A forebodingly deep, immense rift has formed, leaving in its wake huge piles of boulders, tectonic caves, and vast areas that invite exploration.

Directions: From Indian Lake (junction of Rtes. 30 & 28), drive south on Rt. 30 for 0.5 mile and turn left onto Big Brook Road. From Speculator (junction of Rtes. 30 & 8 West), drive north on Rt. 30 for 23.5 miles and turn right onto Big Brook Road.

Proceed southeast on Big Brook Road, crossing over the Lake Abanakee causeway at 1.2 miles. At 3.4 miles, turn right, crossing over a tiny bridge that spans a tributary to Beaver Meadow Brook. When you come to a fork in the road at 4.1 miles from Rt. 30, bear left. At 5.5 miles turn right onto Moulton Road. A sign there indicates that you are heading towards Chimney

Mountain. At 8.1 miles from Rt. 30, you will arrive at the parking area for Chimney Mountain. There are a number of private lodges on the property, so be sure to stay solely on the trail to Chimney Mountain.

Parking fee should be inserted into a locked box at the kiosk.

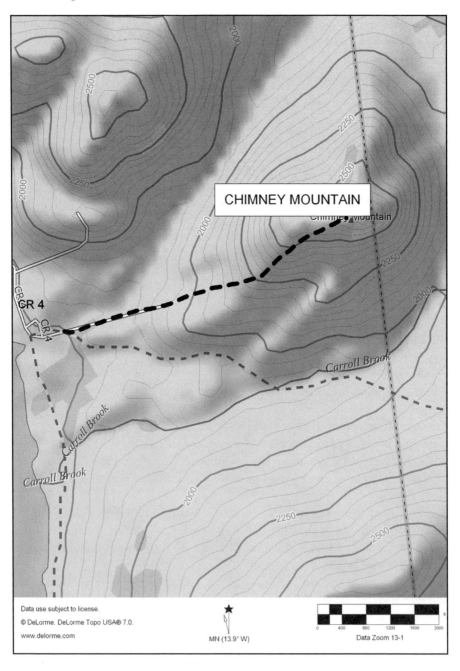

The Hike

From the kiosk, follow the dirt road east for several hundred feet, then veer to your right to the trailhead registry. If you reach the woodshed, then you have gone too far. From the registry, follow the blue-blazed trail leading into the woods. The trail initially parallels a tiny stream on your right. In less than 0.2 mile the trail enters state land.

Blue-Blazed Main Trail

The hike continues steadily uphill. Eventually you will climb up two steep grades. At the crest of the second steep grade, at roughly 0.8 mile, you will come to an unmarked junction where a red-flagged secondary trail goes off to your left. That trail leads to interesting fissure caves and rocky chasms. For now, however, continue climbing uphill following the blue-blazed trail. You will pass by several little paths to your left that lead to small fissure caves and rock shelters.

Within a minute or two, at roughly 1.0 mile, you will come to the false summit of Chimney Mountain where you will encounter the chasm and interesting rock formations. The actual summit is 0.2 mile farther and roughly 200 feet higher, but has none of the interesting features to be found here at the false summit. The blue-blazed trail proceeds directly to a huge series of rock buttresses that rise above the terrain. The farthest block—not immediately visible—is the chimney formation for which Chimney Mountain is named.

The chimney rock formation is what gives the mountain its name. Postcard ca. 1930.

Geological forces have nearly split the top of Chimney Mountain into two. Photograph 1995.

The trail climbs right up to the base of the rock buttresses. You will first encounter a huge declivity between two large rock columns that offers great views into the enormous rift characterizing this part of the mountain. On top of the first rock buttress is a large anvil-shaped rock called Balanced Rock. The space between the two rock columns is partially sheltered by overhanging slabs of rock. Directly opposite these columns is Ship Prow Rock. Birch trees abound, particularly in the rift between the two sides of the chasm.

Continue following the blue-blazed trail for another hundred feet and you will reach the unique chimney formation, the mountain's namesake. View the chimney from its base; do not try to climb to the top. People have been seriously hurt while trying to scale this rock formation. The ascent may look reasonably easy, but the descent can be extremely problematic and should be left to experienced rock climbers with the proper gear. Besides, there are several places on top of the mountain where the views are just as good as, or better than, the view from the chimney, and from those other vantage points you get to see the chimney as well.

Continue along the base of the chimney until you reach a huge overhanging rock slab that forms a shelter cave. At first glance the rock slab seems to be supported by two tiny rocks, but then you notice that the slab extends into the rock formation, giving it added strength. The formation is called The Window, and it provides excellent views into the rift. If you wish to descend into the chasm, this is as good a point as any to do so. Follow a side trail that leads down from here into the chasm.

Chimney Mountain

The unique and distinctive chimney formation that gives Chimney Mountain its name is formed out of Grenville rock and stands thirty-five feet above the eastern rim of the rift. Below, a chasm approximately 250 feet wide and 600 feet long descends to a depth of 200 feet.

As you explore this area of Chimney Mountain, you will discover that there are many crisscrossing paths that allow for leisurely investigation. Many of them are mini-bushwhacks, for often the trail peters out only to start up again in a short distance. Frequently, huge boulders and rocky buttresses have to be side-stepped in order to continue on.

Back near the east rim of the cleft, not far from the Chimney, is a primitive area designated for camping. If you wish to use the camping area, note that you will need to pack in your own water.

Red-Flagged Trail

On the way up the mountain, not far from the section containing the chasm and chimney formation, you will reach a secondary trail to your left that has been flagged with red markers. This will take you along the side of the

mountain approximately 100 feet below the chasm. The trail guides you through enormous blocks of rock and along faults (cracks in the Earth's surface). Along the way you will notice a number of little paths leading upwards. These faint trails will eventually lead up to a rocky spine on top of the west wall of the chasm. Walk north along this spine heading slightly uphill and you will be rewarded with superb views of the chimney formation—located on the opposite side of the chasm—and

Some trails seemingly lead to the ends of the Earth. Photograph 1995.

into the interior of the rift. The paths fade in and out, but they can be easily picked up again by simply descending or ascending.

After viewing the rift from its west wall, return to the red-flagged trail. In less than 0.05 mile from its start, the path seems to end at a small plateau of sandy earth. A vertical cave can be seen here leading underground. It should not be entered, however, unless you are proficient at vertical caving, wear a protective helmet, carry three sources of light, and are accompanied by at least two similarly equipped and experienced cavers. This cave is representative of most of the cave openings on the mountainside.

The plateau seems to be a dead end unless you are ready for a great deal

Large crevices create immense chambers that invite further exploration. Photograph 1996.

of rock scrambling. Backtrack for thirty feet and then follow a faint path that becomes a more discernible trail as it continues. In several hundred feet you will pass by a distinctive, smooth-faced, rust-colored cliff face. Follow along its base, ascending for twenty feet, and then climb back down for another twenty feet, arriving at what feels like a whole different section of the mountain. Here, you will see an enormous cavity that plunges into the earth for fifty to sixty feet.

These directions take you to just a small portion of Chimney Mountain. There is so much to see and do, a seemingly endless number of nooks and crannies and fissures to explore. Having gone, however, to both the east and west rims overlooking the rift, into the chasm, over to the chimney, and having peered into some of the cave and fissure openings, you will have seen a representative sampling of what Chimney Mountain has to offer. But the opportunities for bushwhacking are virtually unlimited and—who knows?—if you explore thoroughly enough, you may even come across something of interest that no one else has seen before.

Geology: The Grenville rocks that form the bedrock at Chimney Mountain are some of the oldest in the world, dating back to around 1.1 billion years ago (the oldest rocks in North America go back as far as 3 billion years). The rift is believed to have formed less than 12,000 years ago, following the end of the Wisconsin glaciation. The major rocks forming the mountain are of Precambrian quartzites and gneisses. Well over one billion years ago, quartz sands, calcium carbonate sands, clays, and volcanic ejecta accumulated at the bottom of a shallow sea. As the bed of sediments collected to a thickness of up to 40,000 feet, the lower layers became compacted under the enormous pressures and were turned into sedimentary rock.

Later, titanic mountain-building processes subjected this sedimentary rock to intense heat and greater pressure, causing the rock to metamorphose into quartzites and gneisses, the rocks that you see at Chimney Mountain today. At the same time, unimaginably powerful forces from deep within the Earth raised the layer of bedrock to as high as the Himalayan plateau, approximately 20,000 feet above sea level. Over eons this lofty mountain range was eventually worn down to stubble, at which time it ended up buried under another shallow sea.

New sedimentary rock, much of it sandstone, began piling up on top of the older bedrock. Three hundred million years ago, new mountain-building processes raised up the land for a second time, eroding the top layer of sandstone and again exposing the quartzites and gneisses (as well as marble, which is found in areas adjacent to Chimney Mountain).

Less than 12,000 years ago, geological forces gradually caused part of Chimney Mountain's top to slide westward, creating a huge rift as the bedrock separated. At the same time, the eastern portion tilted to the north. The canyon formed is reminiscent of the displacement in the earth known as Wolf Hollow that occurred in the Mohawk Valley near Hoffmans (see "Wolf Hollow" chapter). During this slippage, open spaces were created between multiple layers of bedrock, which is how a number of tectonic caves were formed.

A smaller version of the Chimney formation can be seen 400 feet west of the Chimney.

The Caves: There are a number of notable tectonic caves on Chimney Mountain, as well as some lesser-known talus caves (formed where rocks have collapsed on top of each other). These are not solutional caves (which are created by water); they are fractures in the bedrock. Of these tectonic caves, the deepest and most dangerous one is called Eagle Cave,[2] which undoubtedly has been known about since the late 1800s. In *Underground Empire*, Clay Perry gives an account of old-timers lowering a lantern 120 feet into the deep abyss until the light vanished from sight.[3] The full extent of this cave was not known until 1975, when a series of ADK Grotto and Boston Grotto expeditions explored it to a depth of 150 feet and logged in up to 1,800 feet of passageways. To negotiate the main crevasse requires a ninety-foot rappel. The lower chambers of the cave contain a great thickness of ice that lasts well into October and, indeed, perhaps never melts entirely. The cave was named by Roger V. Bartholomew in 1964 after he spotted an eagle's nest above the entrance.[4]

A group of hikers look into a cave. Lacking proper equipment, they wisely decided to go no farther. Photograph 1996.

Since the 1970s, new caves continue to be found, many of them ranging in length from 10 feet up to 400 feet of passage. Robert W. Carroll Jr., one of the Northeast's most recognized and dedicated cavers, spent a considerable amount of time on Chimney Mountain and made a number of discoveries.

In 1983, Roger Bartholomew discovered two more caves—Bajus Cave (named after a youngster who accompanied him and found the main entrance) and Rotunda Cave (named for its dome-like entrance room).[5] Bajus is the second-largest cave on Chimney Mountain, with 600 feet of passages; Rotunda has 300 feet. Bartholomew also visited a number of other caves and gave names to some, such as Bottle Cave (a twenty-foot horizontal crawl).

Other cavers have also been busy at work exploring the rubble of rock near the top, and as of now over forty caves have been discovered.

Anyone desiring to explore the caves should join a caving group and note that the caves are off-limits from mid-September through mid-May while the bat colonies hibernate. Cavers should take extreme care to preserve what remains of the irreplaceable "scale-stone" formations that are contained within several of the caves.

History: The lake near the parking area is called Kings Flow. It was created when a large swamp and several small lakes were dammed. The name can be traced back to the King family, who logged the forests of nearby Humphrey and Puffer mountains. Earlier the lake was known as Lake Humphrey, after the Humphrey family, who lived in a camp at the foot of the Humphrey Mountain and farmed the fields at the north end of the flow from the late 1800s until the early 1900s.[6]

The parking area and buildings were once part of a scout camp.

21 KUNJAMUK CAVE

Location: Speculator (Hamilton County)
Delorme NYS Atlas & Gazetteer: p. 87, D6

Fee: None

Hours: The Speculator Loop Trail is open daily from May 15 until October 12.

Accessibility: 1.3-mile hike (one-way); 2 miles by canoe (one-way)

Degree of Difficulty: Easy to moderate hike; easy bike ride; moderate canoe trip

Restrictions: Stay on the roads (and the trail to Kunjamuk Cave) unless you have a permit from the International Paper Company to use the land for other purposes such as hunting, fishing, or snowshoeing. Follow rules & regulations posted at trailhead kiosk.

Highlights:
- Kunjamuk Cave
- Kunjamuk River
- Beaver pond
- Old logging roads

Description: The Speculator Loop Trail System is a dirt road meant to be used as a bicycle route. It consists of two principal loops. The larger of the two loops is nearly fourteen miles long; the shorter loop, which includes the spur path to Kunjamuk Cave, is seven miles long. The cave can be accessed using part of the shorter loop without having to negotiate its entire length.[1]

The focal point of this adventure is Kunjamuk Cave, a fascinating enigma that has intrigued visitors for generations.

Directions: *To Trailhead*—From Speculator (junction of Rt. 8 West, Rt. 30, and Elm Lake Road), drive east on Elm Lake Road for 1.5 miles. Park in the area near the kiosk. You are at the beginning of the Speculator Loop Trail, which was recently opened as a bike route.

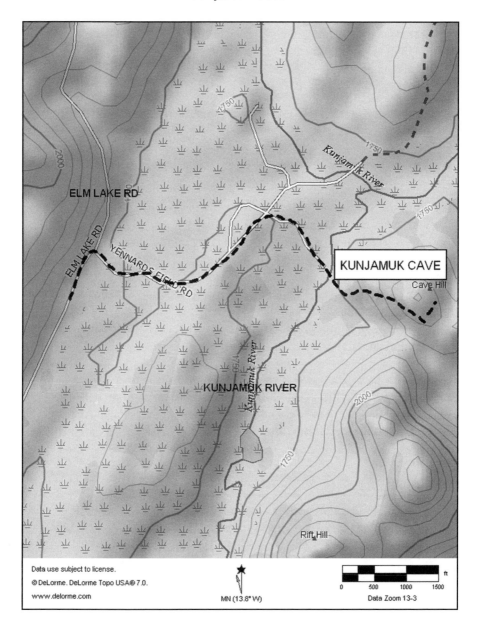

To Canoe Put-In—From Speculator (junction of Rtes. 8 West & 30), drive south on Rt. 30 for 1.8 miles. Pull into a small parking area on your left.

From north of Wells (junction of Rtes. 30 & 8 East) drive northwest on Rt. 30 for 8.0 miles and turn right into the parking area for Kunjamuk Bay.

Two paths lead thirty feet down to the edge of the water at Kunjamuk Bay.

Make your way across the bay, going east until you come to the mouth of the Kunjamuk River. Canoe upstream for nearly 2 miles. The river mostly snakes through the terrain. When you reach a bridge spanning the Kunjamuk River, pull in and secure the canoe. From the top of the bridge, walk east uphill for 0.2 mile along a wide dirt road. Kunjamuk Cave will be to your left.

The Hike

Starting at the kiosk, walk or bike 0.2 miles heading northeast. Turn right where a sign states "1.0 mile to Kunjamuk Cave" (the mileage is actually slightly greater than one mile). In over 0.1 mile you will pass by a pretty pond on your right that is home to a beaver lodge and a colony of beavers. At 0.3 mile continue straight where a secondary road goes off to the right. At 0.7 mile you will reach a junction where turning left leads to Perkins Clearing. Continue straight ahead towards Wells, staying on the main road. At 1.1 mile you will reach a bridge that spans the Kunjamuk River. After crossing the bridge, continue uphill for over 0.2 mile. You will reach a pull-off to your left, just before the road begins climbing steeply again and veers right. Just past this pull-off is a well-worn path on your left that leads in less than 100 feet to the entrance to Kunjamuk Cave. Look for a small roadside sign that states "Historical Kunjamuk Cave".

History: Years ago, a boy's camp named Camp Kun-ja-muk operated on the north shore of Lake Pleasant. In 1880, Silas Call built a hotel called Kun-ja-Muck Inn, which overlooked both Lake Pleasant and Sacandaga Lake. Soon, it became known as Call's Hotel (after the proprietor), and then, when J. Thomas Stearns took over its operation, it was called the Sacandaga Lake Hotel.[2]

The Kunjamuk River passes by Cave Hill as it wends its way up to Elm Lake. Postcard ca. 1930.

Kunjamuk Cave—is
it real or man-made?
You decide.
Photograph 1994.

In 1914, George Tibbitts established Camp-of-the-Woods at Lake Pleasant in Speculator. In 1926, Tibbitts published *The Mystery of Kun-Ja-Muk Cave,* which incorporated local names and places, but slightly disguised. For example, Milt Boyd ended up in the book as Milton Buyce, and so on.[3]

Today, the name Kunjamuk is most closely associated with the Kunjamuk River, a medium-sized stream that rises from South Pond southeast of Humphrey Mountain and flows into Kunjamuk Bay southeast of Speculator. It is a relatively flat river, dropping only twenty-five feet over the course of its fifteen-to-seventeen-mile length as it descends from 1,750 feet to 1,725 feet.[4] It is a very good paddling river for most of its length.[5] There is also a Kunjamuk Mountain (2,969 feet) in Hamilton County near Indian Lake. The Kunjamuk Valley at one time served as the principal stagecoach route to Indian Lake.[6]

Kunjamuk Cave is contained within a tract of land called the Speculator Tree Farm, which in turn is part of a 36,000-acre parcel of land north of the Village of Speculator in the towns of Arietta, Lake Pleasant and Wells in Hamilton County.

Geology: Kunjamuk Cave is located on the shoulder of Cave Hill at the base of a rocky bluff approximately thirty feet high. A tall tree grows nearly above the entrance. The cave is approximately twenty feet long, eight to nine feet

From the inside of Kunjamuk Cave looking out. Photograph 1996.

wide, and nearly fifteen feet high at its highest point. The entrance is over 4.5 feet in height. A smaller, 1.5-feet in diameter, upper opening enters the cave from eight feet above the floor.[7] Some believe that this small opening may have been made by hunters and campers[8] to serve as a vent.

The interior of the cave is shaped like an egg. The walls look chiseled, yet fairly smooth and polished, as though carved out by the action of swirling waters. If you visit the huge post-glacial potholes at Moss Island in Little Falls or the Canajoharie Pothole at Canajoharie (see "Moss Island" and "Canajoharie Gorge" chapters), you will see first-hand the power of moving water as it sculpts potholes and fashions strange formations out of bedrock. Despite appearance, however, the majority opinion is that Kunjamuk Cave is not naturally formed, but rather was excavated by nineteenth-century prospectors looking for gold and silver.[9] Dug Mountain, to the north, once had a little mine in which some traces of silver were found, so a historical precedence of prospecting in this area does exist. Other sources contend that, because the entire Kunjamuk Valley was once a glacial lake, the meltwaters of retreating glaciers may have worn a pothole horizontally into the side of the hill.[10] There are many opinions, but the mystery remains.

22 GRIFFIN, GRIFFIN FALLS & AUGER FALLS

Location: North of Wells (Hamilton County)
DeLorme NYS Atlas & Gazetteer: p. 79, A7

Fee: None

Hours: Open continuously

Accessibility: 0.5 mile of exploration around Griffin and Griffin Falls; 2.4-mile hike round-trip to Auger Falls; both hikes traverse old logging roads and involve short bushwhacks

Degree of Difficulty: Easy to moderate, over mostly level ground

Highlights:
- Waterfalls
- Ruins of tannery buildings and traces of vanished town of Griffin

Description: This hiking area is lovely and remote, with old logging roads traversing a dense forest of birch, maple, pine, and hemlock.

Griffin Falls is formed on the East Branch of the Sacandaga River, a beautiful stream that leaps over granite boulders as it negotiates a series of drops and plunges totaling thirty feet in height. Griffin Falls was named after the town of Griffin, which once existed upstream from the falls. The town of Griffin is gone, but one can walk through the woods and underbrush, paralleling the East Branch of the Sacandaga River, to find hidden traces of this former village.

Auger Falls is over one mile southwest of Griffin. It is a spectacular, seventy-foot-high series of falls formed on the Sacandaga River, tumbling through a very deep, narrow gorge bordered by a hemlock forest.

Directions: From Wells, proceed north on Rt. 30 for approximately 3.0 miles. When you come to the junction of Rtes. 30 & 8, turn right. You will immediately cross over the Sacandaga River. Follow Rt. 8 northeast for 2.5 miles, then turn left onto a dirt road directly across from the trailhead parking for Cod Pond and Willis Lake. Follow the road downhill for over 0.1 mile. When you come to an old iron bridge, cross over it and park in the clearing west of the bridge.

The Hikes

Griffin/Griffin Falls

The hike begins from the west side of the iron bridge that spans the East Branch of the Sacandaga. The bridge was built in 1903 and was repaired in 2004.[1] Griffin Falls is almost directly below the bridge, where the river becomes momentarily compressed, rushes over large granite boulders, and

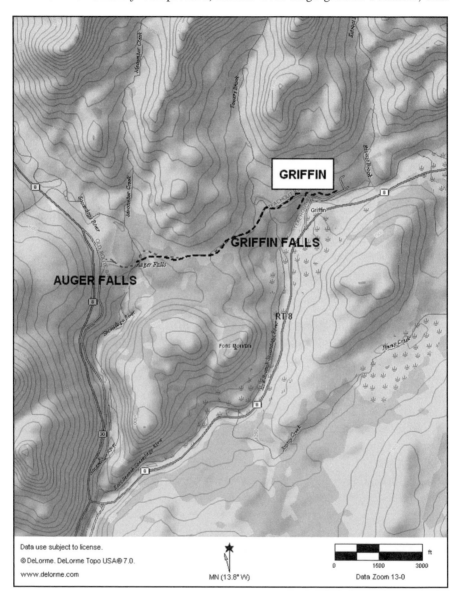

The gorge and falls at Griffin as seen looking upstream towards the iron bridge. Photograph 1998.

drops about thirty feet over inclined ledges. There are several paths that lead down to the base of the falls. One leads from the west end of the bridge, and one leads from the old logging road that heads towards Auger Falls and Austin Flats. On a sunny day there are plenty of sloping rocks on which to lounge or picnic. The river at this juncture is bordered by a profusion of spruce and hemlock trees, creating a pleasant, pine-needle-covered ground.

After pausing to relax by the falls, walk back to the west end of the bridge. From there, follow the old logging road north as it parallels the river upstream. You are now walking along what used to be the main street of Griffin, but you will not see an actual town. All you will observe are the East Branch of the Sacandaga to your right, and woods to your left. In about 0.7 mile the old road disappears entirely, but you can only walk along the first 0.2 mile of the road anyway before it crosses private property.

To "see" the village of Griffin, you need to leave the road and walk directly into the woods, and then zigzag back and forth as you proceed north, paralleling the road.[2] To optimize your chances of encountering old ruins and artifacts, it is best to go in the early spring or late fall when the plant life and foliage is least likely to obscure the view.

Locating the walls of the Griffin Tannery can be tricky, as the surrounding woods and underbrush have all but covered the stone foundations and remaining traces of machinery; however, with some diligence you will find some relics of the past. Begin at the west end of the bridge. Head northwest from there, at about a forty-degree angle from the end of the bridge. The wall that you will come to is 103 feet in length and is the remnant of a "sweating building" that was used to process hides for the Griffin Tannery.

North of the tannery were the company houses for the men who worked in the tannery. Most of these houses didn't have cellars and, therefore, left behind no foundation ruins, but some did have stone stoops that are still evident.

Directly east from the "sweating building" is another stone foundation containing pieces of metal and machinery that you may be able to locate with a little bit of pluck and luck. These remnants are from the tannery building where boilers produced extract from ground bark to tan the hides.

There were many other buildings in Griffin that left no evidence behind—stores, horse barns, a school, a blacksmith's shop, a sawmill, a saloon, boardinghouses, and a lumber company. A map of Griffin's layout can be found in Barbara McMartin's *Hides, Hemlocks and Adirondack History*.[3]

There is one building that still stands in Griffin, however—the former Girard Boarding House, dating back to Griffin's heyday. You won't see it immediately, for it is not located among the ruins of Griffin. It is located along Route 8. Unlike the rest of Griffin's population, which abandoned the town in pursuit of new dreams, the Girard family stayed in the area through successive generations and maintained the residence until the 1970s. This white clapboard building with a metal roof over 0.2 mile up the road on the right from the Cod Pond and Willis Lake parking area is all that remains of Griffin.

The Auger Falls Hike

Auger Falls is the longer of the two hikes, by far. From the west end of the iron bridge, follow the old logging road southwest. Although it initially parallels the East Branch of the Sacandaga River, the road quickly pulls away to the right and wends its way for over a mile through a lovely hardwood forest. You may see trillium, lady slippers, foam flowers, jack-in-the-pulpit, bluets, gay wings, trout lily, and other wildflowers in the spring. In the late summer and fall you will find Queen Anne's lace and day lilies.

In roughly 0.3 mile into the hike, you will cross over a tiny, flat, wooden bridge. When last visited, the creek that once went under the bridge had been diverted by a large beaver dam visible from the road and flowed directly across the road to follow a new channel on the other side.

In roughly 0.4 mile you will come to the end of the drivable road, where a barricade prevents further continuation except by foot. A log cabin sits directly on the left-hand side of the road and should be given a wide berth, since it is privately owned.

After hiking for 1.2 miles, you will hear the roar of the falls off in the distance to your left. A secondary trail, marked off by a warning sign urging caution, bears left from the road and leads directly to the gorge and the falls. Auger Falls is about seventy feet high and is set in an awesome, deep, granite gorge surrounded by tall pine trees. The falls can be partially viewed from the top of the ravine, but caution is strongly advised: the rocks can be very slippery. Unfortunately, try as one may, there is no single, all-encompassing view of the waterfall. The best that one can manage is to see different parts of it at a time.

As an alternate approach, Auger Falls can be reached from a trailhead off Route 30 located 1.7 miles north of the junction of Rtes. 8 East and 30. From this trailhead, the hike in is approximately 0.5 mile and leads you to the top of the west bank of the falls.

Auger Falls can only be partially captured in any one shot. Photograph 1997.

History: When you look at Griffin and Auger Falls today, it is hard to imagine that this area was once populated and busy with tanneries and gristmills, but between 1845 and 1880, Griffin was a town of about 330 people who worked in its mills and attended dances at the Hotel Girard. Today, there are no surviving buildings or even streets to be found—just forest and undergrowth. This is truly a lost village, one that is easy to miss and hard to find. Thanks to bits of recorded history, old photos, and the memoirs of Ouida Girard, a former Griffin resident, some of the town's past can be brought back to life.[4]

Much of what Girard recounted consisted of her or her family's experiences as residents of Griffin. Girard, after completing her education at Cortland Normal School, returned to Griffin to live and teach school. Much later in life she wrote a book titled *Griffin: Ghost Town of the Adirondacks.* Her stories are personal accounts of life in the town. Though Griffin is by no means the only once-thriving village to have vanished in the Adirondacks, it is perhaps the only one to have had its story written in such fascinating, personal detail.

Early on, the East Branch of the Sacandaga River was a natural avenue of travel for Native American hunters as they foraged for fish and game from the Sacandaga to the upper reaches of the Hudson. Many Native American arrowheads have been found in fields along the river.

European colonists Josiah and Philip Wadsworth settled the area along the East Branch near Griffin in 1835. They were pioneers who farmed and hunted the land. Gradually, a few other settlers came to the area to farm and log the virgin pine forests.

With the advent of the logging industry, the settlement underwent a sudden and dramatic expansion. Pine, spruce, and hemlock were cut and sent downriver to the Corinth paper mill. The site on the west side of the river just above the falls was home to a number of sawmills from 1850 through 1880. One of these was operated by Charles Martin, who supplied lumber to the village of Griffin.[5]

It wasn't until the post-Civil War period, however, that the Griffin Tannery was built and the town reached its pinnacle. The tannery, along with the expansion of industry from the nearby community of Wells, created another building boom that caused the population to peak at 330 residents in the 1870s.

The population rapidly expanded in 1872 when the firm of Catlin and Hunt built a mill in the village for extracting tanning liquor from hemlock bark. During this time the settlement oddly, but logically enough, was known as Extract. The name shortly changed to Moon's Mill, however, named for Jim Moon who operated a sawmill in the village.

Also in the same general period of time, a settler named Stephen Griffin purchased 19,000 acres of land along the Sacandaga River Valley and began lumbering operations. He added a supply store, a blacksmith shop, and by 1877 had established two major tanneries and was selling hemlock bark to the other tanners. It didn't take long for the community to change its name again, to Griffin. Now it was truly a tannery town.

Ouida Girard described the main tannery as consisting of several large buildings, six boilers, and 200 vats for soaking the hides. She also tells of a large boardinghouse built by Rice and Emory Co. on the north side of the river, and of twenty-six tannery houses scattered on the hills. There were four stores, a school, and a post office. The stores sold all the needed household items including groceries, cloth, boots, shoes, candy, and a variety of other essentials. Salted mackerel came in big kegs and molasses came in barrels. Oatmeal, beans, cornmeal, and bread were the mainstays of the larder, supplemented by garden produce, fish, and game. Milk was not sold in the stores—people either bought their milk from a dairy or had their own cows.

The village children started school at six years of age and continued there until high school, when they would travel the seven miles to Wells High School by horse and carriage. It took two hours to reach the town of Wells. Travelers had to carry hot bricks in the buggy to keep warm during cold weather.

When the Morgan Lumber Company moved in, it erected a large boardinghouse for its workers. This is the building that still stands today on Rt. 8.

The town stopped growing with the closing of the tannery in 1893. The logging industry had fallen off too, because most of the trees in the surrounding area had been harvested. Around 1895 the Morgan Lumber Company (later to become the International Paper Company) sold the business to H. J. Girard. By 1900 there were many empty tannery houses. Only those who owned land stayed. The rest of the inhabitants were forced to relocate to places where jobs could be found. Many of the buildings were cannibalized and their lumber used for new construction in Wells. Luckily for historians, the Girard family stayed on to farm the land and thus provided future generations with records of the history of Griffin.

ADIRONDACK
Trails *with* Tales

Part VI: Foothills of the Adirondacks: Mohawk Valley Region

T he Mohawk Valley is rich in history dating back to Native Americans, who were hunting and farming in the valley long before the first Europeans set foot on the continent. When Sir William Johnson arrived on the scene in the late 1730s, he had the practicality and foresight to establish good working relationships with the resident Mohawks. In fact, Johnson formed a common-law marriage with Molly Brant, sister of Joseph Brant, a powerful Mohawk chief. This alliance proved fortuitous during the French and Indian War, keeping the valley relatively safe from attempts by the French to drive out the Dutch and British settlers.

Once the French and Indian War ended, a number of settlers began to bristle at the prospect of continued British rule. Soon, war erupted again, this time in the battle cry of American independence, and this time the Mohawk Valley was not spared. William Johnson died in 1774, before the onset of the American Revolution, but his son, John Johnson, remained loyal to the British crown. John Johnson fled to Canada early in the war and returned to the Mohawk Valley with his Mohawk allies to fight against his patriot neighbors. The Mohawk Valley and its river corridor were valuable prizes for either side. As a result, there were bloody battles and skirmishes, and entire communities went up in flames. The eventual victory of the patriots allowed the new nation to take advantage of the power of the river to run industries, as well as to transport goods along a waterway crucial to the country's westward expansion.

The hiking areas described in this section exhibit some awesome geology and are steeped in the stories and historical accounts that have been passed on from these earlier times.

Moss Island: Explore a fourteen-acre island in the Mohawk River with stupendous glacial potholes, atypical flora, a thirty-foot-high rock face, and what at one time was the highest lift-lock in the world.

Tufa Caves & Waterfalls of Van Hornesville: Walk through a nature preserve containing half a dozen waterfalls and a cave made out of an unusual rock, called tufa.

Wolf Hollow: Visit one of the Capital Region's most unusual geological anomalies, where an epic Native American battle took place nearly 400 years ago.

Canajoharie Gorge: Enter a towering gorge to view the renowned Canajoharie Pothole and walk along the top of the upper gorge to an overlook of forty-five-foot-high Canajoharie Falls.

23 MOSS ISLAND

Location: Little Falls (Herkimer County)
DeLorme NYS Atlas & Gazetteer: p. 78, D2

Fee: None

Hours: Daily, dawn to dusk

Accessibility: Requires climbing up metal stairway at Lock 17 to gain entrance to the island. Hike #1—0.5 mile (round-trip) with some scrambling over bedrock to get to the potholes; Hike #2—0.7 mile (one-way).

Degree of Difficulty: Hike #1—Moderate; Hike #2—Easy to moderate

Highlights:
- Glacial potholes
- Sculptured rocks
- Highest lift-lock in the world, at one time
- Views of the Mohawk River and New York State Barge Canal
- Huge cliff face of Precambrian gneiss along south side of island

Description: Moss Island is a fourteen-acre oval-shaped dome of rock 1,500 feet long and 625 feet wide and containing sculptured rocks and magnificent potholes—features that were formed approximately 10,000 years ago during the last glacial retreat.[1] The island is uniquely situated between the Mohawk River and the New York State Barge Canal and is visited by geologists, rock climbers, hikers, and paddlers alike. It is named for its intermittent covering of mosses, which add color and beauty to the large, sculpted boulders on the island. Years ago Moss Island was known as Talequega Park, after the Native American word for "little bushes."

Moss Island is contained in the Little Falls Gorge,[2] which has sloping walls rising to a height of 520 feet to the south and 700 feet to the north. Historically the gorge has been known as the "Gateway to Western New York." In May 1976 the island became a designated National Landmark.

Extending west from Moss Island to Little Falls is a finger-like projection of land bordered by the Mohawk River to the north and the New York State Barge Canal to the south. Adjacent to Moss Island is Lock 17, which at one time was reputed to be the highest lift-lock in the world.[3] In 1958, however, its height was surpassed by the Eisenhower Lock in Massena, which officially opened in 1959 with the inauguration of the Saint Lawrence Seaway.

Directions: From the NYS Thruway (I-90), get off at Exit 29A for Little Falls and drive northwest, continuing on Rt. 169, for 1.9 miles. Along the

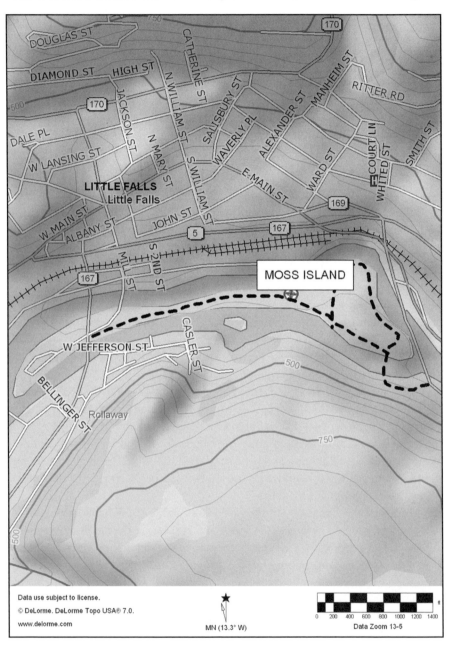

way, looking across the Mohawk River, you will notice high up on the face of an escarpment the impressive ruins of the John Pierce Stone Works and Little Falls Stone Company, which were built in the early 1900s. At 1.9 miles, just before you cross over a bridge spanning the Mohawk River, look for a wooden signpost on the left indicating the way to Moss Island and Lock E17 of the Barge Canal. Turn left and follow the road down to a parking area under the bridge.

From Rt. 5, turn south onto Rt. 169 when you come to the east end of Little Falls, and cross over the Mohawk River. When you reach the end of the bridge, turn immediately right onto a tiny road that takes you down below the bridge to a parking area for Lock E17 and Moss Island.

The Hikes

There are two distinct hikes in the area of Moss Island. One hike leads over and around the island to sculpted rocks, potholes, views of the Mohawk River, and along the top of a forty-foot-high escarpment. The other hike follows a 0.5-mile projection of land leading west from Moss Island to Bentons Landing.

Lock 36 was part of a mile-long system of five locks that predated the Erie Canal by thirty years. Photograph 2001.

Hike #1—Moss Island Hike

The walk begins from the parking lot directly under the Rt. 169 Bridge spanning the Mohawk River. If you look west from the parking lot, you will see Lock 17 approximately 0.1 mile ahead. Just ahead to the left are the remnants of Lock 36, which predates the old Erie Canal by several decades. There is no water in the lock now, just grass surrounded by stone blocks. It is possible to walk right into the lock and marvel at the workmanship that went into its construction. It is a massive structure that is sure to astonish. The stone embankment behind the lock is the supporting wall for an old railroad bed (now a bike and footpath) that runs above it.

Lock 36 measures twelve feet wide by seventy-four feet long. It was initially part of a mile-long, five-lock system at Little Falls, with each lock capable of lifting or lowering a boat nine feet to the next lock level. The canal was constructed by Philip Schuyler and four partners in 1795 in order to bypass the cascades and rapids at Little Falls. The name of their corporation was the Western Inland Lock Navigation Company. In 1825 the mile-long canal was incorporated into the Erie Canal system.

Continue up the road for a few feet farther and you will see a kiosk on your left that contains history about the lock and a map of Moss Island and Little Falls.

Just beyond Lock 36 and the kiosk are metal stairs that lead up to the top of Lock 17. Before climbing the stairs, look around at the massive walls of the lock, which also serve as a dam for part of the barge canal. When you climb up the brightly colored, metal stairs, be sure to take time to look at this historic lock and watch it in operation if boats happen to be passing through.

Lock 17 is historically significant. It was built over a period of eight years, from 1908 to 1916, and upon its completion was considered to be a wonder of industrial engineering. It stands 45 feet wide and 318 feet long, and can raise or lower boats forty feet. According to sources, it was the highest lift-lock in the world when it was first built. Although Lock 17 has since been eclipsed in size by others, it still remains one of the highest operating lift-locks in the United States and is, by far, the highest lift-lock in the New York State Barge Canal System. Particularly notable is the absence of pumps. When boats are raised or lowered, the work is done entirely through gravity alone.

As soon as you step onto Moss Island from the metal and cement walkway paralleling the lift-lock, you will observe to your right a sign describing the geological history of the island and its atypical flora.

There is a trail that begins here. It is one of three trails opposite Lock 17 that leads up to the geological features on Moss Island. Each trail, at its start, has a plaque containing geological and historical information. As soon as you climb up to the top of the ridge above the lock using one of the three trails, you will find

Some of the potholes are big enough to climb down into. Here, Barbara Delaney tries to figure out how to climb back out. Photograph 1995.

that the path turns into a series of unmarked, meandering pathways that criss-cross the rocky terrain. There is no need to worry about getting lost, however. The island is relatively small. If you lose your bearings, just follow the outer perimeter of the island and you will eventually return to where you started.

Moss Island's flora—a combination of mosses, ferns, blueberry bushes, oak trees, and birches—more resembles that of the Adirondacks than the Mohawk Valley. There is a reason for this: the thin cover of topsoil overlying the island's durable mantle of gneiss rock permitted only mosses and lichens, like those found at the arctic tundra, to take hold. From this tenuous beginning, the present flora evolved. Rock is never far away when you hike across Moss Island. It constantly protrudes in the form of ledges, boulders, ravines, cliffs, and rocky outcroppings.

Moss Island's most unique features, however, are its wonderful sculpted rocks and potholes. Most of these formations are located on the northeast side of the island, which means you should keep wending your way to the left as you proceed across the island. There you will find potholes five to thirty feet deep. There are beautiful, naturally carved columns, holes, and crevices that can be explored, climbed in, and in some cases even climbed *through* by the adventurous—as long as care is taken.[4]

The potholes on Moss Island are truly of Brobdingnagian proportions. Several are over twenty feet in circumference. The deepest is thirty feet from top to bottom—higher than a two-story building. Many of the potholes have been carved out at different heights in the bedrock, visible proof that the Mohawk River was at one time markedly higher than it is today.[5]

A number of the larger potholes contain smaller ones, like the craters splattered over the surface of the moon. Some are linked together, forming figure eights. Many, because the river has eroded part of their side walls, look like huge semicircles and can only be truly appreciated when viewed from afar.

The potholes were formed thousands of years ago when the Mohawk River carried a torrent of water equivalent to the Niagara River.[6] Moss Island offered an unusually resistant uplifted block of gneiss against the river's relentless erosive drive. Still, as the island dome was swept over by the mighty Iro-Mohawk River, huge eddies began to wear away at the bedrock and potholes were created. These potholes became further deepened and shaped as stones were trapped in them and were swirled about by the waters. As the height of the river gradually dropped, this process was repeated at lower elevations of bedrock until the island was left with potholes not only at the edge of the river, but fifty feet above it as well.[7]

In the same area can be found huge embankments of rock, one of which is over thirty feet high. These rocky bulwarks have to be climbed over or gotten around in order to fully explore the island's many potholes and to negotiate its northeastern flank. Scampering around these embankments can be lots of fun; however, adults should make sure that children are properly supervised. There are numerous exposed areas where a fall could prove injurious or possibly even fatal.

As you approach the northwest end of the island, in one corner of this labyrinth of paths and towering embankments is a small, box-shaped hut that juts out from a little crevice. When looked at from above, the hut is completely hidden. It is only when you stand directly in front of it that the entrance is visible. Although the opening looks at first like an entrance to a mineshaft, it actually leads nowhere. The hut is very, very small; still, it could make for a shelter during a rain shower and, like a few other oddities on the island, makes for interesting speculation as to what its origin and initial purpose was.

Close to the river along the northwest end of the island is a massive block of rock approximately thirty feet high and freestanding. A path leads to it. Look closely and you will see the cement foundation block of an old structure that once stood next to the towering bluff of rock. This foundation is likely the remains of a nineteenth-century factory building.

Before leaving the northeastern section of the island, stand on one of the overlooks and take a moment to imagine yourself back in the 1700s. Native Americans used the potholes and rocky phalanges to conceal sheep and other spoils they had gathered on raids during the Revolutionary War.[8]

At the northwest end of the island are views of the power plant and industrial buildings, some of which are now vacant or have been turned to other uses.

As you round the western end of the island and head southeast along the top of the escarpment, you will get a birds-eye view of the Barge Canal and Lock 17. From spring to fall, you are likely to see a variety of vessels passing through the lock.

Looking down from the top of the escarpment, don't be surprised if you see rock climbers directly below you making their way up the vertical, forty-

Rock climbers are challenged by the thirty-foot-high cliffs on the island's south side. Photograph 2000.

foot rock face of the southern escarpment. Moss Island is popular with rock climbing enthusiasts. Take note, however, that the city of Little Falls requires that all climbers purchase a permit for a small fee at the police station.

Although Moss Island is not large, its combination of sculpted rocks, potholes, interesting flora, and views of the Mohawk River and New York State Barge Canal can easily consume several hours of time, so plan accordingly.

Hike #2—Moss Island to Little Falls Hike

This hike begins next to Lock 17 and follows a road designated for pedestrians and cyclists that extends for 0.7 mile into the village of Little Falls.

The first thing to note is the huge cliff face, known as Profile Rock, which is approximately forty feet high and extends for hundreds of feet along Moss Island's southern flank, finally ending at the gate of a hydroelectric power plant at the island's western perimeter. The rock comprising the cliffs—and most of the island—is syenite, an igneous rock of Precambrian origin that is extremely resistant to erosion (which explains why Moss Island still stands despite the onslaught of the powerful waters of the Mohawk River).

Directly opposite the cliffs, to the south, is a 100-foot precipice known as Lover's Leap. Like Rogers Rock at Lake George and Sam's Point at Ice Cave Mountain in the Shawangunks, Lover's Leap has a story. According to legend, a Native American maiden and her brave were trying to escape a party of warriors in hot pursuit when they came upon the towering bluff. Preferring death to capture, they leaped off the cliff together and became immortalized in the pages of folklore.[9] If their jump had taken place in the nineteenth century, they would have landed on the New York Central Railroad's tracks, which passed directly below at the base of the cliff. Today, the tracks have been removed and a footpath/bicycle trail now follows the railroad bedding at the base of the escarpment.

As you begin walking between Lock 17 and the cliff face to your right, you will pass by three entry points that lead up to the upper reaches of Moss Island. Each trail is marked by a historic plaque. Between the second and third entry points is a large pothole that you can walk right into. It makes for a great photo opportunity.

The road soon reaches the end of Moss Island, where a hydroelectric plant seemingly blocks further progress. This is just an illusion, however, for the walk continues along a metal walkway that crosses over a dam-created cascade. If water is cresting the top of the spillway, you may wish to stop and listen to the sound of water falling forty feet from the height of the Barge Canal to the Mohawk River.

Nearby, water is being forced through a 14.5-foot-diameter penstock and dropping forty feet to drive the hydroelectric plant's twin, 6,500-kilowatt Kaplan turbines. This generates enough power to provide electricity to over 8,000 homes.[10]

Within a moment you will be past the power-generating plant and onto a thin strip of land. Look to your right and you will see the Mohawk River; look to your left and you will see the New York State Barge Canal. The Mohawk River is full of rapids and tiny falls. That is why the Barge Canal was created—to bypass this section of white water. Postcards from the turn of the twentieth century show this phalange of land inhabited by numerous industries, but virtually nothing remains of them today.

Just before you pass by an old red brick building on your right, follow a little path to your right that leads over to the Mohawk River. You will look down on a small dam that spans a tiny cascade—one of many little falls at Little Falls.

The shape of the valley is more discernible now. On the southern side, huge cliffs tower close to the waters of the barge canal. To the north the valley is more open and rises up gradually. Most of the village of Little Falls is nestled in the cradle of this sloping terrain.

As you continue past the old red brick building, you will see an abandoned bridge to your right, roughly 0.2 mile after passing the power-generating plant. At one time it was possible to stroll out onto the iron bridge for views of the river, but the bridge is no longer safe. It is now posted and has been barricaded.

When the road dips momentarily, you will see the massive wall of the barge canal looming to your left, holding back the water (whose level is above you).

The area to the west of Moss Island was once heavily industrialized.
Postcard ca. 1900.

You will have frequent views of the Mohawk River along the walk. Note
that its north bank is lined with stone walls. A number of buildings of former
industries can be seen above these walls. At one time these industries were
involved in the manufacture of bicycles, velocipedes, milking machines, knit
goods, felt products, bookcases, breakfast foods, and tissue paper. Below, in the
river, promontories of rock can be seen occasionally. Many show clear signs of
having been scoured by the river and contain little potholes of their own.

Just as you begin to feel that you are on an island of the dead, a graveyard
of industry, civilization suddenly returns in the form of a tiny park called
Bentons Landing, where you will find a kiosk with historic plaques telling
about Little Falls. Park benches allow you to sit and enjoy the views of the
barge canal.

Bentons Landing is named after Nathaniel Benton, who lived from 1792
to 1869. Benton was a lawyer, a senator, a district attorney, a canal auditor,
and for twelve years secretary of state for New York. He was also a historian
who wrote a book on the history of Herkimer County. Undoubtedly, however,
the name Bentons Landing originated because Nathaniel Benton was the first
mayor of Little Falls, in 1827.

Take note of the South Ann Street Bridge that takes you across the
Mohawk River into Little Falls. If you walk out to the middle of the bridge
and look downstream, you will see the remnants of an old aqueduct that once
spanned the river.[11] The aqueduct was built in 1822 so that boats could travel
across the Mohawk River. The stone arch supporting the bridge was fashioned
from rectangular slabs of limestone that were cut and precisely fitted together
so that gravity—not mortar—would lock them securely into place.

The aqueduct at Little Falls once consisted of a 214-foot-long bridge with a single, seventy-foot arch forming its center, with smaller arches on each end.[12] The aqueduct was used for only a few decades. In 1881 the bridge was abandoned and its waters drained. About ten years later the northern stone arch was dynamited so that the Victor Knitting Mills and the Paper Box Factory could be expanded. In 1928 the southern arch collapsed. Its ruins are quite visible along the south bank. Finally, in 1993, the central arch collapsed. A pile of rocks still remains in the streambed, and part of the arch near the south bank is still standing, but eventually these vestiges of the past will be washed away as well.

Walk to the north end of the South Anne Street Bridge and look upstream. You will see rapids and little falls amidst jumbles of rocks. These falls generally only come to life during the winter when the barge canal ceases operations, allowing the Mohawk River's full strength to be revealed. The building to your right, looking upstream, was last occupied by Stafford & Holt Co.—manufacturers of knitting machines—which lasted until the 1970s.

From here, retrace your steps and return the way you came.

History: The geological history of Moss Island began about 10,000 years ago at the end of the last ice age. The meltwaters of retreating glaciers created Lake Iroquois, whose overflow exited to the east, thundering through the Mohawk Valley. The torrent of water rearranged and modified great land masses, with Moss Island perhaps its most astonishing piece of sculpturing. Thanks to the placement of this fourteen-acre mound of rock and the continual wash of the

Only the ruins of the aqueduct remain now, lying in a sad heap of stones in the river bed. Postcard ca. 1900.

There are weird formations all over the island. Photograph 1994.

violent waters, a unique area of carved rock evolved and remains today as a geological artifact of beauty and great interest.[13]

The human history of the island did not begin until thousands of years later. The Mohawks were the first permanent Native American residents in the Little Falls area. It is believed that they moved frequently, with the seasons—but this was not always the case. Father Isaac Jogues, a Jesuit missionary, noted the presence of a palisaded village in the area in 1643 when he was brought there as a captive of the Mohawks. Native Americans called the site Astenrogan, meaning "tumbling waters." Early white traders called it Little Falls, distinguishing it from the "Great Falls" of Cohoes near Albany.

By the mid-1700s, Europeans had begun to settle and colonize the Hudson and Mohawk valleys. The Mohawk Valley was the gateway to the west for settlers from the Hudson Valley. This gateway led to the ongoing expansion of colonial territories and to increased trade with Native Americans and

Moss Island by Canoe or Kayak

It is also possible to explore the eastern and northern parts of Moss Island by canoe or kayak, which allows you to approach the island in the same way as it was first seen by Native Americans.

Upstream from the north side of Moss Island, you will eventually encounter the "little falls" of Little Falls. These are not really falls, but impassable rapids. Little Falls acquired its name because the title "Great Falls" had already been bestowed upon Cohoes Falls (located near the eastern terminus of the Mohawk River). Both the little falls at Little Falls and the great falls at Cohoes (to a lesser degree) were greatly modified by the Industrial Revolution.

settlers along both the Mohawk and Hudson waterways. The Burnetsfield Patent, issued in 1725, confirmed the earlier Indian deed of 1722 and granted lots to ninety-two persons, twenty-five of whom were women. These lots were in Herkimer County near Little Falls. In 1741 the islands in the Mohawk River at Little Falls were granted to Peter Winne. Lands to the east of Little Falls were owned by Sir William Johnson's children, whose mother was a Native American.

According to historians, there were German inhabitants in the general area by 1720, but there was only one habitable dwelling and a gristmill occupying the site that is now the town of Little Falls. In 1757, John Joost Petrie—owner of another gristmill, located near the confluence of the Mohawk River and Furnace Creek—and his family were captured by the French and taken to Canada. Twenty-five years later, in 1782, the mill was destroyed by Tory raiders during the American Revolution.

Indeed, the Mohawk Valley corridor was the scene of many battles and raids during the Revolutionary War. When Captain Thompson brought word of the signing of the peace treaty on September 3, 1783, between America and Great Britain, the former residents of Little Falls were finally able to leave the confines of forts Dayton and Herkimer and return to their burned homes and farms to start over again.

In July of that same year, General George Washington and a group of officers made a tour of the Mohawk Valley and its frontier posts. Washington stopped at General Nicholas Herkimer's house and then continued up the south side of the Mohawk River to Fort Herkimer, where he spent two nights. He looked over the carrying place at Little Falls and remarked that a canal for military and commercial purposes should be built around the rapids. These rapids would have been just above and to the north of Moss Island.

The area including Moss Island and Little Falls was a rough frontier town in the days following the Revolutionary War. The Rev. Caleb Alexander wrote during his tour of the area in 1801:

> *Around Little Falls the country is hilly and very rocky near the river. On the northern bank are seven locks and a canal for the conveyance of boats. Here is a village of forty houses, several merchant stores, mechanical shops and a new meeting house of hexagonal construction. The people are principally English. ... The place abounds in vice, especially profanity. Since my arrival on the river I have heard more cursing and swearing, horrid oaths and imprecations than in ten years past. They fell chiefly from the lips of boatmen. In some taverns were English and Dutch farmers drinking and swearing, and the English appeared to be the most abandoned.*[14]

The old canal locks that Alexander referred to were constructed between 1792 and 1795 by the Western Inland Lock Navigation Company, which General Philip Schuyler had a part in developing. This system of waterways connected the Mohawk River with Oneida Lake through Wood Creek, and the Oswego River with Lake Ontario. The canal at Little Falls originally had five wooden locks, which were replaced around 1805 by locks of stone. When the Erie Canal was constructed in 1825, the old canal and locks were purchased by New York State and used as a feeder for the Erie Canal. You wouldn't know it today, but before the Erie Canal was built, part of the Mohawk River ran along the south side of Moss Island. The completion of the Erie Canal was celebrated with great ceremony and festivities at Little Falls, which by that time had a population of around 700 people.

During the 1800s and early 1900s there was an abundance of mills and factories along the Mohawk River in Little Falls. Some were even located on Moss Island itself. One of the mills was George L. Smith's Wool Extract Co. George's father, John Smith, was born in England and came to Little Falls in 1860 to lease the old Anchor Mill from the Loomis Estate. In 1887 a stone building on Moss Island was erected so that wool could be extracted from rags and reused (the cotton component was dissolved). After his father's death, George carried on the business until about 1936, renaming it the Adirondack Woolen Co. After the Woolen Co. ceased operations, the building was used as a warehouse. Then, on January 10, 1946, it tragically collapsed, causing the deaths of four men who were trapped in the debris. George L. Smith died on April 25 of the same year.

It is said that during the Mexican War and the Civil War, the mills at Little Falls ran day and night manufacturing blue woolen cloth for the army, and that every little boy in town had a blue soldier's suit that was made from defective cloth.

Because of the abundance of waterpower, a number of knitting goods businesses gradually developed as Little Falls entered the1890s. In fact, so many residents were engaged in the knit goods business that the knitting machine was adopted in 1895 as Little Falls's official emblem. Ultimately, however, the knit goods business began to decline as steam and electric power and central heating came into vogue.

In 1947 the state purchased Moss Island. Today, virtually all remains of former industries on Moss Island have disappeared except for the foundation stones on the northwest corner of the island. Fortunately, much of the history is carefully preserved and conveyed on signs throughout the town, along the trail to Moss Island, and on the canal walkway from the island to Little Falls.

TUFA CAVES &
WATERFALLS OF VAN HORNESVILLE

Location: Van Hornesville (Herkimer County)
DeLorme NYS Atlas & Gazetteer: p. 64, A2

Fee: None

Hours: Open daily, sunrise to sunset

Accessibility: 0.6–0.8-mile walk (round-trip) over well-maintained trails

Degree of Difficulty: Easy

Restrictions: No swimming, fishing, or hunting. Observe rules posted at entrance.

Highlights:
- Tufa caves
- Waterfalls
- Old ruins

Description: This fascinating, fifty-acre nature preserve containing several small caves and a variety of waterfalls is located at the Robert D. Woodruff Outdoor Learning Center.[1] The preserve's main attractions are the tiny caves that have formed in a huge block of calcareous tufa—a kind of limestone that is honeycombed. At one time the tufa caves were considered so unique that a mural of them was displayed at the 1939 World's Fair.

Several notable waterfalls can be seen next to the tufa caves. The most striking of these is Creamery Falls, a towering, seventy-foot staircase of tumbling water directly across the stream from the tufa caves. Creamery Falls is formed on Creamery Brook, a tiny tributary to Otsquago Creek. Otsquago Creek, which rises near Summit Lake, is the main stream flowing through the preserve.

At the confluence of Creamery Brook and Otsquago Creek is another impressive waterfall—a ten-foot-high plunge over a broad block of bedrock. Because the waterfall is formed at the confluence of the two creeks, it is easy to be fooled into thinking that this fall is merely a continuation of Creamery Falls.

Directions: Take the NYS Thruway (I-90) to Canajoharie (Exit 29), and then Rt. 5S northwest for 3.5 miles until you reach the stoplight at Fort Plain. Turn left onto Rt. 80 and drive southwest for over 11.5 miles until you reach the village of Van Hornesville. Turn left at Owen D. Young Central School and drive down to the lowermost parking level, close to Otsquago Creek. Park there and walk over the bridge spanning Otsquago Creek to the Outdoor Learning Center.

From Rt. 20, drive northeast on Rt. 80 for over 5.0 miles to Van Hornesville. The Owen D. Young Central School will be on the right.

The Hike

The hike begins from the pavilion at the Outdoor Learning Center. A sign states that the park is "intended for the residents and students of the Owen D. Young Central School District," but others are welcomed as well. The trail initially follows an abandoned highway named Plank Road, which at one time was the main route between Fort Plain and Cooperstown. Along the way the trail takes you through a forest of hemlock, quaking aspen, maple, ash, black cherry, white spruce, white pine, and horse chestnut.

From the pavilion, walk north for approximately 300 feet. Turn left and follow a short path down a series of steps to Otsquago Creek. There, a small, six-foot-high waterfall, called Sawmill Falls, can be observed along with stone wall foundations and pieces of old machinery that once powered a sawmill at the site.

Return to the main path and continue north for another 300 feet. Once again follow a side trail going off to your left, which this time leads within twenty feet to the foundation of an old cheese box factory, as well as to the ruins of a small mill that once operated along the bank of Otsquago Creek. You will see a six-foot-high waterfall, as well as a four-foot-high cascade just upstream.

Return again to the main trail. At this point you will notice that the path divides. The old Plank Road continues uphill to a slightly higher elevation, distancing itself from the creek, and a secondary route, called Cave Trail, proceeds north, paralleling the stream. Cave Trail leads directly to the area of the tufa caves.[2] Continue north on Cave Trail for less than 0.1 mile and you will arrive at the caves, which will be down and around to your left.

These caves invite exploration, but none penetrates farther than ten to fifteen feet into the bedrock. The main cave is the one directly facing Creamery Falls. You will notice that much effort has gone into making the area safe for exploration. Wooden platforms and a stairway leading down to the streambed ensure that visitors can avoid the hazards of having to scamper over slippery rocks.

From the top of the wooden platform, you will have a commanding view of Creamery Falls, where the waters come cascading down a seventy-foot-high natural stairway of slate. The massive, ten-foot-high waterfall on Otsquago Creek is equally as fascinating to view since it is composed of the same rock that forms the tufa caves. Walk down to the bottom of the stairway and you can venture right up next to the waterfall for a closer look.

Gazing north from the main fall, you will observe the top of a medium-sized cascade on Otsquago Creek. You will also see numerous huge blocks of tufa rock that lie scattered about along the streambed and up towards the caves.

Climb back up the wooden stairs and follow Cave Trail farther north. Immediately, you will come to a small footbridge that crosses over a little stream. Stand on top of the footbridge and you will overlook the top of a ten-foot plunge waterfall dropping into Otsquago Creek nearly below you. Upstream, along this same tributary to Otsquago Creek, are several small cascades. From the footbridge, look south to see the lower falls upstream on Otsquago Creek.

Cross over the footbridge and you will come to Janet's Lane, which enters on your right. For the moment continue straight ahead (north) for several hundred feet farther. At the point where the hill begins to descend, look to your right. You will see in the near distance another, thirty-foot-high, cascading waterfall formed on a tiny tributary to Otsquago Creek.

To complete the circuit, take Janet's Lane east, going steeply uphill. At the top of the first hill, turn right onto Plank Road and follow it south back to the Outdoor Learning Center's pavilion.

History: In the 1700s a trail developed between Fort Plain and Cooperstown, following a valley that had been carved out by Otsquago Creek. Years later the footpath turned into Plank Road, which passed just east of the tufa caves and waterfalls.

The town of Van Hornesville is named after its founder, Abraham Van Horne.[3] During Van Hornesville's heyday, a number of mills and factories took advantage of Otsquago Creek's powerful current for hydropower generation. Such items as cheese, flour, cigar boxes, distilled spirits, furniture, and even caskets were produced in the factories that proliferated.

By the twentieth century, however, times had changed, and the factories, one by one, fell into ruins. The section of Plank Road by the tufa caves slowly became less traveled and fell into decline, while another road that paralleled the west bank flourished. When the old bridge crossing Otsquago Creek was eventually washed out, no attempt was made to replace it, and the tufa caves became inaccessible to traffic, leaving the area the sole domain of a few locals and fishermen who forded the stream.

In 1984, however, work began on reopening the area to the public. The bridge spanning Otsquago Creek was replaced by members of the 46th

Engineering Battalion of the U.S. Army Reserve, again making it possible for the tufa caves and waterfalls to be accessed with ease.

More information about the area, as well as a colorful display map, can be found at the Outdoor Learning Center. The Learning Center is dedicated to Robert A. Woodruff, who spent his forty-year career as a teacher and principal devoted to the students of Owen D. Young Central School. Owen D.

Creamery Falls bounces down a flight of rocky stairs to reach Otsquago Creek. Photograph 2000.

Young of Van Hornesville had the distinction of having been on the cover of *Time* magazine in 1930 as "Man of the Year." He was an American industrialist, businessman, lawyer, and diplomat at the Second Reparations Conference in 1929 as a member of the German Reparations International Commission. He is probably best known, however, for founding the Radio Corporation of America (RCA) as a subsidiary of General Electric in 1919.

Geology: The limestone bed forming the tufa caves developed after a natural barrier created an impoundment of water. This body of water gradually filled with assorted debris, such as logs, branches, and bushes, and a layer of dissolved calcium carbonate slowly formed on top. Over time, the mass of debris in combination with the dissolved calcium began to harden, ultimately turning into a bed of limestone.[4]

According to geologist Bradford Van Diver: "Precipitation of the dissolved salts, particularly carbonates, results in encrustation of tufa (like flowstone in caves) ... The rapid rate of accumulation is highly conducive to instant fossilization of leaves, twigs, insects, or anything else that happens to fall onto the tufa at the right place and time."[5] (This process can be seen in action today at Geyser Park in Saratoga Springs.)

When the Otsquago Creek cut out its present channel, the block of calcareous tufa became weathered and eroded by the energetic waters of the stream. Ultimately the swirling waters created the caves and blocks of limestone that can be seen along the streambed today.

The astonishing Tufa Caves. Photograph 2001.

25   CANAJOHARIE GORGE

Location: Canajoharie (Montgomery County)
DeLorme NYS Atlas & Gazetteer: p. 64, A4

Fee: None

Hours: Lower gorge and upper gorge trails, daily from 7:00 AM–9:00 PM; Wintergreen Park, open seasonally

Accessibility: *Lower Gorge & Canajoharie Pothole*—0.3-mile walk (round-trip). The hike is short and relatively level, with only slight changes in elevation. Some care must be taken if you venture out onto the streambed, particularly in places where the bedrock has become wet and slippery. *Upper Gorge & Canajoharie Falls*—1.0-mile walk (round-trip). The path along the top of the gorge is essentially level, with slight dips where small streams are encountered. There is no danger unless you approach too closely to the edge of the gorge. The *Wintergreen Park* section of the hike is fairly level.

Degree of Difficulty: Lower Gorge—Easy; Upper Gorge—Easy to moderate; Wintergreen Park—Easy

Highlights:
- Scenic gorge
- Waterfalls
- Pothole rock formations

Description: The Canajoharie Gorge is a massive canyon of shale cut out by Canajoharie Creek at the end of the last glacial epoch, approximately 10,000 years ago. The gorge is one of several dynamic canyons that rise along the south rim of the Mohawk Valley[1] and is characterized by vertically cut walls that tower over 100 feet above the streambed. There are many small cascades contained near Wintergreen Park in the upper gorge, including the famous, forty-five-foot-high Canajoharie Falls.

Canajoharie Creek's most distinctive feature and namesake—the renowned Canajoharie Pothole—can be found in the lower section of the gorge along with several small stair-like cascades. During Revolutionary War days, Canajoharie Creek was known as Bowman's Creek.[2] After the war, mills proliferated along the creek.

Directions: From the NYS Thruway (I-90), take Exit 29 for Canajoharie and turn right onto Rt. 5S. Go west for nearly 0.2 mile. Turn left onto Mitchell Street and drive south for 0.1 mile. Look to your right and you will see that you are now paralleling the east bank of Canajoharie Creek. After coming to the stop sign, continue straight across Montgomery Street onto Moyer Street.

To Lower Gorge: Proceeding south on Moyer Street, turn right onto Floral Street after 0.3 mile and drive to the end to a parking area. This area long ago was used for growing crops. On the land to the left can be seen the greenhouses for Fritz Traudt and Susan Traudt, a brother and sister who have continued a family floral business that dates back to the early 1900s. From the northwest end of the parking area, follow a paved walkway that goes down to the stream. Proceed upstream.

To Upper Gorge and Wintergreen Park: Proceed uphill on Moyer Street for a total of 0.8 mile. After Moyer Street merges with Carlisle Street, continue uphill for another 0.7 mile farther. At the point where Carlisle Street veers to the left, go straight onto Old Sharon Road for 0.1 mile. The entrance to Wintergreen Park will be on your right. Park in the tiny upper parking area on your right to access the scenic rim trail to Canajoharie Falls. Walk over to the top of the gorge and follow a trail north, paralleling the edge of the gorge for 0.5 mile. You will come out to a platform overlooking the fall.

To reach Wintergreen Park, drive down the hill to enter the main section of the park.

The Hikes

There are three different hikes, each with its own appeal and distinctive characteristics.

Hike #1—Lower Gorge & Canajoharie Pothole

This hike begins from the parking area at the end of Floral Street. You will see a paved pathway that leads down to Canajoharie Creek. The town has put a considerable amount of work into stabilizing this path, which previously had eroded significantly in places. As you walk along the path—ten to fifteen feet above the streambed—you will see a number of ledge falls and pools. It is quite a breathtaking stroll.

Almost at once, you will find yourself inside the gorge with sculptured walls rising steeply above you. Continuing along, you will come to the Canajoharie Pothole, which is immediately recognizable because of its enormous size and shape. It is surprisingly round, twenty-four feet in diameter, and over eight feet deep. Unless you are an avid explorer of gorges, it is unlikely that you will have encountered anything like this before.[3]

Canajoharie Gorge

The magnificent Canajoharie Pothole is a notable attraction in the gorge. Native American names for the pothole translate to "the kettle that washes itself" and "the great boiling pot."[4] It has also been called the Devil's Ear and The Kettle in more recent centuries. According to Jeptha Simms, the legendary Mohawk warrior, Joseph Brant, told Judge Isaac Tiffany in 1806 during Tiffany's visit with Brant at his home in Canada that the Mohawk word *canajoharie* translated to "dinner pot" in English.

The pothole was created over a period of thousands of years by swirling eddies of water moving small stones and pebbles around in a circle, causing a round depression to form and then to deepen. If you look into the pothole, you will notice a number of stones resting on the bottom, even now. When the stream gets agitated following large releases of water from snowmelt or heavy downpours, the stones are picked up by the current and continue to grind away at the bottom and sides, further deepening and widening the pothole.

Right next to the pothole and overlooking it looms Sitting Rock,[5] a very distinctive mound of rock whose name is derived from the function it well serves. Look upstream directly behind Sitting Rock and you will observe cement slabs that once encased a conduit made of wooden staves that connected the upstream dam with the Arkell & Smiths Company (which stood on the west bank at some distance farther downstream). The wooden staves have virtually disappeared, but the cement casing remains and can be easily observed.

The remains of the Arkell & Smiths dam, which provided waterpower to a mill that manufactured paper bags, can be seen upstream. According to experts, the dam was erroneously built at a place on the stream where the gorge curved. Because of this, silt and sediment would tend to collect, significantly obstructing the flow. The presence of the dam serves as a reminder of just how highly industrialized the lower gorge has been in the past. The dam also serves as the terminus of the hike. Bypassing the dam and hiking farther into the gorge is not permitted.

On your way back, look closely at sections of the bedrock and you will observe numerous holes that have been drilled in the streambed between the dam and the Canajoharie Pothole. Pipes were inserted into these holes and boards were laid across them perpendicular to the bedrock. In this fashion, plank dams were formed.

Downstream from the Canajoharie Pothole is a deep pool of water called the Devil's Hole, which contains the oldest rock in the gorge. The Bierbauer Brewery Company and a local creamery used to harvest ice thirty inches thick from the Devil's Hole each winter. Stored in insulated buildings, the ice could be used for refrigeration during the hot days of summer.

Hike #2—Upper Gorge & Canajoharie Falls

If you are a waterfall enthusiast, then this is the hike to take. From the upper parking lot above Wintergreen Park, follow a trail that leads north and parallels the east rim of the Canajoharie Gorge. You will be amazed at just how

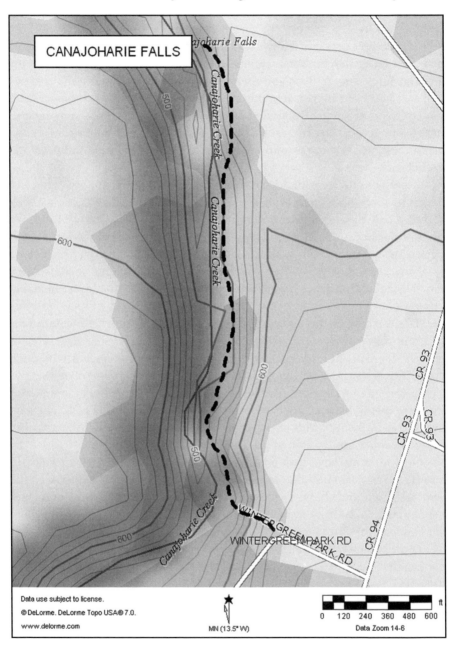

deep-cut and severe this canyon is, with vertical drops of over 100 feet. There is no need to get too close to the rim, however, for there are excellent views of the gorge from the trail. Although you can hear the falls and cascades far below, they can be difficult to see because trees and bushes obscure the view, and also because of the depth of the gorge itself.

Along the way, the trail takes you across two tiny streams that immediately plunge into the gorge, forming waterfalls of their own in the process. The second stream is spanned by a small footbridge. You will see attractive stands of white pine and birch trees, and you will pass by a water tower off to the right near the end of the trail. After a walk of over 0.5 mile, you will arrive at a large wooden platform that looks down seventy-five feet to the top of Canajoharie Falls. The waterfall is an impressive, forty-five-foot-high cascade, but it appears dwarfed by the enormity of the gorge that contains it.

Canajoharie Falls was once farther downstream towards the village of Canajoharie but, like a number of big waterfalls in northeastern New York, it has eroded its way upstream over the eons. As early as 1768, locals proposed calling the waterfall Canajoharic Falls.[6] The views near the top of the falls can be magnificent. On a clear day when foliage does not obscure the view, you can look out north from the hills above Canajoharie Falls to the distant Adirondack foothills.

Visitors must be satisfied to look at the falls from the safety of the wooden viewing platform. There have been a number of fatalities at the falls, mainly of young people who underestimated the danger and became reckless. Entering the gorge to see the falls is no longer permitted and can result in arrest and a hefty fine.

Hike #3—Wintergreen Park Walk (interior of gorge)

Wintergreen Park is a seventy-two-acre recreational area with a pavilion, snack bar, and picnic tables. The picnic area is open from May 15 to September 15.

From the lower parking area at Wintergreen Park, you can walk upstream or downstream along a short trail next to the stream. Take note, however, of large red signs posted next to the stream that state: "No Trespassing. Dangerous Waterfalls. Use Scenic Trail Only." The scenic trail referred to is the one that follows along the rim of the gorge.

During the short walk next to the streambed, you will be struck by the height of the vertical walls that rise up around you like city skyscrapers. But don't spend all your time looking up. The shale beds contain a great number and variety of fossils, which can be studied at will along the bank of the stream. Just be sure not to venture out onto the streambed itself.

Downstream, in an area that is off limits, is a small cascade known as the Lady Slipper. The cascade acquired its name from the rocks forming it.

The village of Canajoharie is named after an impressive pothole that Native Americans called *Canajoharie*—"the kettle that washes itself." Photograph 1999.

Initially, a grayish fold of volcanic ash was laid down between two layers of mud. Millions of years later, the mud beds, after being subjected to high pressure, turned into shale, a sedimentary rock. Like a delicate foot in a slipper, the inner rock is contained within two harder, outer layers.

In addition to the Lady Slipper, the upper gorge is host to a number of little waterfalls that are produced by small tributaries cascading down the side walls. These are meager rivulets, however, with watersheds that quickly become desiccated when the weather turns dry. The most notable waterfall produced is called Cemetery Falls (named for its location next to a cemetery) and is located farther downstream on the west bank below Canajoharie Falls.

Upstream from Wintergreen Park, the gorge becomes less impressive. This part of the gorge is also off limits. Its most unique feature is a sixteen-foot outcropping of crystalline rock along the streambed that doesn't appear to be indigenous to the area. Geologists believe that it is a glacial erratic deposited by retreating glaciers, and that it may have been transported from as far north as the High Peak region of the Adirondacks.

History: The Canajoharie Gorge, born of the last ice age, is over twice as old as the Great Pyramids of Egypt. The first permanent settlers in the area were the Mohawks, who arrived in the early 1500s. It was they who gave the area the name Canajoharie—a name that referenced the Canajoharie Pothole. One of their small villages was on the site later occupied by the Arkell and Smiths sack factory.

Martin Van Alstyne, in partnership with Canajoharie's first settler, Henrick Scrembling, built a mill on the Canajoharie Creek in 1749, according to John Vrooman.[7] Scrembling later sold his interest to Van Alstyne. This mill had massive timbers and stood until 1814, when it burned down.

Around the same time the mill was built, Van Alstyne also built a large, grey, stone home along the creek below the site of the mill. Though many stone houses of this stature were palisaded and used as forts during the Revolutionary War, the Van Alstyne house was spared a similar fate. The house, now privately owned, is still standing and appears to be in good repair. It is located on the east side of the creek before you reach Floral Avenue. There is a plaque in front of the house describing its historical significance.

Later, the site and water privileges of the Van Alstyne–Scrembling mill were sold to George Goertner and Henry Lieber (Goertner's son-in-law), who proceeded to build a stone gristmill about 300 feet below the site of the previous mill and set a stone dam across Canajoharie Creek. Around the same time, Goertner and Lieber also built a sawmill, distillery, carding mill, and fulling mill. At Lieber's death in 1838, Uriah Wood became the new owner of the mills. Ultimately, all of the mills were destroyed by fire and never rebuilt.

The Van Alstyne House, named after Martin Van Alstyne, an early settler. Postcard ca. 1900.

Although forty-five feet high, Canajoharie Falls is dwarfed by the enormity of the gorge containing it. Postcard ca. 1930.

Another gristmill was constructed around 1770 by Col. Hendrick Frey, who also erected a sawmill shortly thereafter. This gristmill stood approximately 800 feet from Van Alstyne's mill and nearly a mile up from Canajoharie Creek's mouth, according to one source. It was built on a high point along the west bank that quickly became known as Upper Mill.

The remains of the Bierbauer Brewery, which made beer for the local populace and dates back to the early 1800s, are still in evidence on the west side of the creek. The stone foundation walls and a grey stone building that has been converted into a home and beauty parlor are on private property, however, and not accessible.

In 1860, James Arkell, Benjamin Smith, and Adam Smith built the Paper & Cotton Flour Sack Company that became known as Arkell & Smiths. With the advent of the Erie Canal, Canajoharie had become a thriving center of commerce that shipped items downstate to New York City. Benjamin and Adam Smith opened up a large store, three stories high, which purchased and sold such commodities as flour, feed, salt, plaster, and cement. James Arkell had his office in the same building on the second floor. At the time, Arkell was the printer and publisher of a small local newspaper called *Radii.* It was Arkell who developed the idea of making cotton bags, and soon the Smith brothers joined in as partners. When the threat of the Civil War caused a shortage in cotton, Arkell designed a machine that was capable of making paper bags, and he went on to patent a series of further innovations in this field. Fueled by their success, Arkell and the Smiths expanded their operation and moved to a new, larger building on Canajoharie Creek in 1861.

From 1839 to 1884, the three men ran the business as a partnership. In 1884 it became incorporated. Bag production led to other enterprises such as packaging coffee, sugar, cement, plaster, and fertilizer. The firm ceased operations in Canajoharie and moved to a preexisting facility in Hudson Falls in 1957. After operating there for a few years, the business was finally bought out by the Chase Bag Company.[8] The Canajoharie factory was dismantled in 1952. You can see still the ruins of the mill's dam that was constructed in 1930 just upstream from the Canajoharie Pothole.

Canajoharie Creek's most famous industry today is the Beech-Nut Company, founded in the late 1800s. The Canajoharie Beech-Nut factory is located farther downstream, near the confluence of Canajoharie Creek and the Mohawk River. Although the company is best known for its baby foods and chewing gum, it started off as a distributor of barrel-smoked Mohawk Valley hams, based upon a homemade recipe.

The confluence of Canajoharie Creek and the Mohawk River is now the site of the Canajoharie Riverfront Park. The park is accessible from Church Street, just before you cross over the Mohawk River into Palatine Bridge.

26 WOLF HOLLOW

Location: Hoffmans (Schenectady County)
DeLorme NYS Atlas & Gazetteer: p. 66, AB1

Fee: None

Hours: Open continuously

Accessibility: Roadside

Degree of Difficulty: Easy

Highlights:
- Scenic ravine
- Miner's cave

Description: Wolf Hollow is a fascinating, 1.0-mile-long ravine that is unique in two distinct and significant ways—it represents a geological anomaly not found anywhere else in the Capital Region, and it carries the history of a fierce and very bloody battle between two Native American tribes.

Although the gorge is readily accessible, there is a downside. Years ago, highway engineers constructed a road through the ravine, which means that you must be ready to put up with the inevitable noise and distraction of passing cars.[1]

A conservation easement was recently established across 37.5 acres of land on the former Swart homestead that parallels the west bank of the Chaughtanoonda Creek.[2] The land donation was made possible through the generosity of the Dudley Crauer family and provides an opportunity to hike without being disturbed by passing cars.

Directions: From Schenectady, take I-890 northwest. Eventually, I-890 veers to the right and crosses over the Mohawk River. At the terminus of I-890, turn left onto Rt. 5. Drive northwest on Rt. 5 for 4.8 miles until you reach Hoffmans.

To Wolf Hollow: Turn right onto Hoffman Hill Road (also called Wolf Hollow Road) and drive uphill, going north, for 0.6 mile. You will come to a fork in the road where Hoffman Hill Road Ext. goes straight uphill and Wolf Hollow Road veers to the left (west). Turn left and follow Wolf Hollow Road into the beginning of the gorge. The ravine ends over 1.1 miles later where Wolf Hollow Road reconnects with Hoffman Hill Road Ext. About halfway up the gorge is an excellent spot to park, at a pull-off on the right-hand side of the road.

To Site of Historic Cement Plant: From Rt. 5, go north on Hoffman Hill Road for 0.05 mile and then turn left onto Touareuna Road. Take note that Touareuna Road is seasonal. Drive northwest for 0.2 mile. You will see the historic marker for the site of the Van Eps Cement plant on your left, over-looking the Mohawk River, railroad tracks, and Rt. 5 below. The actual site was probably thirty feet below the earth and rubble that now forms the shoulder of Touareuna Road. From this lookout you can appreciate the amount of earth and rock that must have been excavated in order to make room for the roads and train lines running parallel to the Mohawk River.[3]

To Site of Algonquin Village: Continue northwest on Touareuna Road for another 0.1 mile. This time you will come to a historic marker on your right, indicating the site of an ancient Algonquin castle (village).

To Site of Van Eps House: From Hoffmans, drive southeast on Rt. 5 for less than 0.2 mile. You will see a historic marker on the left side of the road. Old foundation ruins plus assorted rusted artifacts can be seen slightly to the left after you have walked fifty feet up a grassy road leading north from the sign.

To Conservation Easement: From Hoffman Hill Road (also called Wolf Hollow Road), turn left onto Touareuna Road and drive uphill for roughly 0.3 mile. Just past the historic marker for the Algonquin village/corn pits, you will come to a house on the right belonging to the Crauer family. Ask at the house for permission to access the adjacent land. Bear in mind that certain rules must be obeyed: no motorized vehicles of any kind are allowed on the property; littering and picnicking are prohibited; and archaeological digs are not allowed unless conducted by approved, qualified professionals.

The Hikes

Hike #1—Trek through Wolf Hollow

Although the entire 1.0-mile length of Wolf Hollow can be traversed by car, it is far more enjoyable and rewarding to park about halfway up the ravine and use that as a starting point for exploring the gorge by foot. Doing so will enable you to get a much better feel for the enormity of the ravine and its steeply sloped walls.

Begin by imagining yourself back in the 1600s. You are part of a Mohican war party, quietly making your way up through the hollow after attacking a Mohawk village near Fonda. Suddenly, the unexpected happens! Your way ahead is blocked by a Mohawk war party. You look back and your retreat is blocked as well. The sides of the ravine are steep and barren of protective covering. There is no way out of this death trap. Images grow distorted and grotesque as Chaughtanoonda Creek begins to turn red with the blood of slain warriors.

Today, instead of bodies strewn about the gorge, you are likely to see thirty species of fern scattered about as well as some uncommon orchids (providing, of course, that you visit at the right time of the year). One can easily feel dwarfed by the steeply sloping walls of rock and earth penetrated here and there by tiny tributaries that carry water only during the wet season.

At roughly 0.2 mile into Wolf Hollow, you will come to Johnny Spring, where the gorge turns sharply right. Native Americans would stop here to refresh themselves.

Approximately 0.5 mile from the beginning of the hollow, near where you parked, is a tiny opening in the shale of the east wall of the ravine. This is the entrance to Bear Den's Cave, a short crawl that quickly comes to a dead end. The tiny cave is believed to have been dug out by prospectors in 1884[4] who were hoping to find coal deposits in the black shale. They were unaware that the plants that were to create coal-bearing rock had yet to come into existence at the time when these beds of shale were formed.

Hike #2—Lower Section of Chaughtanoonda Creek

The hike along the easement donated to the Mohawk–Hudson Land Conservancy is short, but historically significant. The path takes you near lower Chaughtanoonda Creek following a route that was once used by Native Americans to access Wolf Hollow.

The beginning of the walk leads you past a number of Native American corn pits. These have been filled in by years of sedimentation, but are still faintly visible if you know what to look for and where to look. The Native Americans dug the pits deep and then covered them with cedar boughs and leaves so that perishables could be stored and preserved in the cool earth.

Close to the corn pits and overlooking the stream is a small cabin built in the early 1900s by Dudley Crauer's grandfather.[5]

The path continues, following the stream for roughly 0.1 mile, ending long before you reach Wolf Hollow.

History of Wolf Hollow: According to a roadside historical marker located at the beginning of the ravine, a major battle was fought in the hollow between the Mohawks and Algonquins (Mohicans). In the end, the Algonquins were roundly defeated and lost over fifty of their warriors, including their chief.[6]

The fierce battle took place on August 6, 1669, and was one of the bloodiest conflicts documented in North America at that time.[7] It was fought over rights to control the Mohawk Valley—an area that not only provided boundless opportunities for agriculture, but also provided a gateway to the mid-western part of the continent where lucrative trade agreements could be pursued. Although the Mohicans were the first tribe to occupy the eastern part of the Mohawk Valley, they had been driven out by the more aggressive Mohawks in the early 1600s and ended up settling in Massachusetts.[8]

For half a century the Mohicans brooded over their defeat and humiliation. Then, after learning that the Mohawks had fared poorly against an Algonquin tribe from Canada, the Mohicans became emboldened and decided that the time had come to avenge themselves. They targeted the Mohawk village of Kahaniaga, near present-day Fonda, choosing the village because of its easternmost position, which made it the most vulnerable to attack.

The Mohicans repeatedly attacked Kahaniaga for two days, but in the end were unable to gain the advantage. With supplies running low, they finally decided to return home to Massachusetts. Retreating east along the Mohawk River, the Mohicans camped out overnight on the hills of Touareuna, which at that time consisted of a steep, rocky ridge that came down to the river's edge close to where a tiny creek issuing from Wolf Hollow flowed into the Mohawk River. A huge section of this ridge no longer exists today. The abutment closest to the river was blasted away by engineers in the 1800s (as was also done to Big Nose near Sprakers) so that there would be adequate room for Rtes. 5 & 5S and the New York Central Railroad to pass through the valley.

In the seventeenth century, however, the spiny ridge and steep vertical slopes of this abutment provided a sense of security for the camped warriors, who considered the rocky spine to be nearly impregnable. The Mohawks, however, were trailing close behind, led by their war chief, the Great Kryn. During the night they took up positions at the top and bottom of the hill.

The next morning the unsuspecting Mohicans began making their way up through Wolf Hollow—the first leg of an elaborate route to Massachusetts that took them through Charlton, up Mourning Creek, over to Round Lake from Ballston Lake, down to Mechanicville, over to Stillwater, and then up the Hoosic River. Much to their horror, they suddenly came face-to-face with a Mohawk war party blocking the way ahead. They were not only boxed in from the front, but from the rear as well, and caught between the massive walls of the ravine.

In the ensuing battle most of the Mohicans were killed, including their chief, Chicataubet. Many died in the ravine; some were slaughtered down by the river as they tried to escape. Only a few managed to elude capture or death.

Prior to this climactic battle, legend has it that a young Mohawk woman named Kateri Tekakwitha traveled through Wolf Hollow in 1667 on her way to Canada after converting to Christianity.[9]

For a short period of time, it was thought that the hollow might harbor coal. A mine was dug into the side wall, but the prospectors came up empty-handed. Postcard ca. 1930.

Geology: As you begin to enter Wolf Hollow, you will see to your left the 150-foot-high wall of the ravine. The upper section of the west wall consists of a nearly vertical cliff face of gray-colored stratified rocks called Canajoharie shale and Amsterdam limestone. The lower portion is a talus slope of Little Falls dolomite. The east wall is considerably lower in height and formed out of Schenectady shale and sandstone.

The hollow itself represents a huge fault where massive geological forces caused the bedrock on the west side to slip or move upward, and the bedrock on the east side to slide downward.[10] This is why there is such a difference between the heights of the walls of the ravine. Quite possibly a preexisting fault line widened suddenly during an ancient earthquake.

The Chaughtanoonda is a small stream that flows through the hollow following the direction of the fissure. Although the hollow has been significantly modified by erosive forces over the last millennia, this reshaping was probably caused as much by rain, snow, ice, frost, and the forces of nature acting on the side walls as it was from the cutting action of the stream.

Limestone was once quarried from both above and below the hollow, and was used in the construction of the Erie Canal.

The Mohawks called the creek issuing from Wolf Hollow, Chaughtanoonda—a reference to the sharp, rocky point that once existed next to the stream's confluence with the Mohawk River. It was this same abutment that gave the Mohicans a false sense of security and impregnability from attack.

Today, nothing is left of this huge abutment that once led to the river's edge. What you will now see is a rock cut west of Hoffman's where a tremendous volume of earth and rock was excavated in order to make room for the highway and railroad.

History of Hoffmans: Southwest of Wolf Hollow, on Touareuna Road, a roadside historic marker points out that this area was once the site of an Algonquin village. According to the sign, "corn pits yet remain," but you will be hard-pressed to see more than a faint outline. This is one of more than a dozen archeological sites in the area. Artifacts from a site known as Kinaquuariones date back as far as 1000 to 2000 BC.[11]

If you get out of the car and walk around, you will notice that the land in this section has been significantly altered. Chaughtanoonda Creek can be seen far below, with jumbles of rocks placed by engineers along the sloping wall of the ravine to stabilize it. To the south, just down the road, an enormous section of the ridge was blasted away to make room for the Mohawk Valley highway (Rt. 5) and railroad tracks.

The first known European to settle in the area was Johannes Van Eps, who established a home in 1720 along what is now Route 5. Seven generations of Van Epses subsequently lived in this homestead over the next 200 years. Only the old foundation of the house and a smattering of artifacts remain today.

During the years 1825 to 1845, John Van Eps and his sons operated the Van Eps Cement Plant southwest of the Wolf Hollow ravine. A roadside marker now marks the spot, which is close to the site of the old Algonquin village.[12] The plant was supposedly the first hydraulic cement mill in this part of New York State.

The area became known as Vedder's Ferry when Harmanus Vedder set up a ferry to take travelers across the Mohawk River in 1790. The name of the hamlet later changed to Hoffman's Ferry in 1835 when John Hoffman acquired the business. Eventually, the hamlet simply became known as Hoffmans.

In the twentieth century the ravine was often visited by Charles Steinmetz—an electrical wizard closely affiliated with the rising fortunes of General Electric—who had a camp close by on the Mohawk River.[13]

Postscript

There are a variety of ways of exploring the Adirondacks without being enclosed by the metallic exterior of a car, boat, or plane, or overwhelmed by the deafening sounds of a snowmobile, dirt bike, or ATV. You just have to look for them. In addition to hiking, there's snowshoeing, cross-country skiing, bike touring, mountain biking (in designated areas) horseback riding, rock climbing, canoeing and kayaking. You can even see parts of the eastern Adirondacks from the Champlain Canal and tour the Mohawk Valley via the Erie Canalway.

Hiking clubs like the Adirondack Mountain Club (www.adk.org) can help facilitate the process of enjoying the Adirondacks, and there are a number of privately run outdoor adventure businesses. For those who take pleasure in bicycling, for instance, and are interested in "biking through history," American Heritage Bicycle Tours (www.americanheritagebicycletours.com.), run by Kyle and Lynn Jenks, offers biking adventures into eastern New York State and western Vermont for all levels of ability—all within the context of French & Indian War and Revolutionary War history.

But whatever your passion may be, the important thing is that you act on it. The Adirondacks represent a smorgasbord of nearly unlimited possibilities for outdoor adventures waiting around every turn of every trail.

Happy *Trails with Tales* to you.

If you enjoyed *Adirondack Trails with Tales,* be sure to pick up its predecessor, *Trails with Tales* (Black Dome Press, 2007). In this photo Mike Canavan plans his next outing.

Adirondack Museums, Historical Sites, Interpretive Centers, and Other Historical Resources

Hikers wishing to learn more about the Adirondacks and regional history can visit the following museums and educational resources. Call ahead to verify days and times when they are open.

Museums

Adirondack History Center Museum: P.O. Box 428, Court Street, Elizabethtown, NY 12932. (518) 873-6466.

E-mail: echs@adkhistorycenter.org. Web site: www.adkhistorycenter.org. Hours: Mon–Sat, 9 AM–5 PM; Sunday, 1 PM–5 PM.
Admission fee. Gift shop.

Adirondack Museum: P.O. Box 99, Blue Mountain Lake, NY 12812. (518) 352-7311. E-mail: info@adirondackmuseum.org.
Web site: www.adkmuseum.org.
Hours: daily from May 22–Oct 18, 10 AM–5 PM; closed Sept 4 and Sept 16.
Admission fee. Gift shop.

Arkell Museum: 2 Erie Boulevard, Canajoharie, NY 13317. (518) 673-2314. E-mail: info@arkellmuseum.org.
Web site: www.arkellmuseum.org.
Hours: Mon–Fri, 10 AM–5 PM; Sat & Sun, 12:30 PM–5 PM; closed New Years, Easter Sunday, Thanksgiving, & Christmas.
Admission fee. Gift shop.

Bolton Historical Museum: 4924 Main Street, Bolton Landing, NY. Web site; www.boltonhistorical.org/museum/museum.html.
Hours: July 4–Labor Day, daily 9 AM–2 PM; 7 PM–9 PM; closed Sunday evenings; weekends only, 9 AM–2 PM, during the spring and fall.

Chapman Historical Museum: 348 Glen Street, Glens Falls, NY 12801. (518) 793-2826. E-mail: ContactUs@ChapmanMuseum.org.
Web site: www.chapmanmuseum.org.
Hours: daily except for major holidays, Tues–Sat, 10 AM–4 PM; Sunday, 12 PM–4 PM.
Free admission. Gift shop.

Clinton County Historical Museum: 98 Ohio Avenue, Plattsburgh, NY 12903. (518) 561-0340. E-mail: director@clintoncountyhistorical.org.
Web site: www.clintoncountyhistorical.org/museum.html.
Hours: Tuesday–Friday, 9:00 AM–2:00 PM, and by appointment; closed weekends and public holidays.
Admission fee. Book shop.

Crown Point State Historic Site Museum: 739 Bridge Road, Crown Point, NY 12928. (518) 597-4666 or (518) 597-3666.
Web site: www.nysparks.com/sites/info.asp?siteID = 8.

Hours: May–Oct, Wed–Mon, 9 AM–5 PM.
Admission fee.

Lake Champlain Maritime Museum: 4472 Basin Harbor Road, Vergennes, VT 05491. (802) 475-2022. E-mail: info@lcmm.org. Web site: www.lcmm.org.
Hours: late May–mid-Oct, daily, 10 AM–5 PM.
Admission fee. Ship's Store gift shop.

Lake George Historical Association Museum: Old Warren County Courthouse, corner of Canada & Amherst Streets (290 Canada Street), Lake George, NY 12845. (518) 668-5044. E-mail: lgha@verizon.net. Web site: www.lakegeorgehistorical.org.
Hours: Mid-May–June, Sat & Sun, 11 AM–4 PM; July & Aug,
Fri, Sat & Tues, 11 AM–4 PM, Wed & Thurs, 3 PM–8 PM;
Sept., Fri, Sat & Sun, 11 AM–4 PM; Oct 1–mid-Oct, Sat & Sun, 11 AM–4 PM.
Admission fee. Book store.

Lake Placid-North Elba Historical Society Museum: Station Street, Box 189, Lake Placid, NY 12946. (518) 523-1608. Web site: www.lakeplacidhistory.com.
Hours: June 1–Sept 30, Tues–Sun, 12 PM–4 PM.

Little Falls New York Historical Society Museum: 319 South Ann Street, Little Falls, NY 13365. (315) 823-0643 (museum), (315) 823-0643 (visitor center). E-mail: lfhistor@ntcnet.com. Web site: http://lfhistoricalsociety.org.
Hours: end of May–Oct, Tues–Fri, 1 PM–4 PM, Sat 10 AM–12 PM.
Free admission. Museum store.

New York State Museum: Cultural Education Center, Albany, New York 12230. (518) 474-5877. Web site: www.nysm.nysed.gov.
Hours: daily from 9:30 AM–5:00 PM; closed Thanksgiving, Christmas & New Years.
Free admission. Gift shop.

Penfield Museum: 703 Creek Rd., Historic Ironville, Crown Point, NY 12928. (518) 597-3804. E-mail: penfield@bluemoo.net. Web site: www.penfieldmuseum.org.
Hours: early June–mid-Oct, Thurs–Sun, 11 AM–4 PM.
Admission fee. Gift shop.

Six Nations Indian Museum: 1462 CR 60, Onchiota, NY 12989. (518) 891-2299. Web sites: www.tuscaroras.com/graydeer/pages/sixnamus.html; www.northcountryfolklore.org/rvsp/sixnations.html.
Hours: July–Labor Day, Tues–Sat, 10 AM–6 PM; May–June & Sept–Oct by appointment only.
Admission fee.

Skenesborough Museum: Skenesborough Drive (off Route 4), P.O. Box 238, Whitehall, NY 12887. (518) 499-1155. E-mail: cbgbird@yahoo.com. Web site: www.museumsusa.org/museums/info/1155278.
Hours: mid-May–Labor Day, Mon–Sat, 10 AM–4 PM & Sun 12 PM–4 PM; Labor Day–mid-Oct, weekends only—Sat, 10 AM–3 PM, Sun, 12 PM–3 PM; other times by appointment only.
Admission fee. Gift shop.

Ticonderoga Heritage Museum: 137 Montcalm St. Ticonderoga, NY 12883. (518) 585-2696. Web site: mysite.verizon.net/unclefvp/indexti.html.
Hours: Memorial Day–late June, weekends only; late June–Labor Day, daily, 10 AM–4 PM; early Sept–Columbus Day, weekends only.
Gift shop.

War of 1812 Museum: 31 Washington Road, Plattsburgh, NY 12903. (518) 566-1814. Web site: www.battleofplattsburgh.org.
Hours: Tuesday–Saturday, 9 AM–3 PM.
Gift shop.

Wild Center: Natural History Museum of the Adirondacks: 45 Museum Drive, Tupper Lake, NY 12986. (518) 359-7800.
Web site: www.wildcenter.org.
Hours: daily, Memorial Day–Oct 31, 10 AM–6 PM; November 1–Memorial Day, Fri, Sat & Sun, 10 AM–5 PM; closed Thanksgiving, Christmas and New Years.
Admission fee. Gift shop.

NYS Adirondack Park Visitor Interpretive Centers

Visitor Interpretive Center (VIC) at Newcomb: 5922 State Route 28N, P.O. Box 101, Newcomb, NY 12852. (518) 582-2067. Web site: www.adkvic.org.
Hours: summer—May 1–Oct 31, daily, 9 AM–5 PM;
Winter—Nov 1–April 30,
Tues–Sat, 9 AM–5 PM; closed Thanksgiving & Christmas.
Free admission.

Visitor Interpretive Center (VIC) at Paul Smiths: 8023 State Route 30, Paul Smiths, NY 12970. (518) 327-3000. Web site: www.adkvic.org./
Hours: summer—May 1–Oct 31, daily, 9 AM–5 PM;
Winter—Nov 1–April 30,
Tues–Sat, 9 AM–5 PM; closed Thanksgiving & Christmas.
Free admission.

Visitor Centers/Forts/Exhibits/Museum Shops

Barton Garnet Mines: P.O. Box 30, North River, NY 12856. (518) 251-2706. Web site: www.garnetminetours.com.
Hours: June–mid-Oct, Mon–Sat, 9:30 AM–5 PM, Sun, 11 AM–5 PM.
Admission fee.

Battle of Plattsburgh Interpretive Center & History Shoppe:
31 Washington Road, Plattsburgh, NY 12903. (518) 566-1814.
E-mail: manager@battleofplattsburgh.org.
Web site: www.battleofplattsburgh.org.
Hours: Tuesday–Saturday, 9 AM–3 PM year-round.

Fort Ticonderoga: P.O. Box 390, Ticonderoga, NY 12883. (518) 585-2821.
E-mail: fort@fort-ticonderoga.org. Web site: www.fort-ticonderoga.org.
Hours: late May–late Oct, daily 9:30 AM–5 PM.
Admission fee to tour fort; no charge to visit gift shop.

Fort William Henry Museum: Canada Street, Lake George, NY 12845.
(518) 668-5471. Web site: www.fwhmuseum.com.
Hours: early May–late Oct, daily, 9 AM–6 PM.
Admission fee. Museum store.

Garnet Hill Lodge & Gift Shop: Thirteenth Lake Road, North River,
NY 12856. (518) 251-2444. (800) 497-4207. www.garnet-hill.com.

Lake Champlain Visitor Center: West end of Crown Point Bridge/
Lake Champlain Bridge, Crown Point, NY 12928. (518) 597-4646.

Lake Champlain Visitor Center: 94 Montcalm Street, Suite 1,
Ticonderoga, NY 12883. (518) 585-6619.

Sagamore, Great Camp: Sagamore Road, P.O, Box 40, Raquette Lake,
NY 13436. (315) 354-5311. E-mail: info@greatcampsagamore.org.
Web site: www.greatcampsagamore.org/great-camp-sagamore.html.
Hours for guided tours & gift shop: Memorial Day–the third weekend in June,
1:30 PM on Saturday and Sunday only; daily in summer, third weekend in
June–Labor Day, 10 AM and 1:30 PM; daily in fall, the Monday after Labor
Day–Columbus Day, 1:30 PM.

Admission fee for guided tour. Members and persons holding Raquette Lake
and Long Lake licenses are admitted free. No fee charged for visiting gift shop.

Additional Resources:

Adirondack Architectural Heritage: 1790 Main St. Civic Center, Suite
37, Keeseville, NY 12944. (518) 834-9328. E-mail: info@aarch.org.
Web site: www.aarch.org/resources/bibliography/comm&preserves.html.

The Adirondack Architectural Heritage is a nonprofit, historic preservation organization that has been heavily involved with the restoration/preservation of the Great Camp Santanoni, as well as other historic sites.

Adirondack Land Trust: www.nature.org/wherewework/northamerica/states/newyork/preserves/art12096.html.

Adirondack Loj: www.adk.org/ad_loj/.

Great Camp Santanoni: www.newcombny.com/newsantanonigreatcamp.html.

High Peaks Information Center: (518) 523-3441.

Endnotes

Champlain Valley Region

Introduction

1. Phil Brown, *Longstreet Highroad Guide to the New York Adirondacks* (Marietta, GA: Longstreet Press Inc., 1999), 91.

2. Max Reid, *Lake George and Lake Champlain: The War Trail of the Mohawk and the Battleground of France and England in their Contest for the Control of North America* (NY: The Knickerbocker Press, 1910), 349.

3. www.reference.com/browse/thirteen + colonies

Valcour Island

1. Dennis Aprill, *Short Treks in the Adirondacks and Beyond* (Utica, NY: Nicholas K. Burns Publishing, 2005), 20. The author devotes a chapter to paddling over to Valcour Island and exploring the island by foot, 19–24.

2. Ibid., 20.

3. www.historiclakes.org/Valcour/valcour_island.htm.

4. Alexandra Roberts, "Valcour Island: This mystical mass of land stands majestically on Lake Champlain," *Adirondack Life* Vol. 15, no. 2 (March/April 1984), 62.

5. Anthony C. Tyrell, "Valcour Island—Past and Present," *The Conservationist* (September–October, 1982), 2.

6. Jack Downs, *Kayak and Canoe Paddles in the New York Champlain Valley: 15 narrated paddling daytrips with maps and photos* (n.p.: Trail Marker Books, 2004), 138–146.

7. Tyrell, op cit., 4. David C. Glenn, Gilliland family historian and genealogist, and author of soon-to-be published *The Battle of Valcour—Myths, Mysteries and Misconceptions Explored*. Information on Limbo Island obtained from *Vive Valcour* by M. H. Yager. Father Moore also named the narrow space between Spoon Island and Valcour Island as "Purgatory Pass."

8. Tyrell, op cit., 5. Glenn, op cit.

9. Ibid., David C. Glenn.

10. www.lighthousefriends.com/light.

11. On-site historical marker.

12. www.lighthousefriends.com/light.

13. www.historiclakes.org/valcour.

14. Tony Tyrell, NYS ranger for Valcour Island.

15. John Howland, ed., *Exploring Lake Champlain and Its Highlands* (Burlington, VT: The Lake Champlain Committee, 1981), 16. David C. Glenn, Gilliland family historian and genealogist.

16. William Sterne Randall, *Benedict Arnold, Patriot and Traitor* (NY: William Morrow and Co., 1990), 291.

17. Alexander Fleck, ed., *The American Revolution in New York State* (Albany, NY: NYS Department of Education, 1926), 149. David C. Glenn, Gilliland family historian and genealogist.

18. Randall, op cit., 278.

19. Ibid., 284.

20. Ibid., 277.

21. David C. Glenn, Gilliland family historian and genealogist.

22. Russell P. Bellico, *Chronicles of Lake Champlain, Journeys in War and Peace* (Fleischmanns, NY: Purple Mountain Press, 1999), 211.

23. http://en.wikipedia.org/wiki/Battle-of-Valcour-Island.

24. David C. Glenn, Gilliland family historian and genealogist.

25. Randall, op cit., 280.

26. David C. Glenn, Gilliland family historian and genealogist.

27. Ibid.

28. Ibid.

29. Ibid.

30. Ibid.

31. Bellico, op cit., 222.

32. Ibid., 223. David C. Glenn, Gilliland family historian and genealogist.

33. Randall, op cit., 308.

34. Ibid., 317.

35. Howland, op cit., 22.

36. *New York Time*s, September 12, 1874.

37. www.historiclakes.org/valcour.

38. Roberts, op cit., 46.

39. Thom Engel, "Valcour Island: A Preliminary Report," The Northeastern Caver Vol. 28, no. 4 (December 1997), 120.

Coon Mountain

1. www.boquetriver.org/newscoonmt.html.

2. David C. Glenn, Gilliland family historian and genealogist.

3. www.nature.org/wherewework/northamerica/states/newyorkpreserves/art11875.html.

4. Virginia Westbrook, *Relishing Our Resources along Lake Champlain in Essex County, New York* (Crown Point, NY: Champlain Valley Heritage Network, 2001). On page 9 can be seen hikers at the summit of Coon Mountain taking in the views.

5. Winslow C. Watson, *Pioneer History of the Champlain Valley, An Account of the Settlement of the Town of Willsborough by William Gilliland* (Albany, NY: J. Munsell Inc., 1863), 20.

6. David C. Glenn, Gilliland family historian and genealogist.

7. Russell Bellico, *Chronicles of Lake Champlain, Journeys in War and Peace* (Fleischmanns, NY: Purple Mountain Press, 1999), 171.

8. Walter Hill Crockett, *A History of Lake Champlain: the Record of Three Centuries, 1609–1909* (Burlington, VT: Hobart J. Shanty, 1909), 89.

9. William L. Wessels, *Adirondack Profiles* (Lake George, NY: Adirondack Resorts Press, Inc., 1961), 31. The first land grant in the Adirondacks was made to Sier Robart (a royal storekeeper in Montreal) in 1737. Although the land was surveyed, Robart never settled on it while it was in French hands, so it became up for grabs after the war.

10. Caroline Halstead Royce, *Bessboro: A History of Westport, Essex Co., N.Y.* (Elizabethtown, NY: n.p., 1904), 108. "He had encompassed a stretch of land as far and fertile as any in the world, rolling from the lake shore to the foot of the mountains, well watered, richly wooded, close under the protection of the fort at Crown Point, and if ever a beautiful prospect had power to touch

an Irish heart, how much his have swelled with joy as he measured those acres for himself."

11. Watson, op cit., preface.
12. Ibid., 25. David C. Glenn, Gilliland family historian and genealogist.
13. Watson, op cit., 33–35.
14. Royce, op cit., 108.
15. Bellico, op cit., 174.
16. Royce, op cit., 112.
17. David C. Glenn, Gilliland family historian and genealogist.
18. Bellico, op cit., 177.
19. William Chapman White, *Adirondack Country* (Syracuse, NY: Syracuse University Press, 1985), 59. Willard Sterne Randall, *Benedict Arnold, Patriot and Traitor* (NY: William Morrow and Company, Inc., 1990) p. 273.
20. Royce, op cit., 138–140.
21. Watson, op cit., 54.
22. Ibid., 54.
23. Ibid., 84.
24. Ibid., 85.
25. Bellico, op cit., 178.
26. Dennis Aprill, "Trail Mix. Low Peaks: Coon Mountain," *Adirondack Life 1998 Annual Guide* Vol. 29, no. 4, 13.
27. Adirondack Land Trust, *Coon Mountain Preserve* (brochure).
28. archiver.rootsweb.com.
29. www.boquetriver.org/newsforgecat.html.
30. Royce, op cit., 443.
31. www.boquetriver.org/newscoonmt.html.

Additional reading:

Scott Edward Anderson, *Walks in Nature's Empire: Exploring the Nature Conservancy's Preserves in New York State* (Woodstock, VT: The Countryman Press, 1995), 165–168.

Dennis Aprill, *Paths Less Traveled: The Adirondack experience for walkers, hikers, and climbers of all ages* (Mt. Kisco, NY: Pinto Press, 2000), 29–32.

Elizabeth Bassett, *Nature Walks in Northern Vermont and the Champlain Valley* (Boston, MA: Appalachian Mountain Club Books, 1998), 248–251.

Phil Brown, *Longstreet Highroad Guide to the New York Adirondacks* (Marietta, GA: Longstreet Press, Inc., 1999), 111.

Alfred L. Donaldson, *A History of the Adirondacks* Vol. I (1921, reprint, Mamaroneck, NY: Harbor Hill Books, 1977), 18–20.

Max Reid, *Lake George and Lake Champlain: The War Trail of the Mohawk and the Battleground of France and England in Their Contest for the Control of North America* (NY: The Knickerbocker Press, 1910). A brief account of Gilliland's life is given on pages 294–296, concluding with a poem: "Found dead. Dead and alone! / Nobody near with love to greet, / Nobody heard his last faint groan, / Alone with God! / Yes. God was near when this wanderer died."

Nick Sayward, "William Gilliland—Tory or Patriot?" *York State Tradition* Vol. 26, no. 1 (Winter 1972).

Crown Point: Fort St. Frederic & His Majesty's Fort of Crown Point

1. Barney Fowler, *Adirondack Album Vol. 2* (Schenectady, NY: Outdoor Associates, 1980). A model of Fort St. Frederic can be seen on page 91.

2. Carroll V. Lonergan, "Fort St. Frederic," *North Country Life* Vol. 12, no. 3 (Summer 1958), 44.

3. Max Reid, *Lake George and Lake Champlain: The War Trail of the Mohawk and the Battleground of France and England in Their Contest for the Control of North America* (NY: The Knickerbocker Press, 1910). Between pages 38 & 39 is a photograph of "The Ruins of Old Fort Amherst, Crown Point." Between pages 196 & 197 is a photo of "The Tottering Walls of Old Fort Amherst, Crown Point."

4. Opinion of Dr. Paul R. Huey, scientist (archaeology), Bureau of Historic Sites, New York State Office of Parks, Recreation, and Historic Preservation.

5. Chas. H. Possons, *Possons' Guide to Lake George, Lake Champlain, and Adirondacks,* 8th ed. (Glens Falls, NY: Chas. H. Possons, 1890), 134–135.

6. NYSDEC brochure on Champlain Memorial Lighthouse.

7. www.lakechamplainregion.com

8. David Starbuck, *The Great Warpath* (Hanover, NH: University Press of New England, 1999), 165.

9. Ibid., 165.

10. Ibid., 166.

11. Possons, op cit., 171.

12. University of Vermont Historic Preservation Program, "Around the Lake," pamphlet, 1996.

Additional reading:

"Crown Point State Historic Site: Walking Tour," brochure.

Tom Anderson, "Crown Point: To keep the past alive, historians labor to save two ruined forts," *Adirondack Life* Vol. 12, no. 3 (May June 1981).

Amy Godine, "The Path of History: Discovering the Champlain Valley's Freedom Trail," *Adirondack Life's 1991 Outdoor Guide* Vol. 22, no. 4.

Arthur S. Hopkins, "Old Fort St. Frederic—French Relic at Crown Point," *Conservationist* (August–September, 1962).

Carroll V. Lonergan, *North Country Life* Vol. 12, no. 3 (Summer 1958), 43–44. In this short article on Fort St. Frederic, Lonergan expressed hope that New York State could be induced to *restore* the fort ruins. Such a response never occurred, to be sure, and today would be considered a moot issue.

Charles Albert Sleicher, *The Adirondacks: An American Playground* (New York: Exposition Press, 1960), 197–201.

Gilbert Tauber, *The Hudson River Tourway: Eleven Scenic Tours by Car of the Historic Hudson River Valley from Westchester to the Adirondacks* (Garden City, NY: Dolphin Books, 1977), 170–171.

Fort Ticonderoga

1. Anonymous, "Fort Ticonderoga—key to a continent," *North Country Life* Vol. 9, no. 3 (Summer 1955), 45.

2. Nicholas Westbrook, director, Ticonderoga.

3. Edward P. Hamilton, *Fort Ticonderoga, Key to a Continent* (Boston: Little Brown and Co., 1964), 36.

4. www.fort-ticonderoga.org.

5. Hamilton, op cit., 51.

6. Ibid., 75.

7. Fred T. Stiles, "1755–59 in the Champlain Valley: Abercrombie at Ticonderoga," *North County Life and York State Tradition* Vol. 16, no. 1 (Winter 1962), 35–37. Stiles gives an account of what happened to Abercromby's forces, who were routed after losing 1,610 men out of 6,000 regulars (including 590 out of 1,000 Black Watch) and 357 provincials. Despite these losses, Abercromby still fielded a massive force of 13,000 soldiers who, with perseverance, undoubtedly could have taken the fort.

8. Hamilton, op cit., 78–81. Dr. Russell Bellico, "The Abercromby Expedition," *Adirondack Life* Vol. 14, no. 4 (July/Aug. 1983). On pages 10–15 the story of how Abercromby snatched defeat from the jaws of victory is recounted.

9. Westbrook, op cit.

10. Hamilton, op cit., 89.

11. David Starbuck, *The Great Warpath,* (Hanover, NH: University Press of New England, 1999), 164.

12. Hamilton, op cit., 102.

13. Ibid., 103.

14. Ethan Allen, *Ethan Allen's Narrative of the Capture of Ticonderoga and of his Captivity and Treatment by the British*, 5th ed. (Burlington, VT: C. Goodrich & S. B. Nichols, 1849). Contains Ethan Allen's own account of how he prevailed at Fort Ticonderoga.

15. Hamilton, op cit., 174.

16. www.fort-ticonderoga.org.

17. Erica Henkel-Karras, *Postcard History Series: Lake George, 1900–1925* (Charleston, SC: Arcadia Publishing, 2005), 97. Postcard shows the ruins at Fort Ticonderoga. Gale J. Halm & Mary H. Sharp, *Images of America: Lake George* (Charleston, SC: Arcadia Publishing, 2000). Photos of the ruins of Fort Ticonderoga are shown on pages 17 & 98. The photograph on page 17 is unusual in that it was taken at the 1875 centennial celebration of the fort's capture by Ethan Allen and his Green Mountain Boys, and the ruins are swarming with people.

18. Westbrook, op cit.

19. Hamilton, op cit., 229–230.

20. Westbrook, op cit.

21. Ticonderoga Historical Society.

22. Anonymous, op cit., 35–36.

23. Hamilton, op cit., 193.

24. Chas. H. Possons, *Possons' Guide to Lake George, Lake Champlain, and Adirondacks*, 8th ed. (Glens Falls, NY: Chas. H. Possons, 1890), 100.

25. Anonymous, op cit., 33.

26. "A Brief History of the Gardens at Fort Ticonderoga," brochure.

Additional reading:

Jane M. Lape, ed., *Ticonderoga: Patches and Patterns from its Past* Vol. I (Ticonderoga, NY: The Ticonderoga Historical Society, 1969), 48.

John Howland, ed., *Exploring Lake Champlain and Its Highlands* (Burlington, VT: The Lake Champlain Committee, 1981). A brief account of the French and Indian War, and the role that Fort Carillon played is described on pages 18–20.

Richard Figiel, "The Second Building of Fort Ticonderoga," *Adirondack Life* Vol. 9, no. 3 (May/June 1978), 12–47.

Edward P. Hamilton, *Fort Ticonderoga: Key to a Continent* (Ticonderoga, NY: Fort Ticonderoga, 1964), 193 & 194.

Robert C. Haas, "But now, please God they must go," *Adirondack Life* Vol. 6, no. 1 (Winter 1975). On pages 57–60 the author recounts Henry Knox's incredible feat of transporting the artillery of Fort Ticonderoga overland to Boston in the middle of winter.

Robert Louis Stevenson, *Ticonderoga: A Legend of the West Highlands* (1887, reprint, Ticonderoga, NY: Fort Ticonderoga Museum, 1947).

Anonymous, "Mt. Defiance," *North Country Life* Vol. 12, no. 2 (Spring 1958), 33–38.

Ironville & Penfield Homestead

1. Tom Henry, "Put Put Fun: He came, he fought, they named things after him," *Adirondack Life* Vol. 38, no. 8 (November/December 2007), 20.

2. Ibid., 20.

3. "The Penfield Homestead Museum," brochure.

4. Patrick Farrell, *Through the Light Hole* (Utica, NY: North Country Books, Inc., 1996), 43.

5. Connie Pope, "Hammondville Essex County Ghost Town," *York State Tradition* Vol. 25, no. 1 (Winter 1971), 34.

6. www.adkhistorycenter.org.

7. Crown Point home page, www.penfieldmuseum.org.

Additional reading:

Barbara McMartin, "Ironville," *Adirondack Life* Vol. 13, no. 4 (July/August 1982), 24–25 & 48–49.

Rock Pond

1. Barbara McMartin, *Guide to the Eastern Adirondacks* (Glens Falls, NY: Adirondack Mountain Club, 1981), 151.

2. Patrick Farrell, *Through the Light Hole* (Utica NY: North Country Press, 1996), 2.

3. Ibid., 5.

4. Lois Moody Gunning, *Up on Chilson Hill: A Story of an Adirondack Hamlet, its times and people* (Burlington, VT: Queen City Printers, 1999), 166.

5. McMartin, op cit., 151.

6. Gunning, op cit., 167.

7. Ibid., 169 & 170.

8. Farrell, op cit., 6.

9. Essex County Historical Society, www.adkhistorycenter.org.

Additional reading:

Bill Ingersoll, "Rock Pond: A Rewarding Short Hike," *Adirondack Sports & Fitness* (May 2007), 15.

Endnotes

Barbara McMartin, Bill Ingersoll, Edythe Robbins & Chuck Bennett, *Discover the Eastern Adirondacks: Guide to the Trails of Lake George & the Pharaoh Lake Wilderness*, 3rd ed. (Barneveld, NY: Wild River Press, 2006), 163–170.

Lake George/Eastern Adirondacks Region

Rogers Rock

1. Chas. H. Possons, *Possons' Guide to Lake George, Lake Champlain, and Adirondacks*, 8th ed. (Glens Falls, NY: Chas. H. Possons, 1890), 94. Max Reid, *Lake George and Lake Champlain: The War Trail of the Mohawk and the Battleground of France and England in Their Contest for the Control of North America* (NY: The Knickerbocker Press, 1910). A photograph of Rogers Rock is shown between pages 66 and 67. On page 179 Reid writes: "Bald Mountain or Rogers's [sic] Rock on the west shore rears its ponderous bulk of granite to an almost perpendicular height of eleven hundred feet, being matched by a similar bulk and height on the east a half-mile away." Later, on page 336, Reid states, "Rogers Rock, which rises from the water's edge at an angle of 45 degrees ... reaches an elevation of three hundred feet."

2. www.dec.ny.gov/outdoors.

3. Thomas Reeves Lord, *More Stories of Lake George: Fact and Fancy* (Pemberton, NJ: Pinelands Press, 1994), 183.

3. Bob Bearor, *The Battle on Snowshoes* (Westminster, MD: Heritage Books, Inc., 1997), 30.

4. Ibid., 30.

5. Ibid., 31.

6. Ibid., 12.

7. Ibid., 62.

8. Ibid., 69.

9. David Starbuck, *The Great Warpath* (Hanover, NH: University Press of New England, 1999), 14.

Additional reading:

Howard Coffin, Will Curtis and Jane Curtis, *Guns Over the Champlain Valley* (Woodstock, VT: The Countryman Press, 2005), 238.

Millard C. Davis, "Up, Up the Storied Mountain: Even the near and familiar can become a new experience for the perceptive hiker," *Adirondack Life* Vol. 9, no. 4 (July/August, 1978), 24–28.

Barbara McMartin, Bill Ingersoll, Edythe Robbins & Chuck Bennett, *Discover the Eastern Adirondacks: Guide to the Trails of Lake George & the Pharaoh Lake Wilderness*, 3rd ed. (Barneveld, NY: Wild River Press, 2006), 113–115.

David R. Starbuck, *Rangers and Redcoats on the Hudson: Exploring the past on Rogers Island, the birthplace of the U.S. Army Rangers* (Lebanon, NH: University Press of New England, 2004). For those interested in learning more about Rogers and his rangers, this book provides much historical and archaeological data of findings on Rogers Island.

Fred T. Stiles, "Tales of Rogers and his Rangers," *North Country Life and New York State Tradition* Vol. 13, no 4 (Fall 1959), 25–28. Although Rogers was considered ruthless and cruel, one has to remember that he lived and fought in desperate times. Rogers never asked for mercy, and he never expected to give any in return, either.

Shelving Rock Mountain & Shelving Rock Falls

1. Barbara McMartin, Bill Ingersoll, Edythe Robbins, Chuck Bennett, *Discover the Eastern Adirondacks: Guide to the Trails of Lake George & the Pharaoh Lake Wilderness*, 3rd ed. (Barneveld, NY: Wild River Press, 2006), 44–46. Carl Heilman II, *Guide to Adirondack Trails 6, Eastern Region*, 2nd ed. (Lake George, New York: Adirondack Mountain Club, 1994), 175–181. David Thomas-Train, ed., with Neal S. Burdick, series editor, *Adirondack Trails: Eastern Region. Forest Preserve Series*, 3rd ed. (Lake George, NY: Adirondack Mountain Club, Inc., 2008), 163–164.

2. McMartin, op cit. A picture of Shelving Rock Falls can be seen on page 43. Frank Leonbruno, *Lake George Reflections: Island History and Lore* (Fleischmanns, NY: Purple Mountain Press, 1998), 145–151.

3. Stuart D. Ludlum, ed., *Exploring Lake George, Lake Champlain 100 Years Ago* (Utica, NY: Brodock & Ludlum Publications, 1972). A line drawing of Shelving Rock Falls is presented on page 27

4. Charles E. Vandrei, "The Lake George Battlefield Park: Looking to the future through the past," *Conservationist* Vol. 55, no. 4 (February, 2001), 26.

5. Fred T. Stiles, "Recollections of the Knapp Estate, Part II," *North Country Life and New York State Tradition* Vol. 15, no.1 (Winter 1961), 41.

6. Leonbruno, op cit. A picture of the gazebo on the summit is shown on page 149.

7. Ibid., 148.

8. Washington County Planning Department, *Introduction to Hudson Resources in Washington County, New York* (Washington County, NY: n. p., 1976), 45. "Mr. Knapp was unique in the fact that when he bought property, the former owner was allowed to stay on the property and work for Mr. Knapp and any produce in excess of that needed for his family was sold to the Knapps. He also paid wages much in excess of the average wage of those days." Leonbruno, op cit., 145–151.

9. William Preston Gates, *Turn-of-the-Century Scrapbook of Jonathan Streeter Gates* (Glens Falls & Bolton, NY: Gates Publishing Company, 1999), 7.

10. Russell Bellico, *Chronicles of Lake George: Journeys in War and Peace* (Fleischmanns, NY: Purple Mountain Press, 1995). Mention is made on page 38 that Knapp's summer home was destroyed in 1917 by an electrical fire started in the basement. Washington County Planning Department, op cit., 56. "The remains of the stone foundation of the mansion, which burned down in 1918, still are visible and the remains of the rose garden are still to be seen among the trees and undergrowth."

11. Fred T. Stiles, "Recollections of the Knapp Estate, Part I," *North Country Life and New York State Traditions* Vol. 14, no. 4 (Fall 1960), 30–31.

12. Betty Ahearn Buckell, *Old Lake George Hotels* (n. p.: Buckle Press, 1986). A picture of the Hundred Island House can be seen on page 79. Gates, op cit., 30. A picture of the Hundred Island Hotel is shown.

13. Ibid., 35.

14. Ibid., 11.

15. Buckell, op cit. Pictures of the Pearl Point House can be seen on pages 80 & 81. Russell Bellico, op cit., 387. The author includes an 1889 map of S. R. Stoddard's that shows the location of the Pearl Point House and Hundred Island House. At the time, the Pearl Point House stood on an extension of land that projected out from the east shore into the narrows.

16. Carl Heilman II, *Guide to Adirondack Trails 6, Eastern Region*, 2nd ed. (Lake George, NY: Adirondack Mountain Club, 1994), 176.

Prospect Mountain

1. David Cross & Joan Potter, *Adirondack Firsts* (Elizabethtown, NY: Pinto Press, 1992), 176.

2. Russell P. Bellico. *Chronicles of Lake George: Journeys in War and Peace* (Fleischmanns, NY: Purple Mountain Press, 1995), 289.

3. Betty Ahearn Buckell, *Old Lake George Hotels* (n. p.: Buckle Press, 1986), 28.

4. www.catskillarchive.com/rrextra/lginclin.html.

5. Erica Henkel-Karras, *Postcard History Series: Lake George, 1900–1925* (Charleston, SC: Arcadia Publishing, 2005), 27. A postcard view from the top of Prospect Mountain is provided.

6. Max Reid, *Lake George and Lake Champlain: The War Trail of the Mohawk and the Battleground of France and England in Their Contest for the Control of North America* (NY: The Knickerbocker Press, 1910), 320. "It is true, that from this precipice we look down upon a wild peak a thousand feet below that has a fearsome name, 'Rattlesnake Cobble.'"

7. Henkel-Karras, op cit., 97.

8. www.nelsap.org/ny/prospectmtn.html.

9. Roy Dean Myers, "When the Bullwheel Turned ... and the mightiest cable railroad of them all climbed Prospect Mountain," *Adirondack Life* Vol. 4, no 2 (Spring 1973), 21.

10. Bellico, op cit., 331.

11. Seneca Ray Stoddard, *Lake George: (Illustrated) A Book of To-day* (Glens Falls, NY: S.R. Stoddard, 1887), 43.

12. Buckell, op cit., 28.

13. www.catskillarchive.com/rrextra/lginclin.html.

14. Meyers, op cit., 21.

15. Buckell, op cit., 28. Martin Podskoch, *Adirondack Fire Towers: Their History and Lore* (Fleischmanns, NY: Purple Mountain Press, 2003), 171.

16. www.lakegeorgehistorical.org/prospect_mt_house.htm.

17. Meyers, op cit., 21.

18. Cross, op cit., 176. Thomas Reeves Lord, *More Stories of Lake George: Fact and Fancy* (Pemberton, NJ: Pinelands Press, 1994), 29.

19. Gale J. Halm & Mary H. Sharp, *Images of America: Lake George* (Charleston, SC: Arcadia Publishing, 2000), 99. An atypical picture of the cable car, looking at it head-on, is shown.

20. Historic marker at top of mountain.

21. www.catskillarchive.com/rrextra/lginclin.html.

22. Buckell, op cit., 28.

23. www.lakegeorgehistorical.org/prospect_mt_house.htm.

Additional reading:

Thomas Reeves Lord, *More Stories of Lake George: Fact and Fancy* (Pemberton, NJ: Pinelands Press, 1994), 29.

Barney Fowler, *Adirondack Album* Vol. 3 (Schenectady, NY: Outdoor Associates, 1982). A photograph of the cable car line can be seen on page 189.

David Thomas-Train, ed., with Neal S. Burdick, series editor, *Adirondack Trails: Eastern Region, Forest Preserve Series*, 3rd ed. (Lake George, NY: Adirondack Mountain Club, Inc., 2008), 136–137.

Barbara McMartin, Bill Ingersoll, Edythe Robbins & Chuck Bennett, *Discover the Eastern Adirondacks: Guide to the Trails of Lake George & the Pharaoh Lake Wilderness*, 3rd ed. (Barneveld, NY: Wild River Press, 2006), 67–68.

Fort George & Bloody Pond

1. Robert B. Roberts, *New York's Forts in the Revolution* (Cranbury, NJ: Associated University Press, 1980), 209. Max Reid, *Lake George and Lake Champlain: The War Trail of the Mohawk and the Battleground of France and England in Their Contest for the Control of North America* (NY: The Knickerbocker Press, 1910). The frontispiece contains an early photograph of the ruins at Fort George. Thomas Reeves Lord, *More Stories of Lake George: Fact and Fancy* (Pemberton, NJ: Pinelands Press, 1994). On page 30 can be seen a photograph of the ruins circa 1850.

2. Thomas Reeves Lord, op cit. On page 16 is a photograph of Bloody Pond covered with lily pads and pond lilies. Reid, op cit. Between pages 156 and 157 is an early photograph of Bloody Pond.

3. Reid, op cit., 317. Donald Fangboner, "Saving the Past," *Lake George ... Ours to Preserve: Centennial Celebration Handbook* (Lake George, NY: The Lake George Association, 1985). On page 38 is a plan of Fort George, taken from notes on the history of Fort George by B. F. Decosta.

4. Seneca Ray Stoddard, *Lake George: (Illustrated) A Book of To-day* (Glens Falls, NY: S.R. Stoddard, 1887), 30.

5. Gale J. Halm & Mary H. Sharp, *Images of America: Lake George* (Charleston, SC: Arcadia Publishing, 2000), 12. A photograph of the E. Williams Monument, erected by the alumni of Williams College in 1854, is shown.

6. David R. Starbuck, *The Great Warpath* (Hanover, NH: University Press of New England, 1999), 111–114.

7. William L. Wessels, *Adirondack Profiles* (Lake George, NY: Adirondack Resorts Press, Inc., 1961), 26. "He [Williams] at once spread his men on a hill and he took a position on a rock which now stands as the monument of his memory." It seems questionable that Williams, knowledgeable about warfare, would expose himself on the rock so openly. Williams was killed by a musket shot; King Hendrick was bayoneted. Chas. H. Possons, *Possons' Guide to Lake George, Lake Champlain, and Adirondacks*, 8th ed. (Glens Falls, NY: Chas. H. Possons, 1890), 32. King Hendrick, because of age and infirmities, was on horseback when he was mortally wounded. Lord, op cit. An illustration of Williams perched on the boulder, sword in right hand, left hand clutching his

chest, having just been shot, and knees buckling, can be seen on page 9.

8. Stoddard, op cit., 56.

9. Possons, op cit., 40.

10. Roberts, op cit., 209.

11. B. F. DeCosta, *Notes on the History of Fort George during the Colonial and Revolutionary Periods, with contemporaneous Documents and an appendix* (New York: J. Sabin and Sons, 1871), 22.

12. Wallace E. Lamb, *Lake George: Fact and Anecdotes*, 2nd ed. (Bolton Landing, NY: n.p., 1938). A photo of the fort ruins is displayed on page 39. Lord, op cit., 30. A photograph of the ruins can be seen on page 15.

13. Historical marker.

Additional reading:

Russell P. Bellico, *Chronicles of Lake George: Journeys in War and Peace* (Fleischmanns, NY: Purple Mountain Press, 1995). The 1878 journal of Francis Parkman states that "the ruins of Fort George [are] chiefly stone laid in mortar. The work is small, but the walls are of very considerable height & thickness."

Verne Steele, "Ephraim Williams—Upstate Character of Earlier Times," *North Country Life* Vol. 9, no. 2 (Spring 1955), 41. Before the fatal encounter with the French, King Hendrick declared, "If we are to fight, we are too few— if we are to be killed, we are too many."

Charles E. Vandrei, "The Lake George Battlefield Park: Looking to the future through the past," *New York State Conservationist* Vol. 55, no. 4 (February 2001), 26–28.

Cooper's Cave & Betar Byway

1. Historic marker.

2. Chas. H. Possons, *Possons' Guide to Lake George, Lake Champlain, and Adirondacks*, 8th ed. (Glens Falls, NY: Chas. H. Possons, 1890), 49. Max Reid, *Lake George and Lake Champlain: The War Trail of the Mohawk and the Battleground of France and England in Their Contest for the Control of North America* (NY: The Knickerbocker Press, 1910). A photograph of Cooper's Cave can be seen between pages 98 and 99. Gwen Palmer, Bob Bayle, & Stan Malecki, *Images of America: Glens Falls* (Charleston, SC: Arcadia Publishing, 2004). Photographs of the cave can be seen on pages 14 & 15. The circa 1890 photograph on page 14 is particularly intriguing, for it looks out from the cave at a group of young people and adult women, several of whom are sitting on logs deposited from the last spring freshet.

3. Louis Fiske Hyde, *History of Glens Falls New York, and Its Settlement* (Glens Falls, NY: n. p., 1936), 45.

4. Seneca Ray Stoddard, *Lake George: (Illustrated) A Book of To-day* (Glens Falls, NY: S.R. Stoddard, 1887), 14–15.

5. Anonymous, *Glens Falls: The "Empire City"* (Glens Falls, NY: Glens Falls Publishing Co., 1908), 3.

6. Palmer, op cit., 20. A picture of the bridge and spiral staircase can be seen.

7. Anonymous, op cit., 4. "The river at this spot has a descent of about sixty feet with numerous falls and rapids. Black fossilferous lime stone forms

the bed and sides of the river. In the progress of the ages, a cave has been worn out of the lime stone formation."

8. Palmer, op cit., 15. "It is actually not a cave, but rather an eroded passageway in the limestone rock."

9. Clay Perry, *Underground Empire: Wonders and Tales of New York's Caves* (New York: Stephen Daye Press, 1948), 190.

10. Hyde, op cit., 44.

Additional reading:

Patricia Edwards Clyne, *Caves for Kids in Historic New York* (Monroe, NY: Library Research Associates, 1980), 101.

Russell Dunn, "Cooper's Cave," *Northeastern Caver* Vol. 23, no. 3 (September, 1992), 95–97. An unsuccessful kayak trek up the Hudson River to Cooper's Cave is described.

Claire K. Schmitt & Judith S. Wolk, *Natural Areas of Saratoga County New York* (Niskayuna, NY: The Environmental Clearinghouse of Schenectady, 1998), 69. Mention is made of the South Glens Falls Historical Trail (the Betar Byway).

High Peaks Region

John Brown's Farm

1. To eliminate any possible confusion, bear in mind that there was another famous John Brown who is associated with the history of Old Forge and whose family founded Brown University. The two Browns are related only in name.

2. Paul Schneider, *The Adirondacks, A History of America's First Wilderness* (New York: Henry Holt and Company, 1997), 110.

3. William Chapman White, *Adirondack Country* (Syracuse, NY: Syracuse University Press, 1985), 195. White's book contains a brief chapter on John Brown, pages 194–200. In White's book, Timbuktu is spelled Timbuctoo. White states that white settlers who resented the blacks came up with this name.

4. David Reynolds, *John Brown Abolitionist* (New York: Vintage Books, 2005), 89.

5. Ibid., 91.

6. Ibid., 144.

7. Ibid., 328.

8. Ibid., 40.

9. Richard Henry Dana, "How We Met John Brown," *Atlantic Monthly* 28 (July 1871), 7. Cornell University Making of America, http//cdl.library.cornell.edu.

10. Ibid., 7, 8.

11. Mary Mackenzie, *The Plains of Abraham* (Utica, NY: Nicholas K. Burns Press, 2007), 122–125.

12. Ibid., 132.

13. Ibid., 133.

14. Reynolds, op cit., 238.

15. Rebecca Schwarz-Kopf, *The Underground Railroad in the North*

Country and early accounts of African-American life, abolitionists, and newspapers in Northern New York and Vermont (Plattsburgh, NY: Studley Printing and Publishing, 2001), 18.

16. Ibid., 18.

17. Karen Whitman, *West Virginia History* Vol. 34, no. 1, www.wvculture. org/history.

18. Reynolds, op cit., 400.

19. Ibid., 32.

20. Edwin N. Cotter Jr., "John Brown in the Adirondacks," *Adirondack Life* Vol. 3, no. 3 (Summer 1972). On page 11 is a sketch by Thomas Nast of the burial of John Brown at Lake Placid that appeared in the December 24, 1859, issue of the *New York Illustrated News*.

Additional reading:

Robert Gordon, "A Mournful Trip," *Adirondack Life* Vol. XV, no. 1. On pages 16–18 & 29–32 the author recounts the journey of John Brown's body back to his Adirondack home.

Mt. Jo & Mt. Van Hoevenberg

1. Fred LeBrun, "The High Peaks United Management Plan Today: What's Working, What's Not, and Where Do We Go from Here?" *Adirondac* Vol. 72, no.1, 17.

2. A breathtaking panoramic photograph of the MacIntyre Range as seen from the summit of Mt. Van Hoevenberg is on permanent exhibit at the New York State Museum in Albany.

3. Sandra Weber, *The Finest Square Mile* (Fleischmanns, NY: Purple Mountain Press, 1998), 31–32.

4. Ibid., 61.

5. William L. Wessels, *Adirondack Profiles* (Lake George, NY: Adirondack Resorts Press, Inc., 1961), 161.

6. Ibid., 162.

7. Weber, op cit., 102.

Adirondac & Indian Pass

1. Lee Manchester, ed., *Tales from a Deserted Village: First-hand accounts of early exploration into the heart of the Adirondacks* (Essex County, NY: n. p., 2007), foreword.

2. Philip G. Terrie, *Contested Terrain: A New History of Nature and People in the Adirondacks* (Syracuse, NY: The Adirondack Museum/Syracuse University Press, 1997), 6.

3. E. R. Wallace, *Descriptive Guide to the Adirondacks (land of the thousand lakes): and to Saratoga Springs, Schroon Lake, lakes Luzerne, George, and Champlain, the Ausable Chasm, the Thousand Islands, Massena Springs, and Trenton Falls*, 12th ed. (Syracuse, NY: Watson Gill, Bible Pub. House, 1887), 344–350.

4. Terrie, op cit., 34.

5. Manchester, op cit., 135.

6. Terrie, op cit., 34.

7. William Chapman White, *Adirondack Country* (Syracuse, NY: Syracuse

University Press, 1985), 234.

8. Manchester, op cit., 407.

9. Open Space Institute Web site, www.osiny.org.

10. Manchester, op cit., 407.

11. Alfred L. Donaldson, *A History of the Adirondacks* Vol. 1 (1921, reprint, Mamaroneck, NY: Harbor Hill Books, 1977), 164.

12. Ibid., 166.

13. Clay Perry, *Underground Empire: Wonders and Tales of New York Caves* (New York: Stephen Daye Press, 1948), 161.

14. Bradford B. Van Diver, *Upstate New York: Field Guide* (Dubuque, IO: Kendall/Hunt Publishing Company, 1980), 32.

15. C. R. Roseberry, *From Niagara to Montauk: The scenic pleasures of New York State* (Albany, NY: State University of New York Press, 1982), 150.

16. Charles Fenno Hoffman.

17. Perry, op cit., 161. Perry quotes A. T. Shorey.

Additional reading:

Open Space Institute Web site, www.osiny.org.

Jim Bailey, "Through Indian Pass, With Backward Glances," *Adirondac* Vol. 54, no. 9 (October/November, 1989), 19–21.

Lincoln Barnett & editors of Time-Life Books, *The Ancient Adirondacks* (New York: Time Inc., 1974). The book contains a chapter on Indian Pass (called "The Great Pass"), 152–165.

Alfred Billings Street, *The Indian Pass: Source of the Hudson* (1869, reprint, Fleischmanns, NY: Purple Mountain Press, 1993).

Phil Brown, "High Peaks gateway to be saved: Tahawus Tract topped conservationists' wish list," *Adirondack Explorer* Vol. 5, no. 6 (July/Aug 2003), 5 & 43.

James R. Burnside, *Exploring the 46 Adirondack High Peaks* (Schenectady, NY: High Peaks Press, 1996), 427–430. A hike through Indian Pass from the north is described.

Robert W. Carroll Jr., "40,000 Square Mile Talus Legacy," *The Northeastern Caver* Vol. 21, no. 4 (December, 1990), 106. Carroll lists TSOD (talus cave) at 13,050 feet in length.

Warder H. Cadbury, "The Early Artists of Indian Pass, Part I," *Adirondac* Vol. 54, no. 9 (October/November, 1989), 22–24.

David Cross & Joan Potter, *The Book of Adirondack Firsts* (Elizabethtown, NY: Pinto Press, 1992), 35. The authors point out that an early sketch of Indian Pass became the basis for an 1837 painting called *The Great Adirondack Pass*—the first oil painting done of the Adirondacks. The painting can be seen at the Adirondack Museum at Blue Mountain Lake.

Henry Dornburgh, *Why the Wilderness is Called Adirondack: the Earliest Account of the Founding of the MacIntyre Mine* (Harrison, NY: Harbor Hill Books, 1980). In addition to the text, there is a line drawing of "Adirondack Village" (Adirondac) on page 19, Indian Pass on page 21, Henderson's Lake on page 25, and of Henderson's Monument on page 32.

Tony Goodwin, ed., & Neal Burdick, series editor, *Adirondack Trails: High Peak Region*, 13th ed. (Lake George, NY: Adirondack Mountain Club, Inc., 2004).

Joe Jillisky, "The Great Passes of the Adirondacks," *Adirondac* Vol. 54, no. 5 (June 1990), 14–17.

Barbara McMartin, *50 Hikes in the Adirondacks: Short Walks, Day Trips, and Backpacks throughout the Park*, 4th ed. (Woodstock, VT: Backcountry, 2003), 239–246.

Barbara McMartin, with Lee Brenning, Phil Gallos, Don Greene, E. H. Ketchledge, Gary Koch, and Willard Reed, *Discover the Adirondack High Peaks* (Utica, NY: North Country Publications, 1989).

Dorothy Taylor, "Noah LaCasse Presidential Hiking Mate," *Adirondack Life* Vol. 3, no. 2 (Spring 1972), 9–11. The author recounts the story of when LaCasse helped Teddy Roosevelt make his historic ride to Buffalo to assume the presidency.

Kenneth Wilson, "The Deserted Village," *Adirondack Life* Vol. 7, no. 4 (Fall 1976), 9–11, 59. On page 9 is a picture of the village in 1976, still looking fairly intact.

East Branch of the Ausable River & Adirondack Mountain Reserve

1. Richard Plunz, ed., *Two Adirondack Hamlets in History, Keene and Keene Valley* (Fleischmanns, NY: Purple Mountain Press, 2000), 69.

2. Edith Pilcher, *Up the Lake Road* (Keene Valley, NY: Centennial Committee for the Trustees of The Adirondack Reserve, 1987), 19.

3. William Schneider, *The Adirondacks, History of America's First Wilderness* (NY: Henry Holt & Co., 1997), 159.

4. Pilcher, op cit., 8.

5. Ibid., 15.

6. Plunz, op cit., 165.

7. Ibid., 122.

8. Ibid., 117.

9. Schneider, op cit., 273.

10. Plunz, op cit., 122.

11. Pilcher, op cit., 28.

12. Schneider, op cit., 273.

Great Camps

Santanoni

1. David A. Steinberg, *Hiking the Road to Ruins: Day Trips and Camping Adventures to Iron Mines, Old Military Sites, and Things Abandoned in the New York City Area…and Beyond* (New Brunswick, NJ: Rivergate Books, 2007), 94.

2. Ibid., 95.

3. Howard Kirschenbaum, ed., Susan Schafstall, and Janine Stuchin, *The Adirondack Guide: an almanac of essential information and assorted trivia* (Raquette Lake, NY: Sagamore Institute, 1983), 62.

4. Kirschenbaum, op cit., 53.

5. www.aarch.org.

6. Ibid.

7. www.newcombny.com/santanoni.htm.

8. Elizabeth Folwell, *The Adirondack Book, A Complete Guide* (Stockbridge,

MA: Berkshire House Publishers, 1992), 156.

9. Lana Fennessey, *The History of Newcomb* (Newcomb, NY: n. p., 1996), 100.

10. www.newcombny.com/santanoni.htm.

Additional reading:

Dennis Conroy, with Shirly Matzke, *Adirondack Cross-Country Skiing: A guide to seventy trails* (Woodstock, VT: Backcountry Publications, 1992). On pages 89–92 the authors describe a cross-country ski trip in to Santanoni.

Alan Darling, "Santanoni," *Adirondack Life* Vol. 12, no. 5 (September/October, 1981), 10–13 & 40.

Robert Engel & Howard Kirschenbaum, "A Great Camp Memoir: The Santanoni spring-party scrapbooks," *Adirondack Life* Vol. 24, no. 3 (May/June, 1993), 46–49.

Bill Ingersoll, "Exploring Camp Santanoni," *Adirondack Sports & Fitness*, January 2008, 13. Ingersoll's article focuses on skiing/snowshoeing in to Camp Santanoni.

Peter Kick, *25 Mountain Bike Tours in the Adirondacks* (Woodstock, VT: Backcountry Publications, 1999), 157–161. The article focuses on biking in to the great camp.

Howard Kirschenbaum, "To Save Santanoni," *Adirondack Life* Vol. 17, no. 1 (January/February, 1986), 53–54.

Paul Malo, "Nippon in the North Country: Japanese inspiration in form and philosophy," *Adirondack Life 1998 Collectors Issue* Vol. 29, no. 7. The Japanese influence on Santanoni is discussed on pages 53 & 54.

Barbara McMartin, *50 Hikes in the Adirondacks: Short Walks, Day Trips, and Backpacks throughout the Park*, 4th ed. (Woodstock, VT: Backcountry, 2003), 221–223.

Laurence T. Cagle, ed., and Neal Burdick, senior editor, *Adirondack Trails Central Region, Forest Preserve Series* Vol. III, 3rd ed. (Lake George, NY: Adirondack Mountain Club, Inc., 2004), 154–156.

Elizabeth Folwell, "Flaking Out in Newcomb: gliding into winter on old roads and woodland trails," *Adirondack Life* Vol. 39, no. 8 (November/December 2008), 44–47. Part of the text and photos include a ski jaunt to Santanoni.

The Sagamore

1. Dick Beamish, "A trip back in time," *Adirondack Explorer 2007 Outings Guide*, 27.

2. Craig Gilborn, *Durant: The Fortunes and Woodland Camps of a Family in the Adirondacks* (Sylvan Beach, NY: North Country Books in collaboration with The Adirondack Museum, 1981), 104–107.

3. William Wessels, *Adirondack Profiles* (Lake George, NY: Adirondacks Resorts Press, 1961), 103–109.

4. Paul Schneider, *The Adirondacks* (New York: Henry Holt and Company Inc., 1997), 258.

5. A photograph of the machinery in the power plant can be seen displayed on the wall in the coffee shop at the Visitor's Center.

Additional reading:

Harold K. Hochschild, *Life and Leisure in the Adirondack Backwoods* (Blue Mountain Lake, NY: Adirondack Museum, 1962). Contains more information on William Durant.

Howard Kirschenbaum, *The Story of the Sagamore* (Raquette Lake, NY: Sagamore Institute, 1990). Kirschenbaum's booklet provides a thorough overview of The Sagamore.

Route 30 Region

Paul Smiths

1. Paul Schneider, *The Adirondacks: A History of America's First Wilderness* (New York: Henry Holt and Company, 1997), 184.

2. Ibid., 184.

3. Helen Escha Tyler, *The Story of Paul Smith: Born Smart* (Utica, NY: North Country Books, 1988), 65.

4. Geraldine Collins, *The Brighton Story* (Saranac Lake, NY: Chauncey Press, 1977), 105.

5. S. R. Stoddard, *The Adirondacks: Illustrated* (Albany, NY: Weed, Parsons & Co., 1874), 78 & 79.

6. Collins, op cit., 66.

7. Andy Flynn, Senior Public Information Specialist at New York State's Adirondack Park Visitor Interpretive Center.

8. Collins, op cit., 56.

9. Ibid., 113.

Additional reading:

Dennis Aprill, *Short Treks in the Adirondacks and Beyond* (Utica, NY: Nicholas K. Burns, 2005). Aprill's book contains a chapter on Paul Smiths, 132–135.

Gayle Carman, "This was Paul Smith," *York State Tradition* Vol. 19, no. 2 (Spring 1965), 32–34. A photograph of the hotel taken by Stoddard in the late 1880s can be seen on page 33.

Geraldine Collins, *The Biography and Funny Sayings of Paul Smith* (Paul Smiths, NY: Paul Smith's College, 1965).

Alfred L. Donaldson, *A History of the Adirondacks* Vol. I (1921, reprint, Mamaroneck, NY: Harbor Hill Books, 1977). Pages 320–329 contain a chapter on Paul Smiths.

Patricia J. O'Brien, "Great Camps of the Adirondacks," *Schenectady & Upstate New York* Vol. III, no. 3 (November 1990), 45.

Maitland C. Desormo, *The Heydays of the Adirondacks* (Saranac Lake, NY: Adirondack Yesteryears Inc., 1974). For those interested in reading about some of the yarns associated with Paul Smith, Desormo has a number of good ones to tell on pages 231–243.

Marjorie L. Porter, "Paul Smith," *North Country Life* Vol. 5, no. 4 (Fall 1951), 24–27. Paul Smith proved to be a versatile man—a caterer, guide, lumberman, real estate operator, merchant, road builder, electric power company builder, and so on.

William L. Wessels, *Adirondack Profiles* (Lake George, NY: Adirondack

Resorts Press, Inc., 1961). A photograph of Paul Smith is shown on page 130, with the depiction "Guide, Host, Capitalist." A brief biography of Paul Smith is on pages 128–132.

Hooper Garnet Mine

1. Barbara McMartin and Bill Ingersoll, *Discover the South Central Adirondacks: Four-Season Guide to the Siamese Ponds Wilderness*, 3rd ed. (Canada Lake, NY: Lake View Press, 1999), 145–146.

2. www.co.warren.ny.us.com.

Additional reading:

Robin Ambrosino, "Garnet Hill's a Jewell: comforts of home in a wild setting," *Adirondack Explorer 2003 Outings Guide*, 23. The author writes about cross-country ski treks that can be taken on the grounds of Garnet Hill.

Chimney Mountain

1. Don Williams, *Images of America: Along the Adirondack Trail* (Charleston, SC: Arcadia Publishing, 2004). On page 73 is a picture looking out from Chimney Mountain. John E. Winkler, *Bushwhacker's View of the Adirondacks* (Utica, NY: North Country Books, 1995). On page 95 is a picture of the chimney formation on Chimney Mountain. Michael Sean Gormley, "Chimney Kindles Kids' Curiosity," *Wild Excursions: An Anthology of Adirondack Adventures* (Saranac Lake, NY: Adirondack Explorer, 2005). A photograph of the chimney formation can be seen on page 16. Frederick A. Hodges, *York State Tradition* Vol. 18, no. 2 (Spring 1964). A picture of the Chimney Mountain formation taken from an unusual perspective is displayed on page 42.

2. Steve Higham, "Carroll's maps of Eagle Cave and Chimney Mountain," *The Northeastern Caver* Vol. 38, no. 1 (March 2007), 20. Higham states, "Eagle Cave is a gneiss fracture and breakdown cave. ... Estimates of the cave's size range up to 1850 feet of passage and 150 feet of relief."

3. Clay Perry, *Underground Empire: Wonders and Tales of New York Caves* (New York: Stephen Daye Press, 1948), 159.

4. Roger V. Bartholomew, "The Naming and Some History of Eagle Cave," *The Northeastern Caver* Vol. 22, no. 2 (June, 1991), 43–50.

5. Robert W. Carroll, Jr., "Chimney Mountain Extras," *The Northeastern Caver* Vol. 15, no 2. (1984), 39.

6. Barbara McMartin, *Discover the Adirondacks, 1: From Indian Lake to the Hudson River, a four season guide to the out-of-do*ors (Somersworth, NH: New Hampshire Publishing Company, 1979), 137.

Additional reading:

Dennis Aprill, *Paths Less Traveled: The Adirondack experience for walkers, hikers and climbers of all ages*, enlarged edition (Mt. Kisco, NY: Pinto Press, 2000). There is a chapter on Chimney Mountain on pages 157–161, with photo of the chimney on page 159.

Roger V. Bartholomew, "Eagle Cave, Chimney Mountain Report," *The Northeastern Caver* Vol. 33, no. 3 (September 2002), 103.

Roger Bartholomew, "Chimney Mountain Notes," *The Northeastern Caver* Vol. 29, no. 1 (March 1998), 25 & 26.

Harold Bishop, "A Peak Frozen in Time," *Adirondack Life* Vol. 16, no. 6 (November/December, 1985), 47–52.

Derek Burnett, "Adirondack Underground: Exploring Chimney Mountain," *Adirondac* Vol. 65, no 1 (January/February, 2001), 18–21.

Russell Dunn, "Great Grottos!" *Adirondack Life 1994 Annual Guide*, 74–79. This brief guide to Adirondack caving includes Chimney Mountain and its tectonic caves.

Michael Sean Gormley and Ethan Gormley, "Chimney Stokes Kids' Curiosity," *Adirondack Explorer* Vol. 5, no. 7 (Sept/Oct 2003), 7. The article addresses hiking up Chimney Mountain with kids to explore caves—something that should always be done with caution and with kids closely supervised.

Barbara McMartin, *50 Hikes in the Adirondacks: Short Walks, Day Trips, and Backpacks throughout the Park*, 4th ed. (Woodstock, VT: Backcountry, 2003), 161–165.

Willard L. Reed, "Chimney Mountain," *Adirondac* (March 1982), 8 & 9.

Laurence T. Cagle, ed., and Neal Burdick, senior editor, *Adirondack Trails Central Region, Forest Preserve Series* Vol. III, 3rd ed. (Lake George, NY: Adirondack Mountain Club, Inc., 2004), 64–65.

Kunjamuk Cave

1. "Speculator Loop Brochure," Adirondacks Speculator Region Chamber of Commerce.

2. Ted Aber & Stella King, *The History of Hamilton County* (Lake Pleasant, NY: Great Wilderness Books, 1965), 639.

3. Ibid., 717 & 718.

4. Anonymous, "Doing It! Our own guide to some canoe trips, ranging from mild to wild, in various areas of the Great Northern Wilderness," *Adirondack Life* Vol. 10, no. 3 (May/June 1979). On pages 30–33 the article describes a canoe trip on the Kunjamuk River, including specific information on the Kunjamuk River on page 31.

5. Aber, op cit. On page 128 is a photograph of early canoeists paddling on the Kunjamuk River.

6. Laurence T. Cagle, ed., and Neal Burdick, senior editor, *Adirondack Trails Central Region, Forest Preserve Series* Vol. III, 3rd ed. (Lake George, NY: Adirondack Mountain Club, Inc., 2004), 103.

7. Robin Ambrosino, "Kanoeing the Kunjamuk," *Adirondack Explorer 2004 Outings Guide*, 19. The author describes the cave as "15 feet deep with an 8-inch hole in the roof."

8. Aber, op cit., 127. "No one recalls who first dug the cave on the Kunjamuk that for years has lured hikers and canoeists to the site. It is only remembered that the egg-shaped artificial hole in the hillside was made by prospectors hunting for minerals. Campers and hunters made the hole through the roof of the cave at a later date."

9. Don Williams, *Inside the Adirondack Blue Line* (Utica, NY: North Country Books, 1999), 67. In the chapter "Thar's gold in them thar hills," Williams mentions that according to local lore Kunjamuk Cave was once a gold mine. Dennis Conroy, with Shirley Matzke, *Adirondack Cross-Country Skiing: A Guide to Seventy Trails* (Woodstock, VT: Backcountry Publications, 1992), 202. Kunjamuk Cave is described as "a small round opening in a vertical frac-

tured wall. It appears shallow and could have been man-made in search for gold or silver."

10. Barbara McMartin & Bill Ingersoll, *Discover the South Central Adirondacks: Four-Season Guide to the Siamese Pond Wilderness*, 3rd ed. (Canada Lake, NY: Lake View Press, 1999), 79.

Additional reading:

Russell Dunn, "On the Low Road with Barbara and Russell: Kunjamuk Cave," *Northeastern Caver* Vol. 25, no. 3 (September 1994), 83–84.

Russell Dunn, "In Search of Kunjamuk Cave," *Adventures around the Great Sacandaga Lake* (Utica, NY: Nicholas K. Burns Publishing, 2002), 141–144.

Griffin, Griffin Falls, & Auger Falls

1. Ouida Girard, *Griffin: Ghost Town in the Adirondacks and other Tales* (n. p., 1980). A picture of the 1903 iron bridge can be seen on page 3.

2. Barbara McMartin, *Hides, Hemlocks, and Adirondack History* (Utica, NY: North Country Books, 1992). On page 245 can be seen a picture of Griffin as it looked back in the 1800s. Girard, op cit. A picture of the town of Griffin is shown on page 6. Ted Aber & Stella King, *The History of Hamilton County* (Lake Pleasant, NY: Great Wilderness Books, 1965), 930. A photo of the old town is shown.

3. McMartin, op cit. A map of Griffin is shown on page 243.

4. Girard, op cit. The author provides extensive history of the life and times of Griffin as only someone who had once lived there could write it.

5. Donald R. Williams, "Griffin: Where are you?" *Adirondack Life* Vol. 5, no. 4 (Fall, 1974), 48–52.

Foothills of the Adirondacks: Mohawk Valley Region

Moss Island

1. Russell Dunn, "Moss Island," *Voice of the Valley* Vol. 1, no. 1 (October 2003), 1. The article contains an overview of Moss Island's geological and industrial history. Barbara Delaney, "Moss Island: A Jewel of the Mohawk," *Mohawk Valley Heritage* Vol. 3, no. 1 (Summer 2005), 22–23. A concise overview of Moss Island is presented.

2. C. R. Roseberry, *From Niagara to Montauk: The Scenic Pleasures of New York State* (Albany, NY: State University of New York Press, 1982). A chapter is devoted to the "Little Falls Gorge" on pages 101–106.

3. Francis P. Kimball, *The Capital Region of New York State* Vol. II (New York: Lewis Historical Publishing Company, Inc., 1942), 233. "The largest lock is at Little Falls, having a lift of 40.5 feet."

4. Russell Dunn, "Exploring Moss Island," *Northeastern Caver* Vol. 22, no. 2 (June 1991). Readers are guided to the island's natural pothole wonders on pages 62–64. Bradford B. Van Diver, *Roadside Geology of New York* (Missoula, MT: Mountain Press Publishing Company, 1985). Page 183 contains a picture of one of the enormous potholes. Roseberry, op cit. A picture of the potholes is included on page 100.

5. Nelson Greene, ed., *The Mohawk Valley: Gateway to the West* Vol. 1 (Chicago: The S. J. Clarke Publishing Company, 1925), 78 & 80. "One of the

most noteworthy evidences of the great postglacial cataract at Little Falls is the existence of potholes of varying sizes worn in the rocky sides of the gorge over which the waters of this tremendous falls overpoured. They are from a few inches to thirty feet wide and the potholes in the Little Falls Gorge are the largest, most remarkable on earth. Some are fully thirty feet deep."

6. Ibid., 77. The power of the Iro-Mohawk River at that time was awesome: "the volume of water which flowed ... across the preglacial divide at Little Falls must have been greater than that which now goes over Niagara Falls."

7. Ibid., 80. In reference to the fossil imprint of the once-mighty waterfall at Little Falls, the author writes, "The largest of the potholes of the Little Falls Gorge is the basin just below the lower falls, with the water over 150 feet deep."

8. Ibid., 80. Greene also substantiates that the potholes at Moss Island were used for many purposes: "During Indian Revolutionary forays, the red men frequently hid sheep and other loot, which they had stolen, in these holes and returned at night to remove them. They were also hiding places for the settlers during the revolution."

9. W. Max Reid, *The Mohawk Valley: Its Legends and Its History, 1609–1780* (1901, reprint, Harrison, NY: Harbor Hill Books, 1979), 367.

10. Historic marker.

11. Reid, op cit., 372.

12. Historic marker.

13. Bradford B. Van Diver, *Upstate New York* (Dubuque, IA: Kendall/Hunt Publishing Company, 1980). Van Diver discusses the geology of Moss Island on pages 188–190. Dean R. Snow, Charles T. Gehring & William A. Starna, ed., *In Mohawk Country: Early Narratives about A Native People* (Syracuse, NY: Syracuse University Press, 1996). A brief description of Little Falls's geology is provided in a chapter taken from DeWitt Clinton's 1810 Private Canal Journal, pages 389–390.

14. "Early Settlers and Events at the Village of Little Falls, Source," *History of Herkimer County, N.Y.*, http://herkimer.nygenweb.net/littlefalls/littlebeers1.html.

Tufa Caves & Waterfalls of Van Hornesville

1. Frank Oppel, compiler, "Richfield Springs (1888)," *New York: Tales of the Empire State* (Secaucus, NJ: Castle, 1988), 168. An illustration of the falls is shown.

2. Michael Nardacci, editor-in-chief, *Guide to the Caves and Karst of the Northeast* (Huntsville, AL: National Speleological Society, 1991). In the chapter on "Caves West of Schoharie County" by Kevin Dumont, a brief write-up of the Tufa Caves is provided on page 102.

3. William M. Gazda, *Place Names in New York* (Schenectady, NY: Gazda Associates, Inc., 1997), 81.

4. Douglas Ayres Jr., "Van Hornesville Caves," *Mohawk Valley USA* Vol. 7, no. 1 (Spring 1986). Extensive geological information about the cave is provided on pages 37–39.

5. Bradford B. Van Diver, *Upstate New York* (Dubuque, IA: Kendall/Hunt Publishing Company, 1980), 174.

Canajoharie Gorge

1. Phyllis Lake, "Canajoharie Gorge." *Mohawk Valley USA* Vol. 1, no. 1 (June 1980). Extensive information is provided about the gorge on pages 22–25.

2. Nelson Greene, *The Old Mohawk Turnpike Book* (Fort Plains, NY: Nelson Greene, 1924), 145.

3. Frederick G. Vosburgh, *Drums to Dynamos on the Mohawk* (Washington, DC: National Geographic Society, 1974). The text includes an excellent picture of the Canajoharie Pothole, complete with skinny-dipper.

4. Gilbert W. Hagerty, *Wampum, War & Trade Goods West of the Hudson* (Interlaken, NY: Heart of the Lakes Publishing, 1985). On page 46, information is presented regarding how the Canajoharie Pothole was named.

5. Kathleen Hanford, Town & Village Historian of Canajoharie.

6. Hagerty, op cit. 47.

7. John Vroman, *Forts and Firesides of the Mohawk Country* (Johnstown, NY: Baronet Litho Co., 1951), 197.

8. Richard Hency, "Remembering Arkell & Smiths," *Courier-Standard-Enterprise*, April 6, 2005, p. 5.

Wolf Hollow

1. Nelson Greene, ed., *The Mohawk Valley: Gateway to the West* Vol. 2 (Chicago: The S. J. Clarke Publishing Company, 1925), 1471. "Kinguariones and Wolf Hollow would make a fine State Park site, being accessible and available to the thousands of motorists on the old Mohawk Turnpike." Alas, since the time these words were written, civilization has captured the hollow and it is now well-traveled by motorists making their way not to it, but through it.

2. Judy Patrick, "Donated easement helps protect historic Wolf Hollow," *The Sunday Gazette*, May 15, 2005, A9.

3. Myron F. Westover, ed., *Schenectady: Past and Present: Historical Papers* (Strasburg, VA: Shenandoah Publishing, Inc., 1931). There is a photo of Touareuna Hill from the Mohawk River with the caption, "At Hoffmans, on the north side of the river, there is a jutting cliff of rock which once stood at the water's edge but has been blasted away to make room for the railroad tracks."

4. Schenectady County Historical Society, *Images of America: Glenville* (Charleston, SC: Arcadia Publishing, 2005), 14. A photo of Wolf Hollow Cave here includes a woman standing near the entrance to provide scale.

5. Information provided by Dudley Crauer. Henrietta Vanderveer & William W. Baird, eds., *History of Glenville: Based upon Historical Data Provided in a Publication by Percy M. Van Epps* (Glenville, NY: n. p., 1982), pages unnumbered. In the chapter entitled "Stories and Legends of our Indian Paths" (1940), a picture of the cabin is displayed.

6. Ibid. In the chapter entitled "The Indian Occupation of Glenville, N.Y." (1929), information is provided on the Algonquins and Mohawks.

7. Hugh P. Donlon, *Outlines of History: Montgomery County, State of New York, 1772–1972,* bicentennial edition (Amsterdam, NY: Printed by Noteworthy Co., 1973), 5. Information is provided on the historic battle in Wolf Hollow.

8. Donald B. Rickey, ed., *Encyclopedia of New York Indians, Vol. One: Tribes, Nations, and People of the Woodlands Areas* (St. Clair Shores, MI: Somerset Publishers, Inc., 1998). A brief chapter on the Mohegans is on pages 182–184.

9. Patrick, op cit. Vanderveer, op cit. In the chapter on "Stories and Legends of our Indian Paths" (1940), the story of Kateri Tekakwitha ("Lilly of the Mohawk") is told.

10. Ibid. "Historical Tablets and Markers of Glenville, N.Y. (Part One)" (1935). James H. Stoller, *Geological Excursions: A Guide to Localities in the Region of Schenectady and the Mohawk Valley and the Vicinity of Saratoga Springs* (Schenectady, NY: Union Book Co., 1931), 13–18. The author devotes a chapter to the geology of Wolf Hollow.

11. Patrick, op cit. Information provided by Dudley Crauer.

12. Roadside historical marker.

13. Patrick, op cit.

Additional reading:

Vincent Schaffer, "Wolf Hollow: Old Rock Scar," Knickerbocker News Union-Star, Monday, Dec. 20, 1971.

Bibliography

Aber, Ted, and Stella King. *The History of Hamilton County*. Lake Pleasant, NY: Great Wilderness Books, 1965.

Allen, Ethan. *Ethan Allen's Narrative of the Capture of Ticonderoga and of his Captivity and Treatment by the British*. 5th ed. Burlington, VT: C. Goodrich & S. B. Nichols, 1849.

Ambrosino, Robin. "Garnet Hill's a Jewell: comforts of home in a wild setting." *Adirondack Explorer 2003 Outings Guide*.

Anderson, Scott Edward. *Walks in Nature's Empire: Exploring the Nature Conservancy's Preserves in New York State*. Woodstock, VT: The Countryman Press, 1995.

Anderson, Tom. "Crown Point: To keep the past alive, historians labor to save two ruined forts." *Adirondack Life*. Vol. XII, no. 3 (May/June 1981).

Anonymous. "Doing It! Our own guide to some canoe trips, ranging from mild to wild, in various areas of the Great Northern Wilderness." *Adirondack Life*. Vol. 10, no. 3 (May/June 1979).

———. "Fort Ticonderoga—key to a continent." *North Country Life*. Vol. 9, no. 3 (Summer 1955).

———. *Glens Falls: The "Empire City"*. Glens Falls, NY: Glens Falls Publishing Co., 1908.

———. "Mt. Defiance," *North Country Life*. Vol. 12, no. 2 (Spring 1958).

Aprill, Dennis. *Paths Less Traveled: The Adirondack experience for walkers, hikers and climbers of all ages*. Enlarged edition. Mt. Kisco, NY: Pinto Press, 2000.

———. *Short Treks in the Adirondacks and Beyond*. Utica, NY: Nicholas K. Burns Publishing, 2005.

———. "Trail Mix—Low Peaks: Coon Mountain." *Adirondack Life 1998 Annual Guide*. Vol. 29, no. 4.

Ayres, Douglas Jr. "Van Hornesville Caves." *Mohawk Valley USA*. Vol. 7, no. 1 (Spring 1986).

Bailey, Jim. "Through Indian Pass, With Backward Glances." *Adirondac*. Vol. 54 no. 9 (October/November, 1989).

Barrett, Lincoln, and editors of Time-Life Books. *The Ancient Adirondacks*. New York: Time Inc., 1974.

Bartholomew, Roger. "The Naming and Some History of Eagle Cave." *The Northeastern Caver*. Vol. 22, no. 2 (June, 1991).

———. "Eagle Cave, Chimney Mountain Report." *The Northeastern Caver*. Vol. 33, no. 3 (September 2002).

———. "Chimney Mountain Notes." *The Northeastern Caver*. Vol. 29, no. 1 (March 1998).

Bassett, Elizabeth. *Nature Walks in Northern Vermont and the Champlain Valley*. Boston: Appalachian Mountain Club Books, 1998.

Beamish, Dick. "Biking through History." *Wild Excursions: An Anthology of Adirondack Adventures*. Saranac Lake, NY: Adirondack Explorer, 2005.

———. "A trip back in time." *Adirondack Explorer 2007 Outings Guide*.

Bearor, Bob. *The Battle on Snowshoes*. Westminster, MD: Heritage Books, Inc., 1997.

Bellico, Russell P. *Chronicles of Lake Champlain: Journeys in War and Peace*.

Fleischmanns, NY: Purple Mountain Press, 1999.

———. *Chronicles of Lake George: Journeys in War and Peace*. Fleischmanns, NY: Purple Mountain Press, 1995.

———. "The Abercromby Expedition." *Adirondack Life*. Vol. 25 no. 4 (July/ Aug. 1983).

Bishop, Harold. "A Peak Frozen in Time." *Adirondack Life*. Vol. 16, no. 6 (November/December, 1985).

Brown, Phil. *Longstreet Highroad Guide to the New York Adirondacks*. Marietta GA: Longstreet Press, Inc., 1999.

———. "High Peaks gateway to be saved: Tahawus Tract topped conservationists' wish list." *Adirondack Explorer*. Vol. 5, no. 6 (July/Aug 2003).

Buckell, Betty Ahearn. *Old Lake George Hotels*. N. p.: Buckle Press, 1986.

Burnett, Derek. "Adirondack Underground: Exploring Chimney Mountain." *Adirondac*. Vol. 65, no 1 (January/February, 2001).

Burnside, James R. *Exploring the 46 Adirondack High Peaks*. Schenectady, NY: High Peaks Press, 1996.

Cadbury, Warder H. "The Early Artists of Indian Pass, Part I." *Adirondac*. Vol. 54, no. 9 (October/November, 1989).

Cagle, Laurence T., ed., and Neal Burdick, senior editor. *Adirondack Trails Central Region, Forest Preserve Series* Vol. III. 3rd ed. Lake George, NY: Adirondack Mountain Club, Inc., 2004.

Carman, Gayle. "This was Paul Smith," *York State Tradition*. Vol. 19, no. 2 (Spring 1965).

Carroll, Robert W. Jr. "Chimney Mountain Extras." *The Northeastern Caver*. Vol. 15, no 2. (1984).

———. "40,000 Square Mile Talus Legacy." *The Northeastern Caver*. Vol. 21, no. 4 (December, 1990).

Clyne, Patricia Edwards. *Caves for Kids in Historic New York*. Monroe, NY: Library Research Associates, 1980.

Coffin, Howard, Will Curtis, and Jane Curtis. *Guns over the Champlain Valley*. Woodstock, VT: The Countryman Press, 2005.

Collins, Geraldine. *The Brighton Story*. Saranac Lake, NY: Chauncey Press, 1977.

———. *The Biography and Funny Sayings of Paul Smith*. Paul Smiths, NY: Paul Smith's College, 1965.

Conroy, Dennis, with Shirley Matzke. *Adirondack Cross-Country Skiing: A Guide to Seventy Trails*. Woodstock, VT: Backcountry Publications, 1992.

Cotter, Edwin N. Jr. "John Brown in the Adirondacks." *Adirondack Life*. Vol. 3, no. 3 (Summer 1972).

Crockett, Walter Hill. *A History of Lake Champlain: the Record of Three Centuries, 1609–1909*. Burlington, VT: Hobart J. Shanty, 1909.

Cross, David, and Joan Potter. *Adirondack Firsts*. Elizabethtown, NY: Pinto Press, 1992.

Dana, Richard Henry. "How We Met John Brown." *Atlantic Monthly*. July 1871.

Darling, Alan. "Santanoni." *Adirondack Life*. Vol. 12, no. 5 (September/ October, 1981).

Davis, Millard C. "Up, Up the Storied Mountain: Even the near and familiar can become a new experience for the perceptive hiker." *Adirondack Life*.

Vol. 9, no. 4 (July/August, 1978).

DeCosta, B. F. *Notes on the History of Fort George during the Colonial and Revolutionary Periods, with contemporaneous Documents and an appendix.* New York: J. Sabin and Sons, 1871.

Delaney, Barbara. "Moss Island: A Jewel of the Mohawk." *Mohawk Valley Heritage.* Vol. 3, no. 1 (Summer 2005).

Desormo, Maitland C. *The Heydays of the Adirondacks.* Saranac Lake, NY: Adirondack Yesteryears Inc., 1974.

Donaldson, Alfred L. *A History of the Adirondacks.* Vol. I. 1921. Reprint, Mamaroneck, NY: Harbor Hill Books, 1977.

Donlon, Hugh P. *Outlines of History: Montgomery County, State of New York, 1772–1972.* Bicentennial Edition. Amsterdam, NY: Printed by Noteworthy Co., 1973.

Dornburgh, Henry. *Why the Wilderness is called Adirondack: the earliest Account of the Founding of the MacIntyre Mine.* Harrison, NY: Harbor Hill Books, 1980.

Downs, Jack. *Kayak and Canoe Paddles in the New York Champlain Valley: 15 narrated paddling daytrips with maps and photos.* N. p.: Trail Marker Books, 2004.

Dunn, Russell. "Cooper's Cave." *Northeastern Caver.* Vol. 23, no. 3 (September, 1992).

———. "Exploring Moss Island." *Northeastern Caver.* Vol. 22, no. 2 (June 1991).

———. "Great Grottos!" *Adirondack Life 1994 Annual Guide.*

———. "Hiking the Waterfall Trail." *Adirondac.* Vol. 62, no. 3 (May/June 1998).

———. "In Search of Kunjamuk Cave." *Adventures around the Great Sacandaga Lake.* Utica, NY: Nicholas K. Burns Publishing, 2002.

———. "Moss Island." *Voice of the Valley.* Vol. 1 no. 1 (October 2003).

———. "On the Low Road with Barbara and Russell: Kunjamuk Cave." *Northeastern Caver.* Vol. 25, no. 3 (September 1994).

Engel, Robert, and Howard Kirschenbaum. "A Great Camp Memoir: The Santanoni spring-party scrapbooks." *Adirondack Life.* Vol. 24, no. 3 (May/June, 1993).

Engel, Thom. "Valcour Island: A Preliminary Report." *The Northeastern Caver.* Vol. 28, no. 4 (December 1997).

Fangboner, Donald. "Saving the Past." *Lake George ... Ours to Preserve: Centennial Celebration Handbook.* Lake George, NY: The Lake George Association, 1985.

Farrell, Patrick. *Through the Light Hole.* Utica NY: North Country Books, 1996.

Fennessey, Lana. *The History of Newcomb.* Newcomb, NY, N.p.,1996.

Figiel, Richard. "The Second Building of Fort Ticonderoga." *Adirondack Life.* Vol. 9, no. 3 (May/June 1978).

Fleck, Alexander, ed. *The American Revolution in New York State.* Albany, NY: NYS Department of Education, 1926.

Folwell, Elizabeth. *The Adirondack Book: A Complete Guide.* Stockbridge, MA: Berkshire House Publishers, 1992.

———. "Flaking Out in Newcomb: gliding into winter on old roads and woodland trails." *Adirondack Life*. Vol. 39, no. 8 (November/December 2008).

Fowler, Barney. *Adirondack Album*. Vol. 2. Schenectady, NY: Outdoor Associates, 1980.

———. *Adirondack Album*. Vol. 3. Schenectady, NY: Outdoor Associates, 1982.

Gates, William Preston. *Turn-of-the-Century Scrapbook of Jonathan Streeter Gates*. Glens Falls & Bolton, NY: Gates Publishing Company, 1999.

Gazda, William M. *Place Names in New York*. Schenectady, NY: Gazda Associates, Inc., 1997.

Gilborn, Craig. *Durant: The Fortunes and Woodland Camps of a Family in the Adirondacks*. Sylvan Beach, NY: North Country Books, in collaboration with The Adirondack Museum, 1981.

Girard, Ouida. *Griffin: Ghost Town in the Adirondacks and other Tales*. N.p.: n.p, 1980.

Godine, Amy. "The Path of History: Discovering the Champlain Valley's Freedom Trail." *Adirondack Life's 1991 Outdoor Guide*. Vol. 22, no. 4.

Goodwin, Tony, ed., and Neal Burdick, series editor. *Adirondack Trails: High Peak Region*. 13th ed. Lake George, NY: Adirondack Mountain Club, Inc., 2004.

Gordon, Robert. "A Mournful Trip." *Adirondack Life*. Vol. 15, no. 1.

Gormley, Michael Sean. "Chimney Kindles Kids' Curiosity." *Wild Excursions: An Anthology of Adirondack Adventures*. Saranac Lake, NY: Adirondack Explorer, 2005.

Gormley, Michael Sean, and Ethan Gormley. "Chimney Stokes Kids' Curiosity." *Adirondack Explorer*. Vol. 5, no. 7 (Sept/Oct 2003).

Greene, Nelson, ed. *The Mohawk Valley: Gateway to the West*. Vol. 1. Chicago: The S. J. Clarke Publishing Company, 1925.

——— *The Mohawk Valley: Gateway to the West*. Vol. 2. Chicago: The S. J. Clarke Publishing Company, 1925.

———. *The Old Mohawk Turnpike Book*. Fort Plains, NY: Nelson Greene, 1924.

Gunning, Lois Moody. *Up on Chilson Hill: A Story of an Adirondack Hamlet, its times and people*. Burlington, VT: Queen City Printers, 1999.

Haas, Robert C. "But now, please God they must go." *Adirondack Life*. Vol. 6, no. 1 (Winter 1975).

Hagerty, Gilbert W. *Wampum, War & Trade Goods West of the Hudson*. Interlaken, NY: Heart of the Lakes Publishing, 1985.

Hall, Robert F. *Pages from Adirondack History*. Fleischmanns, NY: Purple Mountain Press, 1992.

Halm, Gale J., and Mary H. Sharp. *Images of America: Lake George*. Charleston, SC: Arcadia Publishing, 2000.

Hamilton, Edward P. *Fort Ticonderoga, Key to a Continent*. Boston: Little Brown and Co., 1964.

Heilman, Carl II (Neal Burdick, series editor). *Guide to Adirondack Trails 6, Eastern Region*. 2nd ed. Lake George, NY: Adirondack Mountain Club, 1994.

Hency, Richard. "Remembering Arkell & Smiths." *Courier-Standard-Enterprise*, April 6, 2005.

Henkel-Karras, Erica. *Postcard History Series: Lake George, 1900–1925*.

Charleston, SC: Arcadia Publishing, 2005.

Henry, Tom. "Put Put Fun: He came, he fought, they named things after him." *Adirondack Life*. Vol. 38, no. 8 (November/December 2007).

Higham, Steve. "Carroll's maps of Eagle Cave and Chimney Mountain." *The Northeastern Caver*. Vol. 38, no. 1 (March 2007).

Hochschild, Harold K. *Life and Leisure in the Adirondack Backwoods*. Blue Mountain Lake, NY: Adirondack Museum, 1962.

Hodges, Frederick A. *York State Tradition*. Vol. 18, no. 2 (Spring 1964).

Hopkins, Arthur S. "Old Fort St. Frederic—French Relic at Crown Point." *Conservationist* (August–September, 1962).

Howland, John, ed. *Exploring Lake Champlain and Its Highlands*. Burlington, VT: The Lake Champlain Committee, 1981.

Hyde, Louis Fiske. *History of Glens Falls New York, and Its Settlement*. Glens Falls, NY: n.p., 1936.

Ingersoll, Bill. "Exploring Camp Santanoni." *Adirondack Sports & Fitness*. January 2008.

———. "Rock Pond: A Rewarding Short Hike." *Adirondack Sports & Fitness*. May 2007.

Jillisky, Joe. "The Great Passes of the Adirondacks." *Adirondac*. Vol. 54, no. 5 (June 1990).

Kick, Peter. *25 Mountain Bike Tours in the Adirondacks*. Woodstock, VT: Backcountry Publications, 1999.

Kimball, Francis P. *The Capital Region of New York State*. Vol. II. New York: Lewis Historical Publishing Company, Inc., 1942.

Kirschenbaum, Howard. *The Story of the Sagamore*. Raquette Lake, NY: Sagamore Institute, 1990.

———. "To Save Santanoni." *Adirondack Life*. Vol. 17, no 1 (January/February, 1986).

Kirschenbaum, Howard, ed., Susan Schafstall, and Janine Stuchin. *The Adirondack Guide: an almanac of essential information and assorted trivia*. Raquette Lake, NY: Sagamore Institute, 1983.

Lake, Phyllis. "Canajoharie Gorge." *Mohawk Valley USA*. Vol. 1, no. 1 (June 1980).

Lamb, Wallace E. *Lake George: Fact and Anecdotes*. 2nd ed. Bolton Landing, NY: n.p., 1938.

Lape, Jane M., ed. *Ticonderoga: Patches and Patterns from its Past*. Vol. I. Ticonderoga, NY: The Ticonderoga Historical Society, 1969.

Leonbruno, Frank. *Lake George Reflections: Island History and Lore*. Fleischmanns, NY: Purple Mountain Press, 1998.

Lonergan, Carroll V. "Fort St. Frederic." *North Country Life*. Vol. 12, no. 3 (Summer 1958).

Lord, Thomas Reeves. *Stories of Lake George: Fact and Fancy*. Pemberton, NJ: Pinelands Press, 1987.

———. *More Stories of Lake George: Fact and Fancy*. Pemberton, NJ: Pinelands Press, 1994.

Ludlum, Stuart D., ed. *Exploring Lake George, Lake Champlain 100 Years Ago*. Utica, NY: Brodock & Ludlum Publications, 1972.

Malo, Paul. "Nippon in the North Country: Japanese inspiration in form and philosophy." *Adirondack Life 1998 Collectors Issue*. Vol. 29, no. 7.

Manchester, Lee. *Tales from a Deserted Village: First-hand accounts of early explorations into the heart of the Adirondacks* (Essex County, NY: n.p., 2007.

McMartin, Barbara. *Discover the Adirondacks 1: From Indian Lake to the Hudson River, A four season guide to the out-of-doors.* Somersworth, NH: New Hampshire Publishing Company, 1997.

―――. *Discover the Eastern Adirondacks.* Woodstock, VT.: Backcountry Publications, 1988.

―――. *Guide to the Eastern Adirondacks.* Glens Falls, NY: Adirondack Mountain Club, 1981.

―――. *Hides, Hemlocks, and Adirondack History.* Utica, NY: North Country Books, 1992.

―――. *50 Hikes in the Adirondacks: Short Walks, Day Trips, and Backpacks throughout the Park.* 4th ed. Woodstock, VT: Backcountry Publications, 2003.

―――. "Ironville." *Adirondack Life.* Vol. 13, no. 4 (July/August 1982).

McMartin, Barbara, and Bill Ingersoll. *Discover the South Central Adirondacks: Four-Season Guide to the Siamese Pond Wilderness.* 3rd ed. Canada Lake, NY: Lake View Press, 1999.

McMartin, Barbara, Bill Ingersoll, Edythe Robbins, and Chuck Bennett. *Discover the Eastern Adirondacks: Guide to the Trails of Lake George & the Pharaoh Lake Wilderness.* 3rd ed. Barneveld, NY: Wild River Press, 2006.

Meyers, Roy Dean. "When the Bullwheel Turned ... and the mightiest cable railroad of them all climbed Prospect Mountain." *Adirondack Life.* Vol. 4, no 2 (Spring 1973).

Nardacci, Michael, editor-in-chief. *Guide to the Caves and Karst of the Northeast.* Huntsville, AL: National Speleological Society, 1991.

O'Brien, Patricia J. "Great Camps of the Adirondacks." *Schenectady & Upstate New York.* Vol. 3, no. 3 (November 1990).

Oppel, Frank, compiler. "Richfield Springs (1888)." *New York: Tales of the Empire State.* Secaucus, NJ: Castle, 1988.

Palmer, Gwen, Bob Bayle, and Stan Malecki. *Images of America: Glens Falls.* Charleston, SC: Arcadia Publishing, 2004.

Patrick, Judy. "Donated easement helps protect historic Wolf Hollow." *The Sunday Gazette,* May 15, 2005.

Perry, Clay. *Underground Empire: Wonders and Tales of New York Caves.* New York: Stephen Daye Press, 1948.

Pilcher, Edith. *Up the Lake Road.* Keene Valley, NY: Centennial Committee for the Trustees of The Adirondack Reserve, 1987.

Plunz, Richard, ed. *Two Adirondack Hamlets in History, Keene and Keene Valley.* Fleischmanns, NY: Purple Mountain Press, 2000.

Podskoch, Martin. *Adirondack Fire Towers: Their History and Lore.* Fleischmanns, NY: Purple Mountain Press, 2003.

Pope, Connie. "Hammondville Essex County Ghost Town." *York State Tradition.* Vol. 25, no. 1 (Winter 1971).

Porter, Marjorie L. "Paul Smith." *North Country Life.* Vol. 5, no. 4 (Fall 1951).

Possons, Chas. H. *Possons' Guide to Lake George, Lake Champlain, and Adirondacks.* 8th ed. Glens Falls, NY: Chas. H. Possons, 1890.

Reed, Willard L. "Chimney Mountain." *Adirondac* (March 1982).

Reid, Max. *Lake George and Lake Champlain: The War Trail of the Mohawk and the Battleground of France and England in their contest for the control of North America.* NY: The Knickerbocker Press, 1910.

———. *The Mohawk Valley: Its Legends and Its History, 1609–1780.* 1901. Reprint, Harrison, NY: Harbor Hill Books, 1979.

Reynolds, William Sterne. *Benedict Arnold, Patriot and Traitor.* NY: William Morrow and Co., 1990.

Rickey, Donald B., ed. *Encyclopedia of New York Indians, Vol. One: Tribes, Nations, and People of the Woodlands Areas.* St. Clair Shores, MI: Somerset Publishers, Inc., 1998.

Roberts, Alexandra. "Valcour Island: This mystical mass of land stands majestically on Lake Champlain." *Adirondack Life.* Vol. 15, no. 2 (March/April 1984).

Roberts, Robert B. *New York's Forts in the Revolution.* Cranbury, NJ: Associated University Press, 1980.

Roseberry, C. R. *From Niagara to Montauk: The scenic pleasures of New York State.* Albany, NY: State University of New York Press, 1982.

Royce, Caroline Halstead. *Bessboro: A History of Westport, Essex Co., N.Y.* Elizabethtown, NY: n.p., 1904.

Sayward, Nick. "William Gilliland—Tory or Patriot?" *York State Tradition.* Vol. 26, no. 1 (Winter 1972).

Schenectady County Historical Society. *Images of America: Glenville.* Charleston, SC: Arcadia Publishing, 2005.

Schmitt, Claire K., and Judith S. Wolk. *Natural Areas of Saratoga County New York* Niskayuna, NY: The Environmental Clearinghouse of Schenectady, 1998.

Schneider, Paul. *The Adirondacks: A History of America's First Wilderness.* New York: Henry Holt and Company, 1997.

Sleicher, Charles Albert. *The Adirondacks: An American Playground.* New York: Exposition Press, 1960.

Smith, H. Perry. *History of Essex County.* Syracuse, NY: D. Mason & Co., 1885.

Snow, Dean R., Charles T. Gehring, and William A. Starna, eds. *In Mohawk Country: Early Narratives about a Native People.* Syracuse, NY: Syracuse University Press, 1996.

Starbuck, David R. *Rangers and Redcoats on the Hudson: Exploring the past on Rogers Island, the birthplace of the U.S. Army Rangers.* Lebanon, NH: University Press of New England, 2004.

———. *The Great Warpath.* Hanover, NH: University Press of New England, 1999.

Steinback, Elsa Kny. *Sweet Peas and a White Bridge on Lake George when Steam was King.* Utica, NY: North Country Books, 1994.

Steinberg, David A. *Hiking the Road to Ruins: Day Trips and Camping Adventures to Iron Mines, Old Military Sites, and Things Abandoned in the New York City Area ... and Beyond.* New Brunswick, NJ: Rivergate Books, 2007.

Stevenson, Robert Louis. *Ticonderoga: A legend of the West Highlands.* 1887. Reprint, Ticonderoga, NY: Fort Ticonderoga Museum, 1947.

Stiles, Fred T. "Recollections of the Knapp Estate, Part 1." *North Country Life and New York State Traditions.* Vol. 14, no. 4 (Fall 1960).

———. "Recollections of the Knapp Estate, Part II." *North Country Life and New York State Tradition.* Vol. 15, no.1 (Winter 1961).

———. "1755–59 in the Champlain Valley: Abercrombie at Ticonderoga." *North County Life and York State Tradition.* Vol. 16, no. 1 (Winter 1962).

———. "Tales of Rogers and his Rangers," *North Country Life and New York State Tradition.* Vol. 13, no 4 (Fall 1959).

Stoddard, Seneca Ray. *The Adirondacks: Illustrated.* Albany, NY: Weed, Parsons & Co., 1874.

———. *Lake George: (Illustrated) A Book of To-day.* Glens Falls, NY: S.R. Stoddard, 1887.

Street, Alfred Billings. *The Indian Pass: Source of the Hudson.* 1869. Reprint, Fleischmanns, NY: Purple Mountain Press, 1993.

Tauber, Gilbert. *The Hudson River Tourway: Eleven Scenic Tours by Car of the Historic Hudson River Valley from Westchester to the Adirondacks.* Garden City, NY: Dolphin Books, 1977.

Taylor, Dorothy. "Noah LaCasse Presidential Hiking Mate." *Adirondack Life.* Vol. 3, no. 2 (Spring 1972).

Terrie, Philip G. *Contested Terrain: A New History of Nature and People in the Adirondacks.* Syracuse, NY: The Adirondack Museum/Syracuse University Press, 1997.

Thomas-Train, David, ed., with Neal S. Burdick. series editor. *Adirondack Trails: Eastern Region, Forest Preserve Series.* 3rd ed. Lake George, NY: Adirondack Mountain Club, Inc., 2008.

Thurheimer, David C. *Landmarks of the Revolution in New York State: A Guide to the Historic sites open to the Public.* Albany, NY: NYS American Revolution Bicentennial Commission, 1974.

Ticonderoga Historical Society. *Ticonderoga: Patches and Patterns from its Past.* Vol. I. Ticonderoga, NY: The Ticonderoga Historical Society.

Tyler, Helen Escha. *The Story of Paul Smith: Born Smart.* Utica, NY: North Country Books, 1988.

Tyrell, Anthony C. "Valcour Island—Past and Present." *The Conservationist* (September–October, 1982).

Vanderveer, Henrietta, and William W. Baird, eds. *History of Glenville: Based upon Historical Data Provided in a Publication by Percy M. Van Epps.* Glenville, NY: n.p., 1982.

Van Diver, Bradford B. *Roadside Geology of New York.* Missoula, MT: Mountain Press Publishing Company, 1985.

———. *Upstate New York: Field Guide.* Dubuque, IO: Kendall/Hunt Publishing Company, 1980.

Vandrei, Charles E. "The Lake George Battlefield Park: Looking to the future through the past." *New York State Conservationist.* Vol. 55, no. 4 (February 2001).

Vosburgh, Frederick G. *Drums to Dynamos on the Mohawk.* Washington, DC: National Geographic Society, 1974.

Vroman, John. *Forts and Firesides of the Mohawk Country.* Johnstown, NY: Baronet Litho Co., Inc., 1951.

Wallace, E. R. *Descriptive Guide to the Adirondacks (land of the thousand lakes):*

and to Saratoga Springs, Schroon Lake, lakes Luzerne, George, and Champlain, the Ausable Chasm, the Thousand Islands, Massena Springs, and Trenton Falls. 12th ed. Syracuse, NY: Watson Gil, Bible Pub. House, 1887.

Washington County Planning Department, *Introduction to Hudson Resources in Washington County, New York.* Washington County, NY: n.p., 1976.

Watson, Winslow C. *Pioneer history of the Champlain Valley, An Account of the Settlement of the Town of Willsborough by William Gilliland.* Albany, NY: J. Munsell Inc., 1863.

Wessels, William L. *Adirondack Profiles.* Lake George, NY: Adirondack Resorts Press, Inc., 1961.

Westbrook, Virginia. *Relishing Our Resources along Lake Champlain in Essex County, New York.* Crown Point, NY: Champlain Valley Heritage Network, 2001.

Westover, Myron F., ed. *Schenectady: Past and Present: Historical Papers.* Strasburg, VA: Shenandoah Publishing, 1931.

White, William Chapman. *Adirondack Country.* Syracuse, NY: Syracuse University Press, 1985.

Williams, Don. "Thar's Gold in Them Thar Hills." *Inside the Adirondack Blue Line.* Utica, NY: North Country Books, 1999.

Williams, Donald R. "Griffin: Where are you?" *Adirondack Life.* Vol. 5, no. 4 (Fall, 1974).

———. *Images of America: Along the Adirondack Trail.* Charleston, SC: Arcadia Publishing, 2004.

Wilson, Kenneth. "The Deserted Village." *Adirondack Life.* Vol. 7, no. 4 (Falls 1976).

Winkler, John E. *Bushwhacker's View of the Adirondacks.* Utica, NY: North Country Books, 1995.

Index

A

Abercromby, Major General
    James, 39, 45–48, 50, 51
Abolitionist Movement, 120, 122,
    126, 129, 130
Adam's Mountain, 142, 150
Adirondac, 119, 120, 141–144,
    146–152
Adirondack Architectural
    Heritage, 174, 256
Adirondack Camp and Trail
    Club, 140
Adirondack Conservancy
    Committee, 174
Adirondack Electric Company,
    140
Adirondack History Center
    Museum, 253
Adirondack Iron & Steel
    Company, 148
Adirondack Land Trust, 22, 23,
    26, 256
Adirondack Loj, 132, 135, 139,
    140, 146, 256
Adirondack Mountain Club
    (ADK), xv, 252
Adirondack Mountain Reserve
    (AMR), 120, 156, 162–166
Adirondack Museum, 253
Adirondack Northway, 90
Adirondack Park Agency Visitor
    Interpretive Center, 186,
    187, 189, 192
Adirondack Pass, 152
Adirondack State Park, 15, 20,
    106
Adirondack Woolen Co., 231
Adirondack Mountains, The, xv
Adirondacks, The, xv
Adirondacks Illustrated, The, xv,
    155, 191
ADK Grotto, 204
Adventures in the Wilderness,
    xv, 164
Albany, 16, 26, 29, 30, 40, 53, 54,
    63, 110, 131, 173, 229
Albany Academy, 63
Albany Committee of
    Correspondence, 29
Alcott, Bronson, 130
Alexander, Rev. Caleb, 230, 231
Algonquin Peak, 134
Algonquins, 1, 16, 37, 38, 48, 80,
    248, 249
Algonquin village, 247, 251
Allen, Ethan, 3, 29, 40, 53
American Heritage Bicycle Tours,
    252
Amherst, Fort, 4
Amherst, General Jeffrey, 39, 44,
    47, 48, 51, 52, 98
Anchor Mill, 231
Aqueduct, Little Falls, 227, 228
Arietta, Town of, 209
Arkell, James, 244
Arkell & Smith Company, 239
Arkell & Smith Dam, 239
Arkell & Smith Sack Factory,
    243, 244
Arkell Museum, 253
Arnold, Benedict, 3, 5, 6, 8, 9,
    16–19, 29, 40, 53, 68, 103
Arnold Bay, 18
Astenrogan, 229
Atlantic Monthly, 128
Atlantic Ocean, 37
Auger Falls, 185, 211, 213–215
Auriesville, 48, 80
Auriesville Shrine, 80
Ausable Chasm, 27
Ausable Club, 120, 156, 157, 159,
    162, 164–166
Ausable Lakes: Lower, 153, 156–
    158, 161, 162, 166; Upper,
    153, 163, 166
Ausable River, 27
Ausable River, East Branch, 120,
    156–166
Austin Flats, 213
Avalanche Pass, 135, 153

B

Bajus Cave, 205
Balanced Rock, 200
Bald Mountain, 76
Ballston Lake, 249
Barge Canal, New York State,
    219, 222, 224–226
Barker, Dr. Eugene, 62, 63
Barnum, P. T., 191, 192
Bartholomew, Roger V., 204, 205
Barton, Henry, 196
Barton Garnet Mine, 194, 196
Barton Garnet Mine Shop, 255
Barton Mine Corporation, 196
Basin Mountain, 135
Battles: Bloody Morning Scout,
    98, 100–102; Bloody
    Pond, 100, 101; Early
    Morning Scout, 101;
    Lake Champlain, 70;
    Lake George, 98, 99, 101;
    Lexington & Concord, 53;
    Oriskany, 40; Plattsburgh,
    13, 256; Saratoga, 19, 40;
    Snowshoes, on, 76, 78;
    Valcour Island, 6, 8, 19, 40
Bear Den's Cave, 246, 247, 250
Bear Pond, 66–69
Bear Run, 156, 159, 160
Beauty Bay, 12
Beaver Meadow, 166
Beaver Meadow Falls, 156, 157,
    161, 163
Beech-Nut Company, 245
Beede House, Smith, 165
Benedict, Lewis Elijah, 147
Benton, Ed, 86
Benton, Nathaniel, 227
Benton Pond, 86
Bentons Landing, 221, 227
Berkshires, 128
Betar Byway, 72, 104–109
Bicentennial Park, 43
Bierbauer Brewery Company,
    239, 244
Big Boom, 108
Big Cottage, 85
Big Nose, 249
birds, 6, 9
*Birds of the Adirondacks in
    Franklin County, N.Y.*, 191

Birks, General Walker, 11
Black Mountain, 79, 83
Black Point, 69
Black Watch, 45–47
blast furnace, 141, 142, 148–151
Bloody Morning Scout, Battle of,
    98, 100–102
Bloody Pond, 72, 97–99, 101
blue heron rookery, 9
Blue Line, 166
Bluff Point, 6, 13–15
Bluff Point Lighthouse, 6, 12, 14,
    15, 20
Bolton Historical Museum, 257
Booth, John Wilkes, 130
Boquet River, 27–29, 31
Boralex South Glens Falls
    Hydroelectric Project, 109,
    110
borrow pits, 180
Bossom, Alfred, 54, 55
Boston, 3, 26, 45
Boston Grotto, 204
Bottle Cave, 205
Bougainville, Mr., 49
Bourlamaque, Brigadier General, 51
Bowman's Creek, 237
Boyd, Milt, 209
Bradford Corners, 60
Bradley, Reuben, 85
Bradley House, 85
Brant, Joseph, 217, 239
Brant, Molly, 217
breastworks, 46
Brehm, Lieutenant Dietrich, 51
Bridge Cave, 21
British, xiv, 1, 2–4, 6, 9, 13,
    16–19, 24, 26, 29, 32, 39,
    40, 44, 45, 47–49, 51–54,
    70, 76, 77, 97, 100, 102,
    217
Brooklyn, 137, 182
Brown, Frederick, 127, 131
Brown, Jason, 127
Brown, John, 120–131
Brown, (Col.) John, 54
Brown, John Jr., 127
Brown, Mary, 121, 130, 131
Brown, Oliver, 121, 123, 127, 131
Brown, Owen, 127, 128
Brown, Ruth, 128
Brown, Watson, 121, 123, 127,
    131
Brown, Zora, 196
Brown Farm, John, 120–131
Brown Farm State Historic Site,
    John, 121, 131
Brown Memorial Association,
    John, 131
Buck Hollow, 60
Buck Mountain, 79, 82
Buffalo, 143, 149
Bullhead Bay, 6, 9, 15
bullwheel, 88, 93, 95, 96
Bumppo's Cave, Natty, 111
Bureau of Historic Sites of NYS
    Office of Parks, Recreation,
    and Historic Preservation,
    41
Burgoyne, General John, 18, 19,
    40, 47, 53–55, 103

Burlington, 128
Burnetsfield Patent, 230
Butterfly Bay, 12, 14

C

cable car railway, 91, 95, 96
Calamity Brook, 145, 146, 149
Call, Silas, 208
Call's Hotel, 208
Campbell, Major Duncan, 45
"Camp-of-the-Woods", 209
Canada, 1, 3, 13, 17, 26–28, 37,
    39, 40, 51, 53, 80, 103, 137,
    139, 217, 230, 239, 249
Canajoharie, Village of, 210, 237,
    241, 243–245
Canajoharie Creek, 237, 238,
    243–245
Canajoharie Falls, 218, 237, 241,
    242, 244
Canajoharie Gorge, 218, 237–246
Canajoharie Pothole, 210, 218,
    237, 238, 239, 242, 245
Canajoharie Riverfront Park, 245
Canyon, The, 160
Carleton, Sir Guy, 6, 18, 19
Carmichael, Hoagy, 184
Carroll, Commissioner Charles,
    103
Carroll, Robert W. Jr., 205
"carrying place," 37
Cascade Lakes, 153
Casilear, John, 163
Cathedral Rocks, 156, 159, 160
Catlin & Hunt, 216
Catskill Mountain House, 95
Catskill Mountains, 93, 163
caves: Bajus, 205; Bear Den's,
    250; Bottle, 205; Bridge,
    21; Cooper's, 72, 104, 105,
    109–118; Darkroom, 21;
    Eagle, 204; Kunjamuk,
    206–210; Natty Bumppo's,
    111; Rotunda, 205; Spoon
    Pit, 21; Tucker, 21; talus
    (Indian Pass), 153–155;
    tectonic & fissure (Chimney
    Mt.), 197, 199, 204, 205;
    tufa, 218, 232, 233, 236
Cave Hill, 209
Cave Trail, 233, 234
Cedar Point, 10
Cemetery Falls, 242
Chambly, 37
Champlain, Samuel de, 1, 15, 16,
    24, 37, 38, 44, 48, 55
Champlain Canal, 70, 107, 252
Champlain Memorial Lighthouse,
    34
Champlain Valley, 1, 3, 4, 8, 22,
    28, 37, 40, 47, 52–54, 61,
    68, 70
Champlain Valley Farm & Forest
    Project, Adirondack Land
    Trust, 24
Chapman Historical Museum,
    253
charcoal, 31
Charlton, 249
Chase, Commissioner, 103
Chase Bag Company, 245
Chaughtanoonda Creek, 246, 247,
    250, 251
cheese box factory, 233
Cheney, John, xiv, xv, 149

Chepontuo, 113
Chicataubet, Chief, 249
Chilson Hill, 69
Chimney Mountain, 185,
    197–205
Chingachgook, 87, 112, 114
choke point, 37, 38
Churchill, Sylvester, 41
Citadel (Fort St. Frederic), 34, 39
Civilian Conservation Corps
    (CCC), 74
Civil War, 6, 20, 31, 71, 121–123,
    126, 127, 129–131, 163,
    172, 182, 216, 231, 245
Clear Pond, 66, 138
Cleveland, Grover, 191
Clinton Community College, 13
Clinton County Historical
    Association, 20
Clinton County Historical
    Museum, 253
Clinton County Historical
    Society, 15
Cod Pond, 211, 214
Coffin, Marian Cruger, 57
Cohoes, 115
Cohoes Falls, 115
Colchester, Conn., 129
Colden Mountain, 135
Cole, Thomas, 119
Columbia College, 41
Colvin, A. B., 94
Concord, 53
Connecticut, 50, 129
Continental Congress, 17, 18,
    29, 40
Cook, Rev. Joseph, 56,
Cook Mountain, 78
Coon Mountain, 3, 4, 22–31
Coon Mountain panther, 31
Cooper, James Fenimore, 71, 72,
    83, 87, 104, 109, 111–119,
    174
Cooper's Cave, 72, 104, 105,
    109–111, 114–118
Cooper's Cave Bridge, 105, 111
Cooperstown, 111, 233, 235
Corinth, 215
Corlear Lake, 1
Corners, The, 110
corn pits, Native American, 248,
    251
Cortland Normal School, 215
Crab Island, 13
Crauer, Dudley, 246, 248
Creamery Brook, 232
Creamery Falls, 232–235
Crown Point, 2–4, 16, 18, 19,
    22, 26,27, 29, 32–41, 58,
    61–63, 66, 68–70
Crown Point Bridge, 4, 33, 35
Crown Point Iron Company,
    60–62, 69, 70
Crown Point Lighthouse, 36, 37
Crown Point Public
    Campgrounds, 36
Crown Point State Historic Site,
    32, 36, 37
Crown Point State Historic Site
    Museum, 32, 253
Cumberland Bay, 13
Cumberland Bluff, 12
Cystid Point, 10

D

Dacy, Jack, 82
Dana, Henry, 128, 129, 148
Darkroom Cave, 21
Dawn Valcour Agricultural and
    Historical Association, 20
Declaration of Independence, 29
Declaration of Principals, 29
deer, 5, 6
Deer's Head Inn, 130, 131
DeForest, Robert, 120, 165
Delarm, W. Keith, 103
Delarm Bikeway, W. Keith, 103
Delaware & Hudson (D&H)
    Railroad, 13, 80
Delia Spring, 172
de Lotbinière, 50
Department of Environmental
    Conservation (DEC), 8,
    103, 174
Devil's Ear, 239
Devil's Hole, 239
Dewey, Godfrey, 138, 140
Dewey, Melvil, 140
Dieskau, Baron, 38, 98, 100, 101
Discover the Adirondacks (book
    series), xvi
Dix, Governor, 173
Dix Peak, 25
Donaldson, Alfred L., 151
Douglass, Frederick, 126, 130
Duck Hole, 145
Dug Mountain, 210
Dunning, Alvah, xiv, xv
Durand, Asher, 157, 163
Durant, Thomas Clark, 181, 182
Durant, William West, 167, 175,
    176, 181, 182, 184
Dutch, 1, 2, 48, 217, 230

E

Eagle Cave, 204
Earl, Ralph, 30
East Cove, 107
Echo Bay, 76
Eisenhower Lock, 220
"electric age, birthplace of the",
    4, 59, 62
Elizabethtown, 27, 31, 130, 131,
    163
Elizabethtown Town Hall, 131
Elm Lake, 208
Emerson, Margaret, 183, 184
Emerson, Ralph Waldo, 130
Emmons, Professor Ebenezer,
    146, 147, 152
Enoch, 148
Enterprise, 16
Epps, Lyman, 129, 131
Erebus Mountain, 79, 82
Erie Canal, 111, 189, 221, 222,
    231, 244, 250, 252
Essex, 4, 22, 27, 30
Essex County Board of
    Supervisors, 155
Essex County Court House, 131
Extract (hamlet), 216

F

Fahy, Joe and Mary, 196
Ferguson, Dr. James, 93, 94
Ferguson Mt., 93
fern, species of, 248
ferries, 4, 41, 251
Ferris Bay, 18

Index

Finch Pruyn Paper Company, 150
fire towers, 93
Five Mile Point, 76
Flanders house, 126, 128
flowers, 25, 214
Fonda, 247, 249
"forever wild", 8, 166, 174, 184
Forts: Amherst, 4; Carillon, 39, 42, 44, 46, 49–52, 56, 77, 78, 102; Dayton, 230; Edward, 37, 78, 100, 101, 103, 108; George, 40, 71, 72, 84, 97–103; Herkimer, 230; Plain, 233, 234; St. Frederic, 4, 27, 32–35, 38, 39, 52, 68, 76, 77, 100, 102; Stanwix, 40; Ticonderoga, 3, 4, 16, 18, 19, 29, 37, 39, 40, 42–57, 77; William Henry, 38, 103, 112
Fort George Park, 97, 98, 101
Fort Ticonderoga Association, 55, 56
Fort Ticonderoga Museum Shop, 256
Fort William Henry Museum Shop, 256
Fourteen Mile Island, 84
Franklin, Benjamin, 103
Franklin Falls, 191, 192
Free Bridge, 110
French, xiv, 1–4, 13, 16, 24, 27, 32, 34, 36–39, 42, 44, 46, 47, 51, 52, 76–78, 80, 97, 100, 101, 217, 230
French & Indian War, 1, 3, 4, 13, 16, 19, 22, 26, 27, 39, 44, 45, 48, 49, 71, 73, 76, 80, 97, 100, 112, 217, 252
French Lines, 45, 46
French Mountain, 87
Frey, Col. Hendrick, 244
Friends of Santanoni, 174
funicular, 91
Furnace Creek, 230

G

Gamut, 112
Gardener's Cottage, 170
Garden Island, 10, 11
Garden Overlook, 11
Garnet Hill Lodge & X-C Ski Center, 185, 193, 194, 196, 256
Garrison Cemetery, 47
Gates, 17
Gates, General Horatio, 16, 17, 19, 29, 54
"Gateway to Western New York", 219
General Electric Company, 191, 236, 251
Germany, 182, 183, 230
Giant Mountain, 25, 135, 160
giardia, xix
Gilded Age, 172, 176, 181, 184
Gilded Age: A Tale of Today, The, 184
Gilliland, Elizabeth, 26, 29
Gilliland, William, 3, 4, 22, 26–31
Girard, H. J., 216
Girard, Quida, 215, 216
Girard Boarding House, 214
Girard Hotel, 215
Glen, John, 106, 107, 113

Glens Falls, 85, 103, 104, 110–118
Glenville, 110
Goertner, George, 243
Gore Mountain, 194, 196
Gozon, Louis-Joseph de (Marquis de Montcalm), 45, 46
Gray, 135
Great Britain, 26, 37, 38, 42, 45, 55, 230
Great Camps, Adirondack, 167–184; definition, 172, 175
Great Falls, 229
Great Lakes, 1
Great Pyramids, 242
Great Sacandaga Lake, 116
Green Island, 83
Green Mountain Boys, 29, 40
Green Mountains, 22, 25
Grenadier Redoubt, 36
Grenville rock, 201, 203
Griffin, hamlet of, 185, 211–216
Griffin, Stephen, 216
Griffin Falls, 185, 211–213
Griffin: Ghost Town of the Adirondacks, 215
Griffin Tannery, 213, 216
Gunboat Island, 11

H

Hagglund, Lorenzo, 8
Hague, Town of, 103
Haines Falls, 111
Hamilton County, 209
Hamilton's Boat Site, 107
Hammond, C. F., 61
Hammond, John, 62
Hammond's Corner, 60
Hammondville, 3, 60, 62
Harpers Ferry, 121–123, 126, 127, 129–131
Harris Lake, 169, 171
Hartley, Lt. Thomas, 19
Hawkeye, 112–117
Heart Lake, 132, 135, 137–139, 146, 153
Heart Pond, 66, 68
Heart Wilderness Area, 132
Helmes, Ken, 168, 172
Henderson, David, 146, 147, 149, 152
Henderson Lake, 141, 142, 145, 146, 149
Hendrick, King, 98, 101
He-no-do-as-da, 152
Henry, Professor Joseph, 63
Herdman's Cottage, 170
Herkimer, General, 230
Herkimer County, 230
Heron Marsh, 188
Heron Marsh Trail, 187–189
Heron Point, 10
Herwerth, Mary, 20
Herwerth, (Major) William, 20
Hessians, 10
Heyward, Major Duncan, 112–118
Hidden Valley Trail, 24, 25
Hides, Hemlocks and Adirondack History, 214
Higginson, Thomas, 130
Highlanders, 46
High Peaks, 8, 22, 25, 93, 119, 120, 132, 135, 137, 141, 149, 151, 163, 172, 242

High Peaks Information Center (HPIC), 133, 256
High Peaks Wilderness Complex Unit Management Plan, 133
Hinton, George, 131
His Majesty's Fort of Crown Point, 4, 32, 35, 36, 39, 52, 102
Historical Sketches of Northern New York and the Adirondack Wilderness, xv
History of the Adirondacks, A, 151
Hoffman, Charles Fenno, 164
Hoffman, John, 251
Hoffmans, 204, 246, 251
Hoffman's Ferry, 251
Hogstown, 86
Honeymoon Bridge, 171
Hooper, Frank, 194, 195
Hooper Garnet Mine, 185, 193–196
Hoosic River, 249
Horicon Improvement Company, 94
Horseshoe Falls, 139
Hotel Champlain, 13
Howe, Brigadier General George Augustus, 45, 50
Howe, General William, 40, 53
Hoy, Johnny, 180
Hudson, George H., 21
Hudson, Henry, 1, 37, 48
Hudson Falls, 107, 245
Hudson River, 1, 16, 19, 37, 48, 53, 54, 70, 78, 80, 104, 105, 107, 108, 110–112, 114–116, 143, 145, 149, 151, 163, 215, 230
Hudson River School of Painters, 163
Hudson Valley, 6, 16, 40, 54, 119, 229
Hudson Valley Railroad, 99, 103
Hulett's Landing, 77
Humphrey Mountain, 205, 209
Hundred Island House, 85, 86
Hunter, David, 149
Hunter, Robert, 149
Hunter, Sarah, 149
"Hunter's Home," 189
Hurons, 44, 48, 80, 112, 114, 116–118
Hyde, Louis Fiske, 118
hyperthermia, xviii
hypothermia, xix

I

Ice Cave Mountain, 225
ice fishing, 5
Indian Lake, 153, 197, 209
Indian Pass, 119, 120, 129, 135, 140–142, 145–149, 151–155
Indian Pass Brook, 145, 151, 153
Indian Point, 9, 11, 15
Inflexible, 17, 18
Ingham, Charles C., 146
International Paper Company, 206, 216
Irondale, 62
iron ore, 3
Ironville, 3, 4, 58–63, 70
Iroquois, 38, 44
Islands End, 10, 11

J

Jackson, Stonewall, 130
Jackson Point, 12
Jack's Pinnacle, 82
Janesborough, 28, 29
Janet's Lane, 234
Japan, 166, 173
Jefferson, Mr., 128
Jefferson, Thomas, 93, 103
Jenks, Kyle & Lynn, 252
jetty, 9, 10
Johnny Spring, 248
Johnsburg, 196
Johnson, John, 217
Johnson, Sir William, 38, 98, 100, 101, 217, 230
"Joint Caves of Valcour Island," 21
Joques, Father Isaac, 48, 80, 110, 229

K

Kaaterskill Falls, 111
Kahaniaga, 249
Kalm, Peter, 68
Kansas, 127, 129
karst, 9, 10
Keene, 128
Keene Flats, 162
Keene Valley, 162–165
Kensett, John, 163
Kettle, The, 239
Killington, Vt., 93
kilns, 32, 34
Kinaquariones, 251
King family, 205
King George, 35, 80, 100
King George's War, 3, 80
Kings Flow, 205
King's Garden, 42, 44, 56, 57
King William's War, 80
Knapp, George, 71, 79, 83–87
Knox, General Henry, 44, 45
Kryn, Great Chief, 249
Kun-ja-Muck Inn, 208
Kun-ja-muk, Camp, 208
Kunjamuk Bay, 207, 209
Kunjamuk Cave, 185, 206–210
Kunjamuk Mountain, 209
Kunjamuk River, 206–209
Kunjamuk Valley, 209, 210

L

Lac du St. Sacrement, 1, 80, 100
LaChute Falls, 43
LaChute River, 37
LaChute Riverwalk Interpretive Trail, 43, 44
Lady Slipper cascade, 241, 242
Lake Champlain, 1–6, 10, 12, 13, 15–17, 19, 22, 24–27, 29, 36, 37, 42, 43, 46–49, 53, 55, 58, 60, 62, 76, 77, 80, 100, 128, 148, 149, 163, 189
Lake Champlain Maritime Museum, 254
Lake Champlain Visitor Center, 35, 41, 256
Lake Clear, 191
Lake George, 1, 16, 37, 39, 40, 43, 45, 48, 71, 73, 76–80, 82, 85–88, 90, 93, 96, 97, 100–102, 112
Lake George, Battle of, 98, 99

Lake George Battlefield Park, 100, 103
Lake George Historical Association Museum, 254
Lake George Village, 100, 103
Lake Humphrey, 205, 209
Lake Iroquois, 1, 228
Lake Ontario, 40, 231
Lake Placid, 120, 129, 140, 147, 163
Lake Placid Club, 138, 140
Lake Placid–North Elba Historical Society Museum, 254
Lake Pleasant, 208, 209
lakes: Ausable, 153; Ballston, 249; Cascade, 153; Elm, 208; Great Sacandaga, 116; Harris, 168, 171; Heart, 132, 135, 137–139, 146, 153; Henderson, 141, 142, 145, 146, 149; Indian, 153, 197, 209; Iroquois, 1, 228; Long, 151; Loon, 190; Mirror, 140; Newcomb, 168, 170–172; Oneida, 231; Otsego, 111; Raquette, 175, 176, 179, 182, 183; Rich, 169; Round, 249; Sacandaga, 208; Sagamore, 175, 180; St. Regis, 190, 192; Schroon, 108; Thirteenth, 194, 196; Willis, 211, 214. *See also* Lake Champlain, Lake Clear, Lake George, Lake Humphrey, Lake Iroquois, Lake Ontario, Lake Placid, Lake Pleasant
Lakeview Cemetery, 30
"Last Days of John Brown, The" (Henry David Thoreau), 131
Last of the Mohicans, The, 71, 72, 83, 87, 104, 111, 112, 118
Leatherstocking Tales, 111
Lee, Robert E., 130
Legg, Douglas, 174
Le Jardin du Roi, 56
Lent, Lewis S. Jr., 177
Lester Homestead, 188, 189
Lexington, 53
Liberty, 16, 17
Lieber, Henry, 243
lighthouses, 6, 12, 14, 15, 20, 32, 34, 36, 37
Lily Pond, 66
Limbo Island, 12
limestone, 6, 9, 15, 20, 34, 99, 110, 115, 236, 250
Lithgow, David C., 131
Little Buck Mountain, 82
Little Falls (Adirondacks), 31
Little Falls (Mohawk Valley), 210, 219, 222, 225–227, 230, 231
Little Falls dolomite, 250
Little Falls Gorge, 219
Little Falls New York Historical Society Museum, 254
Little Falls Stone Company, 221
Little Rock Pond, 67
Little Santanoni, 172
Lock #17, 219, 221, 222, 224–226

Lock #36, 221, 222
Log House (lodge), 196
Lonergan, James M., 56
Long Lake, 153
Longstreth, T. Morris, xv
Loomis Estate, 231
Loon Lake, 190
Lover's Leap, 225
Lower Wolf Jaws, 158
Lower Works, 150
Loyalists, 53
Lusitania, 183
Lyman Cave System, W. H., 153–155
Lyme disease, xix

M

MacDonough, Captain Thomas, 13
MacNaughton Cottage, 141–143, 145, 149, 150
Madison, James, 103
Magua, 83, 87, 112
Martin, Charles, 215
Mason's Reef, 13
Massachusetts, 15, 50, 60, 101, 102, 128, 148, 249
Massena, 220
Maurepas, Frederic, 38
McAulay, Robert, 28
McCloy, John, 165, 166
McIntyre, Archibald, 147, 149
McIntyre, John, 147
McIntyre's Adirondack and Steel Company, 148
McKinley, William, 13, 141, 149
McMartin, Barbara, xvi, 214
McMartin, Duncan, 148
McMartin, Malcolm, 148
Mechanicville, 249
Megaboulder, 155
Melville, Herman, 130
Melvin family, 174
Memorial Acre, 56
Mental Break (Wallface Mountain), 154
Merriam's Forge, 31
Metcalf, Theodore, 128
Mexican War, 231
mills, 28, 29, 31, 38, 60, 61, 106, 107, 147, 148, 215, 216, 230, 231, 234, 237, 243, 244
Milltown, 27, 29, 30
mines: garnet, 194; graphite, 64, 68, 69; iron, 3, 60, 64, 68–70, 147–149, 152; titanium, 150
Minot, H. D., 191
Minutemen, 29
Mirror Lake, 140
Mohawk–Hudson Land Conservancy, 248
Mohawk River, 48, 116, 218, 221–227, 230, 231, 245, 249, 251
Mohawks, 1, 37, 38, 48, 80, 98, 217, 229, 242, 247–250
Mohawk Valley, 40, 204, 217, 223, 228, 230, 237, 249, 251, 252
Mohican Island, 87
Mohicans, 87, 112, 114, 247–249, 251
Montcalm, Marquis de, 39, 45, 46, 48–50

Index

Montgomery, General Richard, 29, 40, 103
Montreal, 16, 51
Montresor, Col. James, 98
Moon, Jim, 216
Moon's Mill, 216
Moore, "Father" Robert Edward, 12
Moose Pond, 170, 171
Morgan Lumber Company, 216
Moriah, 70
Morse code, 191
Moses Circle, 43
Moss Island, 210, 218–231
mountains: Adams, 142, 150; Algonquin, 134; Ampersand, 135; Basin, 135; Black, 79, 83; Buck, 79, 82; Chimney, 185, 197–205; Colden, 135; Cook, 78; Couchsachraga, 172; Defiance, 42, 43, 54–56; Dix, 25; Dug, 210; Equinox, 93; Erebus, 79, 82; Ferguson, 93; French, 87; Giant, 25, 135, 160; Gore, 194, 196; Gray, 135; Humphrey, 205; Independence, 54, 55; Jo, 120, 132, 135–139; Killington, 93; Kunjamuk, 209; Little Buck, 82; Little Santanoni, 172; Lower Wolf Jaws, 158; Marcy, 93, 123, 134, 137, 138, 149, 166; Marshall, 135, 151, 153; Nye, 135; Panther, 172; Pele, 73, 76; Phelps, 135; Pilot Knob, 82; Prospect, 71, 72, 88–96; Puffer, 205; Rooster Comb, 158; Ruby, 194, 196; Saddleback, 134; Santanoni, 172; Sawteeth, 160; Shelving Rock, 72, 79, 82, 83, 85–87; Sleeping Beauty, 79, 82; Snow, 158; South, 140; Street, 135; Taconic, 153; Tongue, 79; Van Hoevenberg, 132, 133, 135, 136, 140; Wallface, 135, 145, 146, 151, 153, 154
Mourning Creek, 249
Mulholland, Inez, 120
Munro, Alice, 112
Munro, Colonel, 112
Munro, Cora, 111, 112
Murdock, Samuel, 41
Murray, William H. H., xv, 119, 164
Mystery of Kun-ja-Muk Cave, The, 209

N

Narrows: Lake Champlain, 11, 12; Lake George, 79, 80, 82, 85, 87
National Commercial Bank, 173
National Historic Landmark, 131, 219
National Humanistic Education Center, 184
National Lead Company (NLC), 150
National Register of Historic Places, 61

National Veterans Cemetery, 13
Native Americans, xiv, 1, 3, 15, 16, 18, 24, 37, 38, 40, 44, 48, 50, 71, 73, 78, 80, 87, 97, 98, 101, 109, 111, 112, 116–118, 141, 147, 152, 215, 217, 219, 224, 225, 229, 230, 239, 242, 246–250
Natty Bumppo's Cave, 111
Natural History Museum of the Adirondacks, 255
Nature Conservancy, 174
Neilson, William G., 120, 165
New Amsterdam, 80
Newcomb, Town of, 174
Newcomb, Village of, 150, 168, 173,
Newcomb, Visitor Interpretative Center at, 168, 255
Newcomb Lake, 168, 170–172
Newcomb River, 172
New Hampshire, 50, 76
New Jersey, 47, 50
Newport, R.I., 3
New York Central Railroad, 226, 249
New York City, 16, 26–28, 30, 53, 70, 80, 95, 131, 138, 164, 165, 191, 244
New York Mirror, 164
New York National Academy of Design, 146
New York State Museum, 21, 254
New York Times, 108
Niagara Falls, 138, 151
Niagara River, 224
Nichols, Henry E., 85
NL Industries, 142, 150
Nomad, 8, 11
Nomad Trail, 8, 9, 11
Nordberg, Captain John, 102
North Bay, 14
North Creek, 143, 149, 150, 182, 194
Northeast Wilderness Trust, 26
North Elba, 120, 121, 126–131, 147, 148, 152
North River, 193, 196
North River Garnet Company, 196
Northwest Bay, 25
Noses, The, 249

O

Oakwood Cemetery, 140
Ogdensburg, 182
Old Toll Bridge, 110
Oneida Lake, 231
Open Space Conservancy, 150
Open Space Institute (OSI), xii–xiii, 141–144, 150
Oriskany, Battle of, 40
Osawatomie, 127, 131
Os-ten-wanne, 152
Oswego River, 231
Otne-yar-heh, 152
Otsego Lake, 111
Otsquago Creek, 232–234, 236
Outdoor Entertainment Center, 105

Over the Mountain Road, 86

P

Pabst, Fred, 93
Paine, Peter S. Jr., 26
Palatine Bridge, 245
Palenville, 95
Paper & Cotton Flour Sack Company, 244
Paper Box Factory, 228
Paradise Bay, 11, 12
Parks, Daniel, 107
Pavilion, The, 55–57
Peabody, George Foster, 95
Peaked Hill, 67
Pearl Point House, 85, 86
Pearl Village, 110
Peck, William, 94
Pell, Howland, 54
Pell, Stephen, 54
Pell, William Ferris, 56, 57
Penfield, Allen, 60–62, 70
Penfield, Anna, 62
Penfield and Harwood Forge, 62
Penfield Foundation, 61
Penfield Homestead, 34, 58–63
Penfield Museum, 58, 61, 64, 254
Penfield ore bed, 70
Penfield Pond, 58, 61
Pennsylvania, 8, 47, 126
Perimeter Trail, 6, 8
Perkins Clearing, 208
Perry, Clay, 118, 152, 204
Peru, New York, 5
Peru Dock Boat Launch, 5, 6
Petersboro, 126
Petrie, John Joost, 230
Phagan, Elizabeth, 26
Pharaoh Wilderness and Putnam Pond, 66
Phelps, Orra, xv
Phelps, Orson Scofield (Old Mountain Phelps), xiv, xv, 163
Phelps Mountain, 135
Phelps Point, 12
Philadelphia, 40, 131, 164, 165
Philips, Wendell, 131
Pierce Stone Works, John, 221
Pilot Knob Mountain, 82
Pine Knot Camp, 182
Pioneers, The, 111
"Plains of Abraham", 126
Plank Road, 233, 234
Plattsburgh, 4, 6, 13, 20, 48, 191
Pollia, Joseph P., 123, 131
Portens, Mr., 148
Port Henry, 3, 41, 70
Posson, Charles, 102
potholes: Canajoharie, 237–239, 242, 245; Kunjamuk Cave, 210; Moss Island, 219, 223, 224, 229; Shelving Rock, 79, 84
Pottawatomie, 130
Potts, Dr. Jonathan, 103
Powell, Brigadier General, 54
powerhouse, Sagamore, 179, 180, 183
Powerhouse Trail, 175, 177–179
Prescott, William H., 20
Preservation League of New York State, 184
Preston Pond Club, 149
Pringle, Captain Thomas, 6, 18

Profile Rock, 225
Prospect, The, 93
Prospect Mountain, 71, 72, 88–96
Prospect Mountain Hotel, 90
Prospect Mountain House, 88, 94
Prospect Mountain Memorial
    Highway, 88, 92, 93, 96
Providence Island, 11
Pruyn, Robert C., 173
Pruyn, Robert H., 173
Pruyn's Island, 111
Puffer Mountain, 205
Putnam, Major Israel, 60
Putnam Creek, 60, 61
Putnam Point, 18
Putnam Pond, 64, 66
Putnam Pond Campground, 64
Putts Creek, 60, 61
Putts Creek Falls, 58, 61
Pyramid Brook, 159–161
Pyramid Falls, 156, 160, 161

Q

Quebec, 17, 19, 29, 40, 51
Queen Anne's War, 48, 80
"Queen of American Lakes", 71
Queensbury-Moreau Viaduct, 111

R

Raboff, Adolph, 15, 20
Radii, 244
Radio Corporation of America
    (RCA), 236
railroads, 3, 191
Rainbow Falls, 156, 157, 161,
    162, 164
"random scoots," xv
Raquette Lake, 175, 176, 179,
    182, 183
Rattlesnake Cobble, 93, 96
Rattlesnake Hill, 55
Redoubt (Fort St. Frederic), 34
Reid, W. Max, 99
Revenge, 16
Revolutionary War, xiv, 1, 3, 4,
    6, 15, 16, 22, 26, 30, 40,
    41, 44, 46, 48, 53, 56, 70,
    71, 80, 100, 224, 230, 237,
    243, 252
Rhode Island, 50
Rice, Isaac, 47
Rice, Julius, 107
Rice & Emory Co., 216
Richelieu River, 16, 17, 37
Rich Lake, 169
Roaring Brook Falls, 157
Robertson, Robert, 173
rock climbing: Indian Pass, 154;
    Moss Island, 224, 225
Rock Dunder, 16, 48
Rock Pond, 3, 4, 64–70
Roger, Platt, 30
Rogers, Robert, 51, 73, 76–78
Rogers Island, 78
Rogers' Rangers, 51, 76–78
Rogers Rock, 71, 73–78, 225
Rogers Rock State Campground,
    73, 74, 76
Rogers Slide, 75, 78
Roosevelt, Theodore, 141, 143,
    144, 149, 150, 174, 191, 192
Roosevelt Memorial-Highway,
    Theodore, 150

Rooster Comb, 158
Rose Garden, 85
Ross, Daniel, 30
Rotunda Cave, 205
Roubaud, Father, 76
Round Lake, 249
Royal Savage, 8, 16, 18
Royal Savage Trail, 8, 12
Ruby Mt., 194, 196
Rutland, 131
Ryan, W. C. M., 183

S

Sabattis, Mitchell, xiv, xv
Sacandaga Lake, 208
Sacandaga Lake Hotel 208
Sacandaga River, 211, 213, 215,
    216
Saddleback, 134
Sagamore, Great Camp, 167, 172,
    175–184, 256
Sagamore Hotel, 29, 83
Sagamore Institute, 184
Sagamore Lake, 175, 180
Sagamore Lake Trail, 180–181
St. Hubert's, 156, 162, 163, 165
St. Hubert's Inn, 165
St. Johns, Quebec, 17, 29
St. Lawrence River, 1
St. Leger, Colonel Barry, 40, 53
St. Regis Lake, 190, 192
St. Regis Lake House, 190
Salmon River, 28
Sam's Point, 225
Santanoni, 167–174, 256
Santanoni, Little, 172
Santanoni Mountain Range, 172
Santanoni River, 172
Saranac River, 27, 116
Saratoga, Battle of, 19, 29, 40, 54
Saratoga Springs, 182, 236
Sawmill Falls, 233
Sawteeth, 160
Sayonara, 85
Schenectady, 110
Schofield, Josephine, 132,
    135–139
Schroon Lake, 108
Schuyler, Philip, 17, 29, 103,
    222, 231
Schuyler Island, 18
Scott's Clearing, 152
Scrembling, Henrick, 243
Serpent-a-Sonette, 55
Seton, Henry, 9
Seton Mansion, 5, 9
Seven Years War, 3, 26, 27, 45,
    48, 49, 56
Shakers, 20
Shawangunks, 225
Shelburne Point, 48
Shelving Rock, 71
Shelving Rock Bay, 87
Shelving Rock Falls, 72, 79,
    83, 84
Shelving Rock Mountain, 72, 79,
    82, 83, 85–87
Sherman, Darwin W., 85
Shingle Mill Falls, 186, 188, 189
Shingle Mill Falls Trail, 188, 189
Ship Prow Rock, 200
Shorey, A. T., 154
Shurtleff, Roswell M., 163

Siamese Pond Wilderness, 193
Simms, Jeptha, 239
sinkhole, 9
Sitting Rock, 239
Six Nations Indian Museum, 254
Skene, Philip, 68, 69
Skenesborough, 16
Skenesborough Museum, 255
Sleeping Beauty (mountain),
    79, 82
Sloop Cove, 11, 12
Sloop Cove Overlook, 12
Smith, Adam, 244
Smith, Benjamin, 244
Smith, Garrit, 120, 121, 126, 127,
    129, 130
Smith, George L., 231
Smith, John, 231
Smith, Lydia, 190, 191
Smith, Paul, 120, 189–192
Smith, Phelps, 192
Smiths, Paul, 185–192
Smiths, Visitor Interpretive
    Center at Paul, 186, 187,
    189, 192
Smith's College, Paul, 190, 192
Smith's Hotel, Paul, 186, 190–192
Smithsonian Museum, 63
Smuggler Harbor, 8, 11, 12
Snow Mt., 58
Snowshoes, Battle on, 76, 78
Sorel River, 37
South Ann Street Bridge, 227,
    228
South Bay, 167, 176, 177
South Glens Falls, 104, 110,
    111; Feeder Canal, 107;
    Historical Park, 104; Public
    Works, 105; Water Plant,
    107, 108; Water Tower,
    107
South Hero, 11, 12
South Meadow, 132, 133
South Mountain, 140
South Pond, 209
Speculator, 185, 206, 209
Speculator Loop Trail System,
    206
Speculator Tree Farm, 209
Split Rock, 28, 29, 48
Split Rock Mountain Wild Forest,
    26
Spoon Bay, 12
Spoon Island, 12
Spoon Pit Cave, 21
Sprakers, 249
Springfield, Ohio, 126
Stafford & Holt Co., 228
"Stardust", 184
Stearns, J. Thomas, 208
Steinmetz, Charles, 251
Stevenson, Robert L., 45
Stillwater, 249
Stimson, Henry, 165, 166
Stoddard, Seneca Ray, xv, 94, 99,
    102, 110, 138, 155, 157,
    164, 191
Street, Alfred Billings, 119
Sucker Brook, 172
Sugar Hill, 55
Summit Lake, 232
Summit Rock, 120, 141, 146
Summit Trail, 24, 25

Index

Sunset Rock, 155
Swart Homestead, 246
Sylvester, Nathaniel Bartlett, xv
Syracuse University, 184

T

Taconic Mountains, 153
Taft, Howard, 55
Taft, Timothy, 60
Tahawus, 141, 142, 150, 152
Tahawus Club, 149, 150
Talequega Park, 219
Tekakwitha, Kateris, 249
Thirteenth Lake, 194, 196
Thompson, Captain, 230
Thompson, Dyer, 148
Thompson, Henry,126
Thompson and Armstrong
 Lumber Company, 165
Thoreau, Henry David, 130, 131
Thousand Islands State Park
 Commission, 20
Tibbitts, George, 209
Ticonderoga, 3, 47, 51, 69
Ticonderoga, Fort, 3, 4, 16, 18,
 19, 29, 37, 39, 40, 77
*Ticonderoga: A Legend of the
 Western Highlands*, 45.
Ticonderoga Heritage Museum,
 44, 255
Ticonderoga Historical Society,
 55
Tiffany, Judge Isaac, 239
Tiger Point, 11, 12
Timbrel, Heloise Hannah, 182
titanium, 150
Tongue Mountain Range, 79
Tories, 53
Touareuna, 249
Touchy Sword of Damocles
 (TSOD) (cave), 153
Tower, Jonas, 61
Transcendentalists, 130
Traudt, Fritz & Susan, 238
Treaty of Paris, 3, 39, 40, 49
Treaty of Utrecht, 48
Trenton, N.J., 19
Trout Brook, 45, 73
Troy, New York, 60, 131, 137,
 140
Trudeau, Edward Livingston, 191
Truman, Harry, 166
Trumbull, Col. John, 55, 56
Tucker Cave, 21
tufa caves, 218, 232–236
Twain, Mark, 184
Twiss, Lieutenant, 55
Two Years before the Mast, 128

U

Uncas, 83, 87, 112
Uncas Camp, 182
Uncas Island, 87
Underground Empire, 153, 204
Underground Railroad, 120
Union Carbide Corporation, 85
Union College, 41
Union Pacific Railroad, 182
University of the State of New
 York, 173
Upper Duck Hole, 171
Upper Mill, 244
Upper Preston Pond, 150

Upper Works, 148, 149
U.S. Air Force Base, 13
U.S. Army Reserve, 46th
 Engineering Battalion of
 the, 235

V

Valcour Island, 1, 3, 4–21, 40,
 53, 70
Van Alstyne, Martin, 243, 244
Vanderbilt, Alfred Gwynne, 175,
 176, 179, 181, 183
Van Diver, Bradford B., 153, 236
Van Eps, Johannes, 251
Van Eps, John, 251
Van Eps Cement Plant, 247, 251
Van Hoevenberg, Henry, 120,
 132, 135–140
Van Horne, Abraham, 234
Van Hornesville, 232–234, 236
Varick, 17
Vaudreuil, Governor, 51
Vedder, Harmanus, 251
Vedder's Ferry, 251
Vermont, 4, 11, 12, 22, 41, 55,
 61, 93, 103, 128, 131, 163,
 189, 252
viaduct, 110, 111
Victor Knitting Mills, 228
Virginia, 123, 126, 127, 129
Visitor Interpretive Centers:
 Newcomb, 168, 255; Paul
 Smiths, 185, 187, 189, 192,
 255
Visitors Centers: Great Camp
 Sagamore, 176; Lake
 Champlain, 35, 41, 256
Vrooman, John, 243

W

Wadhams, 22
Wadsworth, Josiah, 215
Wadsworth, Philip, 215
Wallface, 135, 145, 146, 151,
 153, 154
Ward Lumber Company, 24
Warner, Charles Dudley, 184
War of 1812, 13
War of 1812 Museum, 255
Warren County Bikeway, 97–99
Warrensburg, 103
Washington, General George, 19,
 45, 54, 103, 230
waterfalls: Auger, 185, 211, 213–
 215; Beaver Meadow, 156,
 157, 161, 163; Buttermilk,
 80; Canajoharie, 218, 237,
 241, 242, 244; Cemetery,
 242; Cohoes, 115, 229;
 Creamery, 232–235; Glens
 Falls, 110; Griffin, 185,
 211–213; Haines, 111;
 Horseshoe, 139; Kaaterskill,
 111; LaChute, 43; Little
 Falls, 229; Lady Slipper,
 241, 242; Niagara, 138,
 151; Putts Creek, 58, 61;
 Pyramid, 156, 160, 161;
 Rainbow, 156, 157, 161,
 162, 164; Roaring Brook,
 157; Sawmill, 230; Shelving
 Rock, 72, 79, 83, 84;
 Shingle Mill, 186, 188, 189;

South Bay, 175, 179; Wedge
 Brook, 156, 160, 162;
 Willsboro, 28
Watson, Winslow, 27
Webb Royce Swamp, 26
Wedge Brook, 160, 161
Wedge Brook Falls, 156, 160, 162
Wells, Bayze, 18
Wells, New York, 209, 211, 216
Wells Dam, 161
Wells High School, 216
Western Inland Lock Navigation
 Company, 222, 231
Westport, 26, 27, 31, 70, 128, 163
White, William Chapman, 166
Whitehall, 16
White Pine (Great Camp), 172
Whitman, Oliver W., xiv
Wild Center: Natural
 History Museum of the
 Adirondacks, 255,
Wilkinson, Col. James, 17
Williams, Ephraim, 97, 98, 101,
 102
Williams College, 102
Williams gravesite memorial,
 Ephraim, 99
Williams Monument, Ephraim,
 97, 99, 100
Williamstown, 102
Willis Lake, 211, 214
Willsboro, 3, 27–31
Willsboro Falls, 28
Willsborough, 27, 30
Willsborough Day Book, 27
windmills, 32, 34–36, 38, 39
Window, The, 200
Winebrook Development, 150
Winne, Peter, 230
Wintergreen Park, 237, 240, 242
Winter Olympic Ski Jumping
 Complex, 122, 124
Wisconsin glaciation, 203
Witherbee and Sherman &
 Company, 41
Wolf Hollow, 204, 218, 246–251
Wolf Jaws, Lower, 158
Wood, Sarah Anne, 177
Wood, Uriah, 243
Wood Creek, 37, 231
Woodruff, Robert D., 235
Woodruff Outdoor Learning
 Center, Robert D., 232,–235
Woodstock, Canada, 139
Wool Extract Co., George C.
 Smith's, 231
World's Fair (1939), 232
World War I, 8, 96
World War II, 94, 150, 165, 166

Y

Yates, Major Christopher, 103
Young, Owen D., 235
Young Central School District,
 Owen D., 233, 235

About the Authors

Adirondack Trails with Tales is a sequel to *Trails with Tales: History Hikes through the Capital Region, Saratoga, Berkshires, Catskills & Hudson Valley* (Black Dome Press, 2006), which Russell Dunn and Barbara Delaney also coauthored. They have conducted an annual weekend of waterfall hikes at Trails End Inn in Keene Valley since 2002, as well as leading hikes to many other regional sites of special natural beauty and historical interest.

Russell Dunn is a New York State Licensed Guide and the author of an ongoing series of guidebooks to the waterfalls of eastern New York State and western New England, including *Adirondack Waterfall Guide: New York's Cool Cascades* (Black Dome Press, 2003), *Catskill Region Waterfall Guide: Cool Cascades of the Catskills & Shawangunks* (Black Dome Press, 2004), *Hudson Valley Waterfall Guide: From Saratoga and the Capital Region to the Highlands and Palisades* (Black Dome Press, 2005), *Mohawk Region Waterfall Guide: From the Capital District to Cooperstown & Syracuse* (Black Dome Press, 2007), and *Berkshire Region Waterfall Guide: Cool Cascades of the Berkshire & Taconic Mountains* (Black Dome Press, 2008). He is also the author of *Adventures around the Great Sacandaga Lake* (Nicholas K. Burns Publishing, 2002), and a soon-to-be-published guidebook on kayaking the waterways of the Capital District Region. He is a frequent contributor of outdoors articles to regional magazines.

Barbara Delaney is a New York State Licensed Guide and avid outdoors-woman. She has written pieces for *Mohawk Valley Heritage* and *Adirondack Sports & Fitness*, and has been the cartographer for Russell Dunn's waterfall guidebooks. Barbara is currently writing a work of historical fiction on the Sacandaga Valley and the lost town of Griffin.

The authors can be contacted at: rdunnwaterfalls@yahoo.com

Photograph by Harry Gnacik.